# CHRISTMAS
*from A to Z*

# CHRISTMAS
## from A to Z

History • Observances • Legends • Customs • Symbols

### By Tanya Gulevich

**Omnigraphics**

Detroit, Michigan

# Omnigraphics, Inc.

Cherie D. Abbey, *Managing Editor*
Peggy Daniels Becker and Helene Henderson, *Contributors*

Peter E. Ruffner, *Publisher*
Matthew P. Barbour, *Senior Vice President*

Elizabeth Collins, *Research and Permissions Coordinator*
Kevin M. Hayes, *Operations Manager*

Allison A. Beckett and Mary Butler, *Research Staff*
Cherry Edwards, *Permissions Assistant*
Shirley Amore, Martha Johns, and Kirk Kauffmann, *Administrative Staff*

Special thanks to Frederick G. Ruffner Jr. for his role in creating this book.

Copyright © 2011 Omnigraphics, Inc.
ISBN 978-0-7808-1244-4

**Library of Congress Cataloging-in-Publication Data**

Christmas from A to Z : history - observances - legends - customs - symbols / edited by Tanya Gulevich.
   p. cm.
Includes bibliographical references and index.
Summary: "Covers the folk and religious customs, traditions, legends, and symbols related to Christmas, from antiquity to the present day. Includes more than 150 alphabetically arranged entries, plus bibliography and index"—Provided by publisher.
   ISBN 978-0-7808-1244-4 (pbk. : alk. paper) 1. Christmas—Dictionaries. I. Gulevich, Tanya.
GT4985.C3846 2011
394.2663—dc23                                                                           2011017404

The information in this publication was compiled from sources cited and from sources considered reliable. While every possible effort has been made to ensure reliability, the publisher will not assume liability for damages caused by inaccuracies in the data, and makes no warranty, express or implied, on the accuracy of the information contained herein.

This book is printed on acid-free paper meeting the ANSI Z39.48 Standard. The infinity symbol that appears above indicates that the paper in this book meets that standard.

Printed in the United States

# Contents

# Introduction

Christmas comes but once a year … yet it lives in our imaginations year-round. What is it about Christmas, more than any other holiday, that is so compelling? For some, Christmas is meaningful because of its religious significance, the miracle of the birth of Jesus. For others, the holiday is meaningful because of the celebrations with family, the chance in this increasingly fragmented age to come together with loved ones. Many people look forward to the social aspects of the Christmas season—the emphasis on friends, parties, and other events. And certainly everyone enjoys Christmas presents. Yet despite the important place Christmas holds in our thoughts, we really know very little about the holiday.

*Christmas from A to Z* addresses this sprawling topic, tracing the history of the holiday and describing its observance today. The book covers a wide range of topics, including folk customs and beliefs, religious practices, symbols, legends, mythological and historical figures, foods and beverages, and major artistic and popular works associated with the celebration of Christmas and the Christmas season.

*Christmas from A to Z* explores the history of Christmas from antiquity to the present day. It contains a number of essays on ancient celebrations and the origins and development of Christmas as a Christian holiday, including the controversy over the date of Jesus' birth and the selection of December 25 as the date of the new festival. Many essays touch on the blossoming of Christmas customs, legends, symbols, and foods in the medieval and Renaissance era. Other essays outline the decline of Christmas following the Protestant Reformation, as well as its resurgence in the Victorian era. The book also covers the continuing evolution of the holiday up to the twenty-first century, noting the development of modern Christmas symbols and customs, including Santa Claus, Christmas trees, and Christmas gifts.

Special attention is paid to the history, customs, and symbols of the holiday as it is celebrated in the United States. Essays detail, for example, how Christmas was celebrated by American slaves as well as how Christmas is celebrated in the White House. They also survey a number of the nation's favorite Christmas books, movies, and television specials, as well as pop culture contributions to the American holiday season, including Christmas villages and holiday light displays and decorations. Other essays discuss Christmas observances in such distinctive American locations as Williamsburg, Virginia; Bethlehem, Pennsylvania; and New York City.

*Christmas from A to Z* will be enjoyed by everyone who loves Christmas—as well as anyone with a fondness for history and folklore who wants to discover the fascinating stories behind one of America's most beloved holidays.

# CHRISTMAS
*from A to Z*

# Adam and Eve Day

According to the Bible's Book of Genesis, God created the first man and woman and invited them to live in a heavenly place called the Garden of Eden. This couple, known as Adam and Eve, lived there in bliss until they took the advice of a serpent and disobeyed God's command not to eat the fruit of the tree of knowledge of good and evil. As punishment for their disobedience, God expelled them from the Garden, thus compelling them to work for their living, suffer pain, and eventually die. Medieval Christians honored Adam and Eve as the father and mother of all people and commemorated their story on December 24, the day before Christmas.

Eastern Christians—that is, those Christians whose traditions of belief and worship developed in the Middle East, eastern Europe, and north Africa—were the first to honor Adam and Eve as saints. Their cult spread from eastern lands to western Europe during the Middle Ages, becoming quite popular in Europe by the year 1000. Although the Roman Catholic Church never formally adopted the pair as saints, it did not oppose their veneration.

Commemorating the lives of Adam and Eve on December 24 promoted comparison of Adam and Eve with **Jesus** and the Virgin **Mary**. Medieval theologians were fond of making such comparisons, the point of which was to reveal how Jesus and Mary, through their obedience to God's will, rescued humanity from the consequences of Adam and Eve's disobedience. Indeed, the Bible itself refers to Jesus as the "second Adam" (Romans 5:14). Whereas humanity inherited biological life from the first Adam, it would imbibe spiritual life from Jesus, the second Adam (1 Corinthians 15: 22, 45, 49). Some theologians took this to mean that Jesus' coming could restore humankind to a state of grace lost when Adam and Eve were exiled from Eden. In like manner, Mary would undo the effects of Eve's disobedience. When the **angel** Gabriel visited Mary and delivered the message that she would bear a divine son, Mary replied, "Behold, I am the handmaid of the Lord; let it be to me according to your word" (Luke 1:38). Medieval commentators relished the fact that in Latin, Eve's name, *Eva*, read backwards spelled *Ave*, meaning "hail." *Ave Maria*, or "Hail Mary" were the first words that the angel **Gabriel** spoke to the Virgin Mary. The spelling of these two short words seemed to them to symbolize God's plan to reverse the consequences of Eve's deed by bring a savior into the world through the Virgin Mary.

Medieval Christians celebrated Adam and Eve's feast day with a kind of mystery play referred to as the paradise play (*for more on the paradise play, see* **Paradise Trees**). This little folk drama retold the story of Adam and Eve in the Garden of Eden. It ended with the promise of the coming of a savior who would reconcile humanity with God. The paradise play was often staged around a single prop called a paradise tree. Actors adorned an evergreen tree with apples and sometimes also with communion wafers. Decked out in this way, it served to represent the two mystical trees in the Garden of Eden: the tree of knowledge of good and evil and the tree of life. Although the church officially banned the performance of mystery plays in the fifteenth century, the people of France and Germany's Rhine river region kept on decorating paradise trees for Christmas. Some writers believe that the paradise tree evolved into what we now know as the **Christmas tree**. Indeed, as late as the nineteenth century people in some parts of Germany customarily placed figurines representing Adam, Eve, and the serpent under their Christmas trees. In some sections of Bavaria, people still hang apples upon their evergreens at Christmas time and refer to the decorated trees as paradise trees.

As the Middle Ages receded into history, so too did the western European feast of Adam and Eve. Adam and Eve have retained a bit more of their ancient importance among certain Eastern Christians. The Greek Orthodox Church still honors Adam and Eve on the Sunday before Christmas.

# Advent

The word "Advent" comes from the Latin word *adventus*, which means "coming" or "arrival." The Advent season serves as a period of spiritual preparation for the coming of Christmas. Advent calls Christians to reflect on both the birth of **Jesus** and on the Second Coming of Christ (*see also* **Jesus, Year of Birth**). In Western Christianity, Advent begins on the Sunday closest to November 30, St. Andrew's Day, and lasts till December 24, extending over a period of 22 to 28 days. In the Orthodox Church, Advent begins on November 15. The Roman Catholic, Orthodox, Anglican, and Lutheran traditions view Advent as the beginning of the Church year. The liturgical color for Advent is purple, reflecting the repentant mood characteristic of early Church Advent observances. By contrast, many popular customs associated with this period joyfully anticipate the coming of Christmas.

## History

In 490 A.D., Bishop Perpetuus of Tours, France, established a period of penance and preparation for Christmas in his diocese. He advocated fasting on Mondays, Wednesdays, and Fridays for a forty-day period preceding Christmas. This fast period began on the day after **Martinmas**, November 11, thereby acquiring the name "St. Martin's Lent" or "The Forty Days' Fast of St. Martin." The observation of a period of penance in preparation for Christmas gradually spread throughout France, and on to Spain and Germany, though it may have been largely restricted to monastic communities. In Spain, groups of Christians were already fasting in preparation for **Epiphany**. In the early years there was little agreement regarding the dates and length of this pre-Christmas fast period. In some areas the fast began on November 11. In others, September 24, November 1, or December 1 might be the starting date. In 581 A.D., the Council of Mâcon ordered the laity throughout France to observe the forty-day period of fasting. Two hundred years later the Advent fast was adopted in England as well.

Advent was not observed in Rome until the sixth century. Pope Gregory I (590-604 A.D.) developed much of the Roman Advent liturgy and shortened the period of observance from six to four weeks. The joyous, festive spirit with which the Ro-

mans celebrated Advent clashed with the somber, penitential mood established in Gallic observances. For a number of centuries Advent celebrations throughout Western Europe varied in tone, length, and manner of observance. Sometime after 1000 A.D., Rome accepted the practice of fasting during Advent, which in those times meant abstaining from amusements, travel for purposes of recreation, and marital relations, as well as certain foods. In addition, no weddings were permitted during fast periods.

By the thirteenth century the observance of Advent in Western Europe had stabilized. It combined the Roman tradition of a four-week observance, the Gallic custom of fasting, and a liturgy that mingled the themes of penance and joy. In recent centuries the Roman Catholic Church reduced, and eventually eliminated, Advent fasting.

## The Orthodox Church

The Orthodox churches of Eastern Europe developed different Advent traditions. Since the eighth century Orthodox believers have fasted in preparation for Christmas, eliminating meat, fish, dairy products, wine, and olive oil from their diets for a set period of time. A common Orthodox term for Advent is "Little Lent." In the Greek tradition, Advent is often called "Christmas Lent," a period that lasts from November 15 until the eve of December 24 and is observed with fasting, prayer, and almsgiving. The Orthodox period of preparation before Christmas may also be called "St. Philip's Fast" because it begins the day after St. Philip's Day. Armenian Orthodox believers fast for three weeks out of a seven-week Advent period that runs from November 15 till January 6.

## Folk Customs

The folk customs of Advent reflect the anticipation and joy that characterize the weeks preceding Christmas. During Advent, **Nativity scenes** are constructed and displayed. Some Christians also create and display a **Jesse tree** or a **Chrismon tree**. Advent may also be a favorite time of year to attend special Christmas concerts and performances. Advent activities for children often include writing letters to the child Jesus or **Santa Claus** (*see also* **Children's Letters**) and participating in **Nativity plays** or pageants recreating the Holy Family's search for a place to spend the night in **Bethlehem** (*see also* **Las Posadas**).

## Advent Calendar

Advent calendars help children count the days remaining until Christmas, usually beginning on December 1. The origin of the Advent calendar is uncertain, although it is thought to have been invented in Germany around the turn of the twentieth century. There is no limit to the design and form of Advent calendars, though most typically include a colorful Christmas or Nativity scene with the numbers one through twenty-five featured prominently. Many Advent calendars are printed on double layers of paperboard, with perforations that allow children to fold back or remove a number each day, revealing a Christmas or Advent themed image printed underneath. Sometimes chocolates or other sweets are revealed behind the fold-back dates on the calendar. Interactive video-game style Advent calendars often feature Christmas music or different animated characters on each day.

## Advent Candles

A number of different Advent customs require the lighting of candles. Placing a lighted candle in a window is perhaps the simplest Advent candle custom. Many residents of Bethlehem, Pennsylvania, keep electric candle lights in their windows at Christmas time (*see also* **Bethlehem, Pennsylvania, Christmas in; Candles**). Christmas time candles also twinkle in the windows of historic Williamsburg, Virginia. The custom there developed as a means of decorating historic district homes in a manner consistent with the town's colonial architecture and décor (*see also* **Williamsburg, Virginia, Christmas in Colonial**). In the American Southwest people decorate the exteriors of their homes with **luminarias**, candles placed in brown paper bags filled with sand. This custom originated in Mexico. Many churches hold special candle-lighting services sometime during Advent. Often, each person attending is given a candle, and the lighting of these candles then becomes part of the service.

## Advent Wreaths

Many Christians enhance their observance of Advent with an Advent wreath. Found in both home and church Advent observances, Advent wreaths are usually fashioned out of **greenery** and are meant to lie on a flat surface or to hang horizontally from the ceiling. These **wreaths** contain four candles, one for each of the four Sundays of Advent. A larger candle, known as the Christ or Christmas candle, is placed in the center of the wreath or off to one side. Purple candles are often found in wreaths designed for church use, because purple is the liturgical color of the Advent season. The Christ or Christmas candle is usually white, which coincides with the white or **gold** liturgical colors for Christmas Day.

One candle in the Advent wreath is lit on the first Sunday of Advent, and another candle is lit on each of the following Sundays until on the fourth Sunday of Advent all four candles burn in unison. Finally, on Christmas or Christmas Eve, the Christ candle is lit alongside the others. The increasing amount of light given off by the candles represents the spiritual illumination hoped for in the Advent season. The Christ candle, bigger and brighter than the rest, symbolizes the arrival of Jesus, "the light of the world" (John 8:12), and Christmas, the culmination of the Advent season.

Some Christians also assign special significance to each of the four wreath candles. Some say they represent the four gifts of the Holy Spirit: hope, joy, peace, and love. Others use them to represent the themes of the Advent season. Thus they may signify hope, preparation, joy, love, or light. Still others tell the story of Jesus' birth with the candles, allowing each to stand for some of the important figures associated with the Nativity, such as the prophets, **angels**, **shepherds**, and the **Magi**.

# Ales

## Christmas Beers, Yule Ales

In recent years a growing number of small American breweries have marketed special Christmas ales during the holiday season. These companies have revived the ancient northern European tradition of celebrating the midwinter holidays with specially brewed beers.

### Yule Ales

In ancient pagan Scandinavian society, the midwinter **Yule** festival included brewing and drinking special beers. Norse mythology taught that the god Odin instructed humans in the brewing of alcoholic beverages, and so the people drank to Odin during Yule. The connection between the Yule season and drinking remained strong as Scandinavia adopted Christianity in the Middle Ages. In Norway, medieval law modified the ancient practice of toasting the gods when drinking Yule ale. It stipulated that Christmas beer should be blessed in the name of Christ and **Mary** for peace and a good harvest. Medieval law also required every household to bless and drink Yule beer. Norwegians usually drank their Christmas ale out of special cups, sometimes reserving ancient drinking horns for this purpose.

### Seasonal Ales

In Norway, the tradition of brewing and blessing special beers for Christmas flourished until the nineteenth century. Tradition dictated that all Christmas baking, slaughtering, and brewing be finished by St. Thomas's Day, December 21. In past times Norwegians visited each other on St. Thomas's Day in order to sample one another's Christmas ale. German beer-makers also developed and maintained a tradition of brewing special seasonal ales, including distinctive Christmas beers.

## Church Ales

In the Middle Ages most monasteries brewed their own beer. In fact, monastic brews were considered among the best in medieval Europe. In the late Middle Ages, parish churches in England began to ferment beers to be sold to the public on feast days. These events, called church ales, raised money for church supplies, repairs, and improvements. The most important church ale of the year occurred at Whitsuntide (Pentecost and the week that follows). Other important church ales took place at Easter, May Day, Christmas, and various patron saints' days. These party-like events featured the consumption of ample quantities of food and drink, along with dancing, game playing, and other forms of revelry. They died out in most places by the eigh-

teenth century, succumbing to long-standing opposition by those who objected to the boisterous behavior that occurred at these church events.

## Christmas Ales

The northern European preference for celebrating the Christmas season with specially brewed ales emerged from all of the above traditions. Midwinter brews tended to be darker, spicier, and slightly more alcoholic than other beers, which made them a special treat. With the rise of industrial breweries, however, handcrafted seasonal beers all but vanished.

American specialty brewing peaked in the late nineteenth century. German immigrants of that era brought to the U.S. their love of malted lagers as well as their brewing knowledge and skills. By 1873, there were more than 4,000 independent breweries operating in the U.S. Competition and consolidation slowly reduced that number, and by the time of Prohibition in 1920, when alcohol was outlawed in the U.S., only about 1,000 breweries remained. After the repeal of Prohibition in 1933, smaller breweries struggled along for many years, never quite regaining the level of success they had previously enjoyed. Production of American seasonal beers all but disappeared after World War II.

During the 1970s, a revival in American craft brewing was driven by hobbyists and entrepreneurs eager to combine traditional European brewing techniques with new flavors. In 1975, a tiny San Francisco firm, the Anchor Brewing Company, reintroduced American beer drinkers to Christmas ale. Their success inspired many other small breweries to follow suit. By 2009, nearly 1,600 craft microbreweries were operating in the U.S., and sales of seasonal brews reached record highs. Contemporary American winter brews and Christmas ales are typically full-bodied, heavier, malt- or wheat-based blends that feature spices and herbs for lingering aroma and flavor. The innovative seasonal recipes of American brewers have begun to influence traditional European brewing practices, helping to revitalize the craft of microbrewing.

# America, Christmas in Colonial

The religious upheaval known as the Reformation divided sixteenth- and seventeenth-century Europeans on many religious issues, including the celebration of Christian feast days. The European immigrants who settled in the thirteen American colonies brought these controversies with them. Among colonial Americans, attitudes towards Christmas depended largely on religious affiliation. In general, **Puritans**, Baptists, Presbyterians, Congregationalists, and Quakers refused to celebrate the holiday. In areas of the country settled primarily by people of these religious affiliations, Christmas withered. By contrast, those who belonged to the Anglican (or Episcopalian), Dutch Reformed, Lutheran, and Roman Catholic traditions generally approved of the holiday. Communities composed primarily of people from these denominations planted the seeds of Christmas in this country.

### The First American Christmas

The first Christmas celebration in what was later to become the continental United States took place in St. Augustine, Florida, in 1565. Old documents inform us that Father Francisco Lopez de Mendoza Grajales presided over a Christmas service held at the Nombre de Dios Mission in that year. The Shrine of Nuestra Señora de la Leche now marks this location. The town of St. Augustine boasts of being the oldest settlement founded by Europeans in what is now the United States. Still, residents of Tallahassee, Florida, suspect that an even earlier Christmas celebration may have been held near the site of their town. In 1539 a party of Spanish colonists, led by explorer Hernando de Soto, camped near the place where Tallahassee now stands. Since the Spaniards stayed from October 1539 to March of the following year, some Floridians speculate that they must have celebrated Christmas there.

### The First Christmas in the English Colonies

In Jamestown, Virginia, a ragged band of Englishmen huddled together on Christmas morning in the year 1607. Although one hundred hopeful settlers had left England in order to found this, the first American colony, less than forty were still alive to celebrate their first Christmas in the New World. Their leader, Captain John Smith, was gone. He had left them to barter for food with the local Indians, and, according to legend, returned alive thanks only to the intervention of a young Indian woman named Pocahontas. Although the settlers had little food with which to rejoice, they still observed Christmas Day with an Anglican worship service.

## Virginia and the South

In Virginia, Maryland, and the Carolinas, the majority of early settlers were Anglicans of English descent. In the second half of the seventeenth century, as their way of life grew more secure, they began to reproduce the festive Christmas they had known in their homeland (*see also* **Williamsburg, Virginia, Christmas in Colonial**). They celebrated with feasting, drinking, dancing, card playing, horse racing, cock fighting, and other games. Although Anglican churches offered Christmas worship services, these apparently did not play a large role in colonial Christmas celebrations. Wealthy plantation owners who lived in large houses aspired to fill the **Christmas season** with lavish entertainments of all sorts. For many, this festive period lasted until **Twelfth Night**. By the eighteenth century these wealthy southerners studded their holiday season with balls, fox hunts, bountiful feasts, and openhanded hospitality. One year guests at a Christmas banquet hosted by a wealthy Virginia planter named George Washington, who later became the first president, dined sumptuously on the following dishes: turtle soup, oysters, crab, codfish, roast beef, Yorkshire pudding, venison, boiled mutton, suckling pig, smoked ham, roast turkey, several dishes of vegetables, biscuits, cornbread, various relishes, cakes, puddings, fruits, and pies. Wines, cordials, and a special holiday drink known as **eggnog** usually rounded out the plantation Christmas feast. Although wealthy parents might give a few presents to their children on Christmas or New Year's Day, this practice was not widespread. More common was the practice of making small **gifts** to the poor, to one's servants, or to one's **slaves**.

The less well-off could not reproduce the splendor of a plantation Christmas, but they could still celebrate with good food and good cheer. In addition, southerners of all classes saluted Christmas morning by shooting off their guns and making all sorts of noise (*see also* **Shooting in Christmas**). Those who did not own muskets banged on pots and pans or lit fireworks. Slaves were usually given a small tip or gift and some leisure time at Christmas. Since they had to prepare the parties and feasts for everyone else, however, their workload increased in certain ways at this time of year.

13

Southern colonists transported a number of old English Christmas customs to the New World, including **Christmas carols, Yule logs,** kissing under the **mistletoe,** and decking homes with **greenery.** Southern schoolboys of this era sometimes resorted to the Old World custom of barring out the schoolmaster in order to gain a few days off at this festive time of year.

### New England

The first bands of settlers to colonize New England were mostly made up of Puritans, members of a minority religious sect in England. They advocated a simplified style of worship and the elimination of many religious holidays, including Christmas. Although they came to America in search of religious freedom, once here, the Puritan settlers established rules and laws favoring their religion above all others, as was the custom in Europe at the time. In Plymouth colony, the first European settlement in New England, Puritan leaders frowned upon Christmas from the very beginning. In 1621, one year after their arrival from England, Governor William Bradford discovered young men playing ball games in the streets on Christmas Day. He sent them back to their work, remarking in his diary that while he may have permitted devout home observances, he had no intention of allowing open revelry in the streets. In 1659 Massachusetts Bay Colony made Christmas illegal. Any person found observing Christmas by feasting, refraining from work, or any other activity was to be fined five shillings. In 1681, however, pressure from English political authorities forced colonists to repeal this law. The anti-Christmas sentiment continued, though, and most people went on treating Christmas like any other workday. Many Puritan colonists resented the presence of the few Anglicans in their midst, especially if they were British officials. On Christmas Day in 1706, a Puritan gang menaced worshipers at the King's Chapel in Boston, breaking windows in protest against the Anglican worship service taking place inside.

The very fact that Puritan leaders passed a law against the holiday suggests that some New Englanders were tempted to make merry on that day. Historic documents record a few instances of seventeenth-century Christmas revelers and mummers being cold-shouldered by their more severe neighbors. The late seventeenth and eighteenth centuries witnessed a slight thawing in Puritan attitudes towards Christmas, as the New England colonies began to fill with people from a wider variety of religious backgrounds. Many still criticized drinking, gaming, flirting, feasting, and **mumming** as unholy acts of abandon that dishonored the Nativity of Christ, but some now accepted the idea of marking the day of the birth of **Jesus** with religious devotions. Nevertheless, noted Puritan minister Cotton Mather clearly warned his congregation against secular celebrations of the holiday in his Christmas Day sermon of 1712:

> Can you in your conscience think that our Holy Saviour is honored by Mad Mirth, by long eating, by hard Drinking, by lewd Gaming, by rude Revelling?… If you will yet go on and do Such Things, I forewarn you That the Burning Wrath of God will break forth among you. [*Christmas in Colonial and Early America,* 1996, 12]

In eighteenth-century New England, Christmas services could be found in Anglican, Dutch Reformed, Universalist, and other churches representing pro-Christmas denominations.

### New York and Pennsylvania

New York and Pennsylvania hosted significant numbers of Dutch and German immigrants. Denominational differences divided many of these immigrants on the subject of Christmas. In general, the Mennonites, Brethren, and **Amish** rejected Christmas. The Lutherans, Reformed, and Moravians cherished the holiday and honored it with church services as well as folk celebrations (*see also* **Bethlehem, Pennsylvania, Christmas in**). Like their English counterparts in the South, the pro-Christmas communities in New York and Pennsylvania ate and drank their way through the Christmas holiday. In addition, both the Dutch and the Germans brought a rich tradition of Christmas baking to this country, including the making of special Christmas cookies, such as **gingerbread**. In fact, the American English word "cookie" comes from the Dutch word *koek*, meaning "cake." This in turn gave rise to the term *koekje*, meaning "cookie" or "little cake."

German immigrants brought other Christmas customs with them as well. As early as the mid-eighteenth century Moravian communities in Pennsylvania were celebrating the day with Christmas pyramids. Other early German communities imported the beliefs and customs surrounding the German folk figures **Christkindel** and **Knecht Ruprecht**, whose gift-giving activities delighted children at Christmas time. Although the Germans probably also introduced the **Christmas tree**, no records of this custom can be found until the nineteenth century.

In addition to its large German population, Pennsylvania became home to many Scotch Irish and Quakers. Both the Scotch Irish, most of whom were Presbyterians, and the Quakers disapproved of Christmas celebrations in general. The Quakers adamantly opposed all raucous street revels, including those of German belsnickelers, mummers, and masqueraders of all kinds. In the nineteenth century, when Quakers dominated Philadelphia and Pennsylvania state government, they passed laws to prevent noisy merrymaking in the streets at Christmas time (*see also* **America, Christmas in Nineteenth-Century**).

The German Christmas blended lively folk customs with devout religious observances. This combination eventually became typical of American Christmas celebrations. At least one researcher has concluded that increased immigration from the German-speaking countries in the second half of the eighteenth century profoundly influenced the American Christmas. The increasing number of Germans permitted their balanced approach to Christmas to spread among the wider population and so encouraged the festival to flourish in the United States.

### Conclusion

The colonial American Christmas differed significantly from contemporary American Christmas celebrations. Many religious people completely ignored the day. Even after the founding of the United States, no state recognized Christmas as a legal holiday. Those people who celebrated it anyway did so without **Santa Claus**, **Christmas cards**, Christmas trees, and elaborate Christmas morning gift exchanges. Instead, the most common ways to observe the holiday featured feasting, drinking, dancing, playing games, and engaging in various forms of public revelry. Although the colonies attracted people from many different countries, English, German, and Dutch settlers exercised the strongest influence on early American Christmas celebrations.

# America, Christmas in Nineteenth-Century

At the beginning of the nineteenth century American Christmas celebrations varied considerably from region to region. These variations reflected religious and ethnic differences in the population. In **Puritan** New England, for example, many people ignored the holiday (*see* **America, Christmas in Colonial**). In Pennsylvania, German-American communities reproduced a number of German Christmas traditions. Prosperous Southerners, especially those of Anglican English or French descent, hosted lavish Christmas meals and parties. All across the country many of those who celebrated Christmas in nineteenth-century America did so with noisy, public, and sometimes drunken, reveling. By contrast, non-observers tried to ignore the noise and the festivities. They treated the day as any other workday, since it was not a legal holiday in most of the century.

During the second half of the nineteenth century, however, more and more people began celebrating Christmas. Regional and religious differences faded as new American Christmas customs emerged. These customs helped to transform the American Christmas into the tranquil, domestic festival we know today. As the century rolled on, larger numbers of people incorporated customs and myths surrounding the **Christmas tree, Santa Claus,** and family **gift** exchanges into their Christmas celebrations. The Civil War served as a watershed in American Christmas observances, after which time the commercial trappings of the holiday—especially **Christmas cards,** store-bought gifts, **store window displays,** and **wrapping paper**—took on greater importance.

## New York and Pennsylvania

In the early nineteenth century some New Yorkers and Pennsylvanians celebrated Christmas with **mumming** and other forms of noisy, public merrymaking. Young men of German extraction carried out their own variation of mumming known as "belsnickeling" (*see* **Knecht Ruprecht**). In Pennsylvania Dutch country, students sometimes celebrated Christmas by barring out the schoolmaster. In New York brazen parties of drunk men sang, played instruments, and shouted in the streets on Christmas Eve, disturbing the sleep of more serious-minded citizens. On New Year's Day, custom dictated that ladies stay at home to exchange New Year's greetings with a string of gentlemen callers, all of whom were entertained with food and drink. For gentlemen with a wide range of female acquaintances, this custom presented yet another opportunity to consume large quantities of alcohol. Christmas mumming occurred in both New York and Pennsylvania, to the dismay of those who favored a more solemn observance of the season.

In addition to those customs it shared with New York, Pennsylvania boasted its own highly developed noisemaking traditions during this era. In Philadelphia young men wandered the streets during the **Christmas season,** drinking, shooting off firecrackers, shouting, and sometimes fighting with one another. Some even strutted about in costume and were referred to as "fantasticals." Many of these celebrants wandered about the downtown blowing horns on Christmas Eve. Those who could not lay their hands on horns added to the pandemonium with tin whistles, sailors' hornpipes, tin pans, hand-held **bells,** sleigh bells, or homemade instruments. In the year 1861 these mock minstrels raised such a racket that they reduced the center of the city to chaos.

The city government, dominated by those who did not celebrate Christmas, made two attempts to outlaw parading, masquerading, and horn playing on Christmas

Eve, once in 1868 and again in 1881. The practice proved too deeply rooted to stamp out, however. Eventually, the city instituted the New Year's Day Mummers Parade, which modified these activities and channeled them into a controlled format. This popular parade continues today. (*For other nineteenth-century Pennsylvania customs, see* Amish Christmas.)

## The South

Southerners also celebrated Christmas by making noise. Men shot off guns both on Christmas Eve and Christmas Day. Firecrackers and gunpowder explosions added to the din. Children without access to either of these items sometimes celebrated by popping inflated hog bladders, the nineteenth-century farm equivalent of a balloon. Southern Christmas celebrations featured so many bangs and explosions that some witnesses said they rivaled Independence Day celebrations. In 1902 an article printed in a New York newspaper claimed that New York manufacturers had sold $1 million worth of fireworks to Southern buyers during the Christmas season.

In addition to noisemaking, residents of many Southern cities also enjoyed dressing in costume on Christmas Eve. In some places they were referred to as "fantasticals," like their fellow celebrants in Pennsylvania. Baltimore, Savannah, Mobile, and St. Augustine hosted versions of this Christmas Eve masquerade. Arrayed in costumes ranging from funny to frightening, residents sallied forth to promenade up and down the main streets of the town. Something similar survives today in New Orleans' Mardi Gras celebrations. Lastly, many residents of the former French territories, which became the states of Louisiana and Missouri, celebrated Christmas with French customs. These customs included assembling **Nativity scenes**, attending **Midnight Mass**, cooking up sumptuous réveillon suppers, and hosting parties in honor of New Year's Eve and **Twelfth Night**.

## The Slaves

The slaves developed Christmas customs of their own (*see also* **Slaves' Christmas**). In North Carolina some celebrated **Jonkonnu**. Some slaves observed an all-night vigil on Christmas Eve during which they sang, danced, and prayed. Throughout the South slaves greeted white folk on Christmas morning with the cry of "Christmas gif'!" According to custom, the white person responded by giving them a present, either a coin or a gift. In addition, slaveowners often distributed presents of clothing, shoes, blankets and other necessities to their slaves at Christmas time. Some slaveowners provided their slaves with extra rations of food at Christmas, including meat, which was something the slaves rarely ate during the rest of the year. Slaveowners frequently provided ample portions of liquor as well. At many plantations slaves celebrated Christmas by dressing in their best clothes, feasting, and dancing. At other plantations slaves worked through the Christmas holidays. Sometimes slaveowners withheld the privilege of celebrating Christmas from those slaves who had displeased them during the year. Others gave presents only to women who had borne babies or to the most productive workers. Abolitionist Frederick Douglass later looked back on the customs of the plantation Christmas as mechanisms for controlling the slaves. He argued that days of drunken carousing subtly convinced some slaves that they were incapable of productive behavior if left to their own devices.

## After Slavery

In the late nineteenth century, African-American Christmas celebrations varied quite a bit. Some African Americans celebrated a modest Christmas, exchanging gifts of homemade food and clothing and attending church. Visitors to the Indiana State Museum's Freetown Village, a permanent, living-history exhibit, can watch a play that reenacts an 1870s African-American Christmas of this type. Others reproduced some of the old customs of the plantation Christmas. The children greeted any adult they could find with the cry of "Christmas gift!" and the adults danced, drank to excess, and refrained from work. African-American educator Booker T. Washington observed these conditions in Tuskegee, Alabama, in the 1880s. As head of the town's newly founded school for African Americans (now Tuskegee University), he made it a point to teach his students to celebrate a sober Christmas, dedicated at least in part to religious observance and to aiding the less fortunate.

## The West

Out on the Western frontier men celebrated Christmas by **shooting** off their guns and banging on tin pans in noisy and often drunken processions (*see also* **Shooting in Christmas**). In Minnesota, settlers of Swedish descent attended *Julotta* services on Christmas morning (*see also* **Christmas Carols and Other Music**). Texans celebrated with Christmas Eve balls. Throughout the Southwest many of Hispanic descent staged Las **Posadas** and Los **Pastores**, traditional Christmas folk plays.

## Christmas Becomes a Legal Holiday

After the Revolution, the newly established American government revoked all British holidays. This act left the United States without any national festivals. In 1838 Louisiana was the first state to recognize Christmas as a legal holiday. One by one, the other states followed suit. Finally, on June 26, 1870, in recognition of the large number of people who already observed the day, Congress declared Christmas to be a national holiday.

## Protestants Embrace Christmas

Just as the states of the nation began to declare Christmas a legal holiday, many Protestant denominations that had previously rejected Christmas began to accept the festival. Between the years 1830 and 1870 Christmas slowly crept into Sunday school curriculums. The middle of the century also witnessed the publication of new American Christmas hymns. A number of these, such as "O Little Town of Bethlehem," "It Came Upon a Midnight Clear," and "We Three Kings"—all composed by clergymen—have become Christmas standards. By the end of the century Presbyterian, Baptist, Methodist, and Congregationalist churches were offering Christmas services on the Sunday nearest Christmas. Perhaps this change signified that the passage of time had finally severed the connections made by many Protestants between Christmas, Roman Catholicism, and the religious oppression of past eras.

## A Festival of Home and Family

The Christmas celebrations that the Protestant denominations were now embracing were not quite the same ones their ancestors had rejected. Several researchers of nineteenth-century American Christmas customs point out that as the century progressed many of the more boisterous elements of the festival diminished. These elements included mumming, belsnickeling, public drinking, and noisemaking. Americans increasingly viewed these activities as unworthy of the season. Instead, they began to create a tranquil celebration that focused on home and family ties. These changes probably encouraged former non-celebrants, including many previously hostile Protestant denominations, to adopt the new version of the holiday. Several new Christmas customs helped to facilitate this transition to a more peaceful, domestic festival, including the Christmas tree, Christmas cards, the family gift exchange, and the new American gift bringer, Santa Claus.

## *Christmas Trees and Gift Giving*

Most colonial Americans who observed the day did not give Christmas gifts to their children. Eighteenth-century Americans were more likely to give gifts to servants or to those who performed services for them during the year. Likewise, many nineteenth-century Americans resisted the idea of exchanging Christmas gifts with friends and family because they viewed Christmas gifts as something one gave to social inferiors. At the turn of the nineteenth century, those who did give presents to family members and neighbors frequently gave simple, homemade gifts, such as handsewn or knitted articles of clothing, wooden toys, or homemade preserves. Family gift giving appears to have been somewhat more frequent in German-American and Dutch-American communities. In these areas children might receive fruits, nuts, and sweets from **Christkindel** or the local belsnickelers. Some adults in these communities also exchanged small gifts, such as handkerchiefs, scarves, or hats. Of those adult Americans who exchanged gifts during the winter holiday season, many did so on New Year's Day rather than on Christmas.

Christmas gifts started to become more common about mid-century. Several factors contributed to this rise in popularity. First, people began to adopt the German custom of installing a Christmas tree in their parlors as a holiday decoration. The Germans covered their trees with good things to eat and small gifts. Hence, the tree focused everyone's attention on giving and receiving. In addition, because it stood at the center of the household, the tree showcased the family gift exchange. Whereas, in the past, some parents may have stuffed a few sweets into their children's **stockings**, they now could hang little gifts from a tree branch. Liberated from the tight quarters of the Christmas stocking, the gifts parents gave to children grew in size and substance. Before 1880 people usually hung their unwrapped gifts from the tree with thread or string. After that time, wrapping paper and fancy decorated boxes slowly became fashionable. As Christmas presents grew too large or heavy to hang on the tree, people began to place them beneath the tree.

Although charity had been an element of Christmas celebrations for centuries (*see also* **Medieval Era, Christmas in**), it became a more prominent theme of the festival during the nineteenth century. Some writers credit the Christmas stories of English author Charles Dickens, especially *A Christmas Carol*, with significantly increasing public interest in Christmas charity. In addition, many ministers preached to their congregations about giving to those less fortunate. The **Salvation Army** took this message to heart in the 1890s, mounting a successful campaign to raise funds to provide the poor with bountiful Christmas dinners in large public halls.

## Santa Claus and Children's Gifts

Santa Claus played an important role in the popularization of Christmas gift giving. This American folk figure became widely known in the second half of the nineteenth century, consolidating and replacing the lesser-known, ethnic gift bringers Christkindel (also known as Kriss Kringle), Belsnickel, and **St. Nicholas**. This bit of American folklore did not spring up from the masses of the American folk, however. Literary and artistic figures, such as Clement C. Moore, the author of "'Twas the **Night Before Christmas**" ("A Visit from St. Nicholas"), and illustrator Thomas Nast, developed the myth and image of Santa Claus that became popular through their works. Nevertheless, the American people quickly adopted him as their own. Santa delivered gifts to youngsters by visiting their homes on Christmas Eve. The increasing popularity of Santa Claus boosted the importance of gifts, especially gifts for children, in American Christmas celebrations.

## Commerce and Cards

The decade following the Civil War witnessed a sudden rise in store-bought gift giving. Researchers have traced this upsurge to two complementary factors: consumer demand and commercial promotion. Although some people objected to the impersonality of store-bought gifts, others desired the new, manufactured goods. Moreover, retailers set about enticing the public into spending money on Christmas with such innovations as lavish store window displays, wrapping paper, and special advertising campaigns. Stores began to schedule special holiday season hours to accommodate the seasonal increase in customers. In **New York City** shop doors remained open until midnight during the Christmas season, generating concern in some quarters for the plight of overworked shop assistants.

Christmas cards achieved widespread popularity by the 1880s, about the time when Americans began celebrating Christmas by exchanging store-bought gifts. According to one researcher, nineteenth-century cards replaced more personal yet more time-consuming ways of sending seasonal greetings, such as writing letters and visiting (*see also* **Children's Letters**). The cards anchored themselves more firmly among America's Christmas customs after the turn of the twentieth century, when people began to use cards to replace cheap gifts for more distant friends and relatives.

## Conclusion

During the nineteenth century, American Christmas celebrations began to coalesce around customs that promoted symbolic exchanges of love and good will both between family members and in the wider community. These customs—the night visit of Santa Claus, Christmas trees, family gift exchanges, Christmas cards, and Christmas charity—still stand at the center of today's festivities. Throughout the nineteenth century, regional differences in the celebration of Christmas diminished, although they never quite disappeared. The twentieth century would witness the further erosion of these regional customs.

# Amish Christmas

The Amish observe Christmas but do not share many mainstream, American Christmas customs. For example, they don't set up **Christmas trees** in their homes, tell their children about **Santa Claus**, and buy lots of expensive presents. Few decorate their homes in any way for the holiday, and those who send cards generally send them to their non-Amish friends. Instead, the Amish Christmas revolves around a few simple, homespun pleasures.

## The Amish

The Amish are Protestant Christians who maintain a lifestyle many Americans associate with centuries past. They reject most modern industrial and technological developments. Amish families continue to work their own farms without the aid of tractors or other motorized farm equipment, ride in horse-drawn buggies, and wear clothes popular two hundred or more years ago. The Amish came to this country in the eighteenth century to escape religious persecution in Europe. Here they found the freedom to worship as they wished and live in the manner they chose. Today's Amish speak English but also preserve the German dialect of their ancestors. Many Amish live in the state of Pennsylvania, but they can also be found in Ohio and other Midwestern states, as well as Canada.

The Amish faith emerged from the Protestant Reformation, a sixteenth-century religious reform movement that gave birth to Protestant Christianity. Like the English and American **Puritans**, the Amish initially rejected the celebration of Christmas as a non-biblical, frivolous, and sometimes even decadent holiday. A touch of this attitude remains today in their restrained observance of Christmas.

## Amish Christmas Customs

Most Amish schools prepare Christmas pageants. Since Amish children attend school right up till Christmas Day, the pageant is generally set for the afternoon of December 24. Parents and other relatives attend and watch with pride as their young people recite poems and take part in skits—many of which contain moral teachings about Christmas charity, faith, and love—and sing **Christmas carols**. Earlier that day the children may have taken part in a **gift** exchange in which each child, having drawn a slip of paper with another child's name on it, brings a present for that boy or girl.

For most Amish, Christmas morning begins with farm chores. Afterwards the family gathers for breakfast and Christmas gifts in the kitchen. In nineteenth-century Amish families, parents set out plates on the kitchen table and piled their children's presents on top. They usually gave their children things like nuts, raisins, cookies, candy, and rag dolls and other homemade toys. Other Pennsylvania Dutch families also set out Christmas plates in past times. The custom of setting out Christmas presents on the kitchen table seems to have died out among other groups, however. Today Amish families exchange a few useful gifts on Christmas morning. Typical gifts include simple toys such as skates and sleds, books, homemade candies and cookies, kitchenware, and household items. A large Christmas dinner completes the day's activities.

On December 26 the Amish celebrate "second Christmas." This custom, once common in Pennsylvania Dutch country, came into being so that those who devoted much of **December 25** to religious observance did not miss out on all the Christmas fun. It's a popular day for family outings, visits, games, and other leisure activities. (*For more on Pennsylvania Dutch Christmas customs, see* America, Christmas in Nineteenth-Century; Bethlehem, Pennsylvania, Christmas in; Knecht Ruprecht.)

# Angels

Images of angels adorn **Nativity scenes**, **Christmas cards**, **Christmas trees**, and many other Christmas displays. These popular Christmas symbols boast an ancient pedigree. They play a prominent role in the New Testament accounts of the birth of **Jesus** (*see also* **Gospel According to Luke; Gospel According to Matthew; Gospel Accounts of Christmas**). Angels also appear in many Old Testament stories.

### Biblical Angels

The Hebrew scriptures (the Christian Old Testament) often use the term *malakh*, meaning "messenger," to refer to the beings we call angels. Writing in Greek, the authors of Christian scripture called these beings *angelos*, a Greek term meaning "messenger" or "herald." This word eventually passed into the English language as "angel." Although the word "angelos" denoted an ordinary, human messenger, biblical authors selected it over another available Greek term, *daimon*, which referred to a guardian spirit. Perhaps they discarded this term because Greek lore taught that the daimon exercised both good and evil influences over people. Eventually, the Greek word "daimon" passed into the English language as "demon."

The angels of biblical tradition frequently acted as messengers. In fact, angels served this function in both scriptural accounts of Jesus' birth. In Matthew's account of the Nativity, an angel appeared to **Joseph** on three separate occasions. The first time the angel came to explain the nature of **Mary's** pregnancy. Later, an angel warned Joseph

of **Herod**'s evil intentions concerning Jesus and advised him to flee into Egypt (*see also* **Flight into Egypt; Holy Innocents' Day**). An angel returned one final time to inform Joseph of Herod's death and to command his return to Israel. In Luke's account of the Nativity, the angel **Gabriel** visited Mary to inform her that she would bear a child by the Holy Spirit. On the night of Jesus' birth an angel appeared to **shepherds** in a nearby field to announce the glorious event. Then a "multitude" of angels suddenly materialized behind the first angel, singing praises to God.

### *What Angels Look Like*

With so many angels involved in orchestrating the events surrounding Jesus' birth, it is no wonder that they became a symbol of the Christmas holiday. Today's Christmas angels frequently appear as winged human beings in flowing white robes with somewhat feminine faces and haloes. This image evolved over the course of two millennia.

The very first Christian depictions of angels date back to the time of the Roman Empire. Early Christian paintings of angels rendered them as ordinary men rather than as winged, spiritual beings. Some artists, however, garbed their angels in white robes, resembling a Roman senator's toga, in order to symbolize their power and dignity. The first winged angels appeared in the fourth century. Some scholars believe that early Christian artists patterned the image of winged angels after the Greek goddess Nike, the winged female spirit of victory. Others trace this image back even further to winged spirits associated with the religion of ancient Babylon. By the fifth century Christian artists from the Byzantine Empire began to depict angels with a disk of light, called a nimbus, behind their heads. This nimbus, or halo, signifies holiness, purity, and spiritual power.

In medieval times most western European artists portrayed angels as masculine in face and form. This trend reversed itself from the fourteenth to the sixteenth centuries. After that time, western European angels acquired softer, more feminine, or androgynous, looks. Sometimes they appeared as chubby children or toddlers. Artists often depicted angels with harps or other musical instruments. These emblems signify what some consider to be the primary occupation of angels—praising God.

# Baboushka

A winter season gift giver is a common figure in folklore from many different regions. Before the Revolution of 1917, Russian children received Christmas **gifts** from Baboushka, an old woman whose story is told in a Russian legend. *Baboushka* means "grandmother" in Russian. After the Revolution, the government discouraged tales about folk characters like Baboushka, whose story refers to religious beliefs. Instead they promoted tales about completely secular characters such as **Grandfather Frost**, who currently serves as Russia's gift bringer. With the fall of Russia's Communist regime in 1991, many old beliefs and practices have been returning, and Baboushka may, too. Baboushka closely resembles the traditional Italian gift bringer, La **Befana**.

### *The Legend of Baboushka*

A long time ago an old woman lived alone in a house by the road. She had lived alone so long that her days and her thoughts were filled only with sweeping, dusting, cooking, spinning, and scrubbing. One evening she heard the sound of trumpets and men approaching on horseback. She paused for a moment, wondering who they could be. Suddenly she heard a knock on her door. Upon opening it she discovered three noble men standing before her (*see* **Magi**). "We are journeying to **Bethlehem** to find the child who has been born a King," they told her. They invited Baboushka to join them. "I haven't finished my work," she replied "and the nights are so cold here. Perhaps it would be better if you came in by the fire." But the strangers would not delay their journey and departed into the night. Sitting by the fire, Baboushka began to wonder about the child and regret her decision to stay home. Finally she gathered a few trinkets from among her poor possessions and set off into the night. She walked and walked, inquiring everywhere for the lordly men and the newborn King, but she never found them. Each year on **Epiphany** Eve (or **Twelfth Night**) Baboushka searches Russia for the Christ child. She visits every house, and even if she doesn't find him, she still leaves trinkets for well-behaved children.

## Variations

In one version of the tale, the wise men ask Baboushka the way to Bethlehem and she intentionally deceives them. In another, the wise men ask for lodgings for the night and Baboushka refuses them. In yet a third the Holy Family passes by her door on their journey from Bethlehem to Egypt (*see* **Flight into Egypt; Holy Innocents' Day**). They beg hospitality from her, but she turns them away with nothing. In spite of their differences, each story concludes in the same way. Baboushka regrets her lack of concern, seeks out the people she has rejected, and eventually becomes a magical figure who travels the world at Christmas time bringing gifts to children.

# La Befana

## La Strega, La Vecchia

A winter season gift giver is a common figure in folklore from many different regions. In Italy, on the night before **Epiphany**, children go to bed expecting La Befana to visit the house during the night. She leaves **gifts** for children who have been good during the past year and warns those who have misbehaved. The name "Befana" comes from the Italian word for Epiphany, *Epiphania*. La Befana may also be referred to as *La Strega*, meaning "the witch," or *La Vecchia*, meaning "the old woman." Although not much is known about the history of this figure from Italian legend, some authorities believe that La Befana may be related to **Berchta**, another witch-like figure who visits homes in central and northern Europe during the **Twelve Days of Christmas** and, especially, on **Twelfth Night**. La Befana also appears to be related to **Baboushka**, a Russian folk figure about whom a nearly identical tale is told.

## The Legend of La Befana

There once was an old woman who lived alone by the side of the road. Her husband and child had died years ago. To forget her loneliness, she busied herself with many household tasks. One day three richly dressed men stopped at her house and asked her the way to **Bethlehem**. They invited the old woman to accompany them on their journey to worship the Christ child who had just been born there. The old woman grumbled, "I'm much too busy with my daily chores to go with you, and besides I've never even heard of Bethlehem." After the Three Kings, or **Magi**, had left, the old woman began to regret her decision. She gathered a few trinkets from among her simple belongings to present to the child as gifts. The she grabbed her broom and hurried after her visitors. The old woman walked and walked, but never caught up with the Three Kings and never found the Christ child. She didn't give up, however. Each year on Epiphany Eve she flies over the world on her broom, searching for the Christ child. She checks each house where children live, diving down the chimney. Even when she doesn't find Him she bestows sweets and gifts on well-behaved children. Naughty children may receive ashes, coal, or a birch rod.

## Customs

Prior to Epiphany, children write letters to La Befana asking her for the gifts they would like to receive (*see also* **Children's Letters**). In some places, rag dolls representing La Befana are hung in windows as seasonal decorations. On Epiphany Eve children hang a **stocking** or a suit of clothes near the fireplace. During the night La Befana fills the stockings or the pockets of their clothes with sweets and gifts. In some cities it was customary for groups of young people to gather on Epiphany Eve and make a great deal of noise with drums and musical instruments to welcome La Befana. In many parts of Italy today, **Santa Claus**, or *Babbo Natale*, has displaced La Befana as the **Christmas season** gift bringer.

# Bells

In the United States we tend to associate bells both with emergencies and with such joyous occasions as weddings and Christmas celebrations. This association between bells and Christmas can be traced back to the Middle Ages, when Church officials began to use bells for worship and celebration. Medieval European bell customs, in turn, developed out of a wide array of beliefs and practices associated with bells in ancient times.

### Bells in the Ancient World

People rang bells for many reasons in the ancient Mediterranean world, especially religious purposes. Jewish high priests hung tiny golden bells from the hems of their robes. The jingling bells repelled any evil spirits who might be lurking about the threshold of the temple. Some evidence suggests that the ancient Greeks also used bells in a number of religious rituals. The ancient Romans sounded bells on many occasions. They rang during civic ceremonies, chimed alongside other musical instruments during festivals and feasts, announced the beginning of religious rituals, publicized the opening of markets and public baths, and warned the people of fires

and other emergencies. Evidence suggests that the Romans associated bells with the dead and believed bells could protect them against evil spirits.

## Church Bells

As Christianity spread throughout Europe, Christian leaders slowly began to adapt bell-ringing traditions to Christian worship. Like the Romans, they used bells as a means of making public announcements. Since they wanted these announcements to carry over longer distances, they began casting large bells in addition to the smaller hand-held bells known since ancient times. They mounted these larger bells in high places and sounded them by the pulling of ropes or other devices. In early medieval times, monasteries began ringing bells to announce the start of religious services. By the tenth century, churches throughout Europe, from cathedrals to tiny rural chapels, were equipped with bells for the same purpose.

## Bell Lore

Like their predecessors in the ancient world, these church bells were credited with mysterious powers. For example, folklore hinted that bells possessed something akin to a life force, a personality, and a soul. Many legends throughout Europe told of bells ringing of their own accord to warn the public of some upcoming disaster. Other legends related stories of bells that refused to sound or that expressed their unhappiness with human actions in other ways. Numerous legends spread word of talking bells. According to folk belief, some bells sounded in tones that seemed to repeat a certain phrase, often praising their makers or lamenting an unjust act. Other bells refused to be silenced, continuing to ring on Christmas Eve even though buried underground or sunk in deep waters. People also commonly believed that church bells had the power to protect them from harm. Church bells were rung to ward off thunderstorms, frighten away witches, and halt outbreaks of disease. Folk belief suggested that the dead ascended to heaven on the sound of ringing church bells.

## Bell Customs

In addition to these folk beliefs and legends, Roman Catholic custom called for the consecration of bells used for church services. This mark of respect reflected the fact that bells served quite literally as the voice of the church building in which they were installed. Bells were prepared for this ceremony, commonly known as baptizing a bell, by draping them in white cloth and festooning them with flowers. During these services the bells were anointed, incensed, and officially named in the presence of their godparents, usually the donors. Some old legends tell of bells that refused to sound until baptized. People equated the sound of ringing bells with the voice of a person in prayer. Therefore, they frequently inscribed brief prayers on the bells so that the bell might offer the prayer to heaven. Other popular bell inscriptions state the bell's purpose or powers—for example, "I call the living, I bewail the dead, I break up storms."

Church bells were most commonly used for worship and celebration. The big bells adopted by churches during the Middle Ages rang to call parishioners to religious services. They also chimed at certain points during the service so that those standing outside or those at home and at work could join in the prayers. In addition, churches tolled their bells to announce local deaths. Many churches had four or five bells. The more important the occasion, the more bells rang to honor it. A high mass warranted three bells, for example. On the principal feast days, such as Easter and Christmas, four or five bells pealed together to celebrate the joyous occasion. In medieval England, Christmas bell ringing began in **Advent**, with a loud clang coming on the first Sunday in Advent to alert parishioners that they had entered the Advent season. Many of these practices were discontinued by Protestant churches after the Reformation, however.

### Bells and Christmas

Today fewer churches carry out the old Christmas tradition of bell ringing, and the folklore surrounding bells has been largely forgotten. Nevertheless, the public imagination still links bells with Christmas. A number of well-known Christmas poems and **Christmas carols** depict pealing or jingling bells as joyful emblems of the holiday. In addition, bells appear as symbols of the holiday on many Christmas decorations. Finally, representatives of charitable causes seeking donations at Christmas time often announce their presence on street corners by ringing hand-held bells (*see also* **Salvation Army Kettles**).

# Berchta

## Bertha, Frau Gaude, Hertha, Holda, Holde, Holle, Perchta

Since ancient times, legends have told of supernatural forces that roam the earth around the time of Christmas. Several very similar female spirits once visited the peoples of northern Europe during the long midwinter nights. Many authors believe these figures to be the remnants of pagan Germanic goddesses. Associated with the home and hearth, spinning, children, and **gift** giving, these pagan goddesses may have been very early ancestors of **Santa Claus**. The coming of Christianity transformed these goddesses into minor magical figures and concentrated the season of their appearances during the **Twelve Days of Christmas** and, especially, **Twelfth Night**. Throughout this transformation, the German goddess Berchta retained the strongest associations with the **Christmas season**.

### *The Winter Goddess of Northern Europe*

The winter goddesses of northern Europe, known as Berchta (or Perchta) and Holde (or Holda, Holle), shared many characteristics and are sometimes spoken of as variants of the same winter goddess. This sky goddess sailed the winds dressed in a mantle of snow. To the people of Alsace-Lorraine she sometimes appeared wearing a crown of fire, a trait that would later provide a tenuous connection to St. Lucy. In attending to the affairs of home and hearth, she acted as the patroness of those who spun thread, rewarding the industrious and punishing the lazy and sloppy. She also spun: not thread, but the fates of human beings. Motherhood and the fertility of the earth also concerned the goddess, who was known as a guardian of children and a protector of fields. Folklore often pictured the goddess flying through the night accompanied by the **ghosts** of children and other supernatural creatures, often phantom dogs, goats, or horses. She appeared most often during the Twelve Days of Christmas. Some believed that she led the **Wild Hunt**, a riotous procession of ghosts who rode across the night skies during **Yule**.

### *Folklore Associated with Berchta*

As Christianity established itself as the dominant religion in Europe, the image of this goddess shrank and changed, although elements of her old concerns and powers re-

mained. In Christian times, people in many German-speaking lands expected the ambivalent figure of Berchta to visit during the winter holidays. Although Berchta herself appeared as ugly and disheveled, she inspected barns and homes for cleanliness. She rewarded the neat and industrious and punished the lazy.

Since Berchta was the patroness of spinners, one custom demanded that women cease their spinning work during the Twelve Days of Christmas out of respect for her. Another custom advised that each house consume a special food on Twelfth Night and leave the remains for Berchta. If a household did not offer food, Berchta would cut open the stomachs of the inhabitants and remove the contents. Although she would punish lazy or naughty children, Berchta rewarded well-behaved children with gifts or good luck, and enjoyed rocking babies' cradles when no one was looking. Mothers would sometimes threaten their children that if they didn't behave, Berchta would come for them. Her nighttime processions frightened those who witnessed them, but in passing she and her followers bestowed fertility on the fields below. The spirits and souls that followed in her train were called Perchten, and, in some German-speaking areas, the night when she was most likely to appear, Twelfth Night, was called *Perchtennacht*. Although it is difficult to trace the relationship of one mythological figure to another, Berchta may also be related to the Italian **Befana** and to another German spirit, **Frau Gaude.**

## Folklore Associated with Holde

Most of the beliefs and practices associated with Berchta are also connected to Holde. Some differ, however. The people of northern Germany spoke more often of Holde than of Berchta. They often imagined Holde, whose name means "the kindly one," as a beautiful woman. When Holde shook out her feather bed in the sky, heavy snowfalls showered the lands below. In Christian times Holde acquired associations with witchcraft, and those thought to be witches were said to "ride with Holde."

## Another Winter Goddess, Hertha

In pagan times, some Norse and Germanic-speaking peoples called their winter goddess Hertha or Bertha. This goddess shares many characteristics with Berchta and Holde and may be related to them. Hertha was the patroness of home and hearth who visited her people around the time of the **winter solstice.** Householders decorated their dwellings with evergreens in order to entice her to visit (*see* **Greenery**). They also made flat stone altars for her and set fire to fir branches on top of them. It was believed that Hertha entered the home through the rising smoke, conferring upon the wise the ability to foretell the futures of those around the flames. At least one author suspects that Santa Claus's descent through the chimney at Christmas time echoes the descent of Hertha through the chimney smoke.

# Bethlehem

Both **Gospel accounts of Christmas** state that **Jesus** was born in the town of Bethlehem. Bethlehem is located in the Palestinian Authority, within the modern nation of Israel. The city of Jerusalem lies just five miles to the north. The town's name means "house of bread" in Hebrew, reflecting its location in a fertile zone of the Judean desert.

### The Birthplace of Jesus

One of the greatest heroes of the Old Testament, King David, was born in Bethlehem. Both gospel accounts of Christmas assert that Jesus was a descendant of David. In fact, in the **Gospel according to Luke** this ancestry indirectly caused Jesus to be born in Bethlehem. In Luke's account, the Romans wanted to conduct a census and ordered everyone to return to their ancestral home in order to be counted. This decree forced **Joseph** and his pregnant wife **Mary** to travel to Bethlehem. Shortly after they arrived, Jesus was born. The **Gospel according to Matthew** does not mention the census and implies instead that Jesus' parents lived in Bethlehem. Matthew's and Luke's claims that Jesus had been born in Bethlehem were especially significant to those who knew Jewish scripture, since the Jewish prophet Micah had declared that the Messiah would be born in that town (Micah 5:2).

### The Church of the Nativity

According to early Christian tradition, Jesus had been born in one of the caves that local people used to shelter animals. As early as the second century A.D., pilgrims began to visit the cave where Jesus was said to have been born. The Roman emperor Hadrian constructed a shrine to the pagan god Adonis over this site. In approximately 325 A.D., after the conversion of the Roman Empire to Christianity, the empress Helena had the temple to Adonis destroyed and built the Church of the Nativity over the presumed site of Jesus' birth. Almost nothing of this original church remains. It was severely damaged in a war that took place several centuries after its construction. According to legend, Persian invaders were about to destroy the church completely, when they noticed a mural depicting the Three Kings, or **Magi**, wearing

Persian dress. Recognizing that the church in some way honored Persian sages of the past, the invaders spared it from total destruction. The great Byzantine emperor Justinian rebuilt the Church of the Nativity in the sixth century A.D. It has been repaired many times since then, but its basic design remains the same. The main door to the church, called the Door of Humility, was built so low that people have to bow down to enter. The original purpose of the design was to prevent Muslims from riding into the church on their horses. Because entering through this door requires one to bow one's head, which also serves as a gesture of reverence for this Christian holy site, Jews have traditionally objected to using the Door of Humility.

Today the Church of the Nativity is an Eastern Orthodox shrine. The cave in which Jesus was born lies underneath the church. Known as the "Grotto of the Nativity," this underground chamber is a site of intense religious devotion for Christians of many different denominations. In the nineteenth century, friction arose over which denomination would exercise the most control over the Grotto. In the midst of this conflict, the star marking the spot where Jesus' manger had lain mysteriously disappeared. Each faction accused the others of the theft. Some writers claim that tensions caused by the star's disappearance helped to provoke the Crimean War. The Sultan of Turkey eventually assisted in resolving this dispute by placing a new fourteen-pointed star in the Grotto. Pilgrims to Bethlehem today can still see this large silver star covering the spot on the floor where, according to legend, Mary gave birth to Jesus. The star bears an inscription in Latin, *Hic De Virgine Maria, Jesus Christus Natus Est*, which means, "Here Jesus Christ was born of the Virgin Mary."

Eastern Orthodox officials share the Grotto of the Nativity with Roman Catholic and Armenian Orthodox clergy. At Christmas time Roman Catholic clergy oversee the **Nativity scene**, while Orthodox clergy control the altar.

In spring 2002, Israeli military forces invaded the West Bank town of Bethlehem as part of Israel's campaign to eliminate Palestinian terrorism. Dozens of people sought refuge in the Church of the Nativity, hoping that such a holy site would not be attacked. Among them were ordinary townspeople, Palestinian gunmen, and clergy members. The Israeli soldiers surrounded the church and prevented people, food, and medical supplies from entering. After a dramatic five-week standoff, the gunmen agreed to go into permanent exile, and the Israelis called off their soldiers. A few windows were damaged during the siege, but no permanent harm was done to the church.

## Christmas in Bethlehem

Bethlehem attracts many Christian pilgrims, especially during the **Christmas season**. The biggest crowds gather on December 24 and 25, when most Western Christians celebrate the Nativity. On December 24 Roman Catholic priests celebrate **Midnight Mass** in St. Catherine's Roman Catholic Church, which lies inside the grounds of the Church of the Nativity. The event begins with a motorcade procession from Jerusalem to Bethlehem, led by the Latin Patriarch of Jerusalem, the highest-ranking Roman Catholic official in Israel. Those practicing Roman Catholics who have obtained advance tickets for the Midnight Mass crowd into St. Catherine's church. This service includes a procession to the Grotto of the Nativity, where the figurine representing the baby Jesus is placed in the Nativity scene. The throng that remains outside can watch a televised broadcast of the service on a screen set up in Manger Square.

Other opportunities for Christmas Eve worship include an Anglican service held at the Greek Orthodox monastery attached to the Church of the Nativity and a Protestant carol service, which takes place at a field just outside Bethlehem. The crowd that assembles in the field sings **Christmas carols**, commemorating the evening two thousand years ago when a small band of **shepherds** received a miraculous announcement of Jesus' birth and witnessed a host of **angels** singing praises to God (*see also* **Gospel According to Luke**). No one knows the exact location of the field mentioned in the Bible. At least three different groups have laid claim to their own shepherds' field. The Christmas Eve carol service takes place at the Y.M.C.A.'s field. The Orthodox Church, however, maintains its own shepherds' field, as does the Roman Catholic Church.

Bethlehem hosts somewhat smaller celebrations on January 7, when many Orthodox Christians celebrate Christmas, and again on January 19, when Armenian Orthodox Christians observe the holiday.

## Rachel's Tomb

Jewish and Muslim pilgrims come to Bethlehem to visit another holy site: the Tomb of Rachel. Rachel's death and burial are mentioned in the Bible (Genesis 35:20). Folk tradition declares that Rachel was laid to rest in Bethlehem, although biblical scholars deny that this is the correct site.

# Bethlehem, Pennsylvania, Christmas in

The town of Bethlehem, Pennsylvania, promotes itself as America's "Christmas City." The city's most notable Christmas customs reflect the religious heritage of its founders, who were Moravian Christians from central Europe.

## The Moravians

The Moravians are mainstream Protestant Christians whose denomination was established in 1457 in what is now the Czech Republic. Many died during religious persecutions that took place in the seventeenth century. In the eighteenth century a German nobleman, Count Zinzendorf, undertook the protection of the remaining Moravians and allowed them to settle on his land. Seeking religious freedom and the opportunity to spread the teachings of **Jesus** to American natives, settlers, and slaves, groups of Moravians began to emigrate from Germany to the American colonies in the eighteenth century.

## Founding of Bethlehem, Pennsylvania

In the mid-eighteenth century Moravians founded two towns along the Lehigh River in Pennsylvania. The first they named Nazareth, after the town where Jesus grew up. They called the second town **Bethlehem**, after the town in which Jesus was born.

In 1741, Count Zinzendorf visited the settlement of Bethlehem and spent Christmas there. His approval of the colonists' proposal to name the town Bethlehem finalized their decision. On Christmas Eve he led the community in singing the German hymn "Jesus, Call Thou Me," which he believed helped to explain why the colonists had made a wise choice in naming the new town. The first verse of the hymn reminds listeners that:

> Not Jerusalem
> Lowly Bethlehem
> 'Twas that gave us Christ to save us,
> Not Jerusalem.

## Christmas Candles and Lights

In 1937, the Bethlehem Chamber of Commerce began to promote the town's Christmas celebrations as a tourist attraction, billing Bethlehem as "Christmas City U.S.A." The city's residents quickly adopted the campaign, organizing a city-wide display of Christmas lights. Bethlehem's most distinctive lighting custom consists of placing a single lit candle in the windows of homes, stores, and other businesses (*see also* **Candles**). Though it can only be traced back to the late 1920s, some researchers claim that early Moravian immigrants brought this custom with them from a Moravian community in Germany. There the flame from a single candle left burning in the window during **Advent** was understood to signal a welcome for the Christ child. By 1940 this custom had spread far beyond Bethlehem's Moravian community to become a city-wide practice. For reasons of safety, many today have replaced real candles with electric lights shaped like candles. Many people in Bethlehem light the candles in their windows on the first Sunday in Advent and keep them lit until **Epiphany**.

The city also hosts an impressive outdoor lighting display. Popular nighttime bus tours led by guides in traditional Moravian dress fill up quickly during the holiday season. On nearby South Mountain a giant, electrically lit star beckons visitors to the Christmas city. First erected in 1935, the "Star of Bethlehem" has been rebuilt several times. Its traditional five-pointed design features extending rays of light measuring 81 feet in height and 53 feet in width, and includes 246 light bulbs. In past times the city of Bethlehem only lit the star during the Christmas season. Since the mid-1990s, the city has kept it illuminated year-round. This star also appears on the city's official seal. There the five points stand for religion, education, music, industry, and recreation, five important components of the city's identity.

## Moravian Stars

The Moravian star constitutes another Moravian-style Christmas decoration that can now be found throughout the town. These three-dimensional stars are made of paper, leaded glass, or plastic and may be illuminated from within by an electric bulb. Although Moravian star-makers shape these ornaments with varying numbers of points, the most common kind of Moravian star has twenty-six points. Moravian stars are displayed in Bethlehem's homes, shops, and Moravian churches.

## Community Putzes

Bethlehem's Moravians have also contributed the Christmas putz to the town's repertoire of Christmas customs. Putzes are miniature **Nativity scenes** depicting not only Jesus' birth in a manger, but also scenes of life in the surrounding countryside (*see also* **Christmas Villages**). In past times members of the Moravian community vied with one another to see who could build the most imaginative and elaborate putz. Between Christmas and Epiphany they visited one another's homes to compare and enjoy the putzes. The custom of putz visiting also caught on with non-Moravians. In the 1930s, one particularly successful putz-building family, that of Edward Neisser, received nearly 1,000 Christmas season visitors.

Neisser suggested that the town build a community putz for the public to enjoy. The Chamber of Commerce took him up on that suggestion in 1937. The first community putz, set up in the office of the Chamber of Commerce, drew 14,000 visitors and so interrupted the Chamber's duties that it was moved to another location the following year. In 1939, the community putz was built in the lobby of Hotel Bethlehem.

Two hundred volunteers helped manage the putz by reading the narration for the display and working the lights. The attraction drew 30,000 visitors, overwhelming the hotel. Several more changes of venue followed until three community putzes were established in local Moravian churches.

Since the beginning of this tradition, members of Bethlehem's Moravian churches have built and managed the community putzes. The process typically begins with an expedition to the Pocono Mountains in November to gather moss used in the display. It then takes volunteers about a week to construct the putz. Viewing begins at the start of Advent. Several times a day, visitors can enter the darkened auditorium to view the putz while a guide reads a narrative describing the scene. The lights in each section of the putz rise as the guide tells the story of those figures.

## Lovefeasts

Bethlehem's Moravian churches hold a religious service called a lovefeast on special days such as Christmas Eve, Good Friday, church anniversaries, or mission occasions. Moravian lovefeasts revolve around a small communal meal. The meal, usually composed of a sweet roll and coffee, should not be confused with the Christian sacrament of Holy Communion. Rather, the sharing of food and drink is intended to foster the growth of love and connectedness among members of the congregation.

Moravian church officials trace the origins of the lovefeast back to the year 1727, when a group of Moravians attending a communion service in Germany felt an outpouring of the Holy Spirit. Grudges melted away and arguments over religious doctrine gently resolved themselves, leaving participants with renewed feelings of love and appreciation for one another. Afterwards people celebrated with communal meals in one another's homes. These historical events inspired the Moravian lovefeast. Some Moravians also note that these incidents recalled the fellowship displayed by the first Christians who shared their meals in common after experiencing the marvelous power of the Holy Spirit (Acts 2:46).

The Central Moravian Church in Bethlehem, Pennsylvania, celebrates two lovefeasts at Christmas time. The first occurs on the first Sunday in Advent. The service begins with a hymn sung by the entire congregation and a prayer. Then several women pass through the church, distributing buns to the congregation. Dressed in old-fashioned lace caps called *haubes*, they are referred to as *deiners*, the German word for "servers." The women are followed by male servers, who distribute mugs of coffee or other beverage to the worshipers. When all have been served, the choir sings and the congregation eats. More hymn singing follows the meal.

The second lovefeast takes place on the afternoon of Christmas Eve. This service is geared towards children and their families, with sugar cookies and chocolate milk often served instead of buns and coffee. This lovefeast resounds with instrumental music and hymns. The hymn first led by Count Zinzendorf in 1741 is typically sung, along with other hymns and **Christmas carols**. The singing of an old Moravian hymn titled "Morning Star" constitutes the highlight of the musical program. Each year a child is chosen to sing portions of this hymn as a solo. To be entrusted with this role is considered a great honor. As the last verse of this hymn begins, servers enter the darkened church carrying trays of lit beeswax candles, trimmed at the bottom with red paper and ribbon. Candles are distributed to the congregation, and everyone sings together.

## Concerts

Visitors to Bethlehem also have the opportunity to hear many Christmas concerts, some featuring Moravian music. Moravians have long encouraged music making within their communities. The early Moravians composed thousands of musical pieces, safeguarded the biggest collection of music in the American colonies, and harbored amongst them many instrument makers. One unusual feature of the distinguished Moravian musical heritage is the trombone choir, an ensemble made up entirely of tenor, bass, alto, and soprano trombones. Moravians brought the first trombones to America in the mid-eighteenth century, where they continued to be a novelty outside Moravian communities until well into the nineteenth century.

## Historic District

People of many different ethnic and religious groups live in Bethlehem, but the town's historic ties with the Moravians give it its most distinctive Christmas customs. In addition to these customs, the town maintains a fine collection of colonial and early American buildings, including the Sun Inn, an establishment that dates back to colonial times and once hosted George and Martha Washington, as well as other famous patriots of the American Revolution. (For more on Christmas in Pennsylvania, *see* **America, Christmas in Nineteenth-Century; Amish Christmas; Knecht Ruprecht.**)

# Birth of the Invincible Sun
## Birth of the Unconquered Sun

In the first centuries after the death of **Jesus**, a new religious cult swept across the Roman Empire. Traditional Roman religion included festivals and ceremonies associated with a wide variety of gods. Followers of the new religion focused their devotions on one god. They called this god "Mithras" or "Sol" and observed his birthday on **December 25** with a festival known as the *Natalis Sol Invicti*, or the Birth of the Invincible Sun.

### Origins of Mithraism

The god Mithras originated in Persia. Ancient Hindu and Zoroastrian texts mention a minor god, Mithra or Mitra, who was associated with the sun, the light that falls between heaven and earth, mediation, and contracts. Most scholars believe that Roman soldiers encountered this god when stationed in the eastern part of the Empire. As their military assignments moved them from one region to another, they spread the cult of Mithras throughout the Roman world. The image of the god changed as the cult of Mithras developed and grew. To his Roman followers Mithras became the god who created the world, the god who would never age or die, the one who was the first and last cause of all things, who upheld standards of justice and truth, and who would bring about a just, new age that would last forever.

### Roman Sun God Worship

Mithraism began to spread throughout the Roman Empire in the late first century. The religion reached the height of its popularity in the second through fourth centuries. The Roman Mithras still retained his association with the sun, an association that grew stronger rather than weaker over time, perhaps due to the rising popularity of the Roman sun god, Sol. Although Sol was only one of the group of gods recognized by traditional Roman religion, the Romans viewed Sol and Mithras as more or less the same deity. During the second century, Sol became increasingly associated with the supremacy of the emperor and of the Roman Empire. One of Sol's new titles, *invictus*, or "the invincible one," may well have been borrowed from those titles customarily applied to the emperor.

In 274 the Roman emperor Aurelian endorsed Sol's rising popularity by naming the sun god the sole protector of the Empire. He also instituted a festival celebrating the birthday of the god, called "the Birth of the Invincible Sun" (also translated as "Birth of the Unconquered Sun"). Most scholars believe that people celebrated this festival on December 25. Mithraism and the cult of Sol Invictus began to die out in the late fourth century and early fifth century as Christianity became the official religion of the Empire and began to gather large numbers of adherents.

## Ceremonies and Celebrations

Very little is known about Roman Mithraism, since it demanded that its followers keep Mithraic beliefs and practices secret from outsiders. Archeological investigations have revealed the basic outlines of the religion, however. These include some striking parallels with the emerging Christian faith. Members gathered together periodically to share a common meal. New members of the religion were brought into the faith through a baptismal ceremony. During this ceremony the officiants "sealed" the new members as devotees of Mithras by branding them on their foreheads. The initiate was expected to progress through seven levels of knowledge, each marked by its own sacrament. Finally, a blissful immortality awaited believers after death.

Mithraism also differed from Christianity in important ways. Only men could join the new cult. In fact, Roman soldiers comprised a large percentage of the membership. The sacrifice of a bull appears to have been a central ritual or mythic image in the worship of the god. Remains of Mithraic churches, built to resemble caves, feature wall paintings depicting the god Mithras slaying a bull. Sacred fires seem to have burned on the altars of these churches. Furthermore, astrology appears to have played an important part in Mithraic beliefs.

Ancient records attest to the fact that horse races were held in the Roman Circus in honor of the sun god's birthday, but little else is known about how the devotees of Mithras celebrated the festival of his birth. According to the ancient Roman calendar, **winter solstice**, the shortest day of the year, fell on December 25. Scholars suggest that worshipers viewed this natural event as symbolic of the birth of the sun god and therefore celebrated the festival on that day.

## *Mithraism and Early Christianity*

Mithraism had enough adherents in the first centuries after Jesus' death to provide some degree of competition for the fledgling Christian faith. Its popularity prompted some early Christian leaders to preach against it. They denounced Mithraic ceremonies as misleading parodies of Christian rituals. In spite of their opposition to the cult, in the middle of the fourth century Christian authorities selected December 25 as the day on which to celebrate the Nativity of Jesus Christ. Scholars believe that they did so largely in order to divert people away from competing, pagan celebrations held on or around that date, such as the Birth of the Invincible Sun, **Saturnalia**, and **Kalends**.

# Black Peter
## Zwarte Piet

A winter season gift giver is a common figure in folklore from many different regions. In the Netherlands, Dutch children receive presents on **St. Nicholas's Day**, December 6. According to old Dutch folk beliefs, each year St. Nicholas and his helper, *Zwarte Piet*, or Black Peter, sail from Spain to Holland in a ship loaded with presents for good children. Nowadays, Black Peter not only carries St. Nicholas's sack of presents, but also brandishes a birch rod which he uses to discipline undeserving children. Truly troublesome youngsters face sterner punishment. Black Peter tosses them into his sack and carries them back to Spain with him (*see also* **Cert**; **Knecht Ruprecht**).

### History

During the Middle Ages "Black Peter" was a common nickname for the Devil. One tale of those times proclaimed that each year on his birthday, St. Nicholas kidnapped the Devil and made the evildoer assist him in his good works. On St. Nicholas's Eve the good saint and his reluctant helper flew from house to house dropping presents down the chimney. Somehow these **gifts** landed in the **shoes** that the children placed by the fire before going to bed.

Black Peter traditionally appears as a dark-skinned man dressed in the costume of a sixteenth-century Spaniard. Perhaps this image of Black Peter developed during the sixteenth century, when the Dutch suffered under Spanish rule. The Dutch may have associated Spain with dark-skinned people since a north African ethnic group known as the Moors ruled parts of Spain from the eighth to the fifteenth centuries. An alternative explanation for Peter's darkened skin links it to his duties as St. Nicholas's assistant. Some speculate that Black Peter may have acquired a permanent coating of ashes and soot from scrambling down so many chimneys. Still, the most likely explanation for Peter's dark skin comes from old folk beliefs. Medieval Europeans often imagined the devil as black-skinned.

## Contemporary Customs

Each year the arrival of St. Nicholas and Black Peter is reenacted in Amsterdam, the capital of the Netherlands. A great crowd gathers to witness the arrival of the ship bearing the saint and his helper. A white horse, St. Nicholas's traditional mode of transport, stands ready to serve the saint. The music of a brass band adds to the festive atmosphere. As the gift bringers descend from the ship, the crowd easily identifies Nicholas by his red bishop's robe and hat and the white beard that flows from his face to his chest. In addition to his embroidered jacket, puffed, knee-length pants, and feathered cap, Black Peter carries a bulging sack of presents, some birch rods, and a large red book in which he has recorded the good and bad deeds of Holland's children. After greetings have been exchanged with the mayor, the saint and his helper lead a parade to Amsterdam's central plaza. There the royal family officially welcomes Holland's **Christmas season** gift bringers.

On St. Nicholas's Eve children may receive home visits from St. Nicholas and Black Peter, usually played by family members or friends. The pair's detailed knowledge of the children's good and bad deeds during the past year often astonishes the younger children. In recent years the increasing popularity of exchanging presents on Christmas Day has somewhat reduced the importance of St. Nicholas and Black Peter in Holland's Christmas celebrations.

# Bonuses

As Christmas approaches, some American workers might look forward to receiving a Christmas bonus from their employer. This bonus might be a lump sum of money added to their December paycheck, or another type of gift. Although the Christmas bonus began as a voluntary gift, over time employees came to expect an increase in their salary for December. More recently, the changing relationship between employers and workers combined with fluctuating economic conditions has made Christmas bonuses a benefit that is no longer guaranteed every year.

In the late nineteenth century, many American employers adopted the custom of distributing Christmas bonuses among their workers. These personalized exchanges

often took place at office Christmas parties, a custom that also developed during this era. The head of the company usually presented each worker with cash or other types of gifts. Often the employer tied the bonus to the employee's performance during the preceding year.

Between 1900 and 1920, these kinds of personalized exchanges all but disappeared. Labor unions grew in numbers and in influence during this period, bringing the issue of the Christmas bonus to the bargaining table. Unionists objected to the nineteenth century practice of bonuses being distributed according to the whims of managers and bosses, which sometimes resulted in favoritism. As the twentieth century rolled on, their arguments prevailed. Christmas bonuses were increasingly calculated according to agreed-upon formulas. These formulas often took into account such things as salary level and years of service.

In recent years the number of companies giving Christmas bonuses has declined. Some firms have switched to year-round incentive programs that reward effective employees. Others provide employees with a lavish Christmas party or paid days off in lieu of a bonus. Instead of yearly bonuses, some employers give symbolic non-monetary gifts to employees on significant employment anniversaries, such as after five or ten years on the job. According to an annual survey conducted by the Bureau of National Affairs in Arlington, Virginia, 41 percent of U.S. employers gave some type of year-end gift or bonus in 2010. This marked the end of a three-year decline in holiday bonuses, and is a significant increase over the previous year. In 2009, only 33 percent of American employers gave out holiday bonuses.

# Boy Bishop

## Bairn Bishop, St. Nicholas Bishop

A long succession of mock rulers have presided over winter holiday merrymaking in Europe. In the Middle Ages the **Christmas season** offered this special delight to a few lucky boys. On December 28, **Holy Innocents' Day**, religious communities, cathedrals, colleges, schools, and parish churches throughout Europe permitted an ordinary choirboy to take over the role of the local bishop. Known as the boy bishop, these kings-for-a-day were enormously popular with the people, in spite of the reservations of some Church authorities. They wore episcopal robes and rings especially made for boys, led processions, officiated at services, preached sermons, made visitations, and received **gifts**. What's more, the administrators of local cathedrals were sometimes expected to entertain the boy bishop and his entourage in a manner befitting their assumed rank. These festivities came to an end around the sixteenth century, when Church and state officials finally prohibited boy bishops. In some areas, however, the custom lingered on. One French diocese supported a boy bishop until 1721. In recent years some English cathedrals have revived the medieval custom of sponsoring a boy bishop at Christmas time.

## Beginnings

During medieval times, custom permitted the low-ranking church staff, such as deacons, sub-deacons, and choirboys, to engage in a number of boisterous celebrations

and mock religious services during the days that followed Christmas. They included the reign of the boy bishop on Innocents' Day. These frolics were sometimes referred to collectively as the **Feast of Fools**. Some experts believe that these customs may have evolved out of the topsy-turvy festivities that characterized the Roman winter feast of **Saturnalia**. During Saturnalia, things were not always as they seemed. Men masqueraded as women or animals, and mock kings were selected to preside over feasts. Some authors believe that the habit of celebrating midwinter with playful role reversals may have persisted into medieval times, inspiring the creation of the boy bishop. The chosen boy was also known as the "bairn bishop," bairn being an archaic word for child.

The origins of this custom are unclear. Some believe that the boy bishop was originally associated with **St. Nicholas's Day**, December 6. They suspect that the boy bishop's reign shifted to Holy Innocents' Day over time. These writers point out that **St. Nicholas** was a bishop in his lifetime and became the patron saint of children after his death. Therefore, they reason, it makes sense for the custom of the boy bishop to have developed around the celebrations held in St. Nicholas's honor. Indeed, in some areas of England the boy bishop ruled on St. Nicholas's Day and was known as the "St. Nicholas Bishop." Furthermore, even though most cathedrals held the ceremonies associated with the boy bishop on Innocents' Day, many held elections for the boy bishop on St. Nicholas's Day. Some researchers have concluded that the boy bishop held office from St. Nicholas's Day to Holy Innocents' Day. During this time he enjoyed many of the privileges of a real bishop and attended to many of the responsibilities. Other writers point out that Innocents' Day also provided an appropriate occasion on which to elevate a boy to the role of bishop, since it commemorated the martyrdom of **Bethlehem**'s male children.

The earliest known historical record of a boy bishop comes from what is now Switzerland. It tells us that in 911 A.D. King Conrad I and the bishop of Constance visited the monastery of St. Gall and attended a service presided over by the boy bishop and his choirboy attendants. The king entertained himself during the service by rolling apples into the aisles in an attempt to distract the children from their solemn duties. Apparently, the children demonstrated more dignity than did the king, since none stooped to pick up these tempting sweets.

## Costumes

Various customs surrounding the boy bishop reveal that this role reversal not only enjoyed popular support, but also received some degree of support from the Church. The institutions that sponsored boy bishops kept vestments specially made for them. These vestments were as luxurious and expensive as those made for real bishops. One old document describes a boy bishop's miter as being made of white silk, covered with flowers embroidered in silver and **gold** threads and ornamented with precious stones.

## Ceremonies

The reign of the boy bishop began on the eve of Holy Innocents' Day in most places. The choirboys, dressed in the silk robes of archdeacons and canons (clerical staff) and led by the regally clad boy bishop, began their procession towards the altar near the end of vespers, the evening prayer service, on December 27. The boy bishop censed the altar, after which the canons rose from their chairs and went to the places vacated by the choir. The choirboys then assumed the seats normally occupied by the clergy. This seating arrangement persisted until vespers on the following day. Moreover, during that time the canons took over the choirboys' duties at services, such as carrying the book, candles, and incense. The boy bishop presided over all services until vespers on Holy Innocents' Day. On Innocents' Day the boy bishop led a procession through the streets, blessing the people as he went. The procession, along with his Innocents' Day sermon, formed the highlights of his brief career.

## Customs

In addition to his clerical duties, the boy bishop was expected to pay visits to churches, monasteries, and dignitaries throughout his diocese. The boy bishop and his entourage carried out this duty with zest, riding out in full regalia to receive the kind of respect, courtesies, gifts, feasts, and entertainments that would normally be offered to a real bishop. Many boys found that it took several days to execute this responsibility properly.

In general, people seem to have been amused by the boy bishop and welcomed his visits. In wealthy households the **Lord of Misrule** arranged food, drink, and gifts for the boy bishop and his entourage. It appears that, in return, the boys often entertained the household with songs or speeches. England's Queen Mary is said to have received the boy bishop of St. Paul's Cathedral, who entertained her with a song. Since many churches, schools, and religious communities sponsored boy bishops, however, any one diocese might contain a small but highly active squad of miniature Christmas bishops, whose trails were sure to overlap. Thus, especially wealthy and high-ranking households and institutions sometimes received visits by more than one boy bishop during the Christmas season.

## Decline

After its introduction in the tenth century, the custom of sponsoring boy bishops at Christmas time spread throughout Europe, becoming a common practice by the thirteenth century. Although known in many lands, boy bishops were especially popular in England, France, and Germany. In spite of the costs and potential inconvenience this custom presented to ordinary people, most did not complain. Church authorities, though, led periodic campaigns to curtail the activities of the boy bishop and his court of choristers. These sporadic crusades appear to have been triggered either by the boys' unruly behavior or by disruptions caused by onlookers.

The custom fell out of favor in the fifteenth century, an era of religious turmoil in which many old practices were questioned or eliminated (*see also* **Puritans**). In England, King Henry VIII issued a proclamation forbidding the boy bishop in 1541.

## Revival

In recent years the boy bishop has sprung back to life in England. A few churches, among them Hereford Cathedral, have reinstituted some of the ceremonies and customs surrounding the boy bishop. On December 6 the boy bishop presides over an elaborate service at Hereford Cathedral. Dressed as a real bishop, the chosen boy walks at the head of a formal procession, gives the sermon, and leads the prayers and blessings. At one point in the service the real bishop of Hereford rises and offers the boy bishop his seat. Contemporary boy bishop ceremonies are observed on St. Nicholas's Day. In this way, they neither conflict with nor find themselves overshadowed by the celebrations and ceremonies already clustered around Christmas Day.

# Candlemas

### Feast of the Presentation of Christ in the Temple,
### Feast of the Purification of the Blessed Virgin,
### The Meeting of the Lord

The Gospel according to Luke tells us that Joseph and Mary brought the baby Jesus to the temple six weeks after his birth (Luke 2:22-24). Once there they observed the Jewish ceremony by which firstborn sons were presented to God. Furthermore, Mary fulfilled the purification rites, which Jewish law required women to undergo forty days after the birth of a son. Another very significant event occurred while the Holy Family was at the temple. Simeon and Anna, a holy man and a prophetess, recognized the infant as the Messiah. Simeon declared that the child would be "a light that will bring revelation to the Gentiles" (Luke 2:32). The Christian feast of Candlemas commemorates all these events. It is celebrated on February 2, forty days after Christmas. Candlemas gets its name from a number of customs related to **candles** that are connected with the feast. By the Middle Ages, the blessing of candles, the distribution of blessed candles among parishioners, and candlelit processions had all established themselves as common elements in western European Candlemas services.

## *History*

The earliest known description of the feast comes from late fourth-century Jerusalem. This early celebration consisted of a solemn procession followed by a sermon and mass. The description named the feast simply "the fortieth day after Epiphany." Since at that time Jerusalem Christians were celebrating both Epiphany and the Nativity on January 6, the festival fell on the fourteenth of February (*see also* December 25). From Jerusalem the new festival spread throughout the East. The Greeks called it *Hypapante Kyriou*, or "The Meeting of the Lord," a name that reflected their emphasis on the meeting between Simeon, Anna, and the infant Jesus. The feast began to appear in the West in the seventh and eighth centuries. Westerners celebrated it on February 2, since by that time Rome had assigned the celebration of the Nativity to December 25. Roman officials called the feast the "Purification of Mary," reflecting their emphasis on Mary's fulfillment of Jewish law.

Several centuries passed before western European Candlemas observances consolidated around a distinctive set of traditions. Candles were used in the services as early as the mid-fifth century in Jerusalem. Nevertheless, Pope Sergius I is generally credited with ordering the first candlelit processions to accompany church services in Rome. In what is now France, the blessing of candles developed during the Carolingian Empire, near the close of the eighth century. By the eleventh century the blessing of candles, the distribution of blessed candles, and candlelit processions had become widespread elements in the western European observance of Candlemas. The feast got its English name, Candlemas, meaning quite literally "candle mass," from these customs. Since the eighteenth century the representatives of various religious communities have offered the pope large, decorated candles on Candlemas.

Contemporary Candlemas services generally emphasize Christ as the Light of the World. In addition, the officiant often blesses and distributes beeswax candles. In some traditions, parishioners bring candles from home to be blessed during the service. In past times Candlemas processions filed out into the churchyard and past the graves of the departed. Contemporary Candlemas processions, however, usually remain within the church.

Some researchers suggest that Christians simply adopted Candlemas and its customs from pagan celebrations held at the same time of year. On February 1 the pagan Celts celebrated Imbolc, a festival associated with the return of the spring goddess Bride (later, St. Bridget). In some areas sacred fires and candles burned through the night in honor of Bride's return. In ancient Rome people observed purification rites throughout the month of February, which included a procession through the city with lit candles. In addition, they celebrated the return of their spring goddess, Ceres, on February first. Pagans in other Mediterranean cultures also welcomed the return of a spring deity. Many of these observances featured fire rituals and torchlit processions.

While some writers believe that these pagan practices gave rise to the observance of Candlemas and its customs, most contemporary scholars doubt that these pagan rituals exerted strong influence on medieval Christians. The doubters point out that these pagan fire ceremonies had died out by the time candles became part of the Christian festival. They also claim a specifically Christian symbolism for the Candlemas tapers. The candles recall the words of Simeon, who proclaimed that Jesus would become "a light" unto the Gentiles.

### Christmas Customs

Jesus' presentation in the temple and Mary's fulfillment of the rites of purification mark the end of the series of events associated with Jesus' birth in the Gospels. In a similar vein, many old European Christmas customs were practiced until Candlemas. For example, in some areas **Nativity scenes** were taken apart and put away on Candlemas. In other areas Christmas **greenery**—such as **rosemary, laurel, mistletoe, holly,** and **ivy**—and other seasonal decorations were finally removed on Candlemas.

# Candles
## Yule Candle

In past centuries many families observed Christmas by lighting especially large candles. Home Christmas celebrations took place in the glow of these enormous tapers. Some families lit the candles on Christmas Eve, in which case custom called for the candle to burn until morning. Others lit their candles on Christmas morning and kept them burning throughout the day. Large candles of this sort were also used in Christmas church services.

People interpreted the meaning of these Christmas candles in several different ways. Many believed the large candle served as a natural symbol for the coming of **Jesus** Christ, "the light of the world." Others said it represented the **Star of Bethlehem**. Many folk beliefs suggest that people commonly viewed the home Christmas candle as representing the family's future in some way. In some parts of England people varied this custom by using many regular-sized candles instead of one extra-large one. In nineteenth-century England many grocers and chandlers (candlemakers) presented their regular customers with the gift of a large candle at Christmas. In parts of Denmark, people lit two candles, one representing the male head of the household, the other representing the female head of the household. Whichever burned out first was said to foretell which of them would die first. Scottish folklore claimed that if the Christmas candle burned out before midnight the family would soon experience some kind of calamity. Scandinavian tradition agreed that bad luck would surely visit any family whose **Yule** candle burned out during the holy night, possibly the death of a family member. While the flame burned, however, many Scandinavians believed that the light of the Yule candle conferred a blessing on all it touched. Families brought good things to eat and drink, money, clothing, and other desirable goods within the circle of candlelight in the hopes that they would be blessed with more of these things in the coming year.

Some peoples believed that the remains of the candle retained their power to bless and protect even after Christmas had passed. In Sweden, people rubbed the stub of their Yule candle against their plows or used it to make the sign of the cross over their animals. In other parts of Scandinavia, people fed the candle stub to their barnyard fowl or saved it as a charm against thunder and lightning.

In Estonia, Germany, and Lithuania people light candles at family gravesites on Christmas Eve. This practice may be linked to old folk beliefs concerning the return of the dead at Christmas time (*see also* **Ghosts**).

# Cert

A winter season gift giver is a common figure in folklore from many different regions. In Slovakia and the Czech Republic, folk beliefs assign **St. Nicholas** the role of Christmas **gift** bringer. According to this folklore, two oddly matched companions aid the good saint in his labors. On December sixth, **St. Nicholas's Day**, Nicholas descends from heaven on a golden rope accompanied by an **angel** dressed in white and a demon known as a cert. The cert wears black clothing and carries a whip and chain. He frightens naughty children, reminding them of the punishment in store for them if they don't mend their ways. (*See also* **Black Peter**.)

# Charitable Giving

In contemporary American society, the end of the year is typically the most popular time for charitable donations and volunteerism. For many people, charitable giving is an important part of the Christmas season. Some see donations and volunteerism as a way to counter the commercialization of the Christmas holiday. Giving to charity helps people to focus on the Christmas spirit of openness, generosity, and goodwill towards those less fortunate. Others make their donations at year end in order to take advantage of allowable income tax deductions. Whatever the reason for the seasonal increase in giving, the practice of charity at Christmas time has its roots in very old traditions.

## Early Charitable Giving

The tradition of Christmas charity can be traced back to England in the Middle Ages. During that time, it was common for churches and nobility to give money to the poor on the day after Christmas. December 26 was originally observed as St. Stephen's Day and later became known as Boxing Day, for this was the day that parish priests customarily opened the church alms-boxes. These boxes collected donations of money from churchgoers throughout the year. On Boxing Day, the donations would be distributed to the needy, many of whom came to rely on their yearly benefit from the boxes.

The idea of Christmas as a season especially appropriate for charitable giving gained popularity in England and America during the second half of the nineteenth century (*see also A Christmas Carol*; **America, Christmas in Nineteenth-Century**). In the early part of that era, Americans who celebrated Christmas sometimes gave gifts to the poor and to servants, following old European customs of Christmas charity. Charitable giving linked Christmas gift giving with the spiritual celebration of the holiday.

As Christmas became a more important holiday in the U.S., charitable gifts made at Christmas time by the wealthy and other notable members of society were sometimes highly publicized. In this way, the idea of Christmas charity was popularized among the general public. For example, there is a long history of the charitable giving of American presidents at Christmas time (*see also* **White House, Christmas in the**).

## Twentieth-Century Giving

**Salvation Army kettles** are one of the oldest public giving campaigns associated with Christmas in America. For more than 100 years, the Salvation Army has stationed volunteer bell-ringers on street corners and at shopping malls to collect money to help those in need. For many Americans, the red kettle and tinkling bell have become an annual holiday symbol and a reminder that the Christmas season is upon us.

In 1947, the United States Marine Corps began its well-known Toys for Tots campaign. Toys for Tots is a program that operates from October to December each year. Volunteers collect donations of toys, which are then distributed to families that are otherwise unable to provide Christmas presents for their children. Toys for Tots was started at the suggestion of the wife of a major in the Marine Corps Reserve. The first toy drive was so successful that the Marine Corps informally adopted the program in 1948. Each year since then, Marines have collected, sorted, and distributed toys in communities throughout the U.S. In 1995, the Marine Toys for Tots Foundation became an official activity of the U.S. Marine Corps and an official mission of the Marine Corps Reserve. Over the years, more than 188 million children have benefitted from the more than 400 million toys donated through the program.

In addition to participating in large-scale organized charitable programs such as Toys for Tots, contemporary Americans have embraced a variety of opportunities to give in a more individual way. "Giving trees," also known as mitten trees or angel trees, are often sponsored by schools, churches, and businesses. These trees provide a focus for donations of items such as clothing, toys, food, or other personal necessities. Mitten trees typically collect mittens, gloves, hats, scarves, and other cold weather gear. Donated items are either given to a local charity for distribution to the needy, or given directly to recipients in the community. Angel trees display paper ornaments containing the names of families or children in need, sometimes including suggestions for specific items such as clothing, coats, or shoes. People select an ornament from the tree and commit to donating items for those named on it. Recipients of angel tree donations are usually identified by such organizations as the Salvation Army or other local agencies, which also coordinate the distribution of donations.

Some people forgo traditional Christmas **gifts** altogether and instead make charitable donations on behalf of their friends and family members. A new development for this type of Christmas giving is the purchase of charity "gift cards," which allow the recipient to choose which charity will receive the donation. Another fairly recent development is the concept of "giving parties." These events, typically held in private homes, are attended by the people with whom the party host would normally have exchanged Christmas gifts. Instead of a traditional gift exchange, the host and guests make monetary donations to one or more charitable organizations that are sometimes pre-selected by the party host.

### Christmas Volunteerism

The Christmas season is also a time when many Americans choose to volunteer for charitable organizations. This practice is not limited to Christians who observe the Christmas holiday, as many Americans of other faiths choose to volunteer their time on Christmas. Some non-Christian Americans routinely volunteer to work on Christmas Eve and Christmas Day so that their Christian co-workers can enjoy the time off. For the past twenty years, Jewish residents in the Detroit area have observed Mitzvah Day each December 25th. "Mitzvah" can be translated as "good deed," and many Jews spend Christmas day volunteering in soup kitchens and other social service agencies. In 2009, the Jewish Community Relations Council and Jewish Federation of Metropolitan Detroit teamed up with the Council of Islamic Organizations of Michigan to create an interfaith collaboration in their annual volunteer drive. These organizations are active throughout the year, but increase their activities on Christmas to allow Christians time to observe the holiday with their families. By 2010, hundreds of Detroit-area Muslims had joined the effort, volunteering to deliver meals and presents on Christmas Day.

An estimated 65 percent of all American households give to charity. There are more than 1.2 million charitable organizations in the U.S. that depend on donations to keep their programs running. These organizations report that 75 percent of all the donations they receive are from individuals rather than corporations or foundations. In 2008, Americans donated an estimated $315 billion, representing the highest recorded giving level since reporting began in 1956. Despite experiencing the worst economic recession since the Great Depression, in 2009 the average annual household donation was about $1,900.

# "A Charlie Brown Christmas"

"A Charlie Brown Christmas" charmed millions of Americans when it made its debut in 1965. This animated television special weaves a story around the Christmas-time antics of the characters from the popular cartoon-strip "Peanuts" by Charles Schulz. While the other kids look forward to Christmas and enjoy winter-time activities, like skating, Charlie Brown alone feels anxious and depressed (*see* **Depression**). He consults Lucy, who fancies herself an amateur psychiatrist. She advises him to "get involved" with something and makes him the director of the school Christmas play. His involvement ends when the other kids laugh at the straggly **Christmas tree** he brings back to adorn the stage. Then Linus, quoting from the Bible, reminds the kids what Christmas is all about (*see* **Gospel Accounts of Christmas**). Afterwards Charlie Brown takes his Christmas tree home. The other kids change their minds about the tree and help Charlie Brown decorate it.

### Charles Schulz's "Peanuts"

Charles Schulz's "Peanuts" was one of the most successful comic strips of all time. More than 300 million people worldwide followed the strip, which was translated into 20 different languages. Schulz's pint-sized characters approach life with a unique combination of wisdom, innocence, anxiety, and hip self-assurance that attracts both adult and juvenile readers. People who knew Charles Schulz find many similarities between the cartoonist and his main character, the worried and hapless Charlie

Brown. Yet Schulz was able to translate his nervousness into an appealing art form, which in turn brought him millions of fans and millions of dollars. Among the many honors given to the cartoonist include his mention in the 1984 *Guinness Book of World Records* when the 2,000th newspaper subscribed to his strip, and his induction into the Cartoonist Hall of Fame in 1986. In 1990 the French government named him a "Commander of Arts and Letters."

On December 14, 1999, Schulz, who was battling cancer, reluctantly announced his retirement to the world. One of the last honors received by this long-time resident of Santa Rosa, California, was given to him by the California state legislature, which declared February 13, 2000, as "Charles Schulz Day." On this day the last "Peanuts" strip was scheduled to run in newspapers across the country and around the world. Schulz died in his sleep on February 12, just hours before a saddened public enjoyed his final original strip. In May 2000 the Congress of the United States posthumously awarded him the Medal of Honor.

### The Making of "A Charlie Brown Christmas"

"A Charlie Brown Christmas" began life as a twinkle in the eye of producer Lee Mendelson. He, Schulz, and animator Bill Melendez had worked together a couple of years earlier on a documentary of Schulz and his cartoon characters. When Mendelson discovered that Coca Cola was looking for a Christmas special and was interested in the Peanuts characters, he assured them of both his and Schulz's interest in the project. Then Mendelson rushed to Schulz's house to inform him of the idea and convince him that it was a good one. Luckily, Schulz readily agreed to work on the project, and together the two of them came up with an outline for the show. The outline specified that the story would contain a school play, winter-time fun and games, a reading from the Bible, and a combination of jazz and traditional Christmas music. Coca Cola liked the outline, and production immediately began on the show.

Mendelson right away invited Bill Melendez to take charge of the animation. The three men met to develop the story. Mendelson contributed the idea of structuring some of the action around a Christmas tree, an inspiration he took from Hans Christian Andersen's short story "The Fir Tree." Schulz qualified the concept by insisting that the tree be a "Charlie Brown" type of tree. The work progressed with Schulz masterminding the dialogue and situations, while Melendez translated them into an animated cartoon.

The three men were eager to hire jazz pianist Vince Guaraldi, whom they had worked with before on the Schulz documentary. They wanted to reuse the "Linus and Lucy" theme developed by Guaraldi several years ago as well as give him an opportunity to create new music. Guaraldi signed on and production went into full swing. The animators produced 10,000 drawings for the half-hour show. Passing them by the camera at the rate of 12 per second made the cartoon characters appear to move.

"A Charlie Brown Christmas" broke new ground in several ways. By having one of the characters recite the biblical narrative of the birth of Jesus, it introduced a moment of serious religious contemplation into a cartoon aimed at children. Although Mendelson was doubtful, Schulz, a quietly religious man, insisted that his Christmas show contain a religious theme. In addition, the three men decided to hire child actors to dub in the cartoon characters' voices. Up till that time, adult actors had typically filled in all the voices in animated cartoons, even those of child characters. Finally, the jazz piano music provided by Vince Guaraldi delighted both adults and children, who previously had been accustomed to cartoons accompanied by simple jingles rather than serious music.

### Reactions to "A Charlie Brown Christmas"

The crew finished work on the show one week before it was scheduled to air on television. Top CBS executives screened the special shortly before it was televised. Disappointed by what they considered its slow pace, they assured Mendelson that although they would air the program, they wouldn't be interested in any further Charlie Brown shows.

This assessment crushed Mendelson, Schulz, and Melendez. Hope revived when the special received a good pre-broadcast review in *Time* magazine. On December 9, 1965, the show was broadcast nationwide. Ratings proved it to be a hit with the American public, and it ranked as the second-most popular show on television during its time-slot. Several months later the three men received an Emmy Award for Best Network Animated Special. "A Charlie Brown Christmas" also received a Peabody Award for excellence in family programming. Rerun in the years that followed, the show continued to receive high ratings.

Charles Schulz went on to create 45 animated television specials based on his famous cartoon-strip characters. "A Charlie Brown Christmas," his first, remained his favorite. Vince Guaraldi's album of music from the show, entitled "A Charlie Brown

Christmas," went platinum (sold over one million copies). Later released as a CD, it continues to be a best-selling Christmas album.

# Cherry Trees

Legend, song, and custom link cherry trees to the **Christmas season**. In all three a cherry tree performs unusual feats in response to the power of God or the magic of the season.

## *Legends*

An old Christian legend, first recorded in the apocryphal Gospel of Pseudo-Matthew, makes the cherry tree the subject of one of the first miracles by the infant **Jesus**. The original Latin text containing the tale dates back to the eighth or ninth century. This version of the story tells of an event that occurred shortly after Jesus' birth. **Joseph, Mary**, and the infant Jesus were traveling in the desert. The couple spied a palm tree and went to rest under its shadow. Joseph worried about how they were going to find water. Mary expressed a wish for the dates she saw hanging high above them. Joseph scolded his wife for asking for something so far out of his reach. Then the baby Jesus spoke to the tree, ordering it to bend down so his mother could gather the fruit. The tree obeyed. Jesus also commanded an underground spring to surface so they could drink and fill their water bags.

As the tale passed from one teller to another, many variations occurred. In later versions of the story, the incident takes place before Jesus is born. Moreover, as the tale became popular in Europe, the tree which Jesus commands to bow down changes to species more familiar to Europeans. In Britain, the newer versions of the story featured a cherry tree. In these later interpretations of the tale, Joseph and his pregnant wife are walking by some cherry trees laden with ripe fruit. Mary asks Joseph to pick some cherries for her. He refuses in a rude manner, with the implication that he still questions the origins of her mysterious pregnancy. Jesus, from inside the womb, then commands the cherry tree to bow down so his mother can pick fruit. Joseph stands by sheepishly and observes this miracle. The earliest recorded version of this

story in the English language appeared in a fifteenth-century miracle play. Eventually this popular tale was set to music in the Christmas song known as "The Cherry Tree Carol" (*see also* **Christmas Carols and Other Music**).

# Children's Letters

The urge to send greetings at Christmas time seizes people of all ages. Businesses prepare hundreds of thank-you notes for their customers. Adults salute family and friends with **Christmas cards**, while children typically write letters to **Santa Claus**.

## Letters to Santa Claus

During the nineteenth century, Santa Claus became known as the bringer of Christmas gifts to children who had behaved themselves particularly well during the previous year. American cartoonist Thomas Nast popularized the notion that Santa Claus lived at the **North Pole**. Once Santa Claus's address became known, American children began writing letters to Santa Claus, hoping to guide him in his choice of gifts for them.

The U.S. Postal Service first began receiving letters addressed to Santa Claus more than 100 years ago. In 1912, the Postal Service began its Operation Santa program, which authorized local postmasters to allow postal employees and volunteers to respond to these letters. By 1940, Operation Santa was becoming overwhelmed by the number of letters received each year. The Postal Service opened the Operation Santa program to charitable organizations and corporations that were interested in participating. Each year since, Operation Santa volunteers read and respond to as many letters as possible. Some volunteers, touched by the earnest requests of letter writing children, find ways to grant at least some of their wishes. The Operation Santa program is now run by numerous post offices located throughout the country. While most of the letters to Santa Claus are forwarded to these locations, many make their way to the tiny town of North Pole, Alaska. Each year since 1954, volunteers there have replied to hundreds of thousands of letters from children all over the world.

In 1997, postal workers all over the country reported the first decline ever in the numbers of letters sent to Santa Claus at Christmas time. Some postal divisions noticed a steep 70 percent drop in these letters. No one knows why so many children all at once lost interest in writing letters to Santa. One possible explanation is the rise of email messaging over traditional postal mail. As technology has changed the way that people communicate, children now have more options to get in touch with Santa Claus. Various web sites now offer the opportunity to send letters to Santa by email, with some promising a personalized reply in return. Some larger department stores, charitable organizations, and telephone service providers also operate telephone hotlines where children can call to hear a message from Santa. Some of these services can also be used by parents to schedule a telephone call from Santa to their child.

# Chrismon Tree

The Chrismon tree adapts the traditional **Christmas tree** to more strictly Christian uses. It consists of an evergreen tree decorated with traditional Christian symbols of **Jesus**. In fact, the word "Chrismon" resulted from the combination of two words, "Christ" and "monogram." Originally, only monograms of Christ decorated the tree. As churches and families adopted the custom, however, they began to create new symbols of Christ to adorn their trees. Only the colors white and **gold** appear on these **ornaments**. These are the liturgical colors for Christmas Day. White represents Jesus' purity and perfection, while gold stands for his majesty and glory. White lights may further embellish the tree, reminding viewers that Jesus is "the light of the world" (John 8:12).

# Christkindel

## Christ Child, Christkind, Kriss Kringle

In parts of Germany, Switzerland, and Austria the *Christkindel* or *Christkind* brings children their Christmas **gifts**. Christkindel means "Christ child" in German. Some people understand the Christ Child to be the child **Jesus**; others view the Christ Child as an **angel** who appears as a young girl with golden wings, long blond hair, and flowing robes.

In past times a rather threatening spirit known as Hans Trapp accompanied the Christ Child in some German-speaking regions. Hans Trapp dressed in furs and carried a rod, making it his duty to punish children who had behaved badly (*see also* **Knecht Ruprecht**). The Christ Child generally intervened on the naughty child's behalf, however.

The Christ Child became a German gift bringer around the seventeenth century. During the Reformation, Protestant reformers wanted to teach children that all blessings come directly from God. Rather than let children continue to believe that **St. Nicholas** brought their gifts, they introduced the concept of the Christkindel. The famous Christmas market in Nuremberg, Germany, which displays hundreds of gift items each year, adopted the name "Christ Child Market" in the seventeenth century.

German immigrants brought the notion of the Christkindel with them to the United States. Over time the customs and lore connected with Christkindel faded and the word itself changed to "Kriss Kringle." The growing popularity of **Santa Claus** in the United States eventually eclipsed any remaining notion of the Christ Child, and Kriss Kringle became simply another name for Santa.

# Christmas Cards

Historians credit the English with the invention and popularization of the Christmas card during the early years of the Victorian era (*see also* **Victorian Era, Christmas in**). By the 1860s an entire industry had grown up around the design and production of Christmas cards in England. This industry soon spread to other countries. Throughout the twentieth century ever-increasing numbers of people embraced the Christmas card, making the practice of sending greeting cards one of the most popular customs of the **Christmas season**.

## *The First Christmas Card*

The first Christmas card was designed by Englishman J. C. Horsley in 1843. Three separate images adorn the front of the card. A large center drawing depicts a family gathered around a table, wine glasses in hand. One woman gives a small child a sip of wine, a detail which caused temperance advocates to object. A smaller side panel depicts a well-dressed woman draping a cloak around a poor woman and child. The other side panel depicts the distribution of food among the poor. The producer of this card printed about 1,000 copies and sold them for one shilling each.

The new custom did not catch on right away. It took two decades for the Christmas card to establish itself as an annual institution in England. The advent of the penny post, begun in 1840, provided an inexpensive means of posting the cards, which undoubtedly permitted the custom of sending Christmas cards to spread. Before that time, not only had postal rates been higher, but also the post office charged the postage to the addressee rather than to the sender. The public responded enthusiastically to the new postal system. Between 1840 and 1845 the number of letters sent in Great Britain nearly doubled.

The first Christmas cards were modeled after Victorian visiting cards and so did not fold in any way. These small rectangles of pasteboard, about the size of an index card, were printed on one side only. The decorated side bore a lithographed or etched drawing, a greeting, and blank space for the names of both the sender and the addressee. By the 1870s manufacturers had started producing larger cards and folded cards. Some of the early folded cards were designed to open out like cupboard doors; others fell into accordion folds.

Trick cards also originated in the 1870s. Their clever designs delighted Victorians. Pulling a paper lever on the face of a card, for example, might add to or subtract something from the design or change it completely. Pop-up cards also tickled Victorian fancies. Some cleverly designed cards contained hidden images that appeared only if viewed from a certain angle or in a certain light.

## Victorian Christmas Cards in Their Heyday

By the 1880s Victorian Christmas cards reflected the ornate taste of the age. Designers embellished the images printed on the cards with a variety of materials, including paper lace, real lace, shells, seaweed, dried grass, flowers, silk, velvet, chenille, tinsel, celluloid, crewel work, metal plates, and small sachets of scented powders. They frosted surfaces with powdered glass or aluminum. For a finishing touch, they embossed or scalloped the edges of their cards, or even finished them with lace, cords, ribbons, or silk.

Some of the most common images found on Victorian Christmas cards are still familiar symbols of the holiday today. These include **holly, ivy, mistletoe,** and, to a lesser extent, **robins,** wrens, winter landscapes, and Christmas feasts and parties. Other images that adorned Victorian cards seem less central to the festival. For example, flowers, shrubs, and trees, often in great profusion, served as perhaps the most popular subjects portrayed on the Victorian Christmas card. Due to the abundance of flowers and leaves, these cards often appear to depict a summer scene, rather than a winter one. Many other cards carried images of children, often at play. Some of these children seem to be unnaturally angelic boys and girls, others clearly pranksters. Animals were another popular theme, and they were often portrayed carrying out human activities and sometimes wearing human clothing. Victorians also enjoyed Christmas cards that featured new inventions, such as the bicycle, the steamship, and the motorcar.

Some Victorian Christmas card illustrations might strike modern viewers as somewhat inappropriate images with which to represent Christmas. Portraits of beautiful girls and women appeared frequently on Victorian Christmas cards, sometimes partially nude or clad only in gauzy robes. The dead robin constitutes another curi-

ous Victorian preference in Christmas card decoration. During the 1880s many of the cards featuring robins depicted a dead bird lying in the snow.

### Early American Christmas Cards

Although the first American Christmas card dates back to the 1850s, the American Christmas card industry did not take off until the 1870s. Historians credit a German immigrant named Louis Prang with developing this industry. In 1875 his print shop introduced a line of visiting cards that included a Christmas greeting. An appreciative public snapped up his entire stock. Prang expanded his line of Christmas cards in the years that followed. At first his designs resembled those of the early Victorian cards from England. These were embellished with flowers, leaves, butterflies and birds, images that evoked springtime rather than illustrating the Christmas sentiments that accompanied them. Soon, however, Prang's workshop began to turn out cards decorated with recognizable Christmas symbols, such as holly, ivy, and **poinsettias**. As these designs became more complex, the cards grew in size, eventually measuring about seven by ten inches. The American public loved Prang's novelties. Many foreign buyers also admired and collected Prang's cards.

Several factors contributed to Prang's extraordinary success. A printer by trade, Prang combined expert printing skills, innovative lithography techniques, and clever marketing ploys to catch the public's attention. But Prang was more than a savvy salesman. He passionately believed that mass-produced images could introduce fine art to those who would never otherwise be exposed to it. Prang's studio developed a reputation for high artistic standards.

In 1880, Prang instituted a yearly competition for the best Christmas card design. He awarded $1,000 to the first-place winner and $500 to the second-place winner. He also gave $300 and $200 prizes. Prang called on well-known figures in the

American art world to serve as judges, including stained-glass artist Louis C. Tiffany, painter Samuel Colman, and architect Richard M. Hunt. Prang also let the public vote on which designs they preferred, and winners of the "Public Prizes" received the same hefty cash awards as those contestants whose work was selected by the panel of artists. Although Prang's competition lasted only a few years, during its day it was considered one of the highlights of the New York art season. Prang's dissatisfaction with the quality of the works presented at his competitions caused him to switch tactics after a few years and commission well-known artists to submit designs.

Unlike his competitors in Victorian England, Prang rejected trick cards and scorned fancy embellishments of lace and other materials as vulgar. During the 1870s and 1880s Christmas cards printed in continental Europe began to infiltrate British and American markets. Prang left the Christmas card business in the 1890s, when his sales figures began to falter.

In spite of his enthusiasm for popularizing refined art, Prang's expensive Christmas cards circulated primarily among the well-to-do. During the 1890s and 1900s the majority of American Christmas gift givers exchanged flimsy knickknacks with their friends. By the second decade of the twentieth century, though, Americans turned towards cards as a tasteful and inexpensive alternative for the useless trinkets everyone gave and, apparently, no one wanted. Inexpensive new Christmas cards quickly grew in popularity, especially during World War I.

The rise in popularity of Christmas cards created an opportunity for some charities. At the turn of the twentieth century a number of charitable organizations hit on a way to use the flood of Christmas mail to raise some badly needed revenue. They began to sell **Christmas seals**, which could be used to decorate envelopes and packages. In the 1960s the U.S. Postal Service began producing special Christmas stamps during the holiday season. Unlike the seals, the stamps function as valid postage. They add a further decorative note to holiday season mail.

## New Traditions

The popularity of Christmas greeting cards continued to grow steadily throughout the 20th century, and several new traditions emerged. Many Americans began to have annual family photos taken specifically for their Christmas cards. The family Christmas newsletter was another popular new custom. Instead of writing a short message inside each card, or simply signing the family's names, some people created newsletters that included updates and personal news from the previous year. These Christmas newsletters typically discussed special achievements, job changes, births, weddings, vacations, or other important family events. Normally typed and then printed in bulk, a copy of the newsletter would be included with each card sent by the family. By 2001, Americans were buying and sending billions of Christmas cards each year, more than all other types of greeting cards combined.

Since then, however, sales of Christmas cards have begun to decline. The rise of new communication technologies such as email, text messaging, and social networking have changed the way that many Americans keep in touch with friends and family. An estimated 77 percent of Americans bought Christmas cards in 2005, but that number dropped to 62 percent in 2009. Many contemporary American teens and young adults seemed to view handwritten Christmas cards sent by postal mail as an outdated tradition.

## High-Tech Cards

In an effort to keep consumers interested in buying and sending Christmas cards, American greeting card manufacturers began to combine traditional paper cards with elements of technology. These new cards featured blinking lights, music that played when the card is opened, or a tiny embedded computer chip that allowed the sender to record a personalized message for the card's recipient. Other recordable cards featured karaoke-style sing-a-longs, allowing the sender to record themselves singing with pre-recorded music for popular **Christmas carols**. Another customizable card allowed the sender to copy up to 50 digital photos to an embedded computer chip. The photos were displayed in a rotating slide show on a small LCD screen also embedded in the card. The recipient was then able to connect the card to a computer, and save copies of the photos. Yet another customizable option allowed people to design their own Christmas card using a special web site, and then have the cards printed, addressed, and mailed by the manufacturer.

# *A Christmas Carol*

*A Christmas Carol*, by Charles Dickens, is perhaps the best-known and best-loved Christmas story of all time. Some writers even credit the tale with changing the way nineteenth-century Britons and Americans celebrated Christmas. *A Christmas Carol* tells the story of a greedy, rich, Christmas-hating old man named Ebenezer Scrooge. One Christmas Eve Scrooge receives a visit from three spirits. These spirits—the Ghost of Christmas Past, the Ghost of Christmas Present, and the Ghost of Christmas Yet To Come—show him scenes from his past, present, and future. This supernatural experience transforms him into a joyous, generous soul who cherishes Christmas above all other times of year.

## *Life and Times of Charles Dickens*

Charles Dickens was born on February 7, 1812, just outside Portsmouth, England. The second of seven children, Charles was brought up in a lower-middle-class household plagued by his father's tendency to fall into debt. In 1821 the Dickens family moved to London, where the young Charles witnessed firsthand the poverty and despair of the city's slums. In 1824, Charles's father was sent to Marshalsea Prison for failure to pay off a debt. The entire family moved into the prison, except Charles, who, at the age of twelve, went to work in a blacking (shoe polish) factory. Although he was not treated cruelly, the young Charles worked twelve hours a day and felt deeply shamed by his family's situation. Several months later, Charles's father inherited a small sum of money, which permitted him to pay the debt and leave prison. Although Charles's mother wanted her son to continue working at the blacking factory, Charles's father insisted that he receive some kind of education. Even after he became a successful novelist, Dickens resented his mother for her willingness to send him back to a life of drudgery.

In 1827 Charles began his adult career as a solicitor's clerk. Shortly thereafter, he mastered shorthand and became a reporter. In 1833 he began to submit sketches and stories to newspapers and magazines under his pen name, "Boz." In a few years he acquired a wide readership. By 1837 *Sketches by Boz* and *The Pickwick Papers*, both published serially, had brought him fame and financial security. He went on to

become one of Victorian England's most prolific and best-loved authors. Dickens never forgot his early brushes with poverty, however, and throughout his life he wielded both his voice and his pen against his society's harsh treatment of the poor. His works of fiction offered middle-class readers disturbing glimpses inside nineteenth-century workhouses (prison-like institutions meting out hard labor to the destitute), painted moving portraits of those confined to debtors' prisons, and sketched the often-desperate plight of the working poor.

### *The Writing of* A Christmas Carol

In an indirect way, Dickens's concern for the poor brought him the inspiration needed to write *A Christmas Carol*. In September 1843, at the invitation of Miss Angela Burdett Coutts, a wealthy philanthropist and a friend of Dickens, he toured one of London's Ragged Schools. Funded by private charity, these schools sought to educate some of the city's poorest children. The visit moved him deeply. Several weeks later he traveled to Manchester to speak at a fund-raising event for the Athenaeum, an organization dedicated to educating workers, where he addressed the link between poverty and ignorance. While in Manchester, the idea of transforming his impressions of the Ragged School into a work of fiction planted itself in his imagination. In October he plunged into a new story called *A Christmas Carol*. To be sure, financial as well as social concerns motivated Dickens to undertake this new project. Sales of his latest novel, *Martin Chuzzlewit*, were floundering. Dickens felt sure that a story like the *Carol* would appeal to readers at Christmas time and thus generate needed cash.

Dickens blazed through the writing of the *Carol*, completing the manuscript in only six weeks. The project seized hold of him, inspiring him to work from morning until late at night. He passed some of these nights striding as many as fifteen or twenty miles through the shadowy, still London streets, meditating on the story. In a letter to a friend he confessed that the work so charged his emotions, he found himself alternately laughing and weeping.

Dickens financed the publication of the slim little book himself, insisting on illustrations and a quality binding. It arrived in bookstores on December 19, 1843. Dickens complained that booksellers seemed uninterested in promoting the story. Nevertheless, the entire first printing, 6,000 copies, sold out in five days. After subtracting what it had cost him to produce the book, though, Dickens earned very little from its first printing. Still, Dickens celebrated Christmas merrily that year, exclaiming in a letter to a friend that he had rarely experienced a **Christmas season** so full of dining, dancing, theatergoing, party games, and good cheer. He even attended a children's party where he entertained the assembled company with magic tricks, to all appearances dumping the raw ingredients of a plum pudding into a friend's hat and pulling out the finished product.

## Public Readings

By March 1844, three months after its first printing, *A Christmas Carol* was in its sixth edition. Enthusiastic letters poured in from an appreciative public. Some readers told Dickens that they kept the book on a little shelf all by itself, others that they read it aloud to their families. In 1853 Dickens himself began a series of public readings of the work that would last the rest of his life.

As the public readings became more frequent, Dickens developed them into polished performances. It took him three hours to read through *A Christmas Carol* as printed, so he began to edit his own little copy of the book, eliminating dialogue and description that he felt could be cut without damaging the tale. He reduced the story to two hours, added some stage directions, and memorized the entire text. The public readings thus became recitations. Just in case his memory failed him, he kept a copy of the book with him on stage.

Dickens performed his first public reading of the *Carol* in December 1853 as a benefit for the Birmingham and Midland Institute. More than two thousand people attended. Charities soon besieged the author with requests that he perform a reading on their behalf. Dickens complied with some of these requests, but also began a series of public readings for which he sold tickets. These readings generated a tidy second income for the author. Dickens incorporated parts of his other works in these public readings as well. *A Christmas Carol*, however, remained one of the most popular and most often requested works in his repertoire.

In 1865 Dickens performed a series of public readings in the United States. He opened in Boston with a reading of *A Christmas Carol*. The ticket line stretched half a mile in length on the night before the box office opened. Although the tickets sold for $2 apiece, scalpers priced tickets to the sold-out performance as high as $26 each. Many prominent American literary figures attended this reading. Dickens continued on to Philadelphia, New York, Baltimore, and Washington, D.C. In New York, five thousand people stood in line on a bitterly cold night waiting for the chance to buy a ticket in the morning. In Washington, Dickens received an invitation to meet President Andrew Johnson.

In spring 1870 Dickens struggled to complete a series of scheduled readings. During intermissions he staggered backstage to lie on a sofa while concerned doctors checked his vital signs. After completing the March 15 reading of *A Christmas Carol*, he returned to the stage for a final round of applause and announced, with tears on his face, that the audience had just witnessed his last public performance. He died three months later, on June 9, 1870, and was buried in Westminster Abbey alongside the composer George Frideric Handel, another great contributor to the artistic legacy of Christmas (*see also* **Messiah**).

## The Carol *as a Ghost Story*

Contemporary readers tend to approach *A Christmas Carol* as a tale about the holiday, thus overlooking the fact that it is also a **ghost** story. In Dickens's day, English tradition called for the telling of ghost stories at Christmas time. Dickens conceived *A Christmas Carol* as an exemplary addition to this genre. He draws our attention to the ghostly aspect of the tale in its full title, which reads *A Christmas Carol in Prose, Being a Ghost Story of Christmas*. The preface continues the ghost theme in a humorous vein: "I have endeavoured in this Ghostly little book to raise the Ghost of an Idea which shall not put my readers out of humour with themselves, with each other, with the season, or with me. May it haunt their houses pleasantly, and no one wish to lay it." Dickens urged his readers to approach the tale as a classic English ghost story. In fact, he advised the public to read the *Carol* out loud, in a cold room by candlelight.

## The Carol *as Personal History*

Dickens's *Carol* is more than a simple ghost story, however. It contains a clear moral message about the perils of selfishness, both for the individual and for society. Readers familiar with Dickens's consistent admiration of humility, simplicity, and familial warmth, as expressed in his many works of fiction, may be surprised to learn that in a letter to a friend Dickens admitted that he based the character of Scrooge on the worst aspects of his own personality. Perhaps because of his own childhood hardships, Dickens sometimes obsessed about the benefits of wealth and the need to make money. In addition, unlike Scrooge's clerk, the poor but noble Bob Cratchit, Dick-

ens was neither affectionate nor attentive as a husband and father.

Dickens plucked several other elements of the *Carol* story out of his own life experience. The Cratchit home resembled the house that Dickens lived in when his family first moved to London. Like Scrooge, Dickens had an elder sister named Frances, whom he called Fanny. Dickens's own younger brother, known to the family as "Tiny Fred," and his nephew, a sickly, disabled boy, inspired the creation of Tiny Tim. Dickens's experience at the Ragged Schools and the Manchester Athenaeum materialized as Ignorance and Want, the two starving children who cling to the legs of the Ghost of Christmas Present. The Spirit cautions Scrooge, and by extension his Victorian audience, to "Beware them both, and all of their degree, but most of all beware this boy [Ignorance], for on his brow I see that written which is Doom, unless the writing be erased."

## The Carol *as Christmas Philosophy*

In *A Christmas Carol* Dickens insists that the Christmas holiday offers a solution to the problems of selfishness and greed. As the story closes, the narrator assures us that Scrooge became a kind, humble, and generous person as a result of his experience with the Spirits. *A Christmas Carol* suggests that Christmas has the potential to awaken all our hearts and thus to transform society. Scrooge's young nephew understands the power of Christmas to renew and transform, as he explains early in the story:

> I have always thought of Christmas time as a good time; a kind, forgiving, charitable, pleasant time; the only time I know of, in the long calendar of the year, when men and women seem by one consent to open their shut-up hearts freely, and to think of people below them as if they really were

fellow-passengers to the grave, and not another race of creatures bound on other journeys. And therefore, … though it has never put a scrap of gold or silver in my pocket, I believe that it *has* done me good, and *will* do me good; and I say, God bless it!

Dickens himself was not an overtly religious man. Nevertheless, the Christmas philosophy outlined in *A Christmas Carol* promotes a secular observance of the festival in keeping with the religious spirit of the holiday. Given Dickens's indifference towards religion, it is somewhat ironic that this approach to the holiday helped to heal the centuries-old breach between those religious sects that celebrated Christmas and those that condemned it (*see* **America, Christmas in Colonial; Puritans**). In its day, however, some critics condemned the *Carol* for purporting to discuss the subject of Christmas with few references to the birth of **Jesus**. This omission may well reflect Dickens's dislike of the Church, which he found sadly out of touch with the social problems of his day.

## Other Christmas Works

Although *A Christmas Carol* became Dickens's best-known treatise on the subject of Christmas, the holiday figures prominently in other writings as well. He wrote a number of short stories concerning Christmas, including "The Chimes," "The Cricket on the Hearth," "The Battle of Life," "The Haunted Man," "The Holly Tree," "The Seven Poor Travellers," "The Poor Relation's Story," and "The Haunted House." In addition, *The Pickwick Papers* contains a delightful depiction of Christmas festivities at a large house in the country. American author Washington Irving's earlier depiction of Christmas celebrations in an English manor house may well have inspired this passage. Indeed, regarding his love of Irving's books, Dickens once confessed, "I don't go upstairs two nights out of seven without taking Washington Irving under my arm." The *Pickwick Papers* also contains the story of a grumpy, old sexton (church custodian) visited by ghosts on Christmas Eve. Dickens expanded and improved upon this plot idea in *A Christmas Carol*.

Dickens's portrayal of Christmas as a season of good cheer among family and friends and good will towards the less fortunate came to represent the ideal version of the holiday for many nineteenth-century Britons and Americans (*see also* **America, Christmas in Nineteenth-Century; Victorian Era, Christmas in;**). These ideals still color contemporary Christmas celebrations, perhaps explaining the *Carol*'s enduring popularity. Indeed, public readings, stage adaptations, and screen versions of this classic Christmas tale continue to delight audiences each year at Christmas time.

# Christmas Carols and Other Music

Over the centuries Christmas has inspired countless songs. Which of the many pieces of vocal music written for Christmas qualify as true Christmas carols? Most writers assume Christmas carols to be those songs about Christmas whose tune and lyrics are widely known and whose popularity is maintained primarily through folk traditions rather than commercial promotions. By this definition, the fine Christmas works written by classical composers are not true Christmas carols, since they are musically complex and known to relatively small numbers of people. The fact that people sing carols for enjoyment and entertainment also figures in their definition. This criterion might exclude a number of lesser-known church hymns, since people usually sing them only during church services. In addition, most carols take as their subject matter the legends, customs, or religious celebration of Christmas. Therefore, some people would not include popular songs such as "I Saw Mommy Kissing Santa Claus" or even the hit song "White Christmas" in a collection of carols, since these songs achieved popularity through commercial means and do not address traditional Christmas themes or religious celebration. Others might quarrel with these criteria, arguing that the subject matter of these songs and the manner in which they achieved popularity simply reflect the commercial interests and cultural outlook of the twentieth century.

Why are these traditional Christmas songs called "carols," anyway? Some scholars trace the English word "carol" all the way back to the ancient Greek word *coros*. In ancient Greek drama the *coros*, or "chorus," appeared from time to time during the play singing commentaries on the plot and often dancing as well. By the late Middle Ages, the word "carol" had come to mean singing and dancing in a circle, as children do when singing "Ring Around the Rosy." In the Middle Ages people caroled on many different occasions. By the sixteenth century, however, this musical genre had acquired a special association with the Christmas season, while its earlier association with dance was fading away. By then, a large number of Christmas carols already circulated throughout Europe. A number of these, such as the English "I Saw Three Ships" and the German "Lo, How a Rose E'er Blooming," are still sung today.

## Earliest Christmas Songs

The earliest recorded Christmas carol was the one that the **angels** sang to the **shepherds** when announcing the birth of **Jesus** (*see* **Gospel According to Luke**):

> Glory to God in the highest,
> And on earth peace among men with whom he is pleased! (Luke 2:14).

Latin hymn writers provided the first Christmas songs sung by the early Christians. "Veni, redemptor gentium" (Redeemer of the Nations Come), written by St. Ambrose, archbishop of Milan, is the earliest surviving example of these works. Others include "A Solis Ortus Cardine" (From East to West, From Shore to Shore) by Sedulius, and works by the Spanish poet Prudentius. These early Christmas hymns were written by monks or other religious scholars for use in worship. They tend to approach Christmas from a theological perspective and emphasize the role of the Nativity in humankind's salvation.

## Medieval Christmas Carols

In the late Middle Ages a new spirit slowly infused the poetry and songs written about Christmas. Artists began to describe the people and events of the Nativity and react to them in emotional terms. Some credit St. Francis of Assisi with instilling a new spirit of simplicity and joy in worship, thereby indirectly bringing about these changes (*see also* **Nativity Scenes**). Some even believe that he wrote Christmas carols. If he did, none have survived. The work of one of his followers, the Franciscan mystic Jacapone da Todi, exemplifies the impact of these new attitudes towards the Nativity. His songs depict the Christmas miracle in homely images, such as that of the Virgin cradling and nursing her child. Whereas earlier church hymns had been written in Latin, a language known only by scholars, da Todi composed joyful songs in Italian so that ordinary people could sing them. These innovations gave birth to the Christmas carol as we know it.

## The Golden Age

The creativity unleashed in the late Middle Ages revealed itself in an outpouring of Christmas songs over the next several centuries. By the fourteenth century, Christmas carols in vernacular languages were sprouting up all over Europe. In Germany carol writers blossomed under the liberating influence of mystics like Meister Eckehart. German carol writers of the fourteenth and fifteenth centuries created such treasures as "Lo, How a Rose E'er Blooming," "In Dulci Jubilo" (Good Christian Men Rejoice), and "Joseph, Lieber Joseph Mein."

In late medieval England, the mystery or miracle plays performed around Christmas time inspired the composition of a number of carols (*see also* **Nativity Plays**). "The Coventry Carol," for example, accompanied the Pageant of the Shearmen and Tailors, a Christmas play produced annually by that guild. The fifteenth and sixteenth centuries gave birth to such well-loved songs as "The First Nowell" (*see also* **Noel**) and "God Rest Ye Merry, Gentlemen."

These English carols played a central role in another English Christmas custom called wassailing, in which people would go house to house carrying a large bowl and crying "Wassail, wassail." In some customs, the bowl would be filled with Christmas ale, which they would exchange for a gift. In other customs, the bowl would be empty and the neighbors would fill it with ale. A number of traditional English and Welsh carols treat such secular Christmas customs as feasting, drinking, and seasonal decorations. Examples include "The Boar's Head Carol," "The Holly and the Ivy," "Deck the Halls," and various wassailing songs. In medieval and Renaissance England people viewed merrymaking as an integral part of the celebration of the Nativity.

Further south in France, carol writing blossomed in the sixteenth and seventeenth centuries. Many songwriters of this era placed the singer in the position of one of the original pilgrims to **Bethlehem**. The songs describe the singer's journey and the people met along the way, who typically turn out to be from neighboring villages. The singer identifies the other pilgrims by their behavior and appearance, which usually exemplifies the negative reputation that their town has acquired in the eyes of its neighbors. By contrast, the seventeenth century Provençal carol, "Bring a Torch, Jeannette, Isabella," sweetly urges villagers to pay reverence to the sleeping Christ child. Perhaps its gentler tone contributes to the song's continuing appeal.

### The Reformation and Beyond

The change in religious beliefs and attitudes associated with the Reformation slowed the creation of carols in many areas of northern Europe, especially Britain. In England, the Puritans' rise to power in the mid-seventeenth century corresponded with

a drop-off in the writing of carols. Nevertheless, common people continued to sing the old carols and so kept many of them alive. Sterner religious authorities gained control in Scotland. In the late sixteenth century these authorities forbade many old Christmas pastimes altogether, including carol singing. In Germany the Reformation also inhibited carol writers, although at the same time it inspired the creation of some fine Christmas hymns. In France the Reformation had little effect on Christmas music. Instead, the change of attitudes that accompanied the revolution of 1789 hushed the singing of noëls and discouraged their composition.

The spirit of the Reformation infused many of the Christmas songs written in the centuries that followed with the flavor of church hymns. Indeed, many of the seventeenth-, eighteenth-, and nineteenth-century carols familiar to us today were written expressly for church use or by members of the clergy. Examples include "Joy to the World," written in 1692 by the famous English hymn writer Isaac Watts; "O Come All Ye Faithful," written in 1742 by another religious Englishman, John Francis Wade; "Angels We Have Heard on High," written in the mid-eighteenth century by an anonymous French composer; "O Holy Night," written in the nineteenth century by Frenchman Adolphe Charles Adam; and "Angels from the Realms of Glory," written in 1816 by the English hymn writer James Montgomery, who wrote the words that were later paired with a tune composed by Henry Smart.

In the early 1800s, an Austrian priest and his organist composed "Silent Night." Its enduring popularity notwithstanding, "Silent Night" came into the world as the slapdash creation of a single evening: Christmas Eve, 1818. Finding himself without a functioning organ for the Christmas Eve service, Father Josef Mohr scribbled down some verse and asked his organist, Franz Gruber, to quickly score it for voices so that the choir could sing it for that evening's Midnight Mass. The song circulated for many years among Austrian folk singers and eventually acquired international popularity before its authorship was traced back to Mohr and Gruber.

### The Nineteenth-Century Revival

The Christmas carol appeared to be dying out in early nineteenth-century England. Observers of English folk customs lamented that only a scattered handful of old people knew and sang the traditional songs. By mid-century the institution of the waits (bands of nighttime carolers) was collapsing. English folklorists predicted the imminent demise of the Christmas carol. These alarm bells inspired the collection and publication of several volumes of English Christmas carols in the early to mid-nineteenth century. The publication of these collections coincided with the budding Victorian interest in the celebration of Christmas (see **Victorian Era, Christmas in**). Soon the flagging tradition of the Christmas carol gained new momentum among the middle classes. By the 1870s, churches began to incorporate these almost forgotten Christmas songs into their holiday services. In 1880 an Anglican bishop, Edward W. Benson, devised the Ceremony of Nine Lessons and Carols, a special Christmas service blending Bible readings with carol singing. The service quickly spread to other congregations, and many churches worldwide offer their version of the service during **Advent**.

The nineteenth century not only hosted a revival of the Christmas carol in Europe, but also witnessed a burst of new interest in the genre in the United States. Americans were just beginning to accept Christmas as a public and religious holiday in the mid-nineteenth century after centuries of opposition by **Puritans** and other religious denominations (see **America, Christmas in Nineteenth-Century**). As if making up for lost time, a number of American clergymen of this era wrote enduring Christmas carols: Unitarian minister Edmund Sears composed "It Came Upon a Midnight Clear" in 1849; Reverend John Henry Hopkins, Jr., authored "We Three Kings of Orient Are" in 1857; and Reverend Phillips Brooks presented "O Little Town of Bethlehem" in 1865.

### Carol Services and Ceremonies

A number of carol services and ceremonies predate the nineteenth-century English Ceremony of Lessons and Carols. Historical evidence suggests that the Welsh attended yearly *Plygain* services at least as far back as the seventeenth century. Each person would bring a **candle** to light up the church during these early morning Christmas services, which included carols, prayers, and an occasional sermon. Las **Posadas**, a Hispanic folk play commemorating the search by **Mary** and **Joseph** for shelter in Bethlehem, also dates back hundreds of years. Other Christmas carol ceremonies include the Scandinavian *Julotta* service, a church service consisting mostly of carol singing that takes place early on Christmas morning in churches glowing with the light of hundreds of candles. The Australian "Carols by Candlelight" represents a twentieth-century addition to the world's carol ceremonies. Radio announcer Norman Banks organized and broadcast the first community carol-sing in Melbourne in the late 1930s. An appreciative public turned the event into a yearly tradition.

Decades later the event flourishes, drawing tens of thousands of people together to sing the traditional songs of the season by candlelight.

## Contemporary American Christmas Carols

Throughout the month of December, contemporary Americans listen to Christmas carols in a variety of formats, from Christmas concerts to church services to radio and television specials to recorded music played in stores. The diversity of songs beloved by Americans reflects our rich historical and cultural heritage. Old European carols such as "The First Noel" and "God Rest Ye Merry Gentlemen" take their place beside popular newer songs like "Let It Snow, Let It Snow, Let It Snow," and "Silver Bells." Gospel favorites like "O Holy Night," "Go Tell It on the Mountain," and "Mary Had a Baby" join commercial hits such as "Santa Claus is Coming to Town," "Rudolph the Red-Nosed Reindeer," and "Frosty the Snowman" in Christmas music compilations. Each year, musicians from a wide range of musical genres—blues, classical, country, pop, R&B, rock, and more—release recordings with modern renditions of favorite carols and other Christmas music.

In 2009, *Billboard* magazine reported that the most popular Christmas songs in America included a mix of old and new twentieth century recordings. The number one Christmas song that year was "All I Want for Christmas is You," recorded in 1994 by Mariah Carey. A 1958 recording of "Rockin' Around the Christmas Tree" by Brenda Lee occupied second place. In third place was the 1996 electronic rock instrumental composition "Christmas Eve/Sarajevo 12/24" by the Trans-Siberian Orchestra. Other top Christmas songs for 2009 included "Jingle Bell Rock" (Bobby Helms, 1957), "Feliz Navidad" (Jose Feliciano, 1970), "A Holly Jolly Christmas" (Burl Ives, 1964), "The Christmas Song" (Nat King Cole, 1960), "White Christmas" (Bing Crosby, 1942), "Last Christmas" (Wham!, 1984), and "The Most Wonderful Time of the Year" (Andy Williams, 1963). These songs reflect twentieth-century Americans' renewed interest in the secular joys of the season and the delights it brings to young and old.

# Christmas Club Accounts

In the United States many banks and credit unions offer their customers the opportunity to save money for Christmas by opening a special "Christmas club" savings account. Account holders make small but regular deposits throughout the year. According to the terms of the Christmas club account, interest may be earned on the deposits, and there may be a penalty fee for early withdrawal of the funds. At a predetermined time, usually a month or two before Christmas, money in the Christmas club account becomes available for withdrawal without penalty. These savings then finance the purchase of Christmas **gifts** and other seasonal expenditures.

A shoe factory owner from Carlisle, Pennsylvania, devised the first Christmas club for his workers in the year 1905. In 1910, a salesman named Herbert F. Rawll got wind of the idea and began to promote the clubs to banks. The opportunity for personal profit fired Rawll's enthusiasm for the project. As a ledger salesman, Rawll not only sold banks on the idea of sponsoring Christmas club accounts, but also provided them with the special forms needed to keep track of the transactions. Both banks and bank customers eagerly embraced the new accounts. Within two years the dynamic Rawll had convinced more than 800 banks to offer the special accounts. By the mid-1920s, about 8,000 banks offered Christmas club accounts to their patrons.

Christmas clubs flourished because they fulfilled the needs of financial institutions and consumers. In the early twentieth century, manufactured items all but replaced the homemade gifts that had characterized American Christmas giving in the nineteenth century. The clubs provided consumers a mechanism through which they could accumulate enough money to buy and to give ready-made Christmas gifts. In the meantime, banks were searching for ways to attract new customers, especially lower- and middle-income people who had previously avoided putting their money in banks. The new accounts succeeded in bringing in these new customers. Moreover, they helped overcome the popularly held image of banks as snobby, coldhearted institutions that served only the well-to-do.

The popularity of Christmas clubs began to wane with the growth of the consumer credit card industry. Credit cards enabled many Americans to pay for purchases over time after the purchase was made, instead of saving in advance. However, credit cards

also enabled people to spend beyond their ability to keep up with payments, and they also charged high rates of interest. The pressure to pay for Christmas gifts and other holiday expenses created problems for some when the bills were due. Though Christmas clubs had all but disappeared by the late 1990s, by the mid-2000s interest in these accounts was growing once again.

Today many Americans still rely on Christmas clubs to fund their Christmas purchases. An estimated 78 percent of credit unions offered Christmas club accounts in 2009. That year, some larger retailers began offering their own Christmas clubs for consumers. These retailer accounts were more like pre-payment plans than savings accounts, as all of the deposited money had to be spent at that retailer.

# Christmas Lads

## Christmas Boys, Jola-Sveinar, Yuletide Lads

Since ancient times, legends have told of supernatural forces that roam the earth around the time of Christmas. In Iceland, thirteen leprechaun-like creatures known as the *Jola-Sveinar*, or Christmas Lads, visit homes during the **Christmas season.** An old Icelandic legend tells us that they are the sons of a giant female troll named Gryla. The first lad arrives on the thirteenth day before Christmas. Another comes on the following day. This continues until the household hosts all thirteen boys on Christmas Eve. One boy departs on Christmas day and another on the following day, until the last withdraws on the twelfth day after Christmas, or **Epiphany.** In some older versions of this folklore, there are only nine Christmas Lads.

The early tales of the Christmas Lads painted them as fearsome creatures. Their mother, Gryla, was reputed to eat misbehaving children; her offspring inherited the same appetite for troublemakers. Adults used to remind children that the Christmas Lads waited for them in the winter time darkness in order to frighten the youngsters into good behavior. This custom inspired so much trauma that in 1746 the government denounced it.

Both the character and the appearance of the Christmas Lads changed over the years. The first record of the Lads dates back to the seventeenth century, when a man named Stephan Olafsson wrote a poem about the ogre Gryla, her husband Leppaludi, and her sons, the malicious **Yule** Boys. At this time Icelanders pictured the Lads as gigantic, lumbering trolls. By the nineteenth century, however, they looked more like peasant farmers. Instead of eating children, these oafish Lads vexed householders during their visits. They stole **candles**, sausages, and the family's best grain. One might leave a room neat and clean only to find it askew upon returning. After Christmas they attempted to steal away with the household's naughty children. In the twentieth century they shrank even further in size and began to resemble miniature Santas. Like **Santa Claus**, they now leave **gifts** of candy for good children, who leave their **shoes** on the windowsills in the days before Christmas to receive this reward.

The names and numbers of Christmas Lads varied over the years. Earlier records account for only nine Lads. In 1864, however, a writer named Jon Arnason named and described thirteen Christmas Lads. He called them Candle-Beggar (or Candle-Scrounger), Gully-Gawk, Hem-Blower, Shorty (also known as Stump), Meat Hook, Spoon-Licker (or Ladle-Licker), Sheep-Cot Clod (also known as Fencepost), Skyr-Gobbler (Skyr is a kind of Icelandic yogurt), Pot-Scraper (or Pot-Licker), Sausage-Swiper, Bowl-Licker, Window-Peeper, and Door-Sniffer (or Keyhole Sniffer). The fact that there were thirteen of them meant that the first would arrive on the eve of St. Lucy's Day, December 13, and the last would come on Christmas Eve. It also meant that the house would host these elf-like creatures throughout the **Twelve Days of Christmas**, since the last Lad would depart on Epiphany. The names given these creatures by Arnason describe their favorite activities and gives an idea of the kind of mischief that nineteenth-century Icelanders attributed to them. Arnason's flight of imagination took root with the Icelandic people, who today generally recognize the same thirteen Christmas Lads.

# Christmas Seals

Many people embellish the **Christmas cards**, letters, and packages they send during the holiday season with special decorative stamps called Christmas seals. Although the seals have no value as postage, the money collected through their sale supports charitable causes.

Danish postmaster Einar Holbøll designed the first mass-produced Christmas seals in 1904. The post office sold four million of the decorative stamps that year, giving birth to a new Danish Christmas tradition. Jacob Riis, an emigrant to the United States, publicized the success of Denmark's Christmas seals in an American magazine article.

In 1907, a fundraiser and Red Cross volunteer named Emily Bissell adopted the idea of selling Christmas seals as a way of raising money for a tuberculosis treatment facility in Delaware. Her success led other organizations to issue Christmas seals the following year, and soon the idea spread across the country. In 1925, the national Kappa Delta Sorority began an annual fundraising drive based on the sale of Christmas seals designed by its members and alumnae. The National Tuberculosis Association, which later became the American Lung Association, remains the largest issuer of decorative Christmas seals in the United States. Today the seals earn millions of dollars a year for the American Lung Association.

Although Christmas seals retain no intrinsic value of their own, they have become highly collectible among stamp enthusiasts. Some collectors have paid hundreds of dollars for a single early issue Christmas seal. In 1980, Emily Bissell was honored with a U.S. postage stamp featuring her name, likeness, and the legend "Crusader Against Tuberculosis."

# Christmas Season

How long is the Christmas season? The answer varies according to different religious and secular customs, and sometimes by Christian denomination. In the United States today, the Christmas season is often equated with the timing of **shopping** for and returning **gifts**. In other times and places, calendar customs or related observances opened and closed the Christmas season.

In past eras Europeans began their Christmas season on a variety of dates on which Christmas-related events and observances took place. In medieval and Renaissance times the English sometimes selected a local **Lord of Misrule**, a kind of clown who presided over Christmas festivities, as early as Halloween or All Saints' Day (November 1). The first day of **Advent**, which occurs on the Sunday closest to November 30, also served as an important date with regard to the European Christmas season. In some parts of Europe the Christmas season began on December 6, **St. Nicholas's Day**.

For many centuries the **Twelve Days of Christmas** stood at the heart of the European Christmas season. The Twelve Days begin on **December 25** and last until **Twelfth Night**. This period includes a number of other observances, such as St. Stephen's

Day, St. John's Day, Holy Innocents' Day, the Feast of the Circumcision, and New Year's Day.

Virtually no one ended their seasonal celebration on December 26, the day after Christmas. Even today, Americans extend the Christmas season through New Year's Day. In the past, however, many Europeans assumed that Christmas ended on **Epiphany**, January 6. In past centuries some English Christmas customs, such as decorating homes with **greenery**, extended as late as **Candlemas**, February 2. In other areas of Europe people finally dismantled their **Nativity scenes** on Candlemas.

Some Orthodox Christian churches celebrate Christmas on December 25, while others still schedule their feast days according to the old, Julian calendar (*see* **Old Christmas Day**). Therefore, some Orthodox Christians celebrate Christmas on or near Epiphany.

In recent years, commercial interests rather than religious observations have defined the Christmas season for many Americans. In the early twentieth century, retailers began to promote the idea that the Christmas season begins on the day after Thanksgiving. More recently, however, many retailers have begun setting out Christmas merchandise and holding Christmas promotions even before Halloween. Regardless of when the season is thought to begin, for most Americans the Christmas season extends through New Year's Day.

# *A Christmas Story*

*A Christmas Story* is a comedy film based on the semi-autobiographical writings of author and radio humorist Jean Shepherd. Released in mid-November 1983, *A Christmas Story* performed moderately well in theaters. The movie's lifetime gross for theatrical release in the U.S. was just over $20 million. However, *A Christmas Story* went on to become a cultural phenomenon with lasting appeal.

The story takes place in a small Indiana town in the 1940s, during the weeks leading up to Christmas. Nine-year-old Ralphie desperately wants a Red Ryder BB gun for Christmas, specifically a 200-shot range model that comes with a compass in the stock. But his mother, his father, and even **Santa Claus** famously insist, "You'll shoot your eye out!" Ralphie is undeterred and launches an intense campaign to convince everyone that a BB gun would make the perfect Christmas gift. In his quest to acquire the longed-for BB gun, Ralphie faces many trials and tribulations. He is terrorized by a bully, gets hit in the face with a snowball, struggles with his teachers at school, gets in a fight, has his mouth washed out with soap, witnesses the horror of another boy getting his tongue frozen to a lamp post, and otherwise suffers through the eccentric behaviors of his family members and neighbors.

One of the movie's highlights is Ralphie's visit to the overworked department store Santa, who rushes kids through an operation resembling an assembly line. Each visit ends with the child being thrust down a chute, sliding to meet their waiting parents on the floor below. When Ralphie refuses to get into the chute, Santa pushes him down the slide with his boot.

Perhaps the most well-known subplot of the movie involves Ralphie's father winning a prize in a contest—a table lamp in the shape of a woman's leg. Claiming that the prize is the most amazing lamp he has ever seen, Ralphie's father puts it in a place of honor in the front window of the house. Now everyone in the neighborhood can see and admire the lamp, much to the consternation of Ralphie's mother. As the movie gained a cult following, the leg lamp went on to achieve fame of its own, with replicas being manufactured and sold to fans of the film.

In addition to the leg lamp, other movie-related merchandise has included a themed Monopoly game, T-shirts, Christmas **ornaments**, jigsaw puzzles featuring scenes from the movie, the *A Christmas Story* board game, a calendar, bobble-head dolls of movie characters, and themed buildings for **Christmas villages**. In 2006, the home where the movie was filmed was restored to its movie set condition and opened to the public for tours. More than 40,000 fans have visited the house, gift shop, and the associated *A Christmas Story* museum. The phenomenon has also spawned an independent documentary film called *Road Trip for Ralphie*, in which two mega-fans chronicle their travels to visit all of the locations where the movie was filmed.

Fans of the movie gather each year for an annual convention, including appearances by cast members, a screening of the movie with commentary from those involved in its production, tours of the *A Christmas Story* house, and other movie-related activities. Every year since 1997, *A Christmas Story* has been shown on television in a continuous twenty-four-hour marathon beginning on Christmas Eve. Each year nearly three million viewers tune in to watch some part of this annual broadcast. This has helped to introduce the movie to new audiences while maintaining its popularity with existing fans.

# Christmas Trees

The Christmas tree originally came from Germany. Today, it is a recognized symbol of the holiday in many parts of the globe. The earliest historical reference to decorated Christmas trees in German homes dates back to the sixteenth century (*see also* **Christmas Villages; Ornaments**). Several theories concerning the beginning of the Christmas tree custom, however, suggest that its origins lie much further in the past.

## Legends

A number of legends offer fanciful explanations for the origins of the Christmas tree. According to one, St. Boniface began the custom in the eighth century. One Christmas Eve this English missionary to the German-speaking peoples came across some pagans preparing a human sacrifice before an oak tree. He struck the oak tree a single blow with his axe, which felled the tree. Duly impressed by this miraculous feat, the people abandoned their old ways and embraced Christianity. The saint pointed to a small fir tree laying among the ruins of the oak and told them to take that as the symbol of their new faith and of the birth of the Christ child.

Legends dating back to tenth-century Europe tell of trees that mysteriously burst into bloom on Christmas Eve (*see also* **Glastonbury Thorn**). Some writers suggest that this myth inspired people to bring decorated trees into their homes at Christmas time. A German legend elaborates on this theme. According to this tale, a humble woodcutter heard a knock on his door one freezing winter night. Upon opening it, he discovered a shivering, poor child. The woodcutter and his wife offered the child hospitality for the night, feeding him and offering him their own warm bed close to the fire. The next morning the grateful child appeared before them, radiant and beautiful. Awareness dawned in them that their guest was in fact the Christ child (*see also* **Christkindel**). Before departing, the Christ child gave them a twig from a fir tree, declaring that it would blossom for them year after year. Unable to imagine how this could occur, they tossed the twig away. Nevertheless, it grew into a beautiful fir tree, which suddenly blossomed with golden apples and silver nuts. The miraculous blooms appeared each year at Christmas time.

Another Christian legend attributes the Christmas tree to Martin Luther. One Christmas Eve the great religious reformer found himself walking through the woods. The beauty of the stars shining through the branches of the fir trees deeply moved him. He cut down a small tree, brought it home with him, and covered it with lit **candles**, explaining to his family that its light and beauty represented Christ, the light of the world. Although this legend helped to increase the popularity of the Christmas tree, it should be pointed out that the earliest known document describing a Christmas tree lit with candles was written about a century after Luther's death.

## *Origins*

No one can confirm the exact origin of the Christmas tree. Some writers base their explanation of the Christmas tree on the theory that in ancient times the pagan peoples of northern Europe revered trees. They propose that the venerable pagan symbol of the tree survived the transition to Christianity by attaching itself to the Christian midwinter holiday, Christmas. Little solid historical evidence exists to support this viewpoint, however. Others believe that the ancient Roman custom of decorating homes and temples with **greenery** during **Kalends** survived for centuries, eventually inspiring the people of the north to decorate their homes with small ever-

green trees at that time of year. Still others view the Christmas pyramid as the ancestor of the Christmas tree.

Finally, a number of researchers disagree with all of these arguments. They point out that the earliest historical records of decorated trees being used to celebrate Christmas come from the Middle Ages. Fir trees decorated with apples served as the central prop for the paradise play, a kind of folk religious drama often performed on December 24 (*see also* **Nativity Plays**). These props were called **paradise trees**, and some researchers believe they were the forerunners of the Christmas tree. The plays eventually fell out of favor with Church officials and the populace. Nevertheless, some writers believe that people from parts of France and Germany retained the custom of celebrating Christmas with a decorated tree, which eventually became known as a Christmas tree.

## *Early History*

The earliest historical reference to Christmas trees as such dates back to sixteenth-century Germany. In 1561 an ordinance posted in Alsace declared that each burgher was allowed only one Christmas tree and that his tree could be no more than "eight shoes" in height. Apparently the custom of bringing a living tree into the home at Christmas time was so popular that deforestation was already becoming something of a problem. In 1605 a traveler to the city of Strasbourg described the German custom of bringing a fir tree into the drawing room at Christmas time and decorating it with apples, wafers, paper roses, gilt, and sugar ornaments. Documents from the same century also record objections to the Christmas tree custom on the part of religious reformers, who argued that it detracted from the spiritual significance of the holiday. On the whole, however, the Christmas-tree-loving Germans appear to have ignored these objections.

The Christmas pyramid found favor with many German families during the seventeenth and eighteenth centuries. Some German families preferred to decorate a pyramid rather than a Christmas tree. Other families had both in their parlors. Still other families preferred to center home celebrations around a **Nativity scene**. For the most part, the Nativity scene held sway in southern Germany, where Catholics were more numerous. The tree dominated in northern Germany, where more Protestants lived. By the nineteenth century, the increasing appeal of the Christmas tree contributed to the decline of the Christmas pyramid.

During the nineteenth century the Christmas tree became increasingly popular in all parts of Germany, but also spread to other countries. Around 1840 the English monarch Queen Victoria and her German-born consort Prince Albert celebrated Christmas with a decorated tree. Although the Christmas tree was known in England before that time, this stamp of royal approval transformed the tree into a fashionable, new addition to the English Christmas. In like manner, the German-born Princess Helene of Mecklenberg started a Christmas tree trend in France in 1837 by celebrating her first Christmas in that country with a decorated tree. Many Scandinavians adopted the Christmas tree in the mid-nineteenth century, as did many Americans, Russians, and other northern Europeans. Southern Europeans, for the most part, stuck with their traditional Nativity scenes. Indeed, the Nativity scene remains the focus of home Christmas celebrations in much of southern Europe.

## The Christmas Tree Comes to America

Some writers claim that Hessian soldiers who fought on behalf of the British in the American Revolution erected the first Christmas trees on American soil. No solid historical evidence exists to back up this claim, however. Several contemporary folklorists instead claim that German immigrants, such as those of the Pennsylvania Dutch country, brought the custom with them to the United States. Occasional references to the novelty of a decorated Christmas tree are scattered throughout newspapers on the East Coast from the early 1800s. In fact, the trees were considered so exotic that some organizations set them up and then charged people money in order to view them.

By the 1840s the Christmas tree was widely known in the United States. Publication of *Kriss Kringle's Christmas Tree* in 1845, a children's book about the custom, helped to popularize the holiday tree. The first American Christmas trees were only a few feet tall and were displayed on tables, following the German fashion. As the size of the tree grew to accommodate an ever-increasing load of ornaments, Americans moved the tree to a stand on the floor. Many of these early American ornaments were in fact Christmas **gifts** and treats. These might include **gingerbread** and other cookies, pretzels, apples, lemons, oranges, raisins, nuts, figs, **sugarplums**, strings of cranberries or popcorn, candy, dolls, books, thimbles, scissors, mittens, **stockings**, shoes, paper roses, glass balls, and ornaments made of egg shells or cotton.

Families gradually began to exchange heavier, more substantial gifts. Before 1880 people usually hung their unwrapped gifts from the tree with thread or string. After

that time, **wrapping paper** and fancy decorated boxes started to become fashionable. As Christmas presents grew too large or heavy to hang on the tree, people began to place them beneath the tree.

## The Christmas Tree Becomes an American Institution

During the second half of the nineteenth century the Christmas tree cast its roots deep into American Christmas celebrations. Its presence undermined the role of the Christmas stocking as a receptacle for gifts in many homes. Christmas trees began to sprout up in school holiday celebrations. They even worked their way into churches, in spite of some initial opposition to what was perceived as a suspiciously heathen custom. Mark Carr, a logger from New York's Catskill Mountains, created the first Christmas tree lot in 1851. For the price of one dollar he rented a sidewalk in **New York City** and sold cut trees to city dwellers. His business appeared to be so profitable that the owner of the sidewalk increased his rent to $100 the following year. In 1856 Franklin Pierce became the first American president to celebrate Christmas in the **White House** with a decorated tree. As the tree became a familiar and cherished part of American Christmas celebrations, people began to make fancy ribbon and lace ornaments as well as to collect store-bought ornaments for their trees. Unlike the gifts and treats which had covered their trees in past years, these ornaments could be saved and reused the following year.

One writer estimates that by the turn of the twentieth century, about one in five American homes displayed a decorated tree at Christmas time. Many of those who could not afford to set up a tree in their homes still enjoyed community or church trees. President Theodore Roosevelt expressed early ecological concerns about the national consumption of evergreen trees at Christmas time. Around the year 1900 he discontinued the use of Christmas trees in the White House. His sons, however, unable to resist the lure of a decorated Christmas tree, smuggled an evergreen into one of their bedrooms. Roosevelt eventually changed his position on Christmas trees after one of his advisors assured him that America's forests could survive the yearly harvest.

In the following decades Christmas trees appeared in more and more American homes. In the year 2000, 79 percent of U.S. homes displayed a Christmas tree during the holiday season. About 31 percent of American homeowners bought real Christmas trees, while 49 percent of homeowners relied instead upon artificial trees (and 2 percent of homes contained both a real and an artificial tree). Christmas tree growers harvest and sell about 33 million real trees annually.

### Symbolic Trees

The Christmas tree has become a potent symbol of peace and goodwill. This symbolism underlies the ceremonies surrounding many public Christmas trees. President Woodrow Wilson presided over the first **National Christmas Tree** ceremony on Christmas Eve in 1913. Although Wilson established the ceremony near the Capitol Building, President Calvin Coolidge moved the national Christmas tree to the vicinity of the White House. In 1923 he led the first ceremonial lighting of the national Christmas tree. This yearly ceremony has continued ever since, with the exception of the years between 1942 and 1945, when wartime blackouts prohibited the festive outdoor lights. After the Korean War, a Christmas "pageant of peace" was attached to the lighting of the national Christmas tree, which entailed rescheduling the lighting ceremony to a date before Christmas Eve (*see also* **Nation's Christmas Tree**).

# Christmas Villages

For many centuries people have delighted in constructing miniature landscapes for Christmas. **Nativity scenes**, life-sized or miniature depictions of the scene of the birth of **Jesus**, date back to the thirteenth century. In the eighteenth century some central Europeans enjoyed creating miniature village scenes—called Christmas gardens—which they set up under their **Christmas trees**. The Moravians brought this tradition with them to America, and from it developed their own custom of Christmas putz building (*see* **Bethlehem, Pennsylvania, Christmas in**). The putz included a Nativity scene within a complicated town and country landscape. The idea of creating a miniature world underneath the Christmas tree soon spread beyond the German-American communities that imported it to this country. It survives to this day, though nowadays most people buy the figurines and buildings from gift shops rather than make them at home.

## *Christmas Gardens and Yards*

In the nineteenth century, many Americans placed a miniature fence around their Christmas trees (*see also* **America, Christmas in Nineteenth-Century**). This fence enclosed an area sometimes referred to as a Christmas garden or Christmas yard. Inside the fenced area families arranged small figurines of people or animals, along with various toys. Magazine articles taught children how to make miniature houses out of cardboard to complement these scenes. Adults also worked on the little settlements. Home crafters created a wide variety of scenes, including vignettes of circus life, clusters of young people skating on frozen lakes, charming gardens, prosperous farms, and snug log cabins.

By the 1890s, manufacturers supplied the public with a steady stream of ready-made miniature cardboard buildings and figures, as well as fences to mark off the magical territory of the Christmas garden. In the 1920s, Germany exported large numbers of Christmas village sets to the U.S. and Canada. In the 1930s Japan added to the supply. During the 1920s and 1930s the buildings came with cellophane windows, designed to permit the consumer to illuminate them from within with an electric light bulb. While some people placed the little homes and shops below their tree, others

113

hung them from the tree as Christmas **ornaments,** or filled them with candy. In the 1940s and 1950s, toy train sets became extremely popular Christmas gifts for boys. The train sets, too—with all their accessories—furthered the tradition of setting up a world in miniature beneath the tree.

### Collectible Village Sets

Beginning around the mid-1970s, Christmas villages became popular collectibles in America. A seemingly endless variety of ceramic buildings, figures, and accessories were manufactured and sold in sets. Among the many available options were sets modeled after Victorian England villages, Alpine ski villages, bustling big cities, and quaint small towns of all time periods. In addition to these more realistic miniatures, there were also fanciful sets, such as North Pole villages featuring Santa, Mrs. Claus, elves, and reindeer. Some of these sets were designed to light up, or included motorized features such as ice skaters that moved around a pond. Collectors built their villages slowly over time, as each year new pieces were introduced to expand the set. Some pieces were cleverly marketed as special editions or limited quantities, their perceived rarity making them more desirable and driving up their value as collectors' items. Many collectors consider their Christmas villages as family heirlooms for the enjoyment of future generations.

# Cookies and Other Treats

No Christmas celebration would be complete without special treats like cookies, candy, and cakes. Many Americans enjoy the yearly tradition of Christmas baking, often using favorite family recipes that have been passed down for generations. For some, Christmas cookies are what makes the holiday truly special. Others prefer a certain kind of cake, or the craft of building and decorating gingerbread houses. Whatever form they take, sweets are an important part of the American Christmas experience.

### Origins of Christmas Sweets

Throughout history, people have celebrated Christmas by preparing a wide variety of foods much fancier than common everyday fare. Early Europeans enjoyed cakes and breads made with spices and sweetened with honey. As innovative medieval cooks developed new baking techniques, these sweet and spicy pastries evolved into early versions of the Christmas cookies favored today. As the centuries passed, recipes were refined and new types of baked goods were created. Christmas cookies had become very popular throughout Europe by the 1500s. These biscuits, or cookies, were brought to America by immigrants who continued the traditional holiday celebrations of their homeland. The first appearance of Christmas cookies in America was in the early 1600s. The first American cookbook, dated 1796, advised bakers to prepare Christmas cookies six months in advance and store them in an earthen pot in the cellar in order to achieve the finest texture and flavor.

Some of these imported treats became familiar American Christmas favorites. Northern Europe's *Pfeffernüsse*, the delicately textured cookies spiced with anise, nutmeg, cinnamon, and cloves, were prized as a once-a-year specialty. Norwegians preferred *krumkake*, thin crumbly wafers flavored with lemon and cardamom. From Germany came *Lebkuchen*, also known as gingerbread, buttery pressed cookies called *Spritz*, rolled and embossed *Springerle* cookies, and the cutout sugar cookies so common in America today. The Spanish brought *biscochitos* to Mexico in the sixteenth century, and this delicate spiced sugar cookie gradually made its way north into the Christmas celebrations of the American southwest.

Traditional holiday fare of many European countries also included enriched breads and cakes, baked with extra fats, dried and candied fruits, and nuts. These also came to the new world with immigrants, and soon became part of American holiday celebrations. Italian *panettone*, German *Stollen*, Swedish *saffransbrod*, Norwegian *Julekake*, and Greek *Christopsomo* were among these imported specialties.

In the nineteenth century, American bakers revived the medieval European tradition of the Christmas "Yule doughs." These pastries were a special holiday treat during the Middle Ages. In that era, bakers shaped the dough like animals or people, most frequently the baby **Jesus.** American bakers called them "Yule dollies" and shaped them like young girls or dolls, and decorated them with icing, colored illustrations (glued onto the cookies with egg white), feathers, or other adornments. These decorated cookies served as **ornaments** for newly popular **Christmas trees.** Today's Christmas bakers still shape and decorate gingerbread cookies in similar ways.

## Modern Traditions

Candy canes are a common symbol of Christmas in contemporary America. These peppermint goodies are often seen hanging from the branches of Christmas trees, or as part of other festive displays. The origin of this favorite treat is uncertain, though several **urban legends** have spread over the years as people speculated on the symbolism of the candy. Some insist that the cane is shaped like the letter "J" in honor of Jesus's name. Others claim the shape represents the hook carried by shepherds who came to the manger when baby Jesus was born. Regardless of any deeper meaning, candy canes are enjoyed by many Americans. Nearly two billion candy canes are sold each year during the month of December.

One common but much maligned Christmas treat is the fruit cake. Fruit cake is a dense loaf-shaped pastry baked with dried fruits and nuts, and sometimes soaked in brandy or other alcohol. The origins of fruit cake can be traced back to the sixteenth century, when people discovered a method of preserving fruit by soaking it in a sugar solution. This proved to be an effective way to prevent European plums and cherries from spoiling while in transit to the American colonies. By the nineteenth century, American bakers were adding many different kinds of dried and candied fruit to the cakes, including pineapple, dates, pears, orange peels, and nuts.

Some Americans celebrate Christmas by preparing a *Bûche de Noël* or Yule Log cake. This sweet treat originated in nineteenth-century France. It consists of thinly rolled sponge cake filled with jam or cream, or slices of sponge cake spread with cream, stacked, and then shaped to resemble a log. The cake is covered with chocolate buttercream frosting that is piped on or scored to resemble tree bark. The **Yule Log** is then decorated with marzipan leaves, meringue mushrooms, or other embellishments.

## Christmas Cookies

Perhaps the most common seasonal treat in America is the Christmas cookie. By 1906, highly detailed cookie molds and cutters from Germany were readily available throughout the U.S. Around the same time, popular cookbooks began featuring cookie recipes that took advantage of these new utensils. Traditional square or round cookies were quickly replaced by elaborate sugar cookies in the forms of animals, flowers, bells, angels, Santas, and many other figures. Shaped sugar cookies remain among the most popular Christmas cookies in America today.

Gingerbread cookies are another traditional American Christmas treat. Typically cut out in the shape of people, gingerbread men are often decorated with frosting or other embellishments. A popular Christmas pastime for many Americans is the construction of gingerbread houses, made from gingerbread that has been baked in sheets. The houses are created by "gluing" gingerbread pieces together with sticky frosting. The houses are then decorated with more frosting and all sorts of different candies, sprinkle decorations, and colored sugars.

Cookie exchanges or cookie swap parties help contemporary American bakers enjoy a variety of Christmas cookies without having to spend days in the kitchen. First popularized in the early 1960s by a suggestion in *Betty Crocker's Cooky Book*, these gatherings provide an opportunity for people to share and trade homemade Christmas cookies. Cookie exchanges are often organized by large families or groups of friends, neighbors, or co-workers. At these events, each person brings enough of one type of cookie to give one dozen to each party guest. Everyone then leaves the party with an assortment of holiday treats that would have otherwise taken many hours to produce. Some churches sponsor a different version of the cookie exchange— parishioners bake hundreds of dozens of a wide variety of cookies, and then community members are allowed to purchase a varied selection of treats, with proceeds going to benefit church programs. These church cookie exchanges have become very popular in recent years, and many sell out quickly.

## Cookies for Santa

For many contemporary American families with young children, setting out a plate of cookies and a glass of milk for **Santa Claus** is an important Christmas Eve ritual. Sometimes this midnight snack also includes a carrot or an apple for Santa's **reindeer**. On Christmas morning the cookies and milk are gone, thus proving that Santa really did visit the house while the children slept. Sometimes children find a thank-you note from Santa next to the empty glass and plate.

The traditions of Christmas baking have become ingrained in American celebrations of the holiday. For some, much of the month of December is given over to indulging in the Christmas cookies and other treats that seem to appear everywhere. These special treats add to the festivity of the holiday season in America.

# December 25

The earliest Christians did not celebrate Christmas. In fact, the first Christian calendar listing December 25 as the Feast of the Nativity was compiled in 336 A.D. Since neither of the two biblical accounts of the Nativity—found in the **Gospel according to Luke** and the **Gospel according to Matthew**—gives the date of the birth of **Jesus**, how did December 25 come to be the date on which Christians celebrate Christmas? (*See also* Gospel Accounts of Christmas; Jesus, Year of Birth.)

### Birthdays in the Ancient World

In the ancient world, various pagan peoples celebrated the birthdays of gods and important individuals. In fact, many pagan myths explained the miraculous births of the gods. This association with paganism caused some early Christian thinkers to oppose the celebration of birthdays on principle. For example, in his commentary on the Gospel of Matthew, the Christian teacher and writer Origen argued that Christians should not observe birthdays since scripture depicts only wrongdoers like the pharaohs and **Herod** celebrating their birthdays.

## *Selection of December 25*

By the fourth century, however, Christian leaders had overcome their reluctance to honor the birthday of Jesus Christ. Now they had to decide upon a date for the new feast. The first mention of Christmas observances taking place on December 25 occurs in the Philocalian calendar, a Church document written in 336 A.D. Some scholars believe that Christian authorities scheduled the Feast of the Nativity for December 25 in order to draw people away from the pagan festivals celebrated on or around that date. The madcap revels associated with the Roman holiday of **Saturnalia** ended on December 23, just two days earlier. On January first the Romans observed **Kalends**, their new year festival. Finally, on December 25 devotees of Mithras and Sol celebrated the **Birth of the Invincible Sun.**

According to the calendar used by the ancient Romans, the winter solstice fell on December 25, making it a perfect day on which to commemorate the rebirth of the sun. The cult of the sun god was especially popular with the Romans between the second and the fourth centuries, a time when Christianity was struggling to establish itself as a legitimate faith. By selecting December 25 as the date for the new Feast of the Nativity, Christian leaders probably hoped to convince sun god worshipers to celebrate the birth of Jesus rather than the birth of the sun.

Some early Christian thinkers offered other, more convoluted explanations for the choice of December 25. They based these explanations not only on their interpretations of scripture, but also on Christian lore and then-popular beliefs concerning the significance of round numbers. According to one scholar, Church leaders tried to figure out the date of Jesus' birth from the date traditionally given for his death, March 25. Since they wanted to come up with a round number for Jesus' age at death, they assumed he was also conceived on March 25. Therefore, he must have been born nine months later on December 25.

Other Christian thinkers drew parallels between Christ and the sun based on Bible passages that describe the Messiah as "the sun of righteousness" (Malachi 4:2) and "the light of the world" (John 8:12). According to this line of thought, Jesus' incarnation represented a new creation, as when God created the world. According to the Book of Genesis, God's first act was to create light, an act that separated light from darkness. Therefore, they reasoned, God must have created the world at the time of the spring equinox, when the world is separated into two equal halves of light and darkness. Since Jesus himself stood for the new creation, Jesus must also have been conceived at the time of the spring equinox. According to the Julian calendar then in use, spring equinox fell on March 25. Allowing for a nine-month gestation period, Jesus would then have been born on December 25.

The solar symbolism attached to Jesus in this explanation concluded with his birth on the winter solstice, the date when the sun "returns" and the days begin to lengthen. By equating Jesus with the sun, Christian leaders adopted and yet subtly undermined the logic of sun god worshipers. For example, one early Christian writer thundered, "They [the pagans] call December twenty-fifth the Birthday of the Unconquered: Who is indeed so unconquered as our Lord? ... or, if they say that it is the birthday of the sun: *He* is the Sun of Justice."

### Division of Christmas and Epiphany

The introduction of Christmas as a separate feast clashed with the way in which many churches had been celebrating **Epiphany**. The first Epiphany celebrations occurred in second-century Egypt. The feast spread to other Christian communities during the next two hundred years, although considerable variation existed among these scattered celebrations. This holiday might commemorate any of the four recognized occasions on which Jesus' divinity revealed itself to those around him: his birth, the adoration of the **Magi**, his baptism, and the miracle at the wedding in Cana. After creating a separate holiday to honor Jesus' birth, the Roman Church shifted the focus of its Epiphany celebrations to the adoration of the Magi. When the Eastern Churches finally accepted Christmas, they used the holiday to honor both Jesus' birth and the adoration of the Magi. Afterwards, their Epiphany celebrations focused on Jesus' baptism.

### Spread of the New Feast

Sometime around the year 350 Pope Julius or Pope Liberius officially adopted December 25 as the Feast of the Nativity. After Church leaders established the holiday in Rome, they attempted to convince the churches in the eastern part of the empire to accept this feast. St. Gregory of Nazianzus introduced the festival in Constantinople in 379. In 386 St. John Chrysostom preached to Christians in Antioch, advising them to accept the festival on this date, in spite of the fact that some still preferred to celebrate the Nativity on January 6. Most of the Eastern Churches accepted the new feast in the years between 380 and 430 A.D. Jerusalem Christians did not accept the new festival until the middle of the sixth century. The Armenians never accepted the new festival. Today, the Armenian Orthodox Church still celebrates the Nativity of Christ on January 6, Epiphany. Those Armenian Orthodox congregations in the Holy Land that still use the Julian calendar celebrate the festival on January 19 (*see* Old Christmas Day).

### Origins of the Word "Christmas"

Since Latin was the official language of the Roman Church, its leaders called the new festival commemorating Jesus' birth *Dies Natalis Domini*, or the "Birthday of the Lord." The more formal name for the holiday was *Festum Nativitatis Domini Nostri Jesu Christi*, or the "Feast of the Nativity of Our Lord Jesus Christ." Our English word for the festival, "Christmas," didn't evolve until centuries later. The term appears in documents from the eleventh and twelfth centuries, written in Old English as *Christes maesse*, which means "Christ's Mass." English speakers soon formed a contraction out of the two words. The name of the festival passed through many forms in the centuries that followed, including *kryst-masse, cristmasse, crystmasse, Chrysmas,* and *Cristmas*. The term "Christmas" came into the English language sometime between the late sixteenth and late seventeenth centuries.

In casual writing, the word Christmas sometimes appears as "Xmas." Some people dislike the informality of this abbreviation and the fact that it removes the word "Christ" from the word Christmas. Others find it less objectionable. They point out that the "x" may be said to stand for the Greek letter "X" (chi), which is the first letter in the Greek word for Christ.

# Depression

For many people the Christmas blues lurk right below the festive reds and greens of the holiday season. According to one national poll, about 45 percent of all Americans confessed to feeling sad around Christmas time.

### Unrealistic Expectations

Our culture bombards us with the message that the **Christmas season** is the happiest time of year, a time for festive parties, loving family get-togethers, lavish gift giving, and constant good cheer. These high emotional, social, and material expectations set us up to be disappointed. Many people find it difficult to fulfill the cultural ideal of non-stop Christmas conviviality. This ideal may easily defeat people with difficult family situations, those who lost a loved one during a previous holiday season, those who are socially isolated, and those estranged or far away from their families. This failure to meet cultural expectations, along with the belief that "everyone else is having a good time," can result in depression.

High material expectations for the holiday may pose similar problems, especially for those on limited budgets (*see also* **Shopping**). So great are the pressures to buy that some people bring financial hardship on themselves by spending more than they can really afford on holiday preparations and **gifts**. The resulting stress may open the door to depression.

Even those who can afford to participate fully in the gift giving, decorating, cooking, eating, drinking, and party going may sink into holiday season sadness, however. Stress and exhaustion brought on by an endless whirl of activities as well as overindulgence in food and drink also contribute to feelings of depression. Women may be particularly prone to this syndrome, as our culture assigns them the primary responsibility for shopping, cooking, decorating, and creating "special" family celebrations.

## *Advice from Therapists*

For those with a tendency to suffer from this form of Christmas season sadness, therapists work to help them discard their unrealistic expectations of the holidays. These often spring from childhood nostalgia and romantic images promoted in the media rather than from a realistic assessment of one's own wishes, needs, limitations, and personal circumstances. In spite of our dreams of instant holiday happiness, these limitations and circumstances seldom vanish underneath the tinsel and colored lights of the Christmas season. Moreover, the stress of holiday preparations, travel, and family visits may aggravate whatever tensions exist in any of these areas. To avoid resentments bred by overwork, psychologists suggest that those saddled with organizing and hosting holiday celebrations delegate responsibilities to others.

Psychologists point out that family tensions that simmer below the surface during the rest of the year very often boil over when the family gathers together for the holidays. Although many people feel that family fights "ruin" holiday get-togethers, it

may be more realistic to assume that if family members quarrel during the rest of the year, they will quarrel on Christmas.

Psychologists also recommend giving oneself, others, and the occasion permission to be less than perfect. They remind us that although the dynamic of family get-togethers often encourages everyone to assume old family roles, we may choose otherwise. Although we may make these choices for ourselves, psychologists counsel us to avoid using Christmas celebrations as a forum for changing family relationships. They point out, for example, that challenging Auntie May about her drinking is likely to lead to a confrontation, and that attempting to squeeze a year's worth of "quality time" with family members into a single holiday is doomed to failure.

Those who have experienced the loss of a loved one in the past year need to accept their current mental, emotional, and physical limits and openly acknowledge that this year's celebrations will be different. Counselors also recommend that those who grieve take time to evaluate which social obligations, family traditions, and religious observances will comfort and strengthen them, and which could overwhelm them. They also suggest that mourners seek the company of comforting people and make occasions to talk about their loved one. It may be best to plan provisionally and be prepared to alter arrangements as necessary to suit one's needs.

## Christmas Suicides

It is widely believed that the rate of suicides increases during the holiday period. Although many Americans admit to feeling sad during the holiday season, studies reveal that the suicide rate does not increase around Christmas time.

## Winter Weather

The winter weather itself seems to plunge some people into depression. Seasonal Affective Disorder (SAD) causes its sufferers to become depressed during the dark days of winter that coincide with the holiday season in the Northern Hemisphere. The exact cause of SAD is not known, but it is believed to be a result of decreased sunlight during the winter months. Experts estimate that between four and six percent of all Americans exhibit symptoms of full-blown SAD. About 10 to 20 percent suffer from a milder version of these symptoms known informally as the "winter blues." Some psychologists claim that among SAD patients, women outnumber men by a four-to-one ratio. In the Northern Hemisphere, the incidence of SAD increases as one travels northward. Researchers have discovered that nearly ten percent of Alaska residents suffer to some degree from SAD, as compared to four percent of Washington, D.C., residents and just one percent of Florida residents.

People suffering from SAD often experience states of lethargy and depression that can last for months. Other symptoms may include increased appetite, an excessive desire for sleep, irritability, anxiety, decreasing self-esteem, and difficulty concentrating. These symptoms can contribute to an already stressful holiday season, when the days are short, the sunlight weak, the skies often overcast, and the nights long. Professional diagnosis and treatment can help those suffering from SAD. Many people affected by SAD have found relief in light therapy treatments, medication, changes in diet, or other lifestyle adjustments.

# Eggnog

Many Americans celebrate the **Christmas season** by imbibing a curious mixture of beaten eggs, spirits, and spices known as eggnog. This drink dates back to the colonial era. In those days, people sometimes called rum "grog." This fact leads some to believe that eggnog's original name was "egg and grog," which was later shortened into "eggnog." In spite of its American credentials, eggnog resembles a number of traditional northern European Christmas specialties, including the English lamb's wool and syllabub, the Dutch *advocaat*, and the Norwegian *eggedosis*. All of these recipes blend beaten eggs with wine, ale, or spirits. Lamb's wool may also contain cream or milk. American eggnog recipes usually call for some combination of beaten eggs, brandy, cream, sugar, and nutmeg.

Eggnog has been enlivening American Christmas festivities for several centuries. George Washington's Christmas guests might well have staggered home after one cup too many of his favorite eggnog preparation. His recipe requires one quart of cream, one quart of milk, one dozen eggs, one pint of brandy, one-half pint of rye, one-quarter pint of rum, and one-quarter pint of sherry (*see also* **America, Christmas in Colonial**). First Lady Dolley Madison entertained her guests with cinnamon eggnog, one of her Christmas specialties (*for more on American presidents, see* **White House, Christmas in the**).

In 1826 cadets at the prestigious West Point Military Academy risked their careers for a taste of the traditional midwinter cheer. They staged a secretive eggnog party in direct disobedience of Superintendent Thayer's order that the academy observe a dry Christmas season. Designated cadets snuck the contraband ingredients past the sentries. On Christmas Eve they blackened the windows in their barracks, posted guards to warn of the approach of officers, and began the festivities. Officials somehow stumbled upon the scene at 4:30 a.m. The encounter between the drunken students and the outraged officers resulted in a bloody melee that left one cadet charged with attempted murder. The so-called "Eggnog Riot" eventually led to the voluntary resignation of six cadets and the court martial of nineteen of their fellows. Eleven of these were dismissed from the academy. Since seventy young men took part in the escapade, one might conclude that most got off easy. Many of these cadets hailed from prominent American families. Jefferson Davis, future president of the Confederate States of America, was one of them. As punishment for his participation in the eggnog conspiracy, school authorities arrested him and confined him to his quarters until February of the following year (*see also* **America, Christmas in Nineteenth-Century**).

In the late twentieth century fewer and fewer Americans seemed willing to abandon themselves to the full-fledged eggnog experience. New low-fat and non-alcoholic versions of the old Christmas favorite sprout up every year, reflecting contemporary health concerns. The following old-fashioned eggnog recipe offers us a glimpse of the uninhibited pleasures of past eras:

> Whisk together six eggs and two cups of sugar until fluffy and light. Continue stirring while slowly adding one quart of bourbon whiskey and one cup of rum. Slowly add four cups of milk, four cups half-and-half, and one cup heavy cream stirring all the while. Add grated nutmeg as desired. Chill and serve.

# Elves

Contemporary Christmas lore suggests that **Santa Claus** lives at the **North Pole**, accompanied by a band of elves. These elves staff Santa's workshop, manufacturing the millions of toys Santa brings to children at Christmas time. What exactly are elves and how did they become associated with Santa Claus and the celebration of Christmas?

## Elves and Fairies

Folk descriptions of a magical and mostly invisible race of beings can be found in the lore of peoples from all parts of the globe. This belief was particularly common among the peoples of Europe and Asia. In Europe these beings were known by many names. Folklorists often refer to them as "fairies," a common English term for these creatures. Some trace belief in fairies back to the ancient Romans and their legends about the deities known as the "Three Fates." Indeed, some folklorists locate the origins of the English word "fairy" in the Latin word for "fate," *fatum*. Eventually, the Three Fates evolved into spirits known as *fata* in Italian and *fada* in Spanish. These beings hovered about babies at the time of their births, bestowing upon them strengths, weaknesses, and destinies. In French-speaking areas, however, these magical creatures were called *fée*, a word some experts link to the Old French verb for "enchant," *féer*. The English adopted the French term for these creatures, translating it as "fay," or later, "fairy."

Ireland and the British Isles were particularly rich in fairy folklore. A multitude of names arose for these magical beings. The Irish knew them as the Síde, or "people of the hills"; the Welsh called them Tylwyth Teg, the "fair family"; and the Scottish talked of two distinct groups—the Seelie (blessed) Court and the Unseelie (unblessed) Court. Other names for them included the Little People, the Good Folk, the Gentry, Puck, Robin Goodfellow, pixies, and brownies. English speakers might also have referred to these beings as elves. The word "elf" came into English from the Nordic and Teutonic languages, apparently arriving in England when Scandinavian peoples invaded in the Middle Ages. The beings known to the English as fairies were called *alfar* in Scandinavia, a word that evokes mountains and water. The English incorporated this word into their own language as "elf."

Fairy folklore taught that, although these magical creatures inhabited the natural world all around us, they often chose to remain invisible. When visible, they frequently appeared in human form. They could, however, take the shape of a flower, a flame, a bird, a jewel, a woodland animal, or any other element of the natural world. Folk beliefs advised people to tread warily if they sensed that these magical and unpredictable creatures were about. On the one hand, elves and fairies often used their powers to aid humans, for example, by providing gifts of food or toys for children, or by breaking evil enchantments. On the other hand, if provoked they could just as easily harm humans. They sometimes stole human children, ruined crops, and caused household accidents.

## European Christmas Elves

The folklore of many European countries warned that spirits of all kinds were particularly active during the Twelve Days of Christmas. British folklore cautioned that fairies and the Will O' the Wisp haunted these long, dark nights. The famous English playwright William Shakespeare disagreed, however. The following lines from the play *Hamlet* voice his dissenting opinion:

> Some say, that ever 'gainst that season comes
> Wherein our Saviour's birth is celebrated,
> The bird of dawning singeth all night long:
> And then, they say, no spirit can walk abroad;
> The nights are wholesome; then no planets strike,
> Nor fairy takes, nor witch hath power to charm;
> So hallow'd and so gracious is the time.

The Scandinavians did not share Shakespeare's sentiments. Their lore reminded them that the arrival of the Christmas season awakened the **Jultomten** (also known as the *Julnissen, Julenissen,* or *Joulutonttuja*). Every homestead hosted at least one of these elf-like creatures. They slept and hid in dark corners for most of the year, but became bold and merry around Christmas time. In fact, they expected householders to provide them with good cheer on Christmas Eve. If the family neglected to leave out an offering of food before going to bed, the Jultomten might curdle the milk or cause other household mishaps. In Sweden, Norway, and Finland, these elves eventually evolved into Christmas gift bringers, a role they still carry out today. In Iceland, prankster elves known as the **Christmas Lads** vex householders at Christmas time.

## *American Christmas Elves*

These European traditions may have influenced the creation of the American Santa Claus, his workshop, and his elven helpers. This vision of Santa's world was constructed in large part by two men over a century ago: classics professor Clement C. Moore and illustrator Thomas Nast. In the early nineteenth century Moore, a professor at General Theological Seminary, scribbled down a little Christmas poem for children. Titled "'Twas the Night Before Christmas" ("A Visit from St. Nicholas"), it described the nocturnal activities of the Christmas gift bringer who would later be known as Santa Claus. This description depicted Santa Claus as a "jolly old elf" who arrives in a "miniature sleigh." Moore's vision of Santa Claus, which had already begun to shape the American public's image of Santa Claus, was further refined by those who followed. Although Thomas Nast was not the first writer or illustrator to place Santa in the company of a band of elves, he was the most influential. In the late nineteenth century Nast published a series of cartoons that elaborated on the image of Santa Claus established by Moore. Nast enlarged Santa to human size and gave him a home, the North Pole. He retained the connection between Santa Claus and elves, however, by depicting them as Santa's labor force.

Whereas the elves of traditional European folklore whiled away the hours dancing in moonlit meadows and sleeping under the stairs, Santa's elves busied themselves in his workshop all year round. Nast's elves seem to have emerged from the imagination of an industrial age, unlike their older, European counterparts. Nevertheless, the fact that both Nast and Moore included references to elves in their creations may well reflect the influence of northern European folklore associating Christmas time with the activities of elves. The American people may have embraced yet another element of European elf lore in their Christmas celebrations. The American custom of leaving a snack of cookies and milk for Santa Claus on Christmas Eve closely resembles the Scandinavian practice of placating the Jultomten. In any case, Nast's vision of Santa and his North Pole workshop gained widespread acceptance in the United States. As Santa Claus became an international folk figure, so, too, did Santa's helpers and year-long companions, the North Pole elves.

# Epiphany

**Blessing of the Waters Day, Día de los Tres Reyes (Three Kings Day), Feast of Baptism, Feast of Jordan, Feast of Lights, Feast of the Three Kings, Fête des Rois, Le Jour de Rois (Kings' Day), Night of Destiny, Old Christmas Day, Perchtennacht, Theophania, Timkat, Twelfth Day, Twelfth Night**

Epiphany is a Christian feast day celebrated on January 6. The holiday commemorates the revelation of Jesus' divinity to those around him. In Western Christianity, the observance of Epiphany focuses on the adoration of the Magi. In Eastern Christianity, the holiday emphasizes Jesus' baptism. Over the centuries European folklore has assigned numerous legends and customs to Epiphany, some of which bear little direct relationship to the life of Jesus. In many countries Epiphany marks the end of the Christmas season.

## The Meaning of Epiphany

The word "epiphany" comes from the Greek term *epiphaneia*, meaning "manifestation," "appearance," or "showing forth." In the ancient world, the term designated occasions on which visiting kings or emperors appeared before the people. The writers of the Gospels used this term to describe occasions on which Jesus' divinity revealed itself to those around him. Ancient writers applied another Greek word, *theophaneia*, or "theophany," to the appearance of a god before human beings. Early Christians also used the word theophany in reference to their Epiphany celebrations. This usage continued in the Greek world, where today the Greek Orthodox Church refers to Epiphany as *Theophania*. Moreover, Eastern Orthodox Christians sometimes call Epiphany the "Feast of Lights." This name reflects their belief that baptism confers spiritual illumination.

## The History of Epiphany

Early Christians were celebrating Epiphany before they began to observe Christmas. The first celebrations of Epiphany occurred in second-century Egypt. Like Christmas, the date chosen for Epiphany has no firm historical or scriptural grounding. Some scholars believe that January 6 was selected by the earliest celebrants in order to upstage a **winter solstice** festival held in honor of an Egyptian sun god on that date. Indeed, according to one ancient Egyptian calendar, winter solstice fell on January 6. Some ancient Egyptians recognized that day as the birthday of the Egyptian god Osiris. Other sacred events held on that day included a festival commemorating the birth of the god Aeon from his virgin mother, Kore.

From the second century onward, scattered celebrations of Epiphany occurred among various groups of Christians, although no consensus emerged as to what events the holiday commemorated. Christian liturgy identifies four instances in which Jesus' divine nature manifested itself on earth: at his birth, at the adoration of the Magi, at his baptism, and when he changed water into wine at the wedding in Cana. Early Epiphany celebrations honored any one or more of these events. By the third century most Eastern Christians were celebrating Epiphany. By the late fourth century most Western Christians had also adopted the feast. Eastern and Western celebrations evolved around different themes, however. When the Western Church designated **December 25** as the Feast of the Nativity in the mid-fourth century, Western Epiphany celebrations consolidated around the revelation of Jesus' divinity to the Magi. When the Eastern Church embraced Christmas, between 380 and 430 A.D., Christmas absorbed the celebration of both the Nativity and the adoration of the Magi. Thus, Eastern Epiphany observances remained dedicated to the commemoration of Jesus' baptism.

In the Middle Ages, popular western European Epiphany celebrations focused on the Magi's journey. People began to refer to the Magi as kings and saints and to Epiphany as the "Feast of the Three Kings." Festivities of the day included **Nativity plays**, many of which featured the story of the Three Kings. Another boisterous medieval ceremony, the **Feast of Fools**, was also sometimes performed in churches on Epiphany.

In 1336 the city of Milan, Italy, hosted a splendid procession and play to commemorate the Feast of the Three Kings. Three men, sumptuously dressed as kings and surrounded by an entire retinue of costumed pages, body guards, and attendants, paraded through the city streets following a gold star which hung before them (*see also* **Star of Bethlehem**). At one juncture, they encountered King **Herod** and his scribes. The Wise Men asked where Jesus was to be born, and King Herod, after consulting the scribes, answered "**Bethlehem**." The kings and their followers continued on to St. Eustorgius Church, bearing their gifts of **gold**, **frankincense**, and **myrrh** ceremoniously before them. The crowd spilled into the church, preceded by trumpeters, horn players, donkeys, apes, and other animals. To one side of the high altar awaited **Mary** and the Christ child, in a manger complete with ox and ass. Although we might consider this noisy and colorful Epiphany celebration unseemly, medieval Europeans enjoyed this mixture of ceremony, carnival, and religion.

In Spanish-speaking countries today, Epiphany retains this strong association with the Magi and is called *Día de los Tres Reyes*, or Three Kings Day. The French call the holiday *Le Jour de Rois* or *Fête des Rois*: Kings' Day or the Feast of the Kings. The British sometimes refer to the holiday as Twelfth Day, and the evening before as **Twelfth Night**, since it occurs twelve days after Christmas. Twelfth Day marks the end of the Christmas season, also known as Twelfthtide or the **Twelve Days of Christmas**. Since late medieval times the British had enjoyed feasts and masquerades on Twelfth Night, but these celebrations have declined since the nineteenth century.

### Folklore and Customs

In Italy and Spanish-speaking countries, children receive **gifts** on Epiphany rather than on Christmas. Furthermore, in Spanish-speaking countries, the Three

Kings, *Los Reyes Magos*, deliver the presents rather than **Santa Claus**. On Epiphany Eve children leave a **shoe** on their doorstep or balcony, along with some straw for the Magi's camels. In the morning they find that the grateful Wise Men have filled their shoes with treats. In Italy, La **Befana**, an old woman from an Italian legend, distributes presents on Epiphany. La Befana was too busy to aid the Magi on their journey to worship the newborn Jesus. As a punishment for her lack of piety, she now wanders the world during the Christmas season bringing gifts to children. In Russian folklore, a woman named **Baboushka** plays a similar role. **Berchta** (or Perchta), a more fearsome female figure, appears on Epiphany Eve in Germany and Austria. She punishes wrongdoers and rewards well-behaved children. In these countries Epiphany is also known as *Perchtennacht*. In Syria and Lebanon Epiphany may be called "The Night of Destiny" (*Lailat al-Qadr*), a name it shares with a Muslim holiday. In these lands the Christmas gift bringer is a mule or a camel.

In Sweden, Norway, Germany, Switzerland, and Poland, groups of costumed children known as the star boys parade through the streets of town singing songs or performing plays about the Three Kings on Epiphany Eve.

An old German tradition encourages people to bring salt, water, chalk, and incense to church on Epiphany Eve to be blessed. Upon returning home, they sprinkle the blessed water over their fields, animals, and homes, and cook with the salt. They burn the incense and waft the smoke throughout their homes as a defense against evil spirits. In both Germany and Austria, the initials CMB—which stand for the names attributed to the Three Kings in legend, Caspar, Melchior, and Balthasar—may be written over doorways with blessed chalk in order to protect the house.

In many European countries, such as France, Austria, Germany, and England, festive meals were once planned for Epiphany featuring a special cake. A coin, pea, bean, or tiny china doll was baked inside the cake, and the person who found the object in their slice was considered "king" or "queen" of the feast (*see also* **King of the Bean**; Twelfth Night). In England, tradition reserves the unwelcome chore of removing and storing Christmas decorations for Twelfth Day.

### Religious Customs

In both Roman Catholic and Orthodox churches, water is blessed on Epiphany and distributed to the faithful for use in home religious observances. Among Orthodox Christians, Epiphany is also known as Blessing of the Waters Day. In past centuries priests blessed Egypt's Nile River. Both Christians and Muslims would then immerse themselves in the now holy waters, often driving their animals into the river as well to share in the blessing. In Palestine, the River Jordan was blessed. Thousands of worshipers then submerged themselves up to three times in the holy currents. Many Orthodox parishes observe similar Epiphany rites today. For example, the congregation may walk to a nearby river or other body of water which the priest then blesses. In some parts of the world, congregants joyfully immerse themselves in the blessed water. Another popular Orthodox observance involves tossing a crucifix into the water. The first to retrieve the cross is often thought to acquire good luck for the coming year.

The blessing of homes is a Roman Catholic ritual connected with Epiphany. The pastor blesses each room of the house using holy water and incense, and recites special prayers. Then he writes the year and the initials CMB inside the door with blessed chalk. In the year 1999, for example, he would write 19 CMB 99. Orthodox priests also bless homes on Epiphany.

Epiphany is not only a Christian feast day, but may also be considered a season of the Christian year encompassing the period between January 6 and the beginning of Lent. The length of this period varies in accordance with the day on which Easter falls each year.

# Farolitos

In the American Southwest, glowing paper sacks decorate the outlines of buildings, patios, walkways, and plazas at night during the **Christmas season**. These ornamental lights are called farolitos (pronounced fah-roh-LEE-tohs), meaning "little lanterns" in Spanish.

Farolitos are made with brown paper lunch bags, votive candles, and sand. To make one for yourself, turn over the rim of a brown paper bag to form a cuff. This helps to keep the bag open. Next pour several inches of sand into the bag. The sand weighs the bag down and anchors the candle. Place the bag outdoors at night, push a votive candle into the sand, and light the wick. The candlelight shining through the brown paper gives off a mellow, golden glow in the darkness.

Although farolitos came to the Southwest from Mexico, their historical roots can be traced all the way back to China. Spanish merchants made this link possible. From the early sixteenth to the early nineteenth centuries, Spain held both Mexico and the Philippines as colonies. Trade relations linked the Philippines with China. These links gave Spanish merchants access to Chinese goods, which they began to export to other places. Chinese paper lanterns, imported from the Philippines to Mexico by Spanish traders, proved popular in the New World. The Mexicans used them for many kinds of celebrations, including Christmas.

By the early nineteenth century the lanterns had spread north to territories now considered part of the United States. Unfortunately, the delicate paper that surrounded the lantern frame quickly perished in the rough conditions to which they were exposed. Frontier settlers soon hit upon a cheaper and sturdier alternative. They began to make lanterns with plain brown wrapping paper made available to them by recently increased trade along the Santa Fe Trail. The new farolitos not only proved hardier but also cast an amber glow that favored the warm colors characteristic of southwestern architecture and landscapes. Today these beautiful lights constitute an important Christmas symbol in the American Southwest.

In some areas of the Southwest farolitos are known as **luminarias.** In other areas the two customs remain distinct. In northern New Mexico, for example, the word "luminarias" refers to small Christmas season bonfires, while the decorative brown paper lanterns are known as farolitos.

# Feast of Fools

A long succession of mock rulers have presided over winter holiday merrymaking in Europe. In the Middle Ages lower clerics in France, Germany, Bohemia, and England celebrated the **Christmas season** by holding mock religious ceremonies that made fun of their usual solemn duties. These lower clerics held low-ranking positions at local churches that involved assisting the priest in his duties or playing a minor role in religious services. Their burlesque rites were known as "The Feast of Fools" and were observed on a variety of days throughout the season. The deacons led the revelry on December 26, **St. Stephen's Day**, the sub-priests (or vicars) on December 27, **St. John's Day**, the choirboys on December 28, **Holy Innocents' Day**, and the sub-deacons on January 1, the **Feast of the Circumcision**. The name "Feast of Fools" was most often given to the rites led by the sub-deacons on January 1. Indeed, these were accounted by some to be the most riotous of all these mock ceremonies.

## History

Some scholars trace the roots of the Feast of Fools back to **Kalends**, the Roman new year celebration that lived on for centuries after the fall of the Empire. Other writers point to similarities between the Feast of Fools and some of the customs surrounding **Saturnalia**. By the twelfth century the Feast of Fools had emerged in full force. It first established itself as an observance of the sub-deacons, but soon expanded to encompass other lower clerics. It appears to have been more popular in France than in any other European country. By the end of the twelfth century Parisians were treated to the spectacle several times over during the Christmas season, as the deacons (St. Stephen's Day) sub-priests (St. John's Day), choirboys (Holy Innocents' Day), and sub-deacons (Feast of the Circumcision, Epiphany, or the Octave of Epiphany) all had a go at leading the mock rites.

Historical documents record several centuries of complaints registered by priests, bishops, and other high-ranking Church officials who, in spite of their authority, seemed unable to stop the raucous revelry. Not only did lower clerics relish their festival, but townsfolk also enjoyed the outrageous spectacle. In 1435 the Council of

Basel forbade the Feast of Fools. Nevertheless, the lower clergy clung to their yearly spree for another 150 years. Clerics from the cathedral of Amiens, France, continued to celebrate the Feast of Fools until 1721.

## Customs

Participants in the Feast of Fools reversed all customary rules of proper church behavior. Instead of presiding over religious services with dignity, seriousness, and reverence, they brought the coarse, lusty, irreverent behavior of the carnival to church. After their wild mass, they often roamed the streets in an equally wild, mock religious procession. In some places merrymakers chose a bishop or archbishop of fools to preside over the celebration. As insignia of his newfound rank he wore a bishop's miter and carried a bishop's staff. Clerical participants in the follies often dressed in street clothing, including women's clothing, masks, garlands of **greenery**, or even in fools' costumes.

Our knowledge of these mock ceremonies comes mostly from the writings of higher clergy who disapproved of the revels. According to one irate cleric who observed the proceedings in mid-fifteenth-century France:

> Priests and clerks may be seen wearing masks and monstrous visages at the hours of the office. They dance in the choir dressed as women, panders or minstrels. They sing wanton songs. They eat black puddings at the horn of the altar while the celebrant is saying Mass. They play at dice there. They cense with stinking smoke from the soles of old shoes. They run and leap through the church, without a blush at their own shame. Finally they drive about the town and its theatres in shabby traps and carts, and rouse the laughter of their fellows and the bystanders in infamous performances, with indecent gesture and verses scurrilous and unchaste. [Miles, 1990, 304]

In a similar observance called the **Feast of the Ass**, a donkey carrying a young woman was led into church and made to stand near the altar. This act may have been meant to represent the flight of **Mary**, **Joseph**, and the baby **Jesus** into Egypt shortly after Jesus' birth (*see also* **Flight into Egypt**). Nevertheless, the revelers took the opportunity to sing the praises of the ass in Latin and to require the officiant to end the mass by braying three times like a donkey. The congregation responded in kind.

In enacting these rites, those of lesser status in the Church temporarily usurped the roles of higher-ups, performing unflattering impersonations of priests, bishops, and archbishops. In this respect the Feast of Fools resembled other Christmas season rites that authorized similar, temporary inversions of power and status. These include the festivities surrounding the **boy bishop,** the **Lord of Misrule,** barring out the schoolmaster, Holy Innocents' Day, Saturnalia, and **Twelfth Night.**

# Feast of the Ass

In the Middle Ages, people in some parts of France commemorated the Holy Family's **Flight into Egypt** with a celebration called the Feast of the Ass. Not only did Christian legends place an ass in the stable where **Jesus** was born, but also medieval people imagined **Mary** and the baby Jesus riding on an ass led by **Joseph** as they plodded towards their Egyptian exile. Later, a donkey would carry the adult Jesus into the city of Jerusalem on the week before his death, an event celebrated on Palm Sunday, the Sunday before Easter (John 12:14-15). The ceremonies associated with the Feast of the Ass honored all the donkeys who played roles in these and other well-known Christian stories. They took place on January 14.

The festivities featured a procession in which a young girl with a baby rode through the city streets on an ass while people sang a silly song honoring the creature:

> Orientis partibus
> Adventavit asinus,
> Pucher et fortissimos,
> Sarcinis aptissimus.
> Hez, Sir asne, hez!
> From Oriental country came
> A lordly ass of highest fame,
> So beautiful, so strong and trim,
> No burden was too great for him.
> Hail, Sir Donkey, hail. [Weiser, 1952, 127]

The ass was then led into a church where religious services took place. Like the **Feast of Fools**, these ceremonies tended to get out of hand. The topsy-turvy ambience of medieval Christmas celebrations encouraged high-spirited excesses that gradually turned the event into a burlesque (*see also* **Medieval Era, Christmas in**). Particularly raucous celebrations took place in the town of Beauvais. After the procession, the ass entered the church, where it was lavished with food and drink. At the same time, the clergy conducted a kind of parody of the evening prayer service, which ended with everyone braying like an ass as they danced around the befuddled creature. Afterwards actors presented humorous folk plays outside the church doors. The last event of the day was a **Midnight Mass**, which the priest brought to a close by braying three times.

These hijinks caused the Roman Catholic Church to officially suppress the Feast of the Ass in the fifteenth century. It lingered for many years after that in some places, however.

# Feast of the Circumcision

### Circumcision of Jesus, Feast of the Circumcision and the Name of Jesus, Feast of the Circumcision of Our Lord, Feast of the Holy Name of Our Lord Jesus Christ, Octave of the Birth of Our Lord, Solemnity of Mary

The Gospel according to Luke (2:21) reports that eight days after Jesus was born, Joseph and Mary named him and had him circumcised. In doing so, they conformed to an old Jewish custom whereby all male infants are circumcised as a sign of the eternal covenant between God and the Jewish people. The Feast of the Circumcision, observed on January 1, commemorates the Holy Family's compliance with this custom. It also celebrates the naming of Jesus and, in the Roman Catholic Church, Mary's role as the Mother of God.

## History

The Feast of the Circumcision received official recognition rather late. Luke's account clearly states that Jesus was circumcised eight days after his birth. After Church authorities established the celebration of Christmas on **December 25**, the obvious date for the remembrance of the Circumcision would be January 1, which falls eight days after the celebration of the Nativity.

In the first few centuries after Christ's birth, however, the vast pagan population of the Roman world was still celebrating **Kalends**, their new year festival, on that date. Numerous early Christian leaders disapproved of the riotous pagan new year celebrations and urged their Christian followers to observe the day with thoughtfulness, fasting, and sobriety instead. In the fourth century A.D., one such leader, a monk named Almacius (or Telemachus) stormed into a crowded Roman stadium on January 1 crying, "Cease from the superstition of idols and polluted sacrifices. Today is the octave of the Lord!" Some report that the enraged crowd stoned the earnest monk to death; others state that the assembled gladiators dispatched him.

This attitude of vehement opposition to the celebrations already taking place on January 1 may explain the reluctance of Church officials to establish a Christian celebration on that day. In an effort to counteract the still-popular festivities surrounding Kalends, the second provincial Council of Tours (567 A.D.) ordered Christians to fast and do penance during the first few days of the new year.

Nevertheless, over the course of the next several centuries, January 1 became a feast day throughout the Christian world. Around the seventh century the Roman Catholic Church introduced a new observance called the "Octave of the Birth of Our Lord" on January 1. In the language of the Church, an "octave" is an eight-day period that includes any great Church festival and the seven days that follow it. Thus, this name signaled that the new observance was to serve as a completion of the Christmas feast. Before that time, however, Christians from Gaul had observed the day as the "Circumcision of Jesus," a name reflecting their emphasis on Jesus' compliance with the

Jewish tradition of circumcision. This idea spread from Gaul to Spain, and, eventually, to Rome.

The Eastern Churches began to observe January 1 as a commemoration of the circumcision in the eighth century. In the ninth century the Roman Church began to blend its original emphasis on the completion of the octave of Christmas with a commemoration of the Circumcision. Before long the Roman Church incorporated yet another theme into its celebrations. Many observed the feast primarily by expressing gratitude and devotion to Mary, the mother of God. Indeed, some historians recognize the festival as the earliest Catholic feast dedicated to Mary. Eventually, it became the most important Marian feast in the Roman Church.

The Feast of the Circumcision falls in the middle of the **Twelve Days of Christmas**. During the Middle Ages, bursts of revelry punctuated this twelve-day period. In spite of the efforts of the early Church to diminish the customary carousing associated with the Roman new year, a new form of riotous display developed around Church celebrations on January 1. From the twelfth to the sixteenth centuries, lower clergy in many parts of Europe took part in the **Feast of Fools** on that date. Scandalized authorities managed to eradicate this observance in most areas by the sixteenth century, although it lingered in France until the eighteenth century.

### Contemporary Observance

The various Christian denominations that observe the feast emphasize different aspects of the events surrounding Jesus' circumcision. In 1969 the Roman Catholic Church changed the name of the observance to the "Solemnity of Mary," a name that reflects their emphasis on Mary's role as mother of the Savior. Orthodox Christians continue to observe the day as the "Feast of the Circumcision of Our Lord." Episcopalians call the festival the "Feast of the Holy Name of Our Lord Jesus Christ." They emphasize the significance of Jesus' name, given to Mary by **Gabriel**—the **angel** of the Annunciation —which means literally "God saves" or "God helps." Lutherans compromise by calling the festival the "Feast of the Circumcision and the Name of Jesus."

# Flight into Egypt

The **Gospel according to Matthew** tells that soon after **Jesus** was born, King **Herod** sent soldiers to **Bethlehem** to kill all the town's male infants (*see* **Holy Innocents' Day**). An **angel** warned **Joseph** of Herod's evil plot and told him to escape with his family to Egypt. The Holy Family obeyed the angel's command and departed. This event, called the Flight into Egypt, has been depicted by many artists over the centuries, including Giotto, Titian, Albrecht Dürer, and Nicolas Poussin. It is commemorated in Orthodox churches on December 26 —or January 8 in churches that still use the Julian calendar—in a service referred to as the Synaxis of the Theotokos (*for more on the Julian calendar, see* **Old Christmas Day**). *Synaxis* means "meeting" and *Theotokos*, a title given to the Blessed Virgin **Mary**, means "God bearer." In the Middle Ages, some western Europeans, particularly the French, remembered the Flight into Egypt with a festival called the **Feast of the Ass**.

When King Herod died, the angel returned again, notifying Joseph that it was safe for him to return with his family to Judea. When Joseph learned that Herod's brutal son, Archelaus, had inherited his father's throne, he decided not to return to Bethlehem, and instead moved his family to Nazareth.

## *Legends*

What happened to the Holy Family on this perilous journey into Egypt? The Bible doesn't say. Perhaps because of this omission, legends and lore soon sprouted up around the event. According to one tale, Herod's soldiers knew the Holy Family had escaped and so pursued them. As Mary, Joseph, and Jesus passed some peasants sowing wheat, Mary said to them, "If anyone should ask if we have been here, tell them that we indeed passed by while you were sowing this field of wheat." Miraculously, the wheat sprouted and grew tall overnight. When Herod's soldiers inquired of the peasants and learned that their prey had passed through the region at the time the wheat was planted, they figured that the Holy Family was many days ahead of them and so lost heart and returned to Judea.

An ancient document known as the Arabic Infancy Gospel records another near escape. In this story, the Holy Family is held up by bandits on their way to Egypt. One

of the highwaymen, however, feels a special sympathy for the fugitives and refuses to rob them. In fact, he tries to convince the other robber to let them go. The other refuses until the first robber agrees to pay him a girdle and forty coins. The kind-hearted thief does so and the other reluctantly allows the prisoners to depart. The baby Jesus predicts that he and the bandits will die on the same day in the same place. Sure enough, according to the Arabic Infancy Gospel, these men turn out to be the two thieves, the one remorseful and the other not, who were crucified alongside Jesus about thirty years later (Luke 23:93-43).

Another tale, this one from a document called the Apocryphal Gospel of Pseudo-Matthew, finds Joseph losing faith as the family trudges through the desert. They stop underneath a date palm tree where Joseph frets about how to find water. Mary asks her husband to pick her some dates. Joseph scolds her for requesting something so far out of his reach. The infant Jesus, however, speaks to the tree, commanding it to bow down so Mary can gather fruit. The tree responds. Then Jesus orders an underground spring to break through to the surface so that they can drink and fill their water bags. As this tale spread through Europe, people changed the date tree to a **cherry tree** and changed the timing of the event so that it takes place before Jesus was born.

Another legend concerning trees reports that the Holy Family passed through a forest on their long journey to Egypt. Every tree except the aspen bowed in reverence as they passed. Irritated by this lack of respect, the baby Jesus then cursed the tree, which is why its leaves tremble in the wind till this day.

Another plant that paid respect to the Holy Family on the Flight into Egypt is the Rose of Jericho. It sprang up wherever they passed. It is sometimes called Mary's Rose.

One final tale popular in the Middle Ages proclaims that the Holy Family encountered a gypsy woman on the road to Egypt. She extended her well-wishes to the Holy Family and, noticing Mary's fatigue especially, she took them to a place where they could rest and offered straw for their donkey. She then proceeded to recount Mary's past history. Afterwards she read Jesus' palm and accurately foretold the major events of his life, including the crucifixion. Then she begged for alms, but not in the usual manner. Knowing the true identity of the child, the gypsy woman asked for the gift of genuine repentance and life everlasting.

# Frankincense

The sap of the frankincense tree (*Boswellia carteri* or *Boswellia thurifera*) dries into hard, yellowish brown lumps of gum resin known as frankincense. In biblical times frankincense was prized as the very best kind of incense. It was one of the **gifts** that the **Magi** presented to the baby **Jesus**.

The English word "frankincense" comes from the Old French words *franc encens,* meaning pure or high-quality incense. Although it was most commonly used as incense in ancient times, frankincense was also prescribed as a medicine to treat a wide variety of ailments. Many ancient peoples, such as the Egyptians, Greeks, Romans, Persians, Jews, and Babylonians, burned incense in home and temple worship. The rising fumes from burning incense may have offered worshipers a visual image of prayers ascending to heaven. Scholars speculate that this imagery explains the widespread use of incense in worship. Frankincense is mentioned numerous times in the Old Testament and was one of the four components of the sacred incense burned by the Jewish priests in the Sanctuary. Because of its close relationship with worship, the Magi's gift of frankincense has traditionally been interpreted as a recognition of Jesus' divinity. Another interpretation suggests that it predicts Jesus' future role as a high priest.

In ancient times, Arabia supplied the Mediterranean and Asia with most of their **myrrh** and frankincense. These products were so highly valued and so difficult to obtain outside of Arabia that they became a luxury affordable only by the rich. Thus, the Magi's valuable gift of frankincense may also have signified their recognition of Jesus' great worth.

Until the mid-1700s tradition dictated that the British monarch offer a gift of frankincense, **gold**, and myrrh at the Chapel Royal on **Epiphany**. Heralds and knights of the Garter, Thistle, and Bath accompanied the King on this reenactment of the Magi's pilgrimage. Under the unstable King George III the procession was abandoned, although the monarch's gift of gold, frankincense, and myrrh is still sent to the Chapel Royal by proxy. A similar royal offering was at one time customary in Spain.

Today frankincense trees can be found in Arabia, Ethiopia, Somalia, and India. Frankincense is still primarily used as incense. Frankincense is a component of the incense burned in Roman Catholic and Orthodox church services. It may also be found in other scented products, such as soap.

# Frau Gaude

## Gaue, Gode, Wode

Since ancient times, legends have told of supernatural forces that roam the earth around the time of Christmas. According to old folk beliefs, Frau Gaude, followed by her pack of phantom dogs, once haunted the streets of German-speaking Europe during the **Twelve Days of Christmas**. If she found a house with an open door, she would send in one of her dogs, which the householders would find impossible to drive away. If they killed the dog, it would turn into a stone. Regardless of where the family left the stone, it would always return to their house at night as a whimpering dog, bringing them bad luck throughout the year.

In some regions, Frau Gaude led the **Wild Hunt**, a riotous procession of **ghosts** and spirits who rode across the stormy night skies during **Yule**. Frau Gaude may be a variant of **Berchta**, a pagan winter goddess who faded into a kind of minor bogey in later times. Other names for Frau Gaude include Gaue, Gode, and Wode.

# "Frosty the Snowman"

Frosty the Snowman is the main character of a popular Christmas song by the same name, as well as numerous animated television specials. The original "Frosty the Snowman" song was written by Walter "Jack" Rollins and Steve Nelson in 1950. It was first recorded by Gene Autry in 1951 and sold more than one million copies. The song has since been recorded countless times by many different artists, but Autry's version remains one of the most popular. Frosty quickly became a well-known symbol of the Christmas season, even though Christmas is not actually mentioned in the song.

In 1969, the first "Frosty the Snowman" animated television special was produced. This cartoon built upon the story told in the song, adding new characters and a plot to fill in the details of Frosty's adventurous life of mischief. In this story, a group of children are being entertained by a magician named Professor Hinkle who, it turns out, is unable to perform any magic tricks. Professor Hinkle throws away his hat in frustration, and the wind blows it onto the head of a nearby snowman, who comes to life. Professor Hinkle realizes the value of his discarded hat and decides to get it back, even though it would cost Frosty his life. In an effort to save Frosty from the evil magician as well as the warming spring temperatures, a girl named Karen strikes out on a journey to take Frosty to the North Pole, where he will never melt. The journey north proves to be more challenging than expected, but hope is restored with Frosty's promise to Karen that he will return again every winter. With its catchy tunes and endearing story, "Frosty the Snowman" was an instant success. It continues to be shown on television every year, helping it to become a holiday classic.

A second animated television special titled "Frosty's Winter Wonderland" was produced in 1976. In this story, Frosty keeps his promise to return to visit the children

again. They make a wife for Frosty, a snow-woman named Crystal who comes to life when she is given a bouquet of flowers made of frost. Frosty and Crystal are happy together, but trouble ensues as jealous Jack Frost plots to ruin everything. The children, Frosty, and Crystal must find a way to include Jack and help him realize the important role he plays as the keeper of winter. The animated "Rudolph and Frosty's Christmas in July" was released in 1979. This sequel has Frosty teaming up with the reindeer Rudolph for an adventure in which the pair must escape the clutches of the evil wizard Winterbolt, who wants to steal Rudolph's famous nose and Frosty's magic hat (*see also* "**Rudolph the Red-Nosed Reindeer**").

The 1992 animated tale "Frosty Returns" represents a further departure from the original story. In this version, Frosty comes to life without the aid of his magic hat. The plot unfolds in the town of Beansboro, in which inventor Mr. Twitchell creates an aerosol spray that instantly removes snow. Frosty and his friends must find a way to stop the spray from being used before it's too late. The 2005 cartoon "The Legend of Frosty the Snowman" takes place in the town of Evergreen, where Mayor Tinkerton's obsession with rules does not allow for a talking snowman. Conflict develops when Frosty encourages the town's children to break the rules. After Frosty meets a terrible fate, it's up to the mayor's son Tommy to set things right.

While the original "Frosty the Snowman" television special enjoyed tremendous success and longevity, subsequent releases were not as popular. The original story appealed to both children and adults, while the sequels seemed to entertain only the youngest viewers. Even so, some of the Frosty sequels continue to be broadcast on television each year during the Christmas season. The popularity of Frosty the Snowman continues in part because of the wide variety of seasonal merchandise featuring the character. The many books, videos, games, toys, and Christmas decorations featuring Frosty have helped him to become a well-known fixture in the contemporary American Christmas scene.

# Gabriel

The Bible names only one of the **angels** who appear in connection with the birth of **Jesus**. The **Gospel according to Luke** states that the angel Gabriel appeared to the Blessed Virgin **Mary** to tell her that she would bear a son whom she should name Jesus (Luke 1:26-35). Christians call this event the Annunciation.

### Gabriel in the Bible

Who is Gabriel and why was he sent to bear such important news? Religious scholars often begin a discussion of the angel by analyzing the meaning of his name. Some say it means "God is my warrior"; others translate it as "man of God." Still others believe it should be translated as "power of God" or "hero of God." Gabriel is one of only two angels mentioned by name in the Hebrew scriptures, or Old Testament (the other is Michael). In the Book of Daniel, Gabriel helps Daniel interpret his visions and informs him of God's plan for the end of time (Daniel 8-12). Gabriel returns again in the New Testament, or Christian scriptures. In the Gospel according to Luke he appears to Zechariah to tell him that he and his wife will conceive a child, John, who will serve as the forerunner to Jesus Christ (Luke 1:11-20). Shortly afterwards Gabriel visits the Virgin Mary to announce her forthcoming pregnancy (Luke 1:26-38). Thus the Bible tends to cast Gabriel as God's herald. Because he frequently brings news of God's doings to human beings, he is sometimes referred to as the Angel of Revelation.

## Gabriel in Christian Art

In the Gospel according to Luke, Gabriel identifies himself as someone who "stand[s] in the presence of God" (Luke 1:19). This has led many Christians to conclude that he is one of the few high-ranking angels known as archangels. Over the centuries Christian artists have portrayed Gabriel as a solemn male figure wearing beautiful robes. In earlier works of art Gabriel often carries a scepter. In more recent works he holds a lily, a symbol of the purity and goodness of the Virgin Mary.

## Jewish and Muslim Beliefs

Jewish lore assigns Gabriel many different jobs. The Book of Enoch portrays him as an overseer of the Garden of Eden (*see also* **Adam and Eve Day**). Other apocryphal texts and legends have shown him as one of the four angels who stand round the throne of God, a participant in the destruction of Sodom and the army of Sennacherib, and one of those who prayed for the world at the time of the Great Flood. Muslims, too, honor the angel Gabriel, whom they know as Jibril. They believe him to be the angel who dictated the Qur'an—the holy book of Islam—to the prophet Muhammad.

## Christian Lore

Christian lore not only places Gabriel at the scene of Jesus' birth but also at the scene leading up to Jesus' death. Perhaps because of his biblical role as a herald, Christian legends have suggested that Gabriel was the unnamed angel that brought the good news of Jesus' birth to the **shepherds** (Luke 2:8-12). Another folk belief places Gabriel in the Garden of Gethsemane as Jesus prayed and waited for the men who would come to arrest him and condemn him to death. Both of these tales emphasize Gabriel's role as the angel of mercy. Michael, by contrast, functions as the angel of judgment. (In Jewish lore these roles are reversed, with Michael serving as the angel of mercy while Gabriel acts as the angel of judgment.)

## Patronage

In 1951 Pope Pius XII gave Gabriel a new role to play, modernizing his ancient task as a transmitter of messages. He declared Gabriel to be the patron saint of all those who work in the field of telecommunications. Gabriel also serves as the traditional patron of messengers, diplomats, clergy members, postal workers, and stamp collectors.

# Ghosts

Spirits of many kinds haunt the Christmas folklore of northern Europe. Since ancient times, legends have told of supernatural forces that roam the earth around Christmas. Some folklorists believe that in ancient times the Germanic and Scandinavian peoples associated the midwinter **Yule** festival with the return of the dead. Old tales tell of a band of ghosts called the **Wild Hunt** that charged through the nighttime sky during the **Twelve Days of Christmas**. In Norway, Estonia, Latvia, and Lithuania old folk beliefs concerning the Christmas time visits of the dead linger on. In the German region of Bavaria, some people believe that restless spirits walk abroad during the Knocking Nights, the Thursday nights in **Advent**. In Estonia, Germany, and Lithuania some people visit family graves on Christmas Eve, leaving behind lit candles (*see also* **Candles**).

In the German-speaking lands **Berchta**, too, wandered through the long, dark evenings. **Elves** peeked out from behind trees and beneath footstools in many countries. In others, trolls lumbered and witches flitted through the darkness. In Scandinavia the **Jultomten** appeared each year at Christmas time. In Iceland the closely related **Christmas Lads** played pranks on householders. Far to the south the **kallikantzari** vexed Greek families.

In England as well, certain folk beliefs warned that ghosts and other supernatural creatures lurked in the long shadows of the Twelve Days.

One old English tradition called for the telling of ghost stories at Christmas time. Perhaps this custom developed out of ancient beliefs concerning the return of the dead during the Yule festival. Indeed, in the eighth century St. Bede, a scholarly English monk, wrote that the Anglo-Saxon people left food on their tables overnight during the **Christmas season** so that visiting spirits could partake of the feast. In spite of these yearly visits, it took the English Christmas ghost another millennia to achieve notoriety. One man, English author Charles Dickens, brought this to pass. His Christmas ghost story, *A Christmas Carol*, became perhaps the most well known and best-loved Christmas tale of the nineteenth and twentieth centuries.

## A Christmas Carol

Contemporary readers tend to experience *A Christmas Carol* as a story about the meaning of Christmas. Nevertheless, Dickens also intended his readers to approach *A Christmas Carol* as a ghost story. He draws our attention to the ghostly aspect of the tale in its full title, which reads *A Christmas Carol in Prose, Being a Ghost Story of Christmas*. The preface continues the ghost theme in a humorous vein: "I have endeavoured in this Ghostly little book to raise the Ghost of an Idea which shall not put my readers out of humour with themselves, with each other, with the season, or with me. May it haunt their houses pleasantly, and no one wish to lay it." Finally, Dickens urged his audience to read the *Carol* out loud, in a cold room by candlelight. Dickens so enjoyed ghost stories that he wrote a number of them over the years, including several more Christmas ghost stories, such as "The Story of the Goblins Who Stole a Sexton," "The Haunted Man," "The Haunted House," and "A Christmas Tree."

# Gifts

The exchange of gifts at Christmas time is now commonplace, though this tradition has a rich history that began long ago. The practice of giving gifts at midwinter has passed through many transformations over the last few centuries. Various midwinter holidays developed gift-giving traditions that evolved over time, and gifts served different purposes in different times and places. Gifts were given to symbolize good wishes for the coming year, affirm one's social rank, generate fun and excitement, or simply demonstrate affection. All of these customs have combined to influence the contemporary practice of Christmas gift giving.

### *Early Traditions*

Historians trace the practice of midwinter gift-giving to the ancient Romans, who exchanged gifts with friends and family during the **winter solstice** festival of Saturna-

lia and the new year festival of **Kalends**. For ancient Romans, traditional gifts included cakes and honey, coins, wax candles, wax fruit, and clay dolls. By the Middle Ages, this practice had spread throughout Europe, where the pagan Saturnalia was replaced by Christmas. In medieval England, Christmas gifts were given according to social hierarchy. For example, peasants who worked on landed estates brought gifts of farm produce to the local lord during the **Twelve Days of Christmas**. Custom dictated that the lord would reciprocate by inviting the peasants to a Christmas feast.

By the sixteenth century, German children were receiving "Christ-bundles" at Christmas time. The traditional bundle contained at least five things: a coin, an article of clothing, a toy, something tasty to eat, and a pencil box or other scholastic item. Parents told their children that the Christ Child had brought them their gifts. In Norway, the Christ Child also provided Christmas gifts to children, placing the gifts in a plate or a bowl that had been left in an obvious place. Norwegians also exchanged gifts with friends and family members. Meanwhile, other German customs encouraged the preparation of simple gifts for the family. The Christmas tree and the Christmas pyramid were decorated with edible treats, such as nuts, apples, cookies, and candy, and provided everyone with holiday sweets.

By the seventeenth century, the English were exchanging New Year's gifts with family and friends. Popular gifts included oranges, gingerbread, rosemary, wine, marzipan, gloves, stockings, and other articles of clothing, jewelry, snuff boxes, tea urns, pens, and watches. Children sometimes received little bound books, often texts of religious instruction. This practice evolved over time, with the date of gift giving eventually shifting from New Year's to **St. Nicholas's Day,** or Christmas.

Another old European tradition of Christmas gift giving comes from Sweden. The Swedes called these gifts *Julklapp*, which means "Christmas knock." This name comes from an old Swedish custom whereby Christmas gift givers would knock on doors, toss in their gift, and run away. Recipients then tried to guess who had delivered the gifts. In addition, *Julklapp* usually arrived in some form of trick packaging. These surprise gifts added a dash of humor to the Christmas season.

## Christmas in Nineteenth-Century America

At the beginning of the nineteenth century, Christmas was not yet a very important holiday in America. In fact, in many states it was not even a legal holiday (*see also* **America, Christmas in Colonial**). In the early part of the nineteenth century, Americans who celebrated Christmas sometimes gave gifts to the poor and to servants, following old European customs of Christmas charity. **Charitable giving** linked Christmas gift giving with the spiritual celebration of the holiday. Personal Christmas gifts were not all that common. Presents to friends and family, often distributed on New Year's Day instead of Christmas, usually consisted of inexpensive, homemade items, such as wooden toys, handmade articles of clothing, or homemade foods. The well-to-do might buy fancier New Year gifts for friends and family members, such as jewelry, watches, pens, pin cushions, gloves, and snuff boxes.

American Christmas celebrations changed significantly during the second half of the nineteenth century. **Puritans** had strongly objected to Christmas festivities, but the holiday became more popular as their objections faded and the customs of Christmas-celebrating immigrant groups such as the Germans and Irish blended with those of more liberal Anglo Americans. The custom of exchanging Christmas gifts among friends and family became widespread during this time (*see also* **America, Christmas in Nineteenth-Century**). Americans adopted the practice of decorating **Christmas trees**, and **Santa Claus** emerged as a uniquely American Christmas gift bringer. Both of these innovations encouraged the growth of Christmas gift giving— the tree by providing a beautiful location to display the gifts, and Santa Claus by serving as a new Christmas gift bringer.

## Modern Gift Preferences

By the twentieth century, most Americans preferred to give and receive store-bought items as Christmas gifts. This movement away from homemade or handcrafted items was spurred in part by the country's shift to a more industrial economy. As more Americans moved into non-agricultural jobs, many people had less leisure time and more discretionary income. Retailers were quick to take advantage of the opportunity to promote manufactured items as ideal gifts. The growth of commercial retail advertising also fueled the shift away from homemade Christmas gifts.

In 1952, the Mr. Potato Head game was the first toy to be advertised on television. Selling for just 98 cents, the game quickly became the must-have Christmas gift for children that year. The 1959 debut of the Barbie doll was another runaway bestseller for Christmas. Gifts for children were not the only store-bought items to become extremely popular as a result of clever advertising. In 1975, a nationwide craze over the Pet Rock made it the top-selling Christmas gift for that year. The Pet Rock was, in fact, a garden-variety rock. It was undecorated and sold in a plain cardboard carton. The power of Christmas advertising drove the popularity of Pet Rocks, even though most Americans could easily see the humor of the gift. Another national obsession began in 1980 with the most popular Christmas gift that year, a puzzle game for all ages called the Rubik's Cube.

Children's toys ruled American Christmas gift-giving throughout the 1980s and 1990s. The unexpected popularity of Cabbage Patch Kids dolls, first introduced in 1983, caused extreme stress for many parents. A shortage of the dolls made it difficult, if not impossible, for many parents to buy one for their child. Scuffles and shoving matches broke out in stores across the country, as desperate parents fought over the last available dolls. Other popular Christmas gifts of that era included Transformers action figures, Care Bears stuffed animals, Beanie Babies miniature stuffed animals, and the Tickle Me Elmo doll that laughed when squeezed.

During the 2000s, American taste in Christmas gifts tended towards high-priced electronic gadgets. Video game systems, portable handheld computers, MP3 players, cell phones, electronic book readers, and battery operated remote controlled toys were among the most popular Christmas gifts during these years. By the middle of that decade, however, Americans began returning to the older traditions of giving handmade items as Christmas gifts. The rise of the DIY (do it yourself) arts and crafts movement in America fueled this trend away from commercially produced gifts. Some people began once again to make their own Christmas gifts, while others rejected mass-produced items in favor of gifts made by local artisans. Contemporary American Christmas gift-giving traditions now encompass a wide variety of customs. Though the gifts themselves may bear little resemblance to some historical traditions, the spirit of giving at Christmas remains the same.

# Gingerbread

The term "gingerbread" encompasses a variety of sweet and spicy cookies, cakes, and breads. These foods originated in medieval Europe at a time when ginger was an especially popular spice. Europeans have celebrated special occasions with gingerbread for centuries. From an earlier association with medieval fairs, gingerbread evolved into a favorite Christmas treat.

## Uses and Recipes

The ancient Romans greatly esteemed ginger for both its culinary uses and curative powers. They used it to flavor sauces as well as to treat upset stomachs and to induce bowel movements. Roman traders bartered with Asian merchants to acquire this useful root. After the fall of the Roman Empire, the trade routes established and maintained by the Romans dissolved, making ginger hard to get in Europe. In medieval times spice merchants charged high prices for ginger. Well-to-do medieval Europeans paid these prices, because they prized the relatively rare root.

Medieval cooks had discovered that ginger lent a preservative effect to pastries and breads. Some of the early recipes for these sweet, spice breads seem a bit crude by modern standards. One simply recommended mixing dry bread crumbs with spices and honey. Another combined bread crumbs with cinnamon, aniseed, ginger, licorice, and red wine. Cooks molded the pasty dough resulting from these recipes into various decorative shapes. This kind of gingerbread survived until the seventeenth century, when a more cake-like gingerbread, composed of flour, sugar, butter, eggs, molasses, ginger, cinnamon, and chopped fruits, began to replace it. "White gingerbread," which mixed ginger with marzipan, also became popular around this time. Bakers often pressed this kind of gingerbread into molds and then covered it in gilt.

## Fairs and Bakers

At the close of the eleventh century gingerbread flourished throughout northern Europe. Gingerbread vendors sold their goods at fairs across England, Germany, France, and Holland. These fairs served as traveling medieval shopping malls, pro-

viding people with opportunities for commerce as well as entertainment. In England, gingerbread was such a popular fairground treat that people began to refer to gingerbread cookies or pastries as "fairings." In addition, gingerbread became such a common item at many fairs that people began to call these commercial gatherings "gingerbread fairs." Several English gingerbread fairs survived into the twentieth century.

Many gingerbread vendors cut their cookies into fanciful shapes, some associated with the time of year, others purely decorative. For example, gingerbread sold at spring fairs might be cut into the shape of a flower. Other popular shapes included windmills, kings, queens, and various animals. Gingerbread sellers delighted in decorating their creations both by cutting them into exquisitely detailed shapes and by adding fancy embellishments. By the eighteenth century gingerbread makers had developed their art to such an extent that English speakers adopted the term "gingerbread work" to refer to fancy, carved, wooden trim on colonial seaport houses or to the gilded, carved prows of ships.

### Gingerbread Becomes an American Tradition

The gingerbread of contemporary American Christmas celebrations probably came down to us from old German traditions. In German-speaking lands, shaped and decorated gingerbreads appeared at autumn fairs and Christmas markets. German cooks often cut their gingerbread dough into the shape of gingerbread men and houses, which they baked, cooled, and decorated. The traditional German gingerbread house plays a prominent role in the famous German fairy tale, "Hansel and Gretel." The witch featured in this story built and lived in a house made out of gingerbread decorated with candy and icing. This tasty exterior tempted children, such as Hansel and Gretel, to venture inside. The Scandinavians also create miniature houses from gingerbread at Christmas time. In the United States, gingerbread men are the more common Christmas treat. Sometimes these cookies briefly serve as **ornaments** for the **Christmas tree** before they are eaten.

# Glastonbury Thorn

The tale of the Glastonbury Thorn has woven itself around some of the most romantic legends ever to have emerged from the British Isles. The thorn takes its name from Glastonbury, England, a location that has hosted many legendary characters and mystical events over the centuries. In the Middle Ages, monks from Glastonbury Abbey claimed to have discovered King Arthur's remains buried in their cemetery. Indeed, Celtic mythology identifies Glastonbury as "Avalon," the enchanted island from which came Arthur's famous sword, Excalibur, and to which the fatally wounded king was carried by fairy queens. Moreover, Christian legends proclaim that Joseph of Arimathea came to Glastonbury in the first century A.D. According to these tales, Joseph brought with him the Holy Grail, a sacred relic sought by many of King Arthur's knights centuries later. Subsequent stories add that Joseph established the Glastonbury Thorn, a mysterious bush that blooms when most others are barren—at Christmas time.

### Life and Legends of Joseph of Arimathea

The Gospels identify Joseph of Arimathea as a "good and upright man," a member of the Sanhedrin (the Jewish high court) who disagreed with their decision to turn

Jesus over to the Roman authorities (Luke 23:50-52). After Jesus' death, Joseph asked Pilate for permission to remove the body for burial. With Pilate's consent, Joseph took Jesus' body from the cross, wrapped it in linen, and sealed it in the tomb.

Later legends added to this sparse biblical account of Joseph's deeds. By the Middle Ages Joseph had become both an important saint and an acclaimed hero. Legends declared that Joseph of Arimathea was the first keeper of the Holy Grail, the vessel Jesus used in the Last Supper. The tales added that Joseph used the chalice to collect the blood that dripped from Christ's wounds.

Years after Jesus' death, Joseph journeyed to Britain as a Christian missionary, bringing the Grail with him (many legends give 63 A.D. as the year of his arrival). A few tales also state that Joseph carried a staff made of hawthorn wood from the Holy Land. Some say it was Christmas Eve when Joseph's ship finally pulled in to the harbor at Glastonbury. Joseph and his companions disembarked and began the climb up steep Wearyall Hill. Finally, cold and tired, the old man thrust his staff into the ground in despair. To his amazement it not only rooted itself, but burst into leaf and bloom. Joseph perceived this miracle as divine confirmation of his faith and his mission of evangelization. Thereafter, the hawthorn bush bloomed every year at Christmas, distinguishing itself from native English hawthorns. Joseph's miraculous tree became known as the Glastonbury Thorn.

Although no solid historical evidence exists to support this tale of Joseph's journey to England, a winter-blooming hawthorn tree did flourish in Glastonbury for many years. Descendants of this plant have been identified as *Crataegus mongyna biflora*, a species of hawthorn native to the Middle East.

### The History of the Glastonbury Thorn

The earliest appearance of the Glastonbury Thorn in written records dates back to an account of the life of Joseph of Arimathea written in the early 1500s. By the early 1600s firsthand descriptions of Glastonbury's hawthorn noted that the plant was suffering from the many carvings made in its trunk and the many cuttings taken from its branches. One Sir William Brereton, after carving his initials in the tree and collecting several branches for his own keeping, thought fit to criticize the people of Glastonbury for neglecting to care for the tree! The Glastonbury thorn reached its yearly peak of popularity around Christmas time, when crowds assembled to witness the tree's miraculous blooming.

Many believed that the buds and flowers had healing powers. These beliefs and customs eventually aroused the ire of the increasingly vocal **Puritans**, who scorned what they saw as evidence of popular belief in magic and superstition. It is said that during the reign of Elizabeth I, the tree met its fate at the hands of an irate Puritan who assaulted it with an axe. After he had destroyed half of the enormous tree, a splinter flew into his eye, blinding him in some versions of the tale and killing him in others. Having avenged itself, the tree lingered another thirty years before finally succumbing to this fatal attack. Other accounts of the tree's demise differ. One simply states that the tree was demolished in 1653 during England's Civil War.

Nevertheless, by this time a number of cuttings from the original plant flourished in Glastonbury and other locations. They continued to bloom on or around Christmas until the calendar reform of 1752, when Britain finally adopted the Gregorian calendar (*see also* **Old Christmas Day**). As a consequence, the nation leaped forward eleven days overnight. Many ordinary people resisted this change. In fact, some explained their allegiance to the old calendar by pointing to the unchanged blooming habits of the Glastonbury Thorn.

### The Glastonbury Thorn in the United States

At the turn of the twentieth century, the once-renowned abbey at Glastonbury lay in ruins (*see also* **Mincemeat Pies**). Stanley Austin, son of England's reigning poet laureate, owned the abbey property. (The abbey has since passed into the hands of the Church of England.) In 1901, when Austin heard of the plans to build the National Cathedral in Washington, D.C., he sent a clipping of the Glastonbury Thorn to the bishop of Washington, the Right Rev. Henry Yates Satterlee. He also sent a sufficient quantity of stones from the ruined abbey to build a bishop's chair in the new American cathedral. Bishop Satterlee saw the English plant established on the Cathedral grounds, where it does occasionally bloom on Christmas Day.

### Christmas at Glastonbury

A descendent of the old tree lives on in Glastonbury today. Each year on Old Christmas Eve, January 5, the keepers of Holy Thorn clip a branch of the tree and send it to the reigning monarch. The sprig serves both as a symbol of respect and as a public affirmation of the town's Christian heritage. This custom dates back about four hundred years.

# Gold

No other metal is named as frequently in the Bible as gold. The Bible most often refers to gold as a form of worldly wealth, but gold also serves as a symbol of spiritual wealth. In biblical times, gold was rarer than today. For the most part, only kings or the very wealthy possessed it. Gold was one of the three gifts that the **Magi** offered to the baby **Jesus**. Therefore, the Magi's **gift** of gold is most often interpreted as recognition of Jesus' kingship or his spiritual authority.

Until the mid-1700s tradition dictated that the British monarch offer gifts of **frankincense**, gold, and **myrrh** at the Chapel Royal on **Epiphany**. Heralds and knights of the Garter, Thistle, and Bath accompanied the king on his royal pilgrimage. Under the unstable King George III the procession was abandoned, although the monarch's gift of gold, frankincense, and myrrh is still sent to the Chapel Royal by proxy. A similar royal offering was at one time customary in Spain.

Gold has been considered rare, valuable, and beautiful throughout history. In addition to its beauty and brightness, gold has some unusual properties. It is nearly indestructible, and yet it is also the most malleable of metals. A single ounce of gold can be beaten into a sheet of gold leaf that measures approximately 200 feet on each side. Gold does not tarnish or corrode, and is extremely resistant to wear. Finally, it is often found in a nearly pure state. These qualities enhance its value, versatility, and mystery.

# Gospel According to Luke

The third book of the Christian Bible, the Gospel according to Luke, offers an account of the events surrounding the birth of **Jesus**. This account, which appears in chapter two, verses one through twenty, has been reprinted below. It begins with the Roman emperor's call for an enrollment, which today we would call a census. Another, slightly different version of the events surrounding Jesus' birth may be found in the **Gospel** according to Matthew (*see also* Angels; Bethlehem; Gabriel; Gospel Accounts of Christmas; Jesus, Year of Birth; Joseph; Mary, Blessed Virgin; Shepherds).

### The Birth of Jesus According to Luke:

In those days a decree went out from Caesar Augustus that all the world should be enrolled. This was the first enrollment, when Quirinius was governor of Syria. And all went to be enrolled, each to his own city. And Joseph also went up from Galilee, from the city of Nazareth, to Judea, to the city of David, which is called Bethlehem, because he was of the house and lineage of David, to be enrolled with Mary, his betrothed, who was with child. And while they were there, the time came for her to be delivered. And she gave birth to her first-born son and wrapped him in swaddling cloths, and laid him in a manger, because there was no place for them in the inn.

And in that region there were shepherds out in the field, keeping watch over their flock by night. And an angel of the Lord appeared to them, and the glory of the Lord shone around them, and they were filled with fear. And the angel said to them, "Be not afraid; for behold, I bring you good news of great joy which will come to all the people; for to you is born this day in the city of David a Savior, who is Christ the Lord. And this will be a sign for you: you will find the babe wrapped in swaddling cloths and lying in a manger." And suddenly there was with the angel a multitude of the heavenly host praising God and saying,

> Glory to God in the highest
> and on earth peace among men with whom he is pleased!

When the angels went away from them into heaven, the shepherds said to one another, "Let us go over to Bethlehem and see this thing that has happened, which the Lord has made known to us." And they went with haste, and found Mary and Joseph, and the babe lying in a manger. And when they saw it they made known the saying which had been told them concerning this child; and all who heard it wondered at what the shepherds told them. But Mary kept all these things, pondering them in her heart. And the shepherds returned, glorifying and praising God for all they had heard and seen, as it had been told them. [Taken from *The Holy Bible*, Revised Standard Version. New York: Thomas Nelson and Sons, 1953.]

# Gospel According to Matthew

The first book of the Christian bible, the Gospel according to Matthew, offers an account of the events surrounding the birth of **Jesus**. This account, which appears in chapter two, verses one through eighteen, has been reprinted below. Another, slightly different version of these events may be found in the **Gospel according to Luke** (*see also* Bethlehem; Flight into Egypt; Gospel Accounts of Christmas; Herod, King; Jesus, Year of Birth; Joseph; Magi; Mary, Blessed Virgin; Star of Bethlehem).

### The Birth of Jesus According to Matthew:

Now when Jesus was born in Bethlehem of Judea in the days of Herod the king, behold, wise men from the East came to Jerusalem, saying "where is he who has been born king of the Jews? For we have seen his star in the East, and have come to worship him." When Herod the king heard this, he was troubled, and all Jerusalem with him; and assembling all the chief priests and scribes of the people, he inquired of them where the Christ was to be born. They told him, "In Bethlehem of Judea; for so it is written by the prophet:

> And you, O Bethlehem, in the land of Judah
> are by no means the least among the rulers of Judah;
> for from you shall come a ruler
> who will govern my people Israel."

Then Herod summoned the wise men secretly and ascertained from them what time the star appeared; and he sent them to Bethlehem, saying, "Go and search diligently for the child, and when you have found him bring me word, that I too may come and worship him." When they had heard the king they went their way; and lo, the star which they had seen in the East went before them, till it came to rest over the place where the child was. When they saw the star they rejoiced exceedingly with great joy; and going into the house they saw the child with Mary his mother, and they fell down and worshiped him. Then, opening their treasures, they offered him gifts, gold and frankincense and myrrh. And being warned in a dream not to return to Herod, they departed to their own country by another way.

Now when they had departed, behold, an angel of the Lord appeared to Joseph in a dream and said, "Rise, take the child and his mother, and flee into Egypt, and remain there till I tell you; for Herod is about to search for the child, to destroy him." And he rose and took the child and his mother by night, and departed to Egypt and remained there until the death of Herod. This was to fulfil what the Lord had spoken by the prophet, "Out of Egypt have I called my son."

Then Herod, when he saw that he had been tricked by the wise men, was in a furious rage, and he sent and killed all the male children in Bethlehem and in all that region who were two years old or under, according to the time which he had ascertained from the wise men. Then was fulfilled what was spoken by the prophet in Jeremiah:

A voice was heard in Ramah,
wailing and loud lamentation,
Rachel weeping for her children;
she refused to be consoled,
because they were no more.

But when Herod died, behold, an angel of the Lord appeared in a dream to Joseph in Egypt, saying, "Rise, take the child and his mother, and go to the land of Israel, for those who sought the child's life are dead." And he rose and took the child and his mother, and went to the land of Israel. But when he heard that Archelaus reigned over Judea in place of his father Herod, he was afraid to go there, and being warned in a dream he withdrew to the district of Galilee. And he went and dwelt in a city called Nazareth, that what was spoken by the prophets might be fulfilled, "He shall be called a Nazarene." [Taken from *The Holy Bible*, Revised Standard Version. New York: Thomas Nelson and Sons, 1953.]

# Gospel Accounts of Christmas

The Christian Bible provides two accounts of the birth of **Jesus**. One account appears in the first two chapters of the **Gospel according to Matthew**, and the other in the first two chapters of the **Gospel according to Luke** (*see also* **Jesus, Year of Birth**). A quick review of these accounts reveals a number of broad similarities as well as some striking differences.

## Similarities

Jesus' parents, **Joseph** and **Mary**, figure in both accounts. Both Matthew and Luke assert that Joseph was a descendant of the Old Testament hero, David. They also agree that Mary was a virgin when she became pregnant with Jesus by the power of the Holy Spirit. An **angel** appears in order to explain the nature of Mary's pregnancy, according to both writers. Both accounts affirm that Jesus was born in **Bethlehem** during the reign of **Herod** the Great. Finally, Matthew and Luke both tell of strangers called by God to witness and worship the birth of the Savior.

## Differences

If probed more closely, a few of these similarities turn out to be only partial, however. Both Matthew and Luke state that Joseph is a descendant of David, but Matthew takes Joseph's lineage back to Abraham, while Luke takes it all the way back to **Adam**. Moreover, Matthew includes five women in Jesus' genealogy, while Luke mentions no women at all. In Luke the angel Gabriel, who explains the nature of Mary's pregnancy, appears to Mary herself, while in Matthew the angel appears to Joseph. Although both writers agree that Jesus was born in Bethlehem, Matthew implies that Jesus' family lived in Bethlehem, while Luke states that Jesus' parents lived in Nazareth and came to Bethlehem only to comply with a Roman census. While Luke's account describes the events that took place on the night of Jesus' birth, Matthew's account leaves vague the issue of whether Jesus was a newborn infant or already a toddler on the night when the **Magi** arrived to worship him.

Some elements of Matthew's story have no parallel whatever in Luke's account. Matthew tells of learned men called the Magi who bring Jesus expensive **gifts** fit for a

king. They find him by following a star which suddenly appeared in the heavens to signal his birth (*see* **Star of Bethlehem**). Moreover, in Matthew's account the Magi inadvertently alert Herod to the existence of the newborn king. As a result, Herod sends soldiers to kill all of Bethlehem's male infants (*see* **Holy Innocents' Day**). Finally, an angel visits Joseph warning him of Herod's intentions and telling him to escape with his family into Egypt (*see* **Flight into Egypt**). After Herod's death the family returns from Egypt, but decides to settle in Galilee, far from Herod's brutal successor.

Turning now to Luke's account of Jesus' birth, we can identify a number of elements that don't appear in Matthew's Gospel. According to Luke, humble **shepherds**, rather than noble Magi, witness Jesus' birth. Moreover, the shepherds learn of the Savior's birth from an angel instead of by studying the stars. In Luke's story, Mary and Joseph must search for lodging because they don't live in Bethlehem. The innkeepers cannot accommodate them, so they end up spending the night in a stable, where Mary gives birth to Jesus.

### Folklore

Scholars have attributed much significance to both the similarities and the differences contained in these accounts. Although these differences may perplex researchers, they do not appear to have inhibited the representation of Jesus' birth in folklore. Around Christmas time **Nativity scenes**, **store window displays**, and Christmas pageants present us with colorful images of Jesus' birth (*see also* **Nativity Plays**). Often these scenes mix together shepherds, wise men, stars, angels, animals, and other figures. These happy scenes suggest that Matthew's and Luke's accounts of Jesus' birth have merged together to form a single story in the popular imagination.

# Grandfather Frost

## Dyed Moroz

A winter season gift giver is a common figure in folklore from many different regions. During the era of Communist rule (1917-91) in Russia, Grandfather Frost became the official winter season gift bringer. Known in Russian as *Dyed Moroz*, Grandfather Frost symbolizes the piercing cold of Russia's winters. Accompanied by his grandchild, the **Snow Maiden**, he travels across Russia bringing **gifts** to children on New Year's Eve.

## *History*

Grandfather Frost existed long before the Communists came to power. In those days, however, he brought his gifts on Christmas Eve rather than on New Year's Eve. Grandfather Frost probably evolved from rural folk beliefs about a spirit known as "the Frost." Country folk did not have an image of what the Frost looked like, but they well knew his rigid and aloof personality. In the nineteenth century, rural people did not dress up like the Frost and did not believe that he brought Christmas gifts. Instead they left gifts of food for the Frost, hoping to satisfy his hunger so that his icy touch would not whither their crops.

By the nineteenth century, a very different image of the Frost had developed in the cities. There, the winter spirit acquired a kindly name, "Grandfather Frost," as well as a kindly reputation. Urban folktales cast Grandfather Frost as a bringer of gifts to well-behaved children at Christmas time. Unlike some of his harsher counterparts in western Europe, Grandfather Frost ignored rather than threatened poorly behaved children (*see also* **La Befana; Berchta; Black Peter; Cert; Jultomten; Knecht Ruprecht; St. Nicholas's Day**). City dwellers pictured Grandfather Frost as an old man with a long white beard who wore a red hat and long, red robe edged with white fur. Their tales told that he lived deep in the forest and rode about on his sleigh.

Before the Communists came to power, Russian children might receive gifts from Grandfather Frost at Christmas or from **Baboushka** on **Epiphany** Eve. A Russian folktale tells how Baboushka rejected the **Magi**'s invitation to accompany them on their journey to worship the newborn **Jesus**. She has wandered the world ever since, bringing gifts to children on Epiphany Eve. The religious content of Baboushka's story made Communist leaders uneasy, since they opposed religion and the celebration of religious holidays on principle. To counteract this story the government promoted the idea that Grandfather Frost alone brought children their presents. Moreover, they changed the date of his arrival from Christmas Eve, a religious holiday, to New Year's Eve, a secular holiday. Grandfather Frost survived the transition to a democratic, capitalist form of government in the 1990s, but now he faces competition from a new, Western import: **Santa Claus.**

### Customs

Some say that Grandfather Frost makes his home in Veliki Ustyug, a town about 500 miles northeast of Moscow. Nevertheless, during the holiday season he makes many public appearances in other towns and cities. He usually wears a full white beard, dresses in a long red, white, or blue robe, and supports himself with a staff. In this eye-catching garb he may be glimpsed at department stores or at public events. For a fee, parents can hire Grandfather Frost and the Snow Maiden to come to their homes as a special treat for the children. More than a thousand Grandfather Frosts crisscross Moscow on New Year's Eve, performing this service for children and parents.

# Greenery

Christmas trees, wreaths, and other seasonal decorations made out of greenery ornament our homes, streets, and churches at Christmas time. Ancient peoples also celebrated winter festivals with decorations of greenery. Over the centuries Christmas appears to have absorbed some of these ancient customs.

### Ancient Beliefs and Customs

Evergreen plants, such as **holly, ivy, mistletoe, laurel** (or bay), **yew, fir, spruce,** and pine stay green all year round (*see also* **Rosemary**). For many ancient peoples, this special property converted these plants into seasonal symbols of the promise of new life or eternal life. Holly, ivy, and mistletoe may have been especially revered, since they not only stay green in winter, but also bear fruit during this harsh season. The pagan peoples of northern Europe garlanded their homes with greenery during their winter festival, **Yule**. Perhaps they wished to honor and imitate the triumph of these living greens over the cold and darkness of winter. Further south, the Romans also decorated their homes with greenery during their winter festivals, **Saturnalia** and **Kalends**. In addition, friends exchanged sprigs of holly as tokens of good will and good wishes for the upcoming new year.

## *Christianity and Winter Greenery*

For hundreds of years, Christian officials waged a campaign against the old pagan European practices. Tertullian, a third-century Christian writer, admonished those followers of the new religion, Christianity, who practiced these old customs. He thundered: "Let those who have no Light burn their (pagan) lamps daily. Let those who face the fire of hell affix laurels to their door-posts.... You are a light of the world, a tree ever green; if you have renounced the pagan temple, make not your home such a temple!" A sixth-century Church council (the Second Council of Braga) forbade Christians the use of green boughs in home decoration. This edict implies that many Christians were still adorning their homes with greenery at that time.

In southern Europe such criticism extinguished this practice, but further north—especially in Germany and England—it continued. In medieval and Renaissance times, many English songs still depicted holly and ivy as special plants associated with the winter season. These songs may indicate that earlier beliefs about winter greenery dimmed but never completely died out, in spite of Church opposition.

Unable to completely destroy this custom, the Church eventually set about reinterpreting these seasonal symbols. Christian legends developed over time, explaining the connection between these evergreens and the **Christmas season** (*see also* **Nativity Legends**). Laurel, for example, represented the triumph of **Jesus** Christ. Holly became a symbol of the Virgin **Mary**'s love for God. Its spiky leaves and blood-red berries also served to remind Christians that Jesus would end his days wearing a crown of thorns.

Not only did the use of greenery persist in seasonal home decorations, but the practice also crept into church decorations. One sixteenth-century observer of English customs commented that parishioners bedecked both home and church with ivy, holly, bay and other greenery at Christmas time. Some authorities claim that mistletoe was sel-

dom adopted for English church decorations, however, due to its strong associations with the pagan past. One notable exception to this trend occurred at York Cathedral during medieval times. A branch of mistletoe was placed on the high altar on Christmas Eve, signaling a general pardon for all wrongdoers for as long as it remained there.

## The Green Branch as a Symbol

For many centuries green branches symbolized hospitality or the reconciliation of differences. During the Middle Ages messengers, negotiators, and heralds carried them in times of battle to signify their peaceful intentions. Taverns and inns hung green boughs, especially ivy, above their doors in lieu of printed signs. Even after literacy spread and lettered signs came into common use, many pubs retained related names, such as The Ivy Bush or The Greenwood Tree.

## Christmas Greenery

Many English folk beliefs suggested that the evergreens most closely connected with Christmas possessed subtle powers. Holly offered protection against witches, and rosemary against evil spirits. Ivy granted good luck to women, while holly bestowed good luck on men. Special customs developed in order to harness the beneficial powers of these plants and deflect the harmful ones. For instance, some believed that winter greenery should not be brought into the house before Christmas Eve or Christmas Day lest it carry ill luck with it. From Christmas to **Epiphany**, however, garlands of greenery inside the home might bring good luck. According to others, a mischievous wood sprite hid behind each sprig of greenery carried into the house for decoration. During the **Twelve Days of Christmas** these sprites kept their peace, but afterwards they might begin to vex the occupants of the household with their pranks (*see also* Elves).

In some parts of England, people dismantled their decorative greenery on Twelfth Day. In other parts of the country, the **ornaments** were left until **Candlemas**. In many cases, folk beliefs cautioned that the withered greens should not simply be tossed away when taken down, but disposed of ceremoniously. Some believed that they should be burned. Others thought that burning them drew bad luck and that feeding them to cattle might preserve their good luck. Still others felt that they should simply be left to decay on their own. Sometimes a sprig of holly or mistletoe was saved for the following year. These sprigs might be used to light the fire under the next year's Christmas pudding.

Although seasonal decorations of greenery have festooned centuries of Christmas celebrations, the style and components of these decorations have changed over time. In Britain, the custom of hanging up a bit of mistletoe, often in the form of a kissing bough, reached the height of its popularity in the eighteenth century and began to fall from favor in the nineteenth. The nineteenth century saw other changes in British Christmas decorations as well. Before that time the English trimmed their homes with laurel, rosemary, ivy, holly, box, and yew. In the nineteenth century holly rose from the ranks to become the favorite plant of English Christmas decorations, replacing, to some extent, the wider variety of winter greenery used. Finally, the British and the Americans adopted the German custom of bringing a Christmas tree into their homes in the nineteenth century. Today the Christmas tree reigns supreme over all other forms of Christmas greenery and has become a widely recognized symbol of the holiday.

# Hanukkah
## Feast of Dedication, Feast of Lights

Hanukkah is a Jewish holiday that is unrelated to Christmas. Because it often falls in the month of December, however, some people have mistakenly assumed that Hanukkah is the "Jewish Christmas." In spite of the difference between the two holidays, many American Jewish families have adapted certain Christmas customs, such as cards and gifts for children, for Hanukkah celebrations.

### What Is Hanukkah?

The Hebrew word *Hanukkah* means "dedication." The holiday is also known as the Feast of Dedication or the Feast of Lights. Hanukkah commemorates a historical event, the Jewish victory in 162 B.C. over the Syrians in the Maccabean War. At that time Judea was part of the Syrian empire, in which Greek culture predominated. Some Jews began to adopt Greek ways of life and thought. A small group of Jews, led by the Maccabee family, resisted this process of assimilation by taking up arms against the Syrian political authorities. After their victory, they cleansed and rededicated the Jewish temple in Jerusalem, which their opponents had occupied and used to offer sacrifices to pagan gods. One record states that those present at the dedica-

tion witnessed a miracle. A small amount of oil, enough to keep the temple lamp lit for one day, lasted a full eight days.

Today's Hanukkah celebrations often downplay the military history behind the festival. Instead, they emphasize the rededication of the temple in Jerusalem, the victory over religious persecution, and the survival of Judaism. The celebrations last for eight days. They feature a special candleholder, known as a *menorah*, with room for nine candles. The middle candle, the *shamash*, or "server," is used to light the other eight. On the first evening of Hanukkah one candle is lit and special prayers are said. On the second evening two candles are lit, and so on. The rest of the evening is spent singing songs, playing games, telling Hanukkah stories, and enjoying special holiday foods.

### Hanukkah and Christmas

Because the Jewish calendar is based on the lunar rather than the solar year, the date of Hanukkah moves about on our calendar. The first day of Hanukkah falls on the twenty-fifth day of the Jewish month of Kislev, which means that it can fall anywhere between November 25 and December 26. In the United States this proximity to Christmas has affected the way in which Hanukkah is celebrated. Originally a minor holiday, Hanukkah has assumed greater importance in the Jewish calendar in order to counter the pervasive presence of Christmas themes and images in the general culture. The old custom of distributing Hanukkah gelt (coins) to children has been expanded to include gifts as well. Many Jewish parents give their children one present for each of the eight nights of Hanukkah. In addition, some people now exchange Hanukkah cards with Jewish friends and family members.

In recent years American presidents have added Hanukkah-related activities to their round of holiday duties. In 1979 Jimmy Carter became the first president to participate in a menorah-lighting ceremony (*see also* **White House, Christmas in the**).

# Herod, King

According to the Bible, **Jesus** was born in the land of Judea. The **Gospel according to Matthew** tells us that King Herod ruled Judea at the time of Jesus' birth. Historians cannot confirm the treacherous deeds attributed to Herod in Matthew's Nativity story. Nevertheless, these barbarities resemble the kinds of brutal acts historians know him to have committed.

### Herod in the Gospel of Matthew

In chapter two of Matthew we learn that **Magi** from the east have arrived in Jerusalem. They inquire about the birthplace of the newborn king of the Jews whose Nativity has been foretold by the rising of a miraculous star (*see also* **Jesus, Year of Birth; Star of Bethlehem**). Herod is disturbed by their questions, seeing in the coming of a great Jewish leader only a potential rival for power. Herod assembles the Jewish priests and scribes and finds out that prophecy dictates that the Messiah will be born in the town of **Bethlehem**. He passes this news on to the Magi, requesting that they first go to Bethlehem and find the child, and then report back to Jerusalem. The Magi journey on to Bethlehem, identify Jesus as the newborn king, and pay him homage. A dream warns them that Herod intends to kill the child they identify as the king of the Jews, so they return to their own countries without going back to Jerusalem. Herod is furious with their failure to return and orders soldiers to kill all the male children in the town of Bethlehem under the age of two. In the meantime, however, an **angel** warns **Joseph**, Jesus' father, of Herod's bloody plan. The angel instructs Joseph and his family to flee into Egypt (*see* **Flight into Egypt**). Herod's massacre of Bethlehem's male children is commemorated on **Holy Innocents' Day**, December 28.

## The Historical Herod

Herod was the family name of a line of kings who ruled Judea at the time of Jesus' birth. Although they were kings in Judea, they were not themselves of Jewish descent. They were Idumeans, a people from outside the land of Judea, many of whom had been forced to convert to Judaism. Some commentators note that Matthew's account of his meeting with the Magi demonstrates Herod's unfamiliarity with Jewish teachings; in order to answer the Magi's questions, he had to consult those who knew Jewish scripture. The Herod who ruled at the time of Jesus' birth was known as Herod the Great.

Herod the Great became King of Judea in 40 B.C. He rose to power by collaborating with the Roman conquerors of Judea. King Herod was hated and feared by his Jewish subjects. He ruthlessly crushed all political opposition, going so far as to execute a wife and several sons whom he suspected might be plotting against him. He impoverished the people with oppressive taxes in order to fund numerous building projects and other lavish expenditures. Finally, he ordered that a number of well-known Jews be executed on the day of his death in order to ensure that the people would actually mourn on that day. Although no historical evidence exists for the massacre of Bethlehem's children reported by Matthew, the act is not inconsistent with the record of Herod's known deeds.

## Herod's Sons

After the death of Herod the Great, the Romans divided his former kingdom among his remaining sons. Herod Archelaus became ruler of Judea, and Herod Antipas ruler of Galilee. The Gospel of Matthew states that after Herod the Great's death, an angel told Joseph that it was safe to return to Israel. When Joseph discovered that the brutal Archelaus had become king of Judea he was too afraid to return there, so he moved his family to Galilee. Thus, the King Herod that interviewed Jesus shortly before his crucifixion (Luke 23) was Herod Antipas, ruler of Galilee.

# Holly

Holly springs up all around us at Christmas time. It ornaments today's **Christmas cards, wreaths, wrapping paper,** and other Christmas decorations. Although holly serves as a very contemporary symbol of the season, folklorists trace holly's association with Christmas back to ancient times.

## *Ancient Beliefs and Customs*

Evergreen plants such as holly, **ivy,** and pine stay green all year round. For many ancient peoples, this special property converted these plants into seasonal reminders of the promise of rebirth or eternal life. Many writers believe that the pagan peoples of northern Europe decorated their homes with **greenery** during their winter festival, **Yule.** Perhaps they wished to honor and imitate holly's triumph over the dark and the cold, for the plant not only remains green during the winter, but also bears bright red fruit during this harsh season. Further south, the Romans also decorated their homes with greenery during their winter festival, **Saturnalia.** In addition, friends exchanged sprigs of holly and other evergreens as tokens of friendship and good wishes for the upcoming new year.

## *Christianity and the Significance of Holly*

Some folklorists think that holly and ivy represented the male and female principles in nature to the pagan peoples of northern Europe. These old beliefs may have lingered on in song and folklore long after Christianity conquered the northern lands. A good number of English songs from the Middle Ages and Renaissance depict a rivalry between holly and ivy in which holly represents masculinity and ivy, femininity. In early Christian times, the Church resisted the pagan European custom of making seasonal decorations out of winter greenery. The sixth-century second Council of Braga forbade Christians the use of green boughs in home decoration.

As time went on, however, Christianity adopted the holly and ivy of pagan winter celebrations, molding their significance to fit Christian beliefs. One authority states that early northern European Christians interpreted holly as a symbol of the Virgin Mary's love for God. Its spiky leaves and blood-red berries also served to remind Christians that **Jesus** would end his days wearing a crown of thorns. The words to the **Christmas carol** titled "The Holly and the Ivy" illustrate similar Christian reinterpretations of these seasonal symbols. After the older beliefs about the plant had faded, some Christian authorities suspected that the word "holly" must be related to the word "holy," a belief that would support their interpretations of its connection with the **Christmas season**. They were mistaken. The modern English word "holly" comes from the older terms for the plant—*hollin*, *holin*, and *holme*—and before that, from the Anglo-Saxon word for holly, *holegn*.

### Folklore and Customs

Old British folklore attributed a variety of special powers to holly. In medieval times, practitioners of folk medicine used holly to treat many conditions, including fever, rheumatism, gout, and asthma. (Holly berries are poisonous, however.) Picking holly on Christmas Day could enhance its medicinal properties. In addition, holly warded off evil spirits. A medieval traveler who had lost his way might shelter under a holly tree for protection against unseen dangers. Placed on doors and around windowsills, holly's spiny leaves would snag any evil spirit that tried to enter the house. One custom advised unmarried women to place a sprig of holly beside their beds on Christmas Eve as protection against witches or goblins. A sprig of holly inside the house might also shield the householders from fire and storms. Holly that had been used in church decorations was believed to be especially powerful. It could confer luck, peace, or happiness, according to English folk beliefs, and protect against lightning, according to German folk beliefs.

Traces of the old association with masculinity and the battle of the sexes lingered on in holly lore. English folklore deemed prickly holly "male" and non-prickly holly "female." (Holly plants are indeed sexed, but the sex difference does not manifest itself

196

in this way). If male holly was brought into the house first, the husband would rule during the upcoming year, and if female holly entered first, the wife would rule. Several hundred years ago, English folk custom still connected competing figures known as the "holly boy" and the "ivy girl" with a number of wintertime observances. During this same period, the Welsh observed "Holming Day" on December 26 with another customary battle of the sexes in which men hit women's bare arms with holly branches (*see also* **St. Stephen's Day**). According to folk belief, holly dealt good luck to men, while ivy granted good luck to women.

Careless dealings with holly could turn good luck into bad, however. Some believed that cutting holly at any other time than Christmas brought bad luck. Bringing holly into the house for Christmas decorations also required special care. Some thought it unlucky to bring it in before Christmas Eve or Christmas Day. The withered greens must also be disposed of respectfully. Some believed that they should be burned. Others thought that burning them drew bad luck and that feeding them to cattle might preserve good luck. Still others felt they should simply be left to decay on their own. Sometimes a sprig of holly was saved for the following year, when it was used to light the fire under the next year's Christmas pudding.

Holly, often alongside its mate, ivy, served as an important Christmas symbol during the nineteenth century. The Victorians wove it into kissing boughs, greenery swags, and other seasonal home adornments, and embellished many a Christmas card with its image. Today, some Americans still hang a wreath of holly on their front doors at Christmas. In Britain many people place similar wreaths on the graves of the family dead at this time of year. In addition, holly continues to trim contemporary holiday decorations, symbolizing for many the mirth of the season. The old yet still popular Christmas carol, "Deck the Halls," expresses this connection between holly and revelry.

# Holy Innocents' Day

## Childermas, Feast of the Holy Innocents, Innocents' Day

In chapter two of the Gospel according to Matthew, the birth of Jesus is followed by a massacre from which the Holy Family narrowly escapes. An angel warns Jesus' father Joseph that King Herod intends to kill the child, whom the Magi have identified as the newborn king of the Jews. The angel instructs Joseph to flee with his family into Egypt (*see* Flight into Egypt). Herod's soldiers arrive in Bethlehem after the Holy Family has departed. They slaughter all the male children in the town and surrounding region who are under two years of age. This event is known as "the slaughter of the Innocents." Holy Innocents' Day, observed on December 28, mourns this act of cruelty.

### Church History

Three Christian festivals follow in close succession after Christmas. St. Stephen's Day occurs on December 26, St. John's Day on December 27, and Holy Innocent's Day on December 28. These commemorative days were established in western Europe by the late fifth century. The individuals they honor share two things in common. Stephen, John, and the Innocents all lived during the time of Jesus and were martyred for him. In addition, Stephen, John, and the Innocents represent all possible combinations of the distinction between martyrs of will and martyrs of deed. The children slaughtered at King Herod's orders in Bethlehem did not choose their fate, but suffered it nonetheless, and so were considered martyrs in deed. St. John willingly risked death in his defense of the Christian faith, but did not suffer death, and so was considered a martyr of will. St. Stephen risked and suffered death for his faith, and thus became a martyr of will and of deed.

Around the year 1000, Holy Innocent's Day acquired a new name. The English began to refer to the observance as "Childermas," a contraction of *childern* (an archaic form of the word "children") and "mass." In the past, if Innocents' Day fell on a Sunday, the liturgical color was red, signifying martyrdom. If the feast fell on any other day of the week, the liturgical color was purple, signifying penitence. This difference reflected the doubt of some early theologians concerning the fate of the children's souls. Although they had died in Christ's place and so might be considered martyrs, they had not been baptized. In 1960 the Roman Catholic Church eliminated this variation in liturgical colors, assigning the red of martyrdom to all observances of the feast.

## Folk Customs

Many of the customs associated with Holy Innocents' Day assign a special role to children. Moreover, a number of Innocents' Day customs encourage activities that reverse power and authority between the older and younger generations. Centuries ago in England, Germany, and France, **boy bishops** held sway in some churches on Childermas (*see also* **Feast of Fools**). On December 28 the boy bishop was expected to deliver a public sermon before stepping down from office. Another old English custom encouraged older family members to swat younger ones with switches on Childermas. Although one writer suggests that the practice served to remind young people of the sufferings of Bethlehem's Innocents, most folklorists view this practice as a remnant of an old, pre-Christian custom intended to drive out evil spirits, ill health, or other harmful forces.

Innocents' Day whipping customs were also popular at one time in central Europe. In some areas groups of children marched from house to house whipping girls and women with twigs and branches. A folk verse that accompanied this practice reveals that it was viewed as a means of imparting health, fertility, abundance, and good luck:

> Many years of healthy life,
> Happy girl, happy wife:
> Many children, hale and strong,
> Nothing harmful, nothing wrong,
> Much to drink and more to eat;
> Now we beg a kindly treat. [Weiser, 1952, 133]

Childermas customs in some regions of Germany permitted children to strike anyone they passed with their whips of twigs and branches. The children demanded coins in exchange for this service, which was known as "whipping with fresh greens." In Hungary boys and men whipped women and girls with switches in order to endow them with health and beauty. In Yugoslavia mothers switched children, hoping to promote their health and strength. Afterwards the children circulated through the neighborhood, smacking adults with switches and receiving treats and coins in exchange.

In Belgium children seized control of the house on December 28. Early in the morning the children would collect all the keys in the house. Later, when any adult ventured into a room or closet for which they had the key, the child would lock him or her in. In order to gain their release the adults promised the child a treat, such as money, candy, fruit, or a toy. The children referred to these ransomed adults as their "sugar uncle" or "sugar aunt." In Austria old folk traditions also allowed children to play tricks on their parents on Holy Innocents' Day and to usurp their parents' authority by sitting in their chairs.

This playful, topsy-turvy spirit also runs through Innocents' Day customs in Mexico, Ecuador, and other Latin countries. Mexicans celebrate the day in much the same way we celebrate April Fools' Day—by playing practical jokes on one another. The one who gets fooled is referred to as an "innocent."

### Folklore

Another, more ominous theme also runs through the lore and customs associated with Innocents' Day, however. Because the feast commemorates such a despicable deed, it came to be viewed as an extremely unlucky day, according to old European folk beliefs. Any undertaking begun on Childermas was bound to fail, according to these superstitions. The Irish called December 28 "the cross day of the year" for that reason. Those who married on that day ran especially high risks of future misery. According to some sources, King Louis XI of France (ruled 1461-83) absolutely refused to conduct or discuss affairs of state on Holy Innocents' Day. It is also believed that the English monarch Edward IV (ruled 1461-70, 1471-83) postponed his own coronation ceremony, originally scheduled for December 28, for fear of tagging his reign with bad luck.

# *How the Grinch Stole Christmas*

Acclaimed children's writer Dr. Seuss, born Theodor Geisel, published *How the Grinch Stole Christmas* in 1957. This story tells how the grumpy Grinch tries to prevent the sweet-tempered citizens of Whoville from celebrating Christmas. He steals the trappings of Christmas—the **Christmas trees**, decorations, **gifts**, and special foods—but discovers that he cannot steal the spirit of Christmas. This realization transforms the Grinch, who then returns the stolen loot.

### *Book, Cartoon, and Movie*

In Dr. Seuss's Christmas story, the spirit of Christmas converts a Scrooge-like main character into a joyful soul. Viewed in this light, Dr. Seuss's story might be seen as a children's cartoon version of Dickens's classic holiday tale, *A Christmas Carol*. Its immense appeal to children led to its being transformed into an animated television special in 1966. Geisel adapted the script from his book, while director and animator Chuck Jones turned Dr. Seuss's drawings into moving cartoon characters. Actor Boris Karloff, famous for his roles in horror films, dubbed in the voice of the Grinch. The show proved an immediate hit, and was rerun year after year. In 1971 Geisel received a Peabody Award for his work on the animated version of *How the Grinch Stole Christmas*. In the years to come, further Grinch television specials brought him two Emmy Awards—*Halloween Is Grinch Night* (1977) and *The Grinch Grinches the Cat in the Hat* (1982).

*How the Grinch Stole Christmas*—both the book and the cartoon—imprinted itself in the minds of millions of American youth—so much so that in the year 2000 Universal Studios, hoping to cash in on the phenomenon, released a live-action movie version of the story entitled *Dr. Seuss's How the Grinch Stole Christmas*. Directed by Ron Howard, the film featured Jim Carrey in the title role. Realizing that the story told in the short book would have to be expanded if it were to become a full-length movie, Howard began adding scenes that developed the characters.

The designers labored to take Dr. Seuss's two-dimensional drawings and recreate a three-dimensional Seussian world for the movie set. Rather than duplicate the exact look of Dr. Seuss's Grinch book, they decided that the sets would reproduce a blend of environments depicted in the books. Dr. Seuss's fantastical settings, buildings, and furniture, often drawn without right angles or much regard for the laws of physics, proved a great challenge to the design team. Make-up artist Rick Baker faced an equally difficult challenge, that of turning Jim Carrey into the Grinch and scores of other actors into the Whos of Whoville. Each morning before filming began, Carrey endured a three-and-a-half-hour makeup session, which included applying makeup over three foam rubber facial pieces as well as inserting false teeth and yellow contact lenses.

In the end, the effort proved worth the trouble. *Dr. Seuss's How the Grinch Stole Christmas* won an Academy Award for Best Makeup and was nominated for two additional awards—Best Art Direction-Set Decoration and Best Costume Design.

## Dr. Seuss

Dr. Seuss was the pen name of Theodor Geisel. His love for doodling and drawing expressed itself at an early age. It continued throughout his formal education at Dartmouth College and Oxford University. Never a particularly dedicated student, he lost patience with the obscurity of advanced academic study while attending Oxford and returned to the United States, where he began to make his living as a cartoonist. As the years went by, Geisel became increasingly fascinated with language and rhyme, and began to work on wedding his rhymes to drawings. Some years later he prepared his first manuscript for a children's book, eventually titled *And to Think That I Saw It on Mulberry Street*. Twenty-seven different publishers rejected it. As Geisel walked the streets of New York, looking for the 28th publisher, he ran into an old college friend, Marshall McClintock, who had just become the children's book editor for Vanguard Press. McClintock gave him the break he needed. Vanguard Press published Geisel's book in 1937.

*And to Think That I Saw It on Mulberry Street*, written in verse, was a success. Though Dr. Seuss's next books were written in prose, he eventually returned to the rhyme schemes for which he became famous.

Over 200 million copies of Dr. Seuss's books have been published in 20 different languages. The enormous popularity of these stories propelled Dr. Seuss and his books into the role of cultural icons. He liked to think of himself as the man who had single-handedly rid American classrooms of the boring "see Dick run" style of early reader. In 1985 the senior class of Princeton University paid a humorous tribute to his role in forming generations of young readers when they stood in unison and recited the entire text of *Green Eggs and Ham* as Seuss mounted the stage to receive an honorary doctorate.

# Interfaith Family Holiday Celebrations

The diversity of contemporary American society has produced challenges that did not exist for previous generations. One of these new challenges is the so-called "December Dilemma" faced by interfaith families. An estimated 28 million American adults are involved in committed relationships with people of different faiths. This number represents 22 percent of all couples who are either married or living together. Complications can arise during Christmas time when one partner is Christian and the other is Atheist, Jewish, Muslim, Hindu, Buddhist, Baha'i, Neo-Pagan, or espouses another non-Christian faith, or practices no religion at all.

In response to the complexities of blending two different belief systems, interfaith families have discovered various ways to navigate the winter holiday season. Most solutions are based on the conviction that enjoying other people's holidays does not diminish one's own faith. With this in mind, many non-Christians will participate in Christmas activities, often with extended family members, a diverse group of friends, or simply as a member of the community in which they live.

Although they do not celebrate Christmas, observant Jews and Muslims recognize **Jesus** as an important historical figure and attribute importance to his birth. For Muslims, Jesus is the second-most important prophet and is considered to be one of God's greatest messengers to mankind. From this perspective, some regard Christmas as a cultural custom of the predominant society. Others view Christmas time as an opportunity to practice tolerance and peacemaking, often reaching out to Christian friends and co-workers during this time of the year. Hindus often embrace the secular aspects of the Christmas holiday, such as exchanging **gifts** and even decorating **Christmas trees**. Neo-Pagans observe the **winter solstice** festival of **Yule**, with some embracing aspects of Christmas that are based on pagan customs, such as decorating the house with **greenery** and lighting a **Yule log**. The colored lights, increased spirit of generosity, and general festivities also hold appeal for many.

### Celebrating Two Holidays

Many mixed-faith families celebrate the holidays of both religions. December may be marked by both **Hanukkah** and Christmas observances, or Christmas and Yule. An estimated 76 percent of Jewish-Christian families plan to celebrate Christmas in some way. Of these, 48 percent plan to celebrate Christmas at their own homes as opposed to limiting Christmas activities to the homes of Christian relatives or friends. The large majority of parents in interfaith marriages emphasize for their children the importance of respecting different religions.

While the date of Christmas is fixed on December 25, some non-Christian religious holidays occur on different dates each year. Because of this, conflicts can arise when, for example, Christmas overlaps with Hanukkah. Interfaith families faced with overlapping holidays typically work together to create a solution. One approach often taken by interfaith families is the creation of family rituals or observances with personal meaning or significance. Sometimes this means celebrating one holiday in the morning and the other in the evening, or having one observance at home and the other at the home of friends or extended family. Another common approach is to highlight the similarities of both holidays on that day—for example, the common theme of light being brought into the world.

### Secular Christmas

Some interfaith families choose to observe Christmas with secular celebrations. This can involve the decorating of a non-denominational holiday tree, or peace tree. These trees might be decorated with **ornaments** that reflect the beauty of nature, winter, or another theme that does not include religious symbols, Santas, or other typical Christmas icons. Non-Christians often buy presents for their Christian partners, children, or friends. Since most businesses are closed and many people have the day off, some interfaith families simply gather with friends for a day of socializing.

### Influence of Popular Culture

Some contemporary non-Christians and interfaith families choose to handle the "December Dilemma" with humor, often with the help of new ideas drawn from American pop culture. Festivus is a holiday popularized in 1997 by the creators of the television sitcom "Seinfeld," which aired from 1989 to 1998. As envisioned on the show, Festivus is a secular holiday observed on December 23. The holiday was introduced by one of the "Seinfeld" characters as an alternative to the commercialism and consumerism that dominate the month of December. Festivus was quickly adopted by "Seinfeld" fans, who mark the day with tongue-in-cheek celebrations. Some interfaith families have adopted the name Festivus—if not all the ways the day was observed on "Seinfeld"—to use for their holiday celebrations.

Chrismukkah, a combination of Christmas and Hanukkah, was invented by the creators of the popular teen television drama "The O.C.", which aired from 2003 to 2007. The holiday, defined as "eight days of presents and then one day with lots of presents," was developed as a plot device for a character whose parents are of different faiths. Chrismukkah gained a cult following among teens and young adult fans of the show. Though the show is no longer in production, the popularity of Chrismukkah has continued to grow.

# It's a Wonderful Life

Many Americans view the 1946 movie *It's a Wonderful Life*, directed by Frank Capra, as the definitive American Christmas story. Some even call it the American version of Charles Dickens's classic Christmas tale, *A Christmas Carol*. The movie tells the story of a responsible but ambitious young man, George Bailey, who never realizes his dream of leaving his hometown for adventure and a big career. Aware of how his departure will hurt the fortunes of others, he decides instead to stay home in order to serve his family and his community. The story begins on a Christmas Eve after

World War II, when a crisis enters George's life and causes him to reconsider the value of all he's done. The final, happy ending celebrates the worth of George's achievements and the importance of friendship.

## The Greatest Gift

Frank Capra based his movie on a short story called "The Greatest Gift" by Philip Van Doren Stern. The main character, George Pratt, despairs over the boredom and triviality of his life. On Christmas Eve he decides to commit suicide by throwing himself over the edge of a bridge. Suddenly a man who he didn't realize was there begins to talk to him. George tells this stranger that he wishes he had never been born. The stranger, an **angel**, grants this wish. George returns to town and visits his family and place of business, finding things and people changed for the worse. He comes back to the bridge and begs the angel for the opportunity to live again. The angel restores everything as it was, and George returns home, realizing that any life, no matter how seemingly unimportant, is a great gift.

Stern penned the brief story in 1938. Unable to find a publisher, he printed up 200 copies of the story as a 24-page pamphlet and sent them to his friends at Christmas time in 1943. His agent, Shirley Collier, thought the story would make a good film. She convinced Stern to let her try to sell the story to a Hollywood studio. In 1944 RKO Pictures bought the film rights to "The Greatest Gift." In that same year *Good Housekeeping* magazine published the short story under the title "The Man Who Never Was." RKO thought the story would provide a suitable lead role for Cary Grant, but was not satisfied with the ideas their screenwriters came up with for turning the short story into a movie script.

## The Story Becomes a Script

In 1945 director Frank Capra, just back from his World War II stint in the armed services, bought the screen rights to Stern's story from RKO. His first concern was to flesh out the brief and thinly developed original story. Capra worked on developing the material himself, but also hired screenwriters Albert Hackett and Frances Goodrich to come up with a script. In the end, the film lists Hackett, Goodrich, and Capra as the authors of the screenplay, and notes that additional scenes were added by Jo Swerling.

Capra loved the new, expanded story. He thought the plot's exploration of the dark themes of despair and contemplated suicide as well as the uplifting themes of love and service to others would be perfect for his first postwar movie.

## The Script Becomes a Film

As Hackett and Goodrich worked on the script, Capra sought the needed actors. He wanted, and got, Jimmy Stewart to play the lead role of George Bailey. Jean Arthur, his first choice to play the role of Mary Bailey, turned him down, however. He considered several more actresses for the part, including Olivia De Havilland, before offering the role to Donna Reed, who accepted. Capra, a meticulous planner, thought as deeply about the casting of the film's small roles as he did its starring roles. When he had finally assembled the perfect cast, he was ready to begin making the movie.

The film's original budget totaled $1.7 million, but the final cost came in at over $3 million. A good portion of this money went to building sets and creating special effects. Set designers recreated several sections of Bedford Falls, the town in which the action takes place, at RKO's Encino Ranch. Covering four acres of land, this was among the longest sets that had yet been created for a movie filmed in the United States. The Main Street set stretched three blocks in length and included 75 buildings and shops. The center of the street was lined with 20 real oak trees, uprooted elsewhere and replanted on the set. The special effects crew labored for three weeks in order to produce the snowstorm that takes place on the night that George Bailey decides to commit suicide. In the process they devised a new way of generating artificial snow, for which they were given a Certificate of Honorable Mention at the 1947 Academy Awards. Although the beautifully filmed wintertime scenes convinced movie viewers, the thermometer on the set registered temperatures in the 80s and 90s on the day they were shot.

## It's a Wonderful Life

The film was released on December 20, 1946. It was not a box office hit, nor did it inspire an unbroken string of rave reviews. Some commentators think that the film's unusual blend of romance, comedy, and dark emotional drama may have confused viewers, thereby contributing to a less than stunning box office return. Moreover, some of America's most prestigious periodicals panned the movie as cloyingly sentimental and unrealistic. Nevertheless, the film charmed scores of other reviewers, and perhaps more importantly, thousands of fans. In addition, it won five Academy Award nominations: Best Actor, Best Picture, Best Director, Best Film Editing, and Best Sound. Though *It's a Wonderful Life* did not receive any Academy Awards, Capra did take home a Golden Globe award for best director from the Hollywood Foreign Correspondents Association.

*It's a Wonderful Life* was the first movie Capra made with Liberty Films, an independent studio formed by Frank Capra, George Stevens, William Wyler, and Sam Briskin after World War II. Financial difficulties soon downed the fledgling company, however. Capra and his partners sold it to Paramount Pictures in 1947, and along with it, the right to any future profits garnered by *It's a Wonderful Life*. The film languished under Paramount's care, and when its original copyright ran out in 1974, no one bothered to renew it. At this point television stations all over the country began to show *It's a Wonderful Life* at Christmas time, because they didn't have to pay for it. These showings revived the interest of older fans and introduced new audiences to the film. This once-forgotten film has now become a beloved Hollywood classic.

## Looking Back

Many movie viewers can imagine no one else but Jimmy Stewart in the role of George Bailey. Although Stewart made over 75 films, *It's a Wonderful Life* remained his favorite. Moreover, he received more fan mail about that movie than any other he ever made.

Donna Reed recalled working harder for Capra than she had for any other director. Still, she later described her days on the set as fun and inspired.

Most of the cast and crew fondly remember their participation in *It's a Wonderful Life*. The same cannot be said of music director Dimitri Tiomkin. Tiomkin had chosen "Ode to Joy" as the song for the last scene in the movie. Capra overruled him and substituted "Auld Lang Syne" instead. He also cut some of the tunes Tiomkin had written specially for the film and replaced them with music written by other composers. Furious, Tiomkin never worked with Capra again. Screenwriters Hackett and Goodrich, too, grew to dislike Capra, who they felt did not respect their contribution to the film.

Though he made scores of movies over his lifetime, Capra loved *It's a Wonderful Life* best of all his creations. He explained his preference in the following way:

213

*It's a Wonderful Life* sums up my philosophy of filmmaking. First, to exalt the *worth* of the individual. Second, to champion man—plead his causes, protest any degradation of his dignity, spirit, or divinity. And third, to dramatize the viability of the individual—as in the theme of the film itself.

I wanted *It's a Wonderful Life* to say what Walt Whitman said to every man, woman, and babe in the world: "The sum of all known reverences I add up in you, whoever you are...." I wanted it to reflect the compelling words of Fra Giovanni of nearly five centuries ago: "The gloom of the world is but a shadow. Behind it, yet within reach, is joy. There is a radiance and glory in the darkness, could we but see, and to see we have only to look. I beseech you to look." ... For myself, I can only say ... it was my kind of film for my kind of people. [Basinger, 1986, ix]

# Ivy

From the **Christmas tree** to the kissing bough, decorations made of **greenery** have adorned our Christmas celebrations for centuries. Of all the evergreens used to represent the season, ivy's connection to Christmas is perhaps the most obscure. Known to botanists as *Hedera helix*, ivy has enjoyed a long association with the **Christmas season** and, before that, with various pagan myths and celebrations.

## Ancient Beliefs and Customs

Evergreen plants, such as ivy, **holly**, and pine, stay green all year round. For many ancient peoples, this special property converted these plants into reminders of the promise of rebirth and eternal life. The pagan peoples of northern Europe decorated their homes with evergreens such as ivy for their winter festival, **Yule**. Perhaps they wished to honor and imitate ivy's triumph over the cold and darkness, for the plant not only remains green during winter but also bears fruit during this harsh season. The ancient Egyptians associated ivy with Osiris, a god who died and was resurrected. To the Greeks ivy symbolized Dionysus, the god of wine. The Greeks told a legend that explained this connection. A nymph had once danced herself to death at the feet of Dionysus in a frenzy of adoration. In recognition of her devotion, the god changed her body into the ivy plant, which casts an adoring embrace around all it encounters.

Further to the south, the ancient Romans also decorated their homes with greenery during their winter festival **Saturnalia**. In addition, they exchanged branches of ivy, holly, and other evergreen plants as symbols of their good wishes for the upcoming new year. Ivy also became the symbol of the Roman god of wine, Bacchus. Wine sellers in ancient Rome sometimes used ivy as a symbol of their trade. A bush or bunch of evergreens, usually ivy or box, tied to the end of a pole was a generally recognized symbol of a wineshop. Pliny the Elder, a famous scholar of ancient Rome, believed that consuming ivy berries before drinking wine or ivy leaves with one's wine could prevent drunkenness. Modern researchers, however, have discovered ivy to be toxic when ingested in large enough quantities.

## Medieval Beliefs and Customs

As literacy was uncommon in the Middle Ages, people continued to use ivy and images of ivy or other greenery to signify a tavern or wineshop. In Britain the decorated pole used by the Romans became known as an alepole or an alestake. Long after lettered signs replaced these old icons, many British taverns retained related names, such as The Ivy Bush or The Greenwood Tree. Ivy not only represented wine, but also was believed to cure drunkenness. Likewise, imbibing from a bowl of ivy wood was thought to cancel out the effects of alcohol.

Some folklorists believe that holly and ivy represented the male and female principles in nature to pagan peoples of northern Europe, and that these early beliefs lingered on in the songs and folklore of later eras. Many medieval and Renaissance songs and **Christmas carols** tell of a rivalry between holly and ivy, in which holly represents masculinity and ivy, femininity.

In early Christian times, the Church resisted the pagan custom of making seasonal decorations out of greenery. The sixth-century second Council of Braga forbade Christians the use of green boughs in home decoration. As time went on, however, Christianity adopted the holly and ivy of pagan winter celebrations, bending their significance to Christian ends. The clinging ivy plant became a reminder of the soul's dependence on God. The words to the Christmas carol "The Holly and the Ivy" depict another Christian reinterpretation of these seasonal symbols. Due to its continuing association with drunkenness, however, some Christians thought it disrespectful to incorporate ivy into Christmas decorations.

## Later Beliefs and Customs

Many diverse and sometimes conflicting beliefs and customs concerning ivy have been recorded during the last two centuries. Because it often grew in cemeteries, ivy acquired an association with death. Some people believed it was therefore unlucky to bring ivy plants indoors. Its persistent association with drunkenness also fueled this belief, especially in continental Europe. Nevertheless, because of its decorative potential, ivy became a favorite houseplant in the Victorian age (*see also* **Victorian Era, Christmas in**).

In the "language of flowers" (a set of meanings attributed to flowers and plants which became popular in the eighteenth and nineteenth centuries), the encircling vines of the ivy plant represented fidelity and undying love. Many attributed magical properties to the plant, especially the ability to reveal the identity of future mates. In England, an ivy leaf dropped into a dish of water on New Year's Eve, covered and left until **Twelfth Night**, could reveal one's own fortune for the upcoming year. If the leaf remained green, one would enjoy good health, but if the leaf spotted, illness threatened. Overall deterioration of the leaf signaled death.

Traces of the old association with femininity and the battle of the sexes echo through the folklore associated with ivy. According to some, holly dealt good luck to men, while ivy bestowed good luck to women. As late as several hundred years ago, English folk customs still connected competing figures known as the "holly boy" and the "ivy girl" with a number of wintertime observances. Ivy, often alongside holly, continued as a symbol of Christmas festivities during the nineteenth century. The Victorians wove it into kissing boughs, greenery swags, and other seasonal adornments, and embellished many a **Christmas card** with its image.

Although less popular than in Victorian times, ivy has gently entwined itself around the edges of contemporary Christmas celebrations. Images of this ancient seasonal favorite still trim our Christmas cards, **wrapping paper**, and other holiday decorations.

# Jesse Tree

The Jesse tree gets its name from a prediction made by the Old Testament prophet Isaiah describing the rise of a great, new Jewish leader as "a branch" growing "from the stock of Jesse" (Isaiah 11:1). In reference to this prophecy, medieval artists frequently painted portraits of **Jesus** and his ancestors on the limbs of a tree, with Jesus at its crown and Jesse at its root. This image was called a "Jesse tree." The identity of Jesus' ancestors played an important role in establishing his identity as the Messiah. In recognition of this fact, both Gospel Nativity stories included an account of Jesus' genealogy. Chapter one of the **Gospel according to Matthew**, which directly precedes Matthew's account of Christ's birth, begins by listing Jesus' ancestors. The **Gospel according to Luke** (3:23-38) offers a slightly different account of Jesus' ancestry (*see also* **Gospel Accounts of Christmas**).

The Jesse tree has long served as a symbol of Jesus' ancestry in Christian art. In recent times, however, people have begun to use the image of the Jesse tree to adapt the modern **Christmas tree** to specifically Christian ends. **Ornaments** representing events in the lives of Jesus' ancestors are hung on an evergreen tree or tree branch. Some people add symbols for other biblical figures and events as well. For example, Moses may be represented by stone tablets, David by a six-pointed star, Jonah by a whale, and Judith by a sword. Decorated this way, the evergreen becomes a living Jesse tree.

# Jesus

Christians view Jesus of Nazareth as the founder of their faith. He spent his adult life as a spiritual teacher and healer who moved from place to place, teaching people about God. In one Bible passage Jesus describes himself as "anointed" by God to "preach good news to the poor … proclaim release to the captives and recovering of sight to the blind, to set at liberty those who are oppressed," and "to proclaim the acceptable year of the Lord" (Luke 4:18-19). Christian scripture also describes Jesus as the Son of God whose sacrificial death renewed humanity's relationship with God and conferred the forgiveness of sins.

The Easter festival commemorates the life, death, and resurrection of the adult Jesus. The Christmas festival, by contrast, celebrates his coming into the world. Theologians call this event the Incarnation, a word that literally means "to be made flesh."

### *The Incarnation*

"Incarnation" refers to the idea that Jesus was both human and divine, and that in him God came to earth in human form. The joy and hope inspired by this event has found a multitude of expressions in the world's Christmas celebrations.

In the **Gospel according to Matthew** and the **Gospel according to Luke**, the accounts given of Jesus' birth state that his mother, **Mary**, conceived Jesus by the power of God's Holy Spirit while still a virgin. Thus Jesus was both human and divine, an idea also expressed in two of his biblical titles, "Son of God" and "Son of Man."

Commentators have remarked that the stories of Jesus' birth reveal something of the nature of the Christian God. The stories show that God is not distant and unmoved by human suffering, but rather cares about particular people in particular places and so enters into the world to effect good. Indeed, Mary is directed by the **angel Gabriel** to name her son Jesus, which means "God saves" or "God heals." Christian scripture expresses Jesus' care for his followers by describing him as a **shepherd**.

In recent years, some theologians have begun to question traditional views of the Incarnation and the Virgin Birth. They point out that "son of God" was a title that the ancient Hebrews gave to people who played a special role in bringing God's help to humanity. The title did not imply divine identity, but rather service rendered to God. These thinkers suggest that the Christian notion of a divine Son of God came about after Jesus' death, as people struggled to understand the nature of Jesus' spiritual authority and to define his identity. The Virgin Birth has similarly been questioned. Some theologians today accord it greater symbolic than literal significance, suggesting that the story of the Virgin Birth was invented to symbolize Jesus' divine origins to a first-century audience. Others interpret Mary's virginity as a symbolic representation of her spiritual wholeness.

## Jesus the Christ

Jesus' followers also gave him the title "Christ," which comes from the Greek word for "anointed." Among the ancient Jews, high religious leaders underwent a ceremony in which they were anointed with oil. Jesus' followers viewed him as the one chosen and anointed by heaven to reconcile humanity with God and so came to call him Jesus Christ.

## Jesus' Birth According to John

Although most people refer to the accounts of Jesus' birth given in Matthew and Luke as the Bible's two Infancy Narratives, the Gospel according to John offers another, more philosophical account of Jesus' coming into the world. It, too, emphasizes Jesus' divine nature and explains that God came into the world through Jesus that humans might come to know God. In this poetical passage Jesus' divine essence is referred to as "the Word" and as "light":

> In the beginning was the Word, and the Word was with God, and the Word was God. He was in the beginning with God; all things were made through him, and without him was not anything made that was made. In him was life, and the life was the light of men. The light shines in the darkness, and the darkness has not overcome it.

> There was a man sent from God, whose name was John. He came for testimony, to bear witness to the light, that all might believe through him. He was not the light, but came to bear witness to the light.

> The true light that enlightens every man was coming into the world. He was in the world, and the world was made through him, yet the world

223

knew him not. He came to his own home, and his own people received him not. But to all who received him, who believed in his name, he gave power to become children of God; who were born, not of blood nor of the will of the flesh nor of the will of man, but of God.

And the Word became flesh and dwelt among us, full of grace and truth; we have beheld his glory, glory as of the only Son from the Father. [John 1:1-14]

## Creeds and Councils

John's passage concerning Jesus' birth raises theological issues not addressed in the other two Gospel accounts. Several hundred years after the birth of Jesus, theologians were still debating the exact nature of Jesus' identity and the mechanics of how he came into being and into the world. Christian leaders decided that they needed to settle these debates once and for all. So they held councils in which they hammered out a general consensus on these matters, creating in the process various creeds and doctrines of the church. Especially important were the Nicene Creed, formulated at the Council of Nicea in 325, and the doctrines that came out of the Council of Chalcedon in 451.

## The Festival of Jesus' Birth

The holiday devoted to the celebration of Jesus' birth, which we call Christmas, dates back to the year 336. It was set for **December 25**, an already important date in the ancient world. Centuries later, Christians would become concerned with establishing the year of Jesus' birth, which had not been recorded in scripture or other early Christian writings (*see* **Jesus, Year of Birth**).

The debate over when Jesus was born continues to this day, as does discussion concerning the appropriate way in which to celebrate Jesus' birth. Five hundred years ago, the **Puritans** objected to celebrations that revolved around eating, drinking, masquerades, and games. More recently, some Americans have begun to question the degree of commercialism that has invaded the festival. Some feel, like the Puritans of old, that contemporary American Christmas celebrations have become so divorced from the story of Jesus' birth that the holiday is more a secular than a religious one. Many are searching for ways to link the spiritual teachings contained in the story of Jesus' birth to their own Christmas celebrations. Indeed, many devotional books advise Christians of various denominations on how to prepare their own heart and spirit to receive the Christ Child (*see also* **Advent**). Some who do not identify them-selves as Christians are looking for ways to celebrate the holiday's secular themes and its universal spiritual themes, while disregarding specific Christian doctrines. These themes include generosity and giving gifts, the celebration of birth and new life, the joys of winter, and the return of the sun (*see also* **Winter Solstice**).

# Jesus, Year of Birth

Christians celebrate the birth of **Jesus** on **December 25**. A quick look at the biblical accounts of the Nativity, however, reveals the fact that neither story mentions the year or the date of Jesus' birth (*see also* **Gospel According to Luke; Gospel According to Matthew;** and **Gospel Accounts of Christmas**). Over the centuries many schol-ars have tried to match details given in the two Gospel accounts of the Nativity with known historical events in order to establish the year and date of Jesus' birth. Al-though debate continues, most scholars now believe that Jesus was born sometime between 7 and 4 B.C.

## The Date

The biblical accounts of Jesus' birth in **Bethlehem** provide only one clue as to the date of this event. Luke's Nativity story mentions **shepherds** who were spending the night with their flocks in the fields. In those days shepherds might well have spent the night with their flocks during the spring lambing season in order to aid the new-born lambs and their mothers. Historians believe that it is much less likely that shep-herds would be sleeping in the fields with their flocks during the winter. This detail from Luke's account would seem to suggest that Jesus was born sometime in the spring. Nevertheless, the first celebrations of the Nativity took place in January. Dur-ing the second and third centuries, a number of Christian communities began to commemorate Jesus' birth on January 6 as part of their **Epiphany** celebrations. In the middle of the fourth century, Church officials in Rome established a separate festi-val to honor the Nativity. They chose to celebrate this festival on December 25, and successfully promoted it throughout the Christian world.

## The Year

The scriptural accounts of the Nativity offer more, but somewhat conflicting, clues to those searching for the year of Jesus' birth. They agree in one regard, though. Both Luke's and Matthew's Nativity stories assert that Jesus was born during the reign of **Herod** the Great, king of Judea. The Gospel of Matthew offers an additional clue, implying that Herod died not long after Jesus' birth. Most historians agree that Herod died in the year 4 B.C., since archeological evidence points to the fact that his successors began their reigns in that year. Taken together, these indications suggest that Jesus was born sometime between 7 and 4 B.C. Luke also mentions that Jesus was born during the reign of the Roman emperor Caesar Augustus. Augustus ruled the Roman Empire from around 42 B.C. to 14 A.D., so this information fits with the assumption that Jesus was born during the reign of Herod the Great, possibly near the time of Herod's death.

A closer look at Luke's account of the Nativity complicates matters, however. Luke declares that Jesus' birth coincided with a Roman census called for by Emperor Augustus and administered locally by Quirinius, the governor of Syria. Historians know that Quirinius became governor of Syria in 6 A.D. Furthermore, they confirm that he conducted a census of Judea around 6-7 A.D. This information fits with the claim that Jesus was born in the days of Caesar Augustus, but contradicts the claim that he was born during the reign of Herod the Great, who presumably died in 4 B.C.

Although scholars have put forward a number of ingenious proposals to reconcile the date of Quirinius's census with the date of Herod's death, most researchers agree that Luke must have erred when he wrote that Jesus was born during the time of the census. Some scholars suggest that Luke may have included the story of the census as a way of locating the birth of Jesus in Bethlehem, since Jewish scripture claimed that the Messiah would be born there. Historians who find Luke's description of the Roman census somewhat unconvincing tend to support this view. They argue that a Roman census would not require people to return to their ancestral homeplaces, since the Romans were interested in where people lived, not where their ancestors came from.

The Gospel of Luke provides another clue to the year of Jesus' birth in a later passage describing the beginning of Jesus' ministry. In chapter three Luke informs us that Jesus was about thirty years old in the fifteenth year of the reign of the Roman emperor Tiberius (42 B.C.-37 A.D.; Luke 3:1, 23). The fifteenth year of Tiberius's reign oc-

curred between the years 27 to 28 A.D. This data fits well with the proposal that Jesus was born sometime between 7 and 4 B.C., but conflicts with a birth date of 6 to 7 A.D.

## The Star

The Gospel of Matthew offers one final bit of information some scholars have used to determine the year of Jesus' birth. According to Matthew, the rising of an unusual star heralded the birth of Jesus. Many ancient peoples studied the night skies and recorded any unusual occurrences. A number of scholars have studied these ancient records in an attempt to identify possible candidates for the Christmas star and so determine the year of Christ's birth (*see also* **Star of Bethlehem**).

Most of these scholars identify the triple conjunction of 7 B.C. as the most likely candidate for the Christmas star, but recently some writers have switched their allegiance to the triple conjunction of 3-2 B.C.

In order to reconcile a Christmas star that appeared in 3-2 B.C. with the claim that Jesus was born during the reign of Herod the Great, they reject the idea that Herod died in 4 B.C. They argue instead that Herod died in 1 B.C. They point to the writings of the ancient Jewish historian Josephus to back up their claim. According to Josephus, in the year Herod died a lunar eclipse preceded Passover. Josephus also recorded a number of events that took place between the eclipse and Herod's death. In the year 4 B.C. ancient astronomers indeed recorded the occurrence of a partial lunar eclipse one month before the Jewish holiday of Passover. In the year 1 B.C., however, a full lunar eclipse occurred three months before Passover. Some scholars argue that Josephus was referring to this eclipse, reasoning that the full eclipse was the more dramatic event and therefore more likely to have impressed historians. Furthermore, because the 1 B.C. eclipse occurred approximately three months before Passover, there was time for all the events that Josephus claimed happened between the eclipse and Herod's demise to play out. This line of reasoning leads to the conclusion that Jesus was born in the years 3 to 2 B.C.

## Continuing Controversy

To date scholars have not been able to reconcile every detail in Matthew's and Luke's Nativity stories with known historical events in a way that everyone can agree on. Debates over the correct date and year of Jesus' birth are nothing new. They can be traced as far back as the third century. In addition, some modern scholars now believe that Matthew and Luke intended their Nativity stories to serve as accounts of Jesus' birth that were spiritually rather than historically accurate. If so, the attempt to correlate the details reported in these stories with historically documented events is somewhat unlikely to provide the correct year and date of Jesus' birth.

## B.C. and A.D.

Although scholars cannot agree on the year of Jesus' birth, our calendar system assumes that Jesus was born in the year 1 B.C. It divides recorded history into two eras, labeled "B.C." and "A.D." B.C. stands for "before Christ" and A.D. stands for *Anno Domini*, a Latin phrase that means "in the year of the Lord." This method of reckoning was devised in the early sixth century by a monk named Dionysus Exiguus. At that time people still relied upon the old Roman system for numbering years. This system reckoned the year in which Diocletian was proclaimed emperor of Rome, 284 A.D., as year one. This methodology distressed Dionysus, who declared that Christians should no longer perpetuate a calendar system associated with Diocletian since he was a noted persecutor of Christians. Instead, he proposed that the birth of Jesus serve as the landmark event from which to date the dawn of a new era. Dionysus accepted the then-established date of Christmas, December 25, and the Roman date for the beginning of the new year, January 1. He calculated the year of Jesus' birth to the best of his abilities and declared that year to be 1 B.C. Dionysus then proclaimed that the new, Christian era began seven days later on January 1, 1 A.D.

St. Bede, a scholarly Anglo-Saxon monk, began the practice of dating historical events from the birth of Christ, and other writers followed his lead. This system of reckoning time gained near universal acceptance over the centuries. In recent years, however, people who object to the Christian bias implicit in this system have replaced the initials B.C. with "B.C.E.," which stands for "before common era." Accordingly, the initials A.D. are replaced with "C.E.," which stands for "common era."

# Jonkonnu
### John Canoe, John Kooner, Junkanoo

At the beginning of the eighteenth century a new Christmas custom arose in the British West Indies. Called Jonkonnu, this Caribbean Christmas celebration blended African and English masquerade and **mumming** traditions. At one time Jonkonnu celebrations spread as far as the southern United States. The festival survives today in Jamaica, the Bahamas, Belize, St. Kitts-Nevis, Guyana, and Bermuda.

### *Jonkonnu in Jamaica*

The origins of Jonkonnu reflect Jamaica's colonial history. The British seized control of Jamaica from the Spanish in 1660 and established a colonial outpost there. Although some African **slaves** already lived on the island, in the late seventeenth century the English colonists began to import slaves from west Africa in great numbers to work on their sugar plantations. The English colonists brought many cultural traditions with them to Jamaica, including the celebration of Christmas with music, dancing, masquerades, and mumming. The African slaves retained their own music, dance, and masquerade traditions, for which they, too, sought an outlet. These two cultural streams flowed together in Jamaican Christmas celebrations, giving rise to Jonkonnu.

Jamaican Jonkonnu celebrations take place on December 26 (*see also* St. Stephen's Day). Most of the Jonkonnu performers are male. Bands of dancers prepare home-made costumes that identify them as specific characters associated with the festival masquerade. Some of these characters, such as "cowhead," clearly reflect African imagery. Others, like "the king" and "the queen," show remnants of British influence. Small bands of musicians accompany these dancers as they briefly parade to some public location. The bands are composed of both African instruments, like the gum-bay drum, and European instruments, such as the fife. The dancing that takes place when the group arrives at the chosen site also illustrates this Afro-European cultural blend. The participants combine African dance movements with old European dance steps, such as those from the quadrille. African cultural influences appear to dominate Jonkonnu dancing, probably because Jamaicans of African descent developed and kept the custom alive over the centuries.

No one knows for sure where the name "Jonkonnu" comes from. Some say it refers to an early eighteenth-century west African king, John Canoe. Others believe it represents a sloppy English pronunciation of a French phrase, *gens inconnu*, meaning "unknown people." They suggest that early observers gave that name to the ritual because they could not recognize the masked and costumed dancers.

### Jonkonnu in the Caribbean

As Jonkonnu spread throughout the Caribbean, the people of different islands varied the costumes, parades, dances, festival name, and festival date. Belize dancers call their tradition "John Canoe" and perform it on Christmas and December 26, Boxing Day. In the Bahamas the festival is called "Junkanoo" and is celebrated between December 26 and January 1, New Year's Day. Bahamians use strips of colored paper to create dazzling costumes for Junkanoo. Today, with government sponsorship of the parade and costume competition, the elaborate costumes worn by top competitors resemble those of Trinidad's fabulous Carnival celebrations.

### Jonkonnu in the United States

During slavery times American blacks in North Carolina also carried out the Jonkonnu ritual at Christmas time. They called the custom "John Kooner" and spoke of going "John Canoeing" or "John Kunering" on Christmas morning. Like their Caribbean counterparts, most participants in American Jonkonnu celebra-

tions were men. They prepared homemade costumes embellished with strips of colorful cloth and also wore masks, some of which sported horns. Thus garbed, and armed with simple musical instruments such as drums, triangles, violins, and jew's harps, they made their way across town. The masqueraders stopped at the houses of the well-to-do, sang and danced for the occupants, and asked for money in return. They also entertained the people they met on their way. Some reports depict plantation slaves celebrating Jonkonnu on the grounds of the estate. The plantation owners enjoyed the music, dancing, and masquerading, and often rewarded the participants with small **gifts**, such as coins or scarves. Some slaveowners convinced themselves that the happiness the slaves enjoyed during this yearly festival justified the institution of slavery.

The nineteenth-century American version of Jonkonnu strongly resembles the Christmas mumming practices common in England at the time. Nevertheless, the custom probably arrived in the United States via Jamaica and the Bahamas. In past centuries, much trade from these areas entered the United States through the port town of Wilmington, North Carolina. Caribbean slaves familiar with Jonkonnu probably passed the custom on to American blacks via this trade route. After the Civil War, African Americans began to abandon Jonkonnu. Oddly enough, as the tradition declined among African Americans, white youths began to adopt it. They called the seasonal masquerade "coonering" and kept it going from the 1890s until it finally died out in the early 1900s. (*see also* **America, Christmas in Nineteenth-Century.**)

# Joseph

The earthly father of **Jesus** was a man named Joseph. The Bible implies that he made his living as a carpenter (Matthew 13:55). In the **Gospel accounts of Christmas,** Joseph emerges as a righteous man of faith who dutifully observes the rituals of his religion.

Joseph plays a relatively large role in the story of Jesus' birth recorded in the **Gospel according to Matthew** (chapters 1 and 2). When he finds out that his betrothed wife, **Mary,** is pregnant, he decides that he will follow Jewish law by breaking his engagement to her. Instead of doing so publicly, however, he looks for some way to call it off quietly. Many commentators have read his desire not to inflict unnecessary shame upon Mary as a sign of Joseph's righteousness. Then an **angel** visits Joseph, informing him that Mary is pregnant by God's Holy Spirit and asking that he take her as his wife. Joseph demonstrates his faith and trust in God by continuing his engagement to Mary and eventually marrying her. In Matthew's account the angel appears once more to Joseph after Jesus' birth. The angel warns him to leave **Bethlehem** immediately, as **Herod** is planning to kill all the town's male babies in an effort to rid himself of the "newborn King of the Jews" (*see* **Holy Innocents' Day**). Once again, Joseph places his trust in the angel's message and hurries his family away to Egypt (**see also Flight into Egypt**).

Joseph plays a much smaller role in the story of Jesus' birth reported in the **Gospel according to Luke.** In this account, the angel appears to Mary with the message of Jesus' divine father. Yet in this version, too, Joseph trusts the divine message and continues his engagement with Mary. Luke says nothing of the Flight into Egypt. Instead, he mentions Jesus' circumcision and naming ceremony, which took place eight days after Jesus' birth, according to Jewish law (*see* **Feast of the Circumcision**). Once again, Joseph is portrayed as a pious man who carefully observes the teachings of his religion.

Joseph does not appear in the gospel accounts of Jesus' adult life. This has led many commentators to assume that Joseph died before Jesus became an adult. Many Christian artists have portrayed Joseph as an old man in accordance with this interpretation.

As the centuries rolled by, Christians became more and more interested in Joseph. Perhaps because the Bible has so little to say about him, an apocryphal, or legendary, literature sprang up, adding further detail to his life and personality. In Roman Catholicism, he became the patron saint of workers, fathers, and happy deaths, as well as the patron saint of Canada, Mexico, Russia, Peru, Korea, Belgium, Vietnam, Austria, and Bohemia.

## Feast Days

Western Christians began to observe March 19 as St. Joseph's Day in the Middle Ages. Researchers have yet to unearth the reason for the selection of that particular date. Orthodox and other Eastern Christians honor St. Joseph on the first Sunday after Christmas. In 1955 Pope Pius XII declared May 1 to be St. Joseph the Worker's Day, in an effort to add religious overtones to workers' celebrations that took place in various communist countries on that date.

## Christmas Customs

Joseph, along with his wife Mary and the baby Jesus, are the central characters in most **Nativity scenes. Nativity plays,** including the Hispanic folk play called Las **Posadas,** accord him an important role. He is also mentioned in a number of **Christmas carols,** such as "Joseph Dearest, Joseph Mine" and the "Cherry Tree Carol."

# Jultomten

### Joulutonttuja, Julenissen, Julnissen

A winter season gift giver is a common figure in folklore from many different regions. In Sweden, Christmas gifts are brought by the Jultomten. The word *Jultomten* combines the Swedish word for Christmas, *Jul*, with the word *tomten*,

which means household fairy or elf. The Jultomten is often depicted as a portly gnome with a white beard and a pointed red cap. During most of the year this creature hides under the staircase, in the attic, or in any other dark corner of the house. The Jultomten emerges on Christmas Eve, tucking small gifts into unlikely locations about the house. Capricious by nature, the Jultomten may reward or punish householders, depending on his mood. Old customs suggest that the family leave small offerings of porridge and milk, or even liquor and tobacco, about the house to appease him.

Each family or neighborhood may elect a member to dress up as the Jultomten. After assuming a disguise intended to hide his or her identity from the children, the Jultomten knocks on the door with a sack of presents. When the door opens, the Jultomten asks, "Are there any good children here?" and distributes presents accordingly.

## Denmark, Norway, and Finland

In Denmark these Christmas elves are known as *Julnissen*, and in Norway as *Julenissen*. Although similar to the Jultomten in appearance, the Danish Julnissen does not distribute gifts. Instead, he lurks about the dark corners of the house, perhaps assuring himself that the family cares properly for the homestead. The Norwegian Julenissen takes after his Swedish cousin and does bring gifts. These Danish and Norwegian sprites become more active during the dark midwinter season. Like the Jultomten, they, too, must be placated with porridge on Christmas Eve if the householders wish to escape their pranks. Finland also has its version of the Christmas gnomes, called the *Joulutonttuja*. Unlike the other Scandinavian Christmas gnomes, the Joulutonttuja are cheerful, helpful creatures. They watch children to find out what they'd like as presents and help Santa make these gifts in his workshop.

## History

In ancient times Scandinavian householders thought that the spirits of the land's past inhabitants lingered on, jealously watching over their old domain. During **Yule**, when the dead were believed to return, the thoughtful, and perhaps fearful, made offerings of food and drink to these **ghosts**. Folk belief gradually transformed these spirits into the Scandinavian household fairies known as *nissen* or *tomten*. These peevish elves guarded household and barn. When unsatisfied with the family's behavior, they punished them with small pranks, like making the milk go sour.

The figure of the Jultomten developed in the late 1800s. Before that time the Yule goat brought Swedish families their Christmas presents. The traditional Swedish tomten, or household sprite, is not associated with any particular season. By contrast, the Jultomten not only appears around Christmas time, but also delivers presents. The importation of German Christmas decorations in the late nineteenth century, featuring the gift-giving **St. Nicholas**, may have suggested the assignment of this function to the Jultomten. The English gift giver Father Christmas may also have influenced this shift. Some writers suggest that the Scandinavian Jultomten, Julnissen, and Joulutonttuja, in turn, inspired the invention of the helpful elves who became **Santa Claus**'s assistants in the frozen **North Pole**.

# Kalends

## Calends

Kalends, the Roman new year festival, began on January 1 and lasted until January 5. The Romans celebrated Kalends in much the same way they did **Saturnalia**. Early Christian writers condemned the carousing crowds. Nevertheless, some of the customs associated with Kalends were eventually absorbed into the celebration of Christmas.

In 45 B.C. the Roman emperor Julius Caesar introduced a new calendar (called the Julian calendar) which shifted the date of the Roman new year from March 25 to January 1. The Romans called the festival that began on this day "kalends" (or "calends"). They also used this word to refer to the first day of each month. On this day Roman officials posted the calendar for each month. The English word "calendar" comes from the old Latin term "kalends."

## *Customs*

The Romans celebrated Kalends by decorating their homes and temples with lights and **greenery**. They exchanged **gifts** with one another as well. A sprig of greenery taken from the groves dedicated to the goddess Strenia was considered a very traditional gift. Later the Romans added cakes and honey (symbolizing a "sweet" new year) and coins (symbolizing wealth) to the roster of traditional new year gifts. The Romans called these gifts *strenae*, after Strenia. This Latin word finds echo in the modern French word for new year's gift, *Étrenne*. In addition to exchanging gifts with friends and family, many Romans offered gifts and *vota*, wishes for prosperity, to the emperor. The mad emperor Caligula went so far as to require these gifts and good wishes, and stood outside the palace to collect them in person.

Other Kalends customs included fortune-telling and informal masquerades in which men cavorted through the streets dressed as animals or as women. Their bold and sometimes rude antics entertained some onlookers and outraged others. Some researchers trace the origins of **mumming** back to this Kalends custom. During the Kalends festival, slaves enjoyed time off and even sat down with their masters to play dice. Feasting, drinking, and merrymaking rounded out the festival. Certain superstitions also attached themselves to the holiday. The Romans believed bad luck would follow any who lent fire or iron to a neighbor at this time.

Kalend's Eve celebrations resembled our own New Year's Eve festivities. A fourth-century Greek scholar named Libanius wrote that almost everyone stayed up on Kalend's Eve to usher in the new year with drinking, singing, and revelry. Instead of spending the evening at home, crowds of people roamed through the streets, returning to their houses near daybreak to sleep off the night's overindulgence. Coins were distributed among the people on the first day of the new year. Indeed, all Kalends gift giving took place on the first of January. On January second most people stayed at home and played dice. Races entertained the populace on the third of January. Kalends festivities wound down on the fourth of January and finally came to a close on the fifth.

## Similarity to Christmas

Libanius left future generations a lengthy description of the attitudes and activities that characterized the celebration of the Roman new year. This description reveals many striking similarities between Kalends and contemporary Christmas celebrations:

> The festival of Kalends ... is celebrated everywhere as far as the limits of the Roman Empire extend.... Everywhere may be seen carousals and well-laden tables; luxurious abundance is found in the houses of the rich, but also in the houses of the poor better food than usual is put upon the table.

240

The impulse to spend seizes everyone. He who the whole year through has taken pleasure in saving and piling up his pence, becomes suddenly extravagant. He who erstwhile was accustomed and preferred to live poorly, now at this feast enjoys himself as much as his means will allow.… People are not only generous towards themselves, but also towards their fellowmen. A stream of presents pours itself out on all sides.… The highroads and footpaths are covered with whole processions of laden men and beasts.… As the thousand flowers which burst forth everywhere are the adornment of Spring, so are the thousand presents poured out on all sides, the decoration of the Kalends feast. It may justly be said that it is the fairest time of the year.… The Kalends festival banishes all that is connected with toil, and allows men to give themselves up to undisturbed enjoyment. From the minds of young people it removes two kinds of dread: the dread of the schoolmaster and the dread of the stern pedagogue. The slave also it allows, so far as possible, to breathe the air of freedom.… Another great quality of the festival is that it teaches men not to hold too fast to their money, but to part with it and let it pass into other hands. [Miles, 1990, 168-69]

## *Christian Opposition*

Many of the customs and attitudes associated with Kalends and Saturnalia gradually attached themselves to the celebration of Christmas. Ironically, this transfer took place in spite of the overwhelming rejection of these holidays and their customs by Christian officials. For centuries Christian authorities condemned the drunkenness, disorder, fortune-telling, gambling, and masquerading associated with the celebration of Kalends. Nevertheless, these customs proved remarkably difficult to stamp out, even after Christianity became the dominant religion and Christmas an important winter holiday. One researcher has counted at least forty separate Church documents containing official denunciations of the kinds of midwinter masquerades associated with Kalends. These documents range from the fourth to the eleventh centuries and come from authorities in many European lands as well as north Africa and the Near East.

Church officials urged their followers to abandon riotous pagan practices and instead to observe the day with thoughtfulness and sobriety. In 567 the second provincial Council of Tours tried to counteract the still popular festivities surrounding

Kalends by ordering Christians to fast and do penance during the first few days of the new year. In the seventh century Church officials made a new effort to reclaim the day from pagan celebrations. They introduced a new Christian holy day, the **Feast of the Circumcision**, to be celebrated on January 1. By the time Kalends finally withered away, however, the peoples of Europe had already transferred many of its customs to the **Christmas season**.

# Kallikantzari
## Callicantzari, Kallikantzaroi

Since ancient times, legends have told of supernatural forces that roam the earth around the time of Christmas. According to traditional Greek folklore, the kallikantzari rampaged across Greece during the **Twelve Days of Christmas**. These diminutive demons spent the rest of the year deep inside the earth gnawing at the tree that supports the world. The tree renewed itself each year during the season of Christ's birth. Thus thwarted, the enraged kallikantzari swarmed up to the surface of the earth to bedevil humanity. The holy ceremonies occurring on **Epiphany** drove them back underground. Belief in the kallikantzari was especially strong in the region of Mt. Parnassos.

## Appearance

Reports concerning the appearance of these demons varied. According to some, the kallikantzari appeared half human and half animal. Many claimed to have caught a glimpse of long, curved talons, red eyes, hairy bodies, or donkey's ears. Others told frightening tales of tiny imps who rode astride lame or deformed chickens.

## Activities

According to Greek folklore, the kallikantzari knew many ways of vexing human beings. Some reports said that they entered homes by the door or the chimney, relieved themselves in any open containers of food and drink, upset furniture, and

extinguished the fire. Others credited them with direct attacks on human beings. For example, they hopped on peoples' backs and drove them to dance until they collapsed. The presence of the kallikantzari during the Twelve Days of Christmas posed special problems for expectant mothers. Children born at this time of year ran the risk of becoming kallikantzari themselves. From sunset to dawn the demons roamed the countryside looking for opportunities to harass humanity. They tended to retreat into hiding places at daybreak, however.

## Remedies

Just as traditional beliefs warned of the dangers presented by the kallikantzari, they also offered methods for warding off these attacks. Keeping a fire burning in the hearth during the Twelve Days of Christmas prevented the demons from entering the home through the chimney. In addition, the kallikantzari found the smell of burning shoes, salt, wild asparagus, or other substances that produced a foul smoke especially repugnant. Of course, so did human beings. Greek folklore apparently did not address the subject of whether this method of repelling the kallikantzari also repelled family, friends, and neighbors. Traditional lore also recommended hanging a pig's jaw bone by the door as a method of preventing the kallikantzari from crossing the threshold. To protect babies born during the Twelve Days of Christmas from becoming kallikantzari, mothers wrapped their infants in garlic or straw, or scorched their toes in the fire.

The religious ceremonies associated with Epiphany offered the most effective method of driving off the malicious pranksters. According to Greek custom, priests visited homes on Epiphany, filling them with the scent of burning incense and sprinkling them with holy water. Greek folklore insisted that the kallikantzari fled before this onslaught of holiness, retreating to their underground lair until the following Christmas.

## Parallels

According to various European folk traditions, demons, spirits, and magical creatures of all kinds roamed the earth during the Twelve Days of Christmas. Some of these demons served as the unlikely companions of **St. Nicholas** (*see also* **St. Nicholas's Day**). The good saint somehow tamed the **cert** from Slovakia and the Czech Republic, **Black Peter** from the Netherlands, and the German **Knecht Ruprecht** from Germany. Yet many other supernatural creatures still wandered freely through the dark nights. In some parts of northern Europe traditional lore asserted that werewolves, bears, or trolls prowled for victims during the Twelve Days of Christmas. Legends from some countries warned that the fearsome spirits known as the **Wild Hunt** raced across the night skies at this time of year. German lore cautioned that the supernatural figure known as **Berchta** toured the countryside with her entourage during these cold, dark days. Often, **Frau Gaude**, too, appeared to German villagers at this time of year. Other folklore told of frolicking elves and fairies, such as the Swedish **Jultomten** and the Icelandic **Christmas Lads**.

# King of the Bean
## Bean King, Epiphany King

A long succession of mock kings have ruled over winter holiday merrymaking in Europe. In ancient times they presided over feasts held in honor of the Roman festival of **Saturnalia** (*see also* **Zagmuk**). In the Middle Ages the **boy bishop** and the **Lord of Misrule** directed certain Christmas festivities (*see also* **Feast of Fools**). **Twelfth Night** celebrations, however, came under the special supervision of another mock ruler: the King of the Bean.

In past centuries the English, French, Spanish, German, and Dutch celebrated Twelfth Night, or **Epiphany** Eve, with a feast. The Twelfth Night cake not only provided dessert, but also helped to facilitate an old custom. While preparing the cake, the cook dropped a bean, coin, or other small object into the batter. The man who found this object in his slice of cake was declared "King of the Bean." If a woman received the bean, she became queen and appointed a man as king.

The king presided over the rest of the evening's activities. In some areas the king chose his own queen. In others, a pea was also added to the cake batter and the woman who found the pea in her serving of cake enacted the role of "queen." Everyone else became a member of the royal court. At some parties the courtiers carried out their role by announcing the mock ruler's every action. Cries of "the king drinks" or "the king coughs" cued others to follow suit. The mock rulers might also give silly commands that the court was expected to carry out. The French saying, *il a trouvé la fève au gâteau*, which means "he found the bean in the cake," comes from this Twelfth Night custom and means "he's had some good luck."

## History

**Christmas season** mock kings sprouted up regularly in the courts of medieval Europe. Records indicate that in late medieval France these kings were selected by a kind of edible lottery. All candidates received a piece of a special cake into which a bean had been baked. Whoever found the bean in their slice of cake became the king of the feast. The title conferred upon these mock monarchs, "Bean King" or "King of the Bean," referred back to this custom. It may also have alluded to their lack of real power. In the sixteenth century, ordinary Dutch and German households celebrated Twelfth Night by baking a coin into a cake and acknowledging whoever received the coin in their slice of cake as king of the feast. In the next century, this Twelfth Night custom spread to England, France, and Spain.

The English added an innovation of their own to the Twelfth Night feast. In 1669 English diarist Samuel Pepys described his enjoyment of a new custom whereby Twelfth Night merrymakers drew slips of paper from a hat on which were written the names of characters found at the bean king's court. They were expected to impersonate this character for the rest of the evening. In this way everyone present at the celebration, not just the king and queen, got into the act.

The King of the Bean continued to preside over English Twelfth Night celebrations until the nineteenth century. In this era people began to substitute metallic objects for the bean and pea embedded in earlier Twelfth Night cakes. These objects stood for future fortunes rather than for characters. For example, a ring might foretell marriage, and a thimble spinsterhood. The importance of Twelfth Night declined throughout the nineteenth century. Rather than fade into oblivion, however, this fortune-telling custom transferred itself to Christmas. The tokens found a new home inside the plum pudding so popular at English Christmas dinners. By the end of the nineteenth century the English had all but abandoned the Twelfth Night king. The custom of baking a bean into the Twelfth Night cake survived into the twentieth century in the southern French region of Provence. In Germany the bean king and his cake still appear at Epiphany celebrations.

# Knecht Ruprecht

## Aschenklas, Belsnickel, Bullerklas, Butz, Hans Muff, Hans Trapp, Klaubauf, Krampus, Pelz Nicholas, Pulterklas, Ru-Klas, Schimmelreiter

According to old European folklore, a variety of frightening figures lurk in the long, dark nights of the **Christmas season**, including the ghostly personnel of the **Wild Hunt** and mysterious wanderers like **Berchta**. Many folklorists interpret these figures

as remnants of old pagan spirits that blended into the emerging Christian folklore of the Christmas season. The folklore associated with **St. Nicholas's Day** offers a clear example of this dynamic. **St. Nicholas,** a fourth-century bishop from Asia Minor, became the Christmas **gift** bringer in much of northern and central Europe. According to folklore, however, this clearly Christian figure travels about with a variety of somewhat sinister companions. In German-speaking lands scruffy Knecht Ruprecht trails behind St. Nicholas, meting out punishment to naughty children. Some folklorists trace Knecht Ruprecht's roots back to ancient times.

### Ruprecht's Many Names

St. Nicholas's German helper goes by many different names. In Austria and some areas of Germany, many children know him as Knecht Ruprecht, which means "Knight" Ruprecht or "Servant" Ruprecht. Some of the names assigned to this bogeyman reveal that somewhere along the line his identity merged with that of St. Nicholas. Some know him as *Ru-Klas*, or "Rough Nicholas," while others identify him as *Pelz Nicholas*, or "Fur Nicholas." Still others call him *Aschenklas*, or "Ash Nicholas." In some areas a figure known as *Pelzmartin*, or "Fur Martin," blended the identity of St. Martin with the Christmas season bogey (*see also* **Martinmas**). The Pennsylvania Dutch brought Pelz Nicholas with them to America when they began to settle in Pennsylvania in the eighteenth century. There the name "Pelz Nicholas" eventually slurred into *Belsnickel* (sometimes written as "Bellsnickle," "Bellschniggle," or "Pelznichol"; *see also* **America, Christmas in Colonial**).

### Folklore

The appearance and activities of these folk figures vary in a number of details, but a rough composite image does emerge. Knecht Ruprecht startles onlookers with his menacing demeanor and unkempt appearance. He wears clothing made of rags, straw, or furs, and often adds a soot-blackened face, beard, or a frightening mask. In past times he sometimes sported devil's horns. In addition, he carries one or more of the tools of his trade: a whip, stick, sack, or **bell**. The bell warns of his approach. He cows all children into good behavior and punishes badly behaved children with his whip or stick. The sack contains treats for well-behaved children and items that serve as symbolic warnings to wrongdoers that their misbehavior has not gone unnoticed.

According to folklore, St. Nicholas and his companion visit homes on St. Nicholas's Eve, often entering through the chimney. They leave treats, such as nuts, fruit, and cookies, for good children, and ashes, birch rods, or other warnings for naughty ones. In some areas the pair makes their rounds on Christmas Eve instead of St. Nicholas's Eve.

### European Customs

Until the early part of the twentieth century, men dressed as Knecht Ruprecht and St. Nicholas visited homes on St. Nicholas's Eve in German-speaking lands. St.

Nicholas quizzed the children on their behavior, their prayers, and their lessons, while Ruprecht posed threateningly in the background. In some areas the Christmas bogey worked alone and arrived on other dates during the Christmas season, such as Christmas Eve. Although Knecht Ruprecht's looks and manners often intimidated, his brash and erratic behavior entertained. Children still prepare for his visit by leaving their shoes by the fireplace, on the doorstep, or in some other place where the gift bringer was sure to notice them. In the morning well-behaved children find their shoes filled with treats, while those whose behavior needs improvement find birch rods, ashes, or other warnings.

### Belsnickeling in the United States

In the early years of the United States people from different countries adopted elements of each other's lore and traditions, giving rise to new customs. By the nineteenth century the English custom of mumming had grafted itself onto the Pennsylvania Dutch figure of the Belsnickel to create the custom of belsnickeling.

Groups of young men or single individuals dressed themselves in rags, overcoats, or furs, and hid their faces behind beards, hats, or masks, or covered them with soot. They carried whips, bells, and sacks as they marched from house to house. After gaining entrance to a neighbor's home, they entertained the householders with their comic antics and horseplay while family members tried to guess their identities. In return for their visit, the belsnickelers expected to receive hospitality in the form of food and drink. The belsnickelers took nuts and sweets out of their pockets and tossed them onto the floor, cracking their whips over the heads of any children bold enough to retrieve them. Sometimes they also pulled pranks on their neighbors under the cover of their disguise.

Although Belsnickel was originally associated with St. Nicholas's Day, Pennsylvania belsnickelers shifted the dates of their activities closer to Christmas, visiting their neighbors in masquerade on the dark nights between Christmas and New Year's Day. Belsnickelers also plied their trade in Canada's Nova Scotia province.

### Opposition

Christmas season masquerading met with some resistance by the more subdued groups who made up Pennsylvania's population. In the eighteenth century, Quakers in Philadelphia vigorously opposed this custom. Court records indicate that some masqueraders were brought before juries for their unruly behavior. In the early nineteenth century the Pennsylvania House of Representatives formally outlawed Christmas season masquerading. Those who dared to flaunt this edict faced fines of between $50 and $1,000, and prison sentences of up to three months. A Philadelphia ordinance forbade Christmas Eve masquerading and noisemaking in 1881. Nevertheless, belsnickelers continued their seasonal activities in rural areas settled by people of Germanic descent who were friendly to the custom.

### Decline

Belsnickeling died out in the early twentieth century, about the time when authorities ceased to oppose it. In 1901 Philadelphia issued its first permit for a New Year's Day mummers' parade. This parade developed out of the mumming and noisemaking traditions of a variety of Philadelphia's immigrant groups, among them the German-American tradition of belsnickeling. Philadelphia's New Year's Day Mummers Parade continues to this day. Today's parade, however, revolves around a competition between highly organized groups wearing elaborate and expensive costumes. (*For more on Christmas in Pennsylvania, see* America, Christmas in Nineteenth-Century; Amish Christmas; Bethlehem, Pennsylvania, Christmas in).

# Kwanzaa

Kwanzaa is an African-American holiday that is unrelated to Christmas. Nevertheless, its founder, Dr. Maulana Karenga, a University of California at Los Angeles professor from Nigeria, placed the seven-day holiday between Christmas and New Year's Day. He did so in order to provide an African-American alternative to Christmas, which he viewed as a European holiday. He also wanted to make Kwanzaa easy to celebrate by placing it during a week when many people were already celebrating and had time off from work or school. Kwanzaa begins on December 26 and lasts until January 1.

Karenga hoped that the new holiday, based on principles and symbols associated with African harvest festivals, would provide an ethnic celebration all African Americans could observe, regardless of religious affiliation. He also sought to create a holiday that

emphasized communal and spiritual values, rather than the materialism he found rampant in American Christmas celebrations.

Karenga created the word "Kwanzaa" from the Swahili phrase *matunda ya kwanza*, which means "first fruits." Many African first fruits celebrations, or harvest festivals, last between seven and nine days. Accordingly, Karenga decided to have the new American festival continue for seven days. He added the extra "a" to the Swahili word *kwanza* so that the name of the new holiday, Kwanzaa, would contain seven letters.

Karenga selected seven principles from among the values most commonly held in high esteem by the peoples of Africa and honored in their harvest celebrations. One of the seven principles of Kwanzaa is celebrated on each of the seven days of the festival. The seven principles include *umoja* (unity), *kujichagulia* (self-determination), *ujima* (collective work and responsibility), *ujamaa* (cooperative economics), *nia* (purpose), *kuumba* (creativity), and *imani* (faith). Kwanzaa celebrations also feature a seven-branched candleholder called a *kinara*. The kinara holds red, green, and black candles—colors symbolic of African identity. One candle is lit on each of the seven nights. On December 31 celebrants participate in a communal feast. On January 1, the last day of the festival, modest gifts are exchanged.

Since its founding in 1966 Kwanzaa has steadily grown in popularity. Estimates of the number of Americans who observe the holiday each year vary widely, with estimates ranging from 2 million to more than 18 million. Millions more are thought to celebrate the festival in Africa, Canada, the Caribbean, and Europe.

# Laurel

## Bay

Seasonal decorations of **greenery** have embellished European Christmas celebrations for centuries. Laurel's association with the season can be traced back even further, however. The Romans celebrated their new year festival, **Kalends**, by adorning their homes and temples with evergreen branches. Both the Greeks and the Romans crowned the victors of their athletic and other contests with **wreaths** of laurel, since the laurel branch served as a symbol of victory. In later times northern Europeans gathered laurel, or bay, for their Christmas garlands. In the seventeenth century the English poet Robert Herrick noted that, according to local custom, "**Rosemary** and baies [bays] that are most faire were stuck about the houses and the churches as Christmas decorations." Christian authorities explained this use of laurel with reference to its ancient association with victory, declaring that when used in Christmas trimmings the fragrant leaves represented the triumph of **Jesus** Christ.

# Light Displays and Decorations

The first string of electric lights was fashioned by Thomas Edison for Christmas 1880. Edison strung these lights around the outside of his Menlo Park Laboratory, creating the first outdoor display of electric Christmas lights in America. This display likely fascinated passengers travelling by on the nearby railway, but Christmas lights would not become widely used until some forty years later.

Before 1903, pre-made strings of electric lights were not available to the general public. The skills of a wireman, the term used to identify early electricians, were required to manually assemble the electrical cords, light bulb sockets, and lights. Due to the high cost of hiring a wireman, strings of Christmas lights were generally available only to the wealthy. In 1903, General Electric introduced pre-made Christmas light kits for use by the average person. But many American homes did not yet have electrical service at this time, and so electric Christmas lights still did not catch on.

The first outdoor electric Christmas lights were introduced in 1927 by General Electric. These early outdoor light strings included seven round light bulbs that were painted in different colors. In 1928, flame-shaped bulbs were introduced. During this era, the General Electric and Edison Electric companies sponsored neighborhood outdoor lighting competitions at Christmas time. These contests were held to encourage the use of electric Christmas lights. The competitions quickly became popular events that spread to communities across the country.

### Christmas Decorating at Home

After World War II, the national interest in outdoor Christmas decorating grew substantially. With the economic prosperity of the post-war era, many Americans had the means and the opportunity to invest in new kinds of Christmas lights and decorations. More people began to use Christmas decorations on the outside of their homes as well as the inside.

Today, Americans buy an estimated 150 million sets of Christmas lights each year. It is estimated that each year, more than 80 million American homes have out-

# Laurel

## Bay

Seasonal decorations of **greenery** have embellished European Christmas celebrations for centuries. Laurel's association with the season can be traced back even further, however. The Romans celebrated their new year festival, **Kalends**, by adorning their homes and temples with evergreen branches. Both the Greeks and the Romans crowned the victors of their athletic and other contests with **wreaths** of laurel, since the laurel branch served as a symbol of victory. In later times northern Europeans gathered laurel, or bay, for their Christmas garlands. In the seventeenth century the English poet Robert Herrick noted that, according to local custom, "**Rosemary** and baies [bays] that are most faire were stuck about the houses and the churches as Christmas decorations." Christian authorities explained this use of laurel with reference to its ancient association with victory, declaring that when used in Christmas trimmings the fragrant leaves represented the triumph of **Jesus** Christ.

# Light Displays and Decorations

The first string of electric lights was fashioned by Thomas Edison for Christmas 1880. Edison strung these lights around the outside of his Menlo Park Laboratory, creating the first outdoor display of electric Christmas lights in America. This display likely fascinated passengers travelling by on the nearby railway, but Christmas lights would not become widely used until some forty years later.

Before 1903, pre-made strings of electric lights were not available to the general public. The skills of a wireman, the term used to identify early electricians, were required to manually assemble the electrical cords, light bulb sockets, and lights. Due to the high cost of hiring a wireman, strings of Christmas lights were generally available only to the wealthy. In 1903, General Electric introduced pre-made Christmas light kits for use by the average person. But many American homes did not yet have electrical service at this time, and so electric Christmas lights still did not catch on.

The first outdoor electric Christmas lights were introduced in 1927 by General Electric. These early outdoor light strings included seven round light bulbs that were painted in different colors. In 1928, flame-shaped bulbs were introduced. During this era, the General Electric and Edison Electric companies sponsored neighborhood outdoor lighting competitions at Christmas time. These contests were held to encourage the use of electric Christmas lights. The competitions quickly became popular events that spread to communities across the country.

### Christmas Decorating at Home

After World War II, the national interest in outdoor Christmas decorating grew substantially. With the economic prosperity of the post-war era, many Americans had the means and the opportunity to invest in new kinds of Christmas lights and decorations. More people began to use Christmas decorations on the outside of their homes as well as the inside.

Today, Americans buy an estimated 150 million sets of Christmas lights each year. It is estimated that each year, more than 80 million American homes have outdoor Christmas displays. The decorating schemes of many American homes are simple and understated, often involving colored lights strung on trees or shrubs, and sometimes around windows or along the roofline. Lighted inflatable figures are sometimes arranged in front of the house, such as snowmen, Santas, reindeer, angels, toy soldiers, and so on. Many Americans are content with these modest displays, but a few go to far greater lengths to create the ultimate extreme Christmas display.

Each year, in communities all across America, there are amateur decorators who install home Christmas displays of impressive scale. It is not uncommon for these dedicated hobbyists to use thousands or even millions of lights on their homes. Some also incorporate an abundance of lighted figures representing every possible theme related to Christmas or the winter holiday season. Still others invest in complicated computer software that allows them to program lights to blink and twinkle in time to Christmas tunes that are broadcast for the listening pleasure of their neighbors. Many of these enthusiasts have special electrical circuitry installed at their homes in order to power these extravagant displays.

In some communities, groups of neighbors join together to create such showy Christmas displays that people come from miles around to see the lights each year. The Tacky Light Tour in Richmond, Virginia, began in the late 1980s at the encouragement of a local radio personality. A list of Tacky Light homes is published annually by the *Richmond Times-Dispatch* newspaper, and fierce competition drives those who want to be included on the list. In order to be listed, homes must be decorated with a minimum of 30,000 lights. Most participants far exceed that requirement, with some dazzling displays using many thousands of lights. Participation has grown to such a degree that it is now impossible to see all of the Tacky Light Tour in one night.

Another example of community decorating, albeit on a much smaller scale, takes place each year in the Hampden neighborhood of Baltimore, Maryland. There the residents of 34th Street create the annual Miracle on 34th Street display, a local tradition that began in 1990. Each of the twenty-two traditional Baltimore row homes lining both sides of the street is decorated to the hilt, the tiny front yards stuffed with all manner of Christmas items and strings of Christmas lights festooned across the roadway. It takes six months to plan each year's display, and about three months to take it all down. An estimated 100,000 people visit 34th

Street each year to see the sights, which include an eight-foot-tall Christmas tree made of 134 car hubcaps, and a motorized train set that travels a circular track running inside and outside the house. The homeowners of 34th Street pool their money to create a general fund that pays the excessive electricity bills generated during the Christmas season.

Extreme Christmas decorating has become such a national trend that television specials now document the phenomenon. Shows like HGTV's "Extreme Christmas" and "What's With That Christmas House" provide a tour of some of the most outlandishly decorated homes in America.

## Municipal Displays

In the eighteenth century, German immigrants brought to the United States the tradition of creating extravagantly detailed **Nativity scenes** called *putz* (from the German word for "decorate"). In these displays, dozens or hundreds of figurines might be placed amidst gardens, fountains, arbors, villages, streams, bridges, waterfalls, and other delightful scenery. The town of **Bethlehem, Pennsylvania**, builds a large community putz every year that is visited by thousands of tourists.

In the early twentieth century it was customary for many cities and towns throughout the country to set up public Nativity scenes at Christmas time, often on the grounds of city hall. In the early 1970s, these displays became the focus of legal questions about local government promoting one particular religion over others. In 1973, the American Civil Liberties Union won a landmark lawsuit that ruled Nativity scenes on government land to be in violation of the U.S. Constitution. As a result, many cities and towns have discontinued the practice of displaying public Nativity scenes. However, many families and churches continue to enjoy this Christmas tradition, and outdoor Nativity scenes can often be found displayed on privately owned land.

Contemporary municipal Christmas displays are often built around secular symbols of the holiday, such as **Christmas trees**, tableaus of arctic animals like polar bears and penguins, snowmen, Santa, or simply an abundance of colored lights. One of the most well-known governmental displays is installed each year at the White House, where the President also lights the **National Christmas Tree** each year (*see also* **White House, Christmas in the**).

# Lord of Misrule

## Abbot of Unreason, Christmas Lord, Master of Merry Disports

A long succession of mock rulers have presided over winter holiday merrymaking in Europe. In late medieval and Renaissance England, towns, colleges, noble houses, and the royal court often chose a mock king to preside over their Christmas festivities. Temporarily elevated from his ordinary, humble rank to that of "king," he was known by a variety of names, including the Lord of Misrule, the Abbot of Unreason, the Christmas Lord, and the Master of Merry Disports. These colorful titles reflect the kind of madcap revelry associated with these parties.

## *Activities*

The Christmas festivities over which the Lord of Misrule presided might include feasts, dances, **mumming**, musical entertainments, plays, and masques, as well as a good deal of general merriment. According to an irate **Puritan** of the sixteenth century, Christmas Lords sometimes led their retinue of giddy followers through the streets of the town and into churches while services were being held. Perhaps in imitation of the **Feast of Fools**, the motley band careened down the aisle, dancing, singing, jingling **bells**, and brandishing their hobbyhorses. Many worshipers laughed at the spectacle and stood on their pews to get a better view. Apparently, the Puritans did not find the interruption at all amusing.

Of course, the noble and wealthy enjoyed the most elaborate Christmas celebrations, and also left the best records of the Lord of Misrule and his activities. One of the earliest records of an English Christmas celebration presided over by a mock king dates back to the time of King Edward III. In 1347 Edward enjoyed a number of extravagant Christmas masques and dances prepared for him by his "Master of Merry Disports." King Henry VIII found the Lord of Misrule and his diversions vastly entertaining. His enthusiasm for the custom was such that in a few cases he ordered others to follow suit. For example, when he founded Cambridge University's Trinity College, he mandated that a Lord of Misrule preside at its Christmas festivities.

### Term of Office and Duties

The duties of the Lord of Misrule varied from place to place, as did the type of entertainment offered and the duration of the Christmas holiday. The Lord of Misrule's most fundamental duty, however, was to attend the Christmas festivities in the character of a mock king. His temporary elevation of status permitted him to command all present, but he was primarily expected to foster a merry atmosphere.

In some cases the Lord of Misrule also helped to plan the various **Christmas season** entertainments. At this time Christmas celebrations in wealthy households usually lasted throughout the **Twelve Days of Christmas.** In some places, though, Christmas festivities began as early as All Hallow's Eve (Halloween), October 31, with the selection of the Lord of Misrule. Indeed, the period between Halloween and **Twelfth Night** coincided with the theater season in London, a period of parties and entertainments of all sorts for the well-to-do.

### Rise and Decline

The Lord of Misrule was known in England as early as the fourteenth century. The custom reached the height of its popularity in the fifteenth and sixteenth centuries and declined in the seventeenth century. Some writers believe he evolved out of the mock bishops associated with the Feast of Fools. Others guess that the **King of the Bean**, already popular in parts of continental Europe, may have inspired the creation of this custom. Whatever his origins, the Lord of Misrule did resemble these and other temporary kings of the Christmas season, including the **boy bishop** and the mock kings associated with **Saturnalia.**

# Luminarias

*Luminarias* (pronounced "loo-mee-NAR-ee-yahs") means "lights" or "illuminations" in Spanish. The word also refers to the small bonfires that illuminate the dark nights of the **Christmas season** throughout the American Southwest (*see also* **Farolitos**). These bonfires are made from piñon pine logs that have been stacked in log-cabin fashion to form a box about three feet in height. Although one may spot luminarias throughout the Christmas season, they are most common on Christmas Eve. On that evening the little bonfires blaze in front of churches, homes, and in public plazas, guiding worshipers to mass, enlivening public and family celebrations, and welcoming the coming of the Christ child.

Some believe that the custom of celebrating Christmas Eve with luminarias can be traced all the way back to the fires that warmed the **shepherds** to whom the birth of **Jesus** was announced in the **Gospel according to Luke**. Others say the custom came from Native American traditions, which Spanish missionaries later incorporated into the celebration of Christmas. Still others think that Spanish missionaries brought the custom with them to Mexico. They note that the Spanish custom evolved out of various pagan European practices (*see also* **Candles; Martinmas; Yule**). Whatever its origins, the earliest historical record of the practice in the New World dates back to the sixteenth century. Spanish missionaries, sent to evangelize the native peoples of Mexico, wrote that on Christmas Eve the people celebrated by singing, drumming, and lighting bonfires on church patios and on the roofs of their flat-topped houses.

Today, the custom of lighting luminarias on Christmas Eve continues in New Mexico. Although city conditions sometimes make the lighting of outdoor fires difficult, many people and organizations strive to continue this old custom. In Albuquerque, New Mexico, organized tours guide interested viewers through the neighborhoods that tend to offer the best displays. The custom has spread around the U.S., as neighborhoods gather together to light luminarias on Christmas Eve and other evenings during the Christmas season.

# Macy's Thanksgiving Day Parade

For many Americans, Macy's Thanksgiving Day Parade, which takes place in **New York City**, symbolizes the start of the holiday season. It also announces the beginning of the Christmas **shopping** season. Macy's, a department store chain that began in New York City, launched the yearly parade in 1924 as a means of advertising its stores at the start of the year's busiest shopping season. Each year, the parade includes an array of giant helium balloons, a multitude of floats and falloons (float and balloon combinations), marching bands, music and dance ensembles, groups of clowns, and performances from current Broadway shows. The Radio City Rockettes, a group of New York City dancers, also appear in the parade, in addition to a number of celebrities. The two-and-one-half-mile parade requires a huge staff, including 4,000 Macy's employees. Although similar Thanksgiving Day parades take place in other cities, national television coverage has helped to make the New York parade an American institution.

### Thanksgiving Day in Nineteenth-Century New York

In the nineteenth century many cities hosted military parades on Thanksgiving Day. In addition to the military parade, the citizens of New York City celebrated Thanksgiving Day with a few unique customs that may have helped to inspire the format of

Macy's parade. One such custom involved a public masquerade on Thanksgiving Day. Bands of working-class men dressed in costumes and paraded around the streets. Known as "fantasticals," they often fueled their costumed hijinks with liberal amounts of alcohol. Their parades began early in the morning and were accompanied by blaring horns, much to the annoyance of those who preferred to sleep in. They usually ended their march about town with a meal in one of the city's parks and in the evening often attended costumed balls.

Children who participated in Thanksgiving Day masquerades were called ragamuffins. They did not march with the adults but rather begged for coins or treats under the cover of costume, much in the way children do today at Halloween. Frequently, boys dressed as girls and girls dressed as boys. White children blackened their faces with soot, while black children whitened their faces with powdered talc. The sight of children dressed up in old clothes and make-up was so common that some New Yorkers called Thanksgiving "Ragamuffin Day."

"Target Companies" provided another Thanksgiving Day public spectacle for 19th-century New Yorkers. These bands of young men, most of whom belonged to a slightly higher social class than did the fantasticals, enjoyed being soldiers for a day. They gave their "company" a name, dressed in boots and military costumes, and marched to a city park to practice target shooting. Since most practiced only once a year, there were not many good shots among them. Proper military parades also took place in New York and other U.S. cities on Thanksgiving Day.

Some commentators believe that the November antics of the ragamuffins and fantasticals began as celebrations of the final withdrawal of British troops from the city, which took place on November 25, 1783. Others view them as Carnival customs that somehow migrated from early spring to autumn. At least one researcher has suggested that they might instead have grown out of early Guy Fawkes Day celebrations—commemorated by the British on November 5—which moved to Thanksgiving Day as the city's inhabitants began to think of themselves less as British and more as Americans. As the twentieth century dawned, fewer and fewer people celebrated Thanksgiving Day as fantasticals or ragamuffins. These customs died out around the time of World War II.

## Macy's Thanksgiving Day Parade Begins

Thus, when Macy's launched its first parade in 1924, the sight of people marching through the streets of New York in costume on Thanksgiving Day was nothing new.

Though the organizers of Macy's parade may have found inspiration in New York's older parade and masquerade customs, the most immediate influence was likely to have been the parades sponsored by Gimbel's department store in Philadelphia in 1921 and Hudson's department store in Detroit in 1923. These stores had used the parades to convince the public that the Christmas shopping season began as early as Thanksgiving and to draw shoppers into their store. Macy's thought the gimmick was a good one and followed suit.

The first parade featured Macy's employees dressed in costumes, animals on loan from the Central Park Zoo, and **Santa Claus**, who unveiled Macy's **store window displays** as the finale of the parade. The parade was a hit with New Yorkers and a great boost for the store. In fact, Macy's estimated that the parade contributed to bringing 5,000 children per day to visit the Santa who held court at the store. A few years after the parade's installation, however, devout citizens began to complain that the popular event drew people away from morning church services held in honor of the day. The complaint led Macy's to change the parade from the morning to the afternoon hours. Several years later, however, Macy's reinstated the morning parade. Parade administrators didn't want their event to conflict with the increasingly popular afternoon football games that were beginning to draw even bigger audiences than the church services.

## Balloons

The first few parades did not include the gigantic balloons that characterized the event in later years. These first appeared in 1927 and were the invention of Tony Sarg, an expert puppeteer and designer that Macy's hired to help jazz up their show. Sarg got rid of the wild zoo animals because they frightened away the little children, and replaced them with papier mâché creatures. Finding inspiration in the dirigible and zeppelin—the helium-inflated flying airships of the era—and drawing on his experience as a puppeteer, he designed a number of huge airborne balloons shaped like a dragon, a toy soldier, an elephant, and a cartoon character named Felix the Cat. Sarg viewed his creations as enormous, upside-down marionettes, manipulated by ropes from below rather than by strings from above. He called them "balloonatics."

Making the balloonatics required the help of expert manufacturers. Sarg sent his designs to the Goodyear Tire & Rubber Company in Akron, Ohio. Goodyear executed the designs in rubber and fabric and sealed them with airship cement.

In the early years, the public not only loved the sight of the tethered giants careening down broad city streets, but also thrilled to the sport of hunting them down afterwards. At the end of the parade the balloon wranglers simply let the big behemoths go, knowing that they would eventually deflate and sink to earth. Macy's gave a cash reward to anyone who found and returned the deflated balloons. In 1931, world-class pilot Clarence Chamberlin caught sight of the unleashed Jerry the Pig balloon bobbing over Brooklyn's Prospect Park on Thanksgiving Day. He roped the balloon and towed it back to the ground, winning not only Macy's cash reward but also a good deal of publicity. Nevertheless, the policy of releasing the balloons with cash rewards for their return caused unexpected problems. Some people shot the balloons down, damaging them for future use. The most alarming incident occurred in 1932, however, when a student pilot and her instructor nearly collided with a giant cat balloon that had ascended to 5,000 feet. After that, Macy's quietly deflated the balloons at the end of the parade route.

The big balloons have continued to cause problems over the years. A Santa Claus balloon exploded during inflation in 1941. High winds took out all but one balloon during the 1956 parade. A helium shortage in 1958 meant that the balloons had to be filled with air and then suspended from cranes for the duration of the parade. In 1971 strong winds led to the cancellation of the parade balloons. Nevertheless, the big balloons are the most noted feature of the parade. Since the big balloons are capable of lifting over 600 pounds, wranglers must work the giant, inflatable puppets in groups at all times. Each wrangler must weigh at least 125 pounds.

## World War II

The Thanksgiving Parade was cancelled in 1942, 1943, and 1944 due to World War II. In 1942, Macy's surrendered its balloons to wartime officials in response to the government's call for citizens to donate rubber to the military. Making a spectacle out of the event, parade officials inflated one of the balloons—a giant green dragon—and escorted it to city hall. When they arrived, Mayor Fiorello La Guardia, also head of the Office of Civilian Defense, took a long knife and "slew" the beast. By handing over its balloons, Macy's contributed 650 pounds of rubber to the war effort.

## National Popularity

The parade resumed in 1945, drawing a crowd of two million observers. It was first televised locally in 1946. In 1947 television coverage went nationwide, expanding the parade's potential viewing audience from coast to coast. The 1947 Christmas film *Miracle on 34th Street* generated further publicity for the event by setting the opening scenes of the story at the Macy's Thanksgiving Day parade. By the 1950s the opportunity to ride in the parade drew well-known celebrities. In 1957, the first high school marching band participated. The marching bands, as well as other groups of young entertainers, would become a regular feature of the parade, with hopeful candidates auditioning yearly before Macy's judges. In 1969, the first floats entered the parade. The 1970s saw the first falloons—part float, part balloon—enter the parade.

## Commercial Effects and Influences

From its modest beginnings, the parade has grown to become big business for the Big Apple. Each year, the parade generates millions of dollars of economic activity in New York City. In particular, hotels and businesses located along the parade route get a boost from the influx of tourists and local New Yorkers who come to see the parade in person. The economic effects of the parade are also felt far away from the city. About 60 million people watch the parade each year, either in person or on television. This enormous audience, glued to television sets right at the start of the Christmas shopping season, creates plenty of opportunity for what some have termed holiday commercialism. Companies typically pay hundreds of thousands of dollars to place a balloon in the parade or to sponsor one of the parade floats. A large number of the characters represented by the Macy's parade balloons are licensed images. In recent years, some of these "commercial" balloons have included Buzz Lightyear (sponsored by Disney-Pixar), Kermit the Frog (sponsored by Disney), Kung Fu Panda and Shrek (sponsored by Dreamworks Animation), Spider Man (sponsored by Marvel Entertainment), and Snoopy the Flying Ace (sponsored by Peanuts Worldwide). Recent non-commercial novelty balloons have included elves, candy canes, snowflakes, stars, and Chloe the Holiday Clown.

## Where and When

The parade normally begins at 9:00 a.m. on Thanksgiving Day. The parade route changes each year, usually ending around noon at the Macy's store in Herald Square. Located at 34th Street and Sixth Avenue, this store is Macy's flagship branch and bills itself as the largest department store in the world. Just as he did in the early days, Santa Claus still brings up the rear of the parade. Promoters bill his arrival at Herald Square as the official start of the holiday season in New York.

# Magi

## Three Kings, Three Kings of Cologne, Wise Men of the East

Christian lore and tradition assigns several different titles to the Magi, sages from the East who traveled to **Bethlehem** to pay tribute to the baby **Jesus**. They are referred to as the Wise Men of the East, the Three Wise Men, the Three Kings, the Three Kings of Cologne, or by the names most commonly associated with them in legend—Melchior, Caspar (or Gaspar), and Balthasar. Their association with Christmas begins in Christian scripture. Of the two **Gospel accounts of Christmas** recorded in the Bible, the **Gospel according to Matthew** is the only one to mention the Magi and their pilgrimage. However, this brief account of their actions neither reveals their identities nor elaborates on the source of their prophetic knowledge. Over time, tangled vines of legend have grown up around the slender trunk of Matthew's account, creating a rich heritage of story, custom, and celebration around these mysterious witnesses of the first Christmas.

### The Magi in Matthew's Gospel

In chapter two of the Gospel according to Matthew, Magi from the East, led by a star, journey to Jerusalem. They arrive at the court of King **Herod** asking for the whereabouts of the newborn king of the Jews. Herod, secretly troubled by news of a potential rival, consults Jewish priests and scribes. He discovers that prophecy dictates that the Messiah will be born in Bethlehem. Herod relays this information to the Magi, asking them to return with news of the child's identity. The Magi then continue on their journey, again guided by the star. They find Jesus in Bethlehem, worship him, and offer him costly **gifts: gold, frankincense**, and **myrrh**. A dream warns the Magi not to return to Herod, who is planning to kill the child they identify as the king of the Jews, and they set off for their own countries by another route.

### The Magi in History

Although the Gospels give no further information about these prophets from the East, scholars of ancient history can tell us something about the people known in biblical times as magi. The word "magi" comes from the ancient Greek term *magoi*,

plural of *magos*, and from the Old Persian word *magu*. Both terms referred specifically to a class of scholar-priests originally from the ancient land of Media (Medes), now part of Iran. In biblical times, magi could be found throughout Persia and in many other Near Eastern countries.

The magi were famed for their knowledge of astronomy, astrology, dream interpretation, philosophy, and religious ritual, hence the translation often given for the term magi is "wise men." They often served as councillors to kings and as tutors to princes. Their teachings were studied and recorded by some of the most renowned thinkers of ancient Greece, including Plato, Aristotle, Pythagoras, and Herodotus. The magi were also associated with what we today would call magical or occult practices, such as divination. Indeed, the English word "magic" comes to us from the ancient word "magi." Because of the magi's strong association with magic, the term magi was sometimes used more loosely and negatively by ancient Greek and biblical writers to refer to anyone who claimed occult knowledge from Eastern lands.

When Media was conquered by Persia in the sixth century B.C., the magi adopted many of the ideas of Persian Zoroastrianism, an ancient religion. They became important proponents and developers of Zoroastrian ideas, spreading their influence beyond Persia. One of these beliefs corresponds well with their role in the Christmas story. Like the ancient Jews, Zoroastrians believed in the coming of a savior, a *saoshyant*. Zoroaster had been the first saoshyant. The last of the three saoshyants, who would be born to a virgin mother, was to be the greatest. He would have the power to defeat the forces of evil, resurrect the dead, banish old age and decay from the world, and would usher in a new age for humanity.

### Early Christian Interpretations

This historical background helps to explain the presence of magi in Matthew's account of Jesus' birth. As believers in the coming of a saoshyant, they would be expecting the birth of a savior. Since they were skilled in divination practices, they might be keenly interested in predicting this event. As astrologers, they might expect that the prophet's birth would correspond with a heavenly event, such as the rising of an unusual star. As astronomers, they would know and watch the night sky and notice immediately any such event. As scholars and religious experts, they might be interested in making the journey to Judea to discover the identity of the child and to worship him. Finally, as experts in the study of dreams, they would understand the dream imagery warning them of Herod's evil intent. Because of the intellectual and occult prestige of the magi in the ancient world, readers of Matthew's account would be likely to interpret their recognition of Jesus' birth as confirmation of his identity as the Messiah.

Although we do know something of the activities and beliefs of magi in ancient times, we know literally nothing about the individuals who appear in Matthew's account. He states that the Magi journeyed to Bethlehem from the East, but he does not mention their names, their nationalities, or their exact number. They could have been from any number of countries, such as Arabia, Persia (or Iran), Mesopotamia, or even India. The lack of detail given in the scriptures led to speculation about the Magi by religious figures, as well as much embellishment of the story in folk tradition. Early Christian artwork depicts two, three, four, or more Magi. Eastern Christians believed that there were twelve Magi. By the sixth century A.D., the idea that there had been three Magi became firmly established among Western Christians. This belief was probably based on the three gifts mentioned in the scriptures, which became associated in folk tradition with three individuals.

By the end of the second century A.D., Christians began to celebrate a special holiday, called **Epiphany**, in honor of the Magi's pilgrimage. The word "epiphany" means "manifestation," "appearance," or "showing forth." The feast of Epiphany thus celebrates the first manifestation of Jesus' divinity, as witnessed by the Magi. Epiphany predates Christmas by well over a century, illustrating its importance to early Christians.

### Folk Beliefs and Legends

By the early Middle Ages, folk and Church tradition had converted the enigmatic wise men of Matthew's Gospel into three kings. Some scholars attribute this transformation to the influence of prophetic writings in the Old Testament (Psalms 72; Isaiah 60:3-6) linking the future conversion of the gentiles with the homage of foreign kings and gifts of gold and frankincense.

The most widespread Western legend about the Magi assigns them the following identities: Melchior, king of Arabia; Caspar (or Gaspar), king of Tarsus (located in southern Turkey); and Balthasar, king of Ethiopia or king of Saba (in modern-day Yemen). Not only did legend assign them names and nationalities, but they were also assigned various characteristics. Melchior is most often described as an elderly, light-complexioned man with white hair and beard who bears the gift of gold. Caspar, a young and beardless man of "ruddy" complexion, offers frankincense. Balthasar, a middle-aged African man, brings the infant Jesus a gift of myrrh. (Sometimes the ages of Balthasar and Caspar are switched).

Once these identities became firmly established in the folk imagination, they, too, began to excite speculation. St. Bede suspected that the diverse kings represented the continents of Europe, Africa, and Asia. Others believed that the ethnic and racial diversity of the three kings represented the belief that Jesus' teachings were to spread to all nations. The gifts of the Magi also acquired symbolic meanings. The gold was said to represent Jesus' kingship, the frankincense his divinity, and the myrrh his early death or his ability to heal.

In addition to providing answers about the names, ages, and fates of the Magi, folk tales also speculated about their ancestry and origins. One legend affirms that they were descendants of Balaam, a Mesopotamian seer from the Old Testament, who some also called a magus. Balaam predicted that "a star out of Jacob" (Numbers 24:17) would foretell the birth of a great Jewish leader. The legend suggests that Balaam kept watch for the appearance of the star, passing the search to his sons, who in turn passed it on to their descendants. Another account, again credited to St. Bede, speculates that the Magi were descended from Noah's sons, Shem, Ham, and Japheth. Yet another tale declares that the kings of Persia and Chaldea sent the twelve wisest men of their courts to follow the star.

## Magi Tales from the East

In the late thirteenth century, Venetian explorer Marco Polo returned to Italy from his years of travel in central and east Asia. He brought with him many exciting, foreign tales, including some Eastern stories concerning the Magi. In one, Melchior, the eldest, first entered the shelter where Jesus lay. There he encountered an old man who spoke with the wisdom of many years. The middle-aged king went next, and found Jesus to be a learned man of his own age. When the youngest stepped over the threshold he discovered a young man full of passion and inspiration. After comparing and marveling over their varied experiences, the kings entered the shelter together bearing their gifts and found Jesus to be an infant.

Another tale of Eastern origins suggests that the Magi's gifts were meant to test the baby Jesus. If he chose the gold, he was a king; if he chose the incense he was a priest;

and if he chose myrrh he was a healer. The child took them all, and the Magi concluded that Jesus was all three things at once.

One more story states that the Magi received a small gift in return for their pilgrimage, some say from **Mary**, others say from the infant Jesus. When the Wise Men opened the box, they found only a stone inside. The stone was meant as a sign that their faith should be as firm as a rock. The Magi did not understand this, however, and, thinking the stone worthless, they tossed it down a well. As they did so, fire streamed down from heaven towards the well (or, some say, ascended from the well towards heaven). The amazed Wise Men transported the fire back to their own countries, where it was worshiped. This tale presents us with an interesting link back to Zoroastrianism. In the Zoroastrian religion, fire represents the divine. In Zoroastrian fire temples, flames are kept burning perpetually and are used in religious ceremonies and worship.

### The Fate of the Magi

Many legends suggest that, after returning to their own lands, the Magi devoted the rest of their lives to good works and to spreading the news of Christ's birth. One tale declares that they were baptized by St. Thomas the Apostle and later became Christian priests and bishops. Another suggests that the Star of Bethlehem appeared to them once more, shortly before their deaths. Some believed that they died in the city of Sewa, now in Iran. Marco Polo, who visited that city during his thirteenth-century travels, declared that the inhabitants showed him the tombs of the three ancient kings, called Melchior, Caspar, and Balthazar, who in their lifetimes had made a great journey to worship a newborn prophet.

### Relics

In the tenth century the citizens of Milan, Italy, turned to the well-known legends concerning the Three Kings to interpret an unusual discovery. The embalmed bodies of three men, one young, one middle-aged, and one old, had been found in the church of St. Eustorgius. These remains were quickly assumed to be those of the Three Kings. The emperor Frederick Barbarossa had the relics transferred to Cologne, Germany, in 1164, where a special shrine was built to house them in the city's cathedral. In this way, the Magi acquired yet a new name: the Three Kings of Cologne.

But how did the three Middle Eastern kings end up buried in Italy? It was believed that the Empress Helena (St. Helena, c. 248-c. 328) had originally retrieved the bodies from the East during her travels to the Holy Land. Legend had it that she brought the remains to Constantinople, and that later they were moved to the city of Milan. The bodies appeared not to have aged since the Magi's momentous meeting with

Jesus, but it was not difficult for people to believe that, in death, the bodies of the kings had been preserved as they had been during that holy encounter. The long tale of the Magi's bones took a final turn in 1903, when the Cardinal of Cologne approved the return of some of the relics to Milan.

## Enduring Popularity

The story of the Magi's quest has kindled the imaginations of Christians for centuries. The Magi's journey was one of the most popular images depicted by early Christians in the Roman catacombs. The Magi often appear as characters in medieval **Nativity plays**. A multitude of artists, including the famous painters Diego Velázquez, Sandro Botticelli, and Leonardo da Vinci, have created memorable images of the adoration of the Magi. Gian Carlo Menotti's twentieth-century opera, *Amahl and the Night Visitors,* revolves around a small boy's encounter with the Magi. The Magi are the central figures in such familiar **Christmas carols** as "We Three Kings of Orient Are." The initials of each of the three kings, CMB, are still inscribed over the doors of houses during the **Christmas season** in Germany, Austria, Poland, Lithuania, the Czech Republic, and Slovakia in order to protect the house. Roman Catholic priests sometimes bless the homes of their parishioners at Epiphany by writing the initials CMB inside the door with blessed chalk, surrounded by the numbers representing that calendar year. In the year 1999, for example, the priest would write 19 CMB 99. Finally, the Magi are often represented in the **Nativity scenes** that Christians all over the world assemble during the Christmas season.

## Significance

For close to two millennia, folk tales and legends have embroidered additional details around Matthew's spare outline of the Magi's pilgrimage to Bethlehem. For some, however, Matthew's original text is rich in spiritual significance. The Magi's journey may be said to represent the universal search for God. Some Christians see the Magi's story as a demonstration of an active faith; the Magi act on the inspiration and understanding that they have, while others, who presumably also see the star, do nothing. The story's assertion that the non-Jewish Magi are the first people inspired to worship Jesus is also believed to be significant by many Christian commentators. It symbolizes that seekers of all ethnic and religious backgrounds will be drawn to Jesus, that his message is to be offered to all peoples, and that his teachings will spread throughout the entire world.

# Martinmas

## Funkentag, Martinalia, Martinsfest, Martinstag, St. Martin's Day

Martinmas, or St. Martin's Day, falls on November 11. This Christian feast day honors St. Martin of Tours, but many of the popular customs that have been associated with it over the centuries resemble those connected to a much earlier pagan autumn festival. In medieval Europe, the arrival of Martinmas signaled the beginning of winter. In early medieval times, the festival marked the beginning of **Advent** in some parts of Europe.

### Life and Legends of St. Martin

Born into a pagan family in Hungary in the late fourth century A.D., St. Martin became interested in Christianity and a monastic life at an early age. His military father forced him to become a soldier, however. Many tales about the saint's life illustrate his generosity. In the most famous of these, Martin, while stationed as a soldier in Amiens, France, encountered a beggar shivering miserably in the cold. Martin quickly removed his cloak, cut it in half with his sword, and covered the beggar with the cloth. That night **Jesus** appeared to Martin in a vision, declaring, "Martin the catechumen hath clothed me in this garment." Shortly afterwards Martin was baptized. At the age of forty he left the army and began a life of religious devotion. He was elected bishop of Tours in 371 A.D.

One legend tells that when the retiring saint heard the news of his election, he was so flustered that he ran away and hid in a barn, but the squawking of a goose soon announced his presence. The goose thereafter became a symbol of the saint. As bishop of Tours, Martin gained a reputation for religious fervor by converting his entire diocese to the new religion of Christianity and replacing the pagan temples with Christian churches. St. Martin eventually became one of the most popular saints of the medieval era.

### Precedents

In pre-Christian times the Germanic peoples of north-central Europe celebrated a great autumn festival. As pastures thinned with the coming of cold weather, they

slaughtered the animals that could not be kept alive and preserved most of their meat for the winter. At this time the people gathered together, feasted on fresh meat, and drank. They may also have honored the dead and lit ceremonial bonfires at these celebrations. This festival probably marked the end of the old year and the beginning of the new year in pre-Christian times. According to several scholars, some of the customs associated with medieval **Yule** celebrations were actually transferred to that season from earlier celebrations of this great autumn festival. At least one researcher has identified the date of this ancient Germanic new year festival as November 11 or 12.

### History

The Christian festival of Martinmas developed in the several hundred years that followed the saint's death in the late fourth century. In 490 A.D. Bishop Perpetuus of Tours called for a forty-day period of partial fasting in preparation for Christmas. This period began on November 11, a day already associated with the veneration of St. Martin, and was known as the "Forty Days' Fast of St. Martin" or "St. Martin's Lent." In later times these weeks of spiritual preparation for Christmas came to be called Advent. Pope Martin I established Martinmas as a great

Church festival. He may have been attempting to provide a Christian rationale for the celebrations that pagan northern Europeans still held around this time of the year.

The customs associated with medieval celebrations of Martinmas closely resemble those connected with earlier pagan celebrations. In the Middle Ages the feast of Martinmas marked the beginning of winter. Customs in some regions suggest that it may have been treated as a kind of new year as well. In areas of England, France, and Germany, leases ended at Martinmas, rents were due, and servants left households in search of new employment. In his eighth-century chronicles, St. Bede noted that the Anglo-Saxon term for November was *Blot Monath*, or "Blood Month," in reference to the customary slaughtering of animals that took place during that month. Not only did this old custom attach itself firmly to Martinmas, but so also did the feasting and drinking of earlier November celebrations. In medieval times Martinmas may have served as a kind of thanksgiving festival during which the people rejoiced at the close of the harvest and their full barns and larders. In Germany, St. Martin became the patron saint of the harvest, as well as the champion of the poor.

The sixteenth-century Protestant Reformation created a new rationale for this traditional November festival. Rather than forbid the celebration of the day because it venerated a Roman Catholic saint, Protestant authorities dedicated the celebrations to Martin Luther, the German founder of the Protestant movement who was born on November 10, 1483. In some areas of Germany the celebrations were shifted to November 10; in others the people continued to celebrate on November 11 in the belief that the Protestant reformer was baptized on that day. In Germany the holiday acquired the name *Martinsfest* or *Martinstag*, meaning "Martin's Festival" or "Martin's Day."

### Martinmas Folklore

Long after pagan European religions disappeared, early November retained its association with the commemoration of the dead. Old Scottish and Irish folk beliefs declared that the ghosts of the dead returned to their old homes on Martinmas. In the twentieth century, the festivals of early November still link the season to the remembrance of the dead. On November 5, Guy Fawkes Day, the British commemorate the capture and execution of a group of men who tried to blow up the Houses of Parliament. In Britain and North America many celebrate October 31 as Halloween, a folk festival associated with spirits of the dead. Christians in many countries observe All Saints' Day on November 1 and All Souls' Day on November 2. Even the secular calendar retains November 11 as a date sacred to the memory of the dead. After World War I, November 11 was established as Armistice Day and dedicated to the memory of the soldiers who died in that war. (In Britain and Canada the day is known as Remembrance Day). In 1954 Armistice Day became Veterans Day in the United States, and its purpose was broadened to include the recognition of all those who have served in the United States armed forces.

In some European countries St. Martin became a gift-bearing folk figure, much like **St. Nicholas.** He was often depicted as a bishop garbed in red robes riding a white horse. In Belgium and other European countries he distributes sweets to well-behaved children on St. Martin's Eve, but badly behaved youngsters may receive a rod instead.

A variety of folk beliefs and sayings link Martinmas with the weather. In Europe the temperate days that often surround Martinmas may be referred to as "St. Martin's Summer." Legend has it that God first sent mild weather at this time of year to shield St. Martin from the cold, since he had just given half of his cloak to a beggar. An English folk belief suggests that if Martinmas is mild, the coming winter will be severe, whereas if frost occurs before Martinmas, the winter will be gentle.

## Martinmas Fires

In Germany and the Netherlands, great bonfires once roared on Martinmas or Martinmas Eve. In the fifteenth century, the festival acquired the nickname *Funkentag* (Spark Day) in Germany, due to the many fires that blazed in honor of the occasion. In the centuries that followed, people in Austria, Germany, Denmark, and Belgium also participated in lantern parades on Martinmas Eve, marching through the darkened streets of town with lanterns or jack-o'-lanterns fashioned out of turnips or pumpkins.

In the twentieth century Martinmas Eve fires still blazed along the banks of the Rhine and Moselle rivers in Germany. Although fire safety has become an issue in recent decades, the fires burn on in some parts of Germany. Excited children collect cardboard, tree branches, and other tinder for weeks in anticipation of the event. Lantern parades continue to be celebrated in Germany, although they have become primarily a children's custom. Children fashion elaborate lanterns from paper or recreate the traditional turnip lanterns. The finished lanterns dangle from a wooden pole. In some

areas the lantern processions end with a reenactment of St. Martin's most famous deed, sharing his cloak with a beggar. Afterwards the children disperse, singing songs (*Martinslieder*) and reciting rhymes for neighbors and shopkeepers. In return, they are given small gifts (*Martinswecken*), such as nuts, candies, apples, cookies, and coins.

## Martinmas Feasts

The central and enduring customs of Martinmas feature the preparation and consumption of meat and drink. The date at which the holiday falls in the agricultural cycle anchored these customs to it. In Britain the customary slaughter of cattle on Martinmas produced "Martlemas Beef," the salted and dried meat that sustained people throughout the lean winter months. In Germany, Denmark, Ireland, and Scandinavia, goose became the traditional Martinmas feast, perhaps in reference to the Christian legend connecting the saint with a goose. Another possible explanation for this association between Martinmas and geese arises from an old German agricultural custom; in past centuries people fattened geese for the fall season, when they could be used to pay the taxes due on Martinmas. Not every European country favored roast goose for their Martinmas feast, however. In Portugal the traditional St. Martin's Day feast featured roast pig.

According to old German and Italian traditions, the year's new wines were sampled for the first time on Martinmas. People who got drunk on Martinmas were often called "Martinmen," as were people given to spending their money on short-lived good times. Indeed, so important was this association between Martinmas and wine that St. Martin became the patron saint of tavernkeepers, wine makers, and drunkards. Indulging in large quantities of meat and drink persists as a perennial feature of the holiday. In France the upset stomach that often follows the consumption of too much food and drink is known as *mal de Saint Martin*, or "Saint Martin's sickness." St. Martin's Day is still observed in Europe with traditional festive meals, most commonly of roast goose.

# Mary, Blessed Virgin

Jesus was born to a human mother named Mary and a human father named Joseph. The Bible tells that Mary conceived the child by the power of God's Holy Spirit before the couple was married, however. For this reason she is known as the Virgin Mary, or the Blessed Virgin Mary. Although she is present at various events recorded in Christian scripture, Mary figures most prominently in the biblical passages describing the events surrounding Jesus' birth. In Roman Catholic and Orthodox Christianity, Mary is the most revered of all the saints, honored both as the mother of the Lord and for her own spiritual attributes: purity, faith, humility, love, steadfastness, and introspection. Artists have often pictured Mary in blue robes, as the color blue symbolizes truth, love, fidelity, and constancy in Christian art.

## The Annunciation

The **Gospel according to Luke** gives the most detailed portrait of Mary's miraculous pregnancy. In an event that later became known as the Annunciation, she receives a visit from **Gabriel,** an **angel** who greets her with the phrase "Hail, O favored one, the Lord is with you" (Luke 1:28). He then tells her that she is to bear a son, conceived by the Holy Spirit, whom she will name Jesus and who shall be acclaimed as "the Son of the Most High" (Luke 1:32). Generations of Christians have interpreted the angel's greeting, along with heaven's selection of Mary to be Jesus' mother, as signs of her great purity and virtue. She demonstrates her steadfast faith in God and her humility by assenting to the decree delivered by the angel, saying, "Behold, I am the handmaid of the Lord; let it be to me according to your word" (Luke 1:27).

## The Visitation

After receiving the angel's visit, Mary hurries to see her kinswoman Elizabeth, who is also pregnant with a son who will become the prophet called John the Baptist. During the meeting between the two women, often referred to as the Visitation, Elizabeth honors Mary as the mother of the Lord. Mary exults in the fulfillment of God's promise to bring both mercy and justice to those on earth in a long speech known as the Song of Mary, or the Magnificat (Luke 1:46-56). The title Magnificat, which means "it magnifies," comes from the first word of the Latin version of the hymn:

My soul magnifies the Lord,
And my spirit rejoices in God my Savior,
For he has regarded the low estate of his handmaiden.
For behold, henceforth all generations will call me blessed;
For he who is mighty has done great things for me,
And holy is his name.
And his mercy is on those who fear him
From generation to generation.
He has shown strength with his arm,
He has scattered the proud in the imagination of their hearts,
He has put down the mighty from their thrones,
And exalted those of low degree;
He has filled the hungry with good things,
And the rich he has sent empty away.
He has helped his servant Israel,
In remembrance of his mercy,
As he spoke to our fathers,
To Abraham and to his posterity for ever. [Luke 1:47-55]

Various branches of the Christian church have incorporated this beautiful hymn of praise into the liturgy of daily religious services. In addition, numerous composers have set it to music. Mary's hymn not only underscores her faith and humility, but also reveals her love of God, her gratitude for the gift God has made to her, and her joy at the prospect of seeing God come to the rescue of the needy and downtrodden.

## Jesus' Birth

In both the Gospel according to Luke and the **Gospel according to Matthew**, Mary and Joseph receive visitors around the time of Jesus' birth. Matthew's account implies that the Holy Family lived in **Bethlehem**. He tells of a mysterious star that guided a number of learned men from Eastern lands, the **Magi**, to the site of Jesus' birth in order to pay him homage.

By contrast, Luke's story has the couple journeying to Bethlehem in order to comply with a Roman census. Since the Bethlehem inn was full, the couple spent the night in a stable, where Mary gave birth to Jesus. **Shepherds** received notice of the holy birth from angels and came to Bethlehem to worship the newborn Son of God.

The shepherds explain to Mary and Joseph how they came to know of the child's birth, and Mary "kept all these things, pondering them in her heart" (Luke 2:19). Thus Luke's account also shows Mary to be a seeker of spiritual wisdom. Because of her faith and her heart's inclination to "ponder" God's ways, many Christians view Mary as a model of contemplation and the contemplative life.

### The Flight into Egypt and the Circumcision

The Gospel according to Luke and the Gospel according to Matthew also differ in their accounts of the events following Jesus' birth. Matthew fails to mention Mary's role in these events. Nevertheless, Luke's account gives us one more clue as to Mary's character. Matthew reports that King **Herod** ordered soldiers to kill all the male infants in Bethlehem so that he might rid himself of the child the Magi identified as the King of the Jews (*see* **Holy Innocents' Day**). The Holy Family escapes the slaughter because an angel warned Joseph about what was soon to occur. Following the angel's mandate, the family journeys to Egypt. This event, called the **Flight into Egypt**, is not reported in Luke's gospel. Luke instead says that eight days after his birth, Jesus' parents had him circumcised and gave him the name Jesus. These events illustrate Mary's obedience to Jewish law and her continuing cooperation with the divine plan announced to her by the angel Gabriel.

### Early Christian Ideas

Early Christian writers and teachers, such as Justin Martyr, Irenaeus, and Tertullian, compared Mary to Eve, the first woman, whose story is told in the Bible's Book of Genesis. Eve heard God's command and disobeyed, but Mary listened to the angel Gabriel and gave her assent to God's plan. Thus Mary was cast as a "second Eve," the woman who would bring a savior into the world to undo the damage done by Adam and Eve's disobedience. This comparison was heightened by the medieval calendar of Christian holy days, in which Adam and Eve were commemorated on December 24, and Jesus' birth on **December 25**.

Early Christian leaders sometimes disagreed on the nature of the role Mary played in the birth of the Savior and the degree of veneration that should be accorded to her. They resolved some of these issues in the year 431 at the Council of Ephesus. The Council declared that Mary was the Theotokos, or "God bearer," paving the way for greater devotion to be dedicated to her.

## Feast Days

Over the centuries many festivals evolved to pay tribute to the important events in Mary's life. The first festival scheduled in honor of Mary was called the Commemoration of St. Mary and dates back to the fifth century. Some researchers report that it was scheduled for the Sunday before Christmas; others believe that it was held on December 26 or even on January 1. It celebrated Mary's death, which was viewed as her birth into heaven. This observance eventually evolved into the Feast of the Assumption, and the date was changed to August 15.

Other Marian festivals still celebrated today commemorate events related to the Nativity. The **Feast of the Circumcision** (January 1), for example, honors the fact that Mary and Joseph complied with Jewish law by taking their son to be circumcised on the eighth day after his birth. In the Roman Catholic Church the day celebrates Mary's role as the mother of God. **Candlemas** (February 2) commemorates Mary's purification in the temple 40 days after Jesus' birth. The Annunciation (March 25) recalls the angel Gabriel's visit to the Virgin Mary and her acceptance of the mission with which God entrusted her.

Other important Marian festivals include the Birthday of the Blessed Virgin Mary (September 8) and a Roman Catholic observance called the Feast of the Immaculate Conception (December 8). In addition, many people celebrate Marian festivals particular to their community. Mexicans, for example, honor the Virgin of Guadalupe on December 12. All told, the major feasts dedicated to Mary, plus those feasts celebrated only in certain places or observed by certain monastic communities, numbered about 1,000 by the early twentieth century. This number reflects the love and respect accorded to the Blessed Virgin Mary by generations of Christians.

## New Views

In recent decades feminist theologians have begun to question some of the traditional doctrines concerning Mary. Some of these views are critical, suggesting, for example, that in upholding Mary as both virgin and mother, religious authorities have encouraged both women and men to view female sexuality as dirty and shameful. Others object to the emphasis placed on Mary's humility in her role as exemplary woman, noting that church officials have used this image of Mary to support the subordination of women in society. Nevertheless, for many people Mary models a deeply faithful Christian spirituality to be adopted by all those who follow the teachings of Jesus, both men and women.

# Medieval Era, Christmas in

In the medieval era, people celebrated Christmas without **Santa Claus, Christmas trees**, and Christmas morning **gift** exchanges. Not only would we fail to spot these familiar elements of contemporary Christmas celebrations if transported back in time, but we would also witness a number of extinct Christmas customs now strange to us. Nevertheless, the **Christmas season** and a few of its enduring customs first took shape during this era.

## Christmas Season

In the fourth century Church authorities chose **December 25** as the date on which Christians would celebrate the Nativity. They placed Christmas near two important Roman feasts, **Saturnalia** (December 17 to 23) and **Kalends** (January 1 to 5). Moreover, they scheduled it on the same day as the **Birth of the Invincible Sun**, a festival dedicated to the sun god. This meant that the major Christian feasts of Christmas and **Epiphany** (January 6) opened and closed a thirteen-day period during which many recent converts were already accustomed to celebrate.

Eventually, the Church decided to accept this inclination to celebrate a midwinter festival rather than fight it. In 567 the Council of Tours declared the days that fall between Christmas and Epiphany to be a festal tide. This decision expanded Christmas into a Church season stretching from December 25 to January 5. This Church season became known as "Christmastide," but ordinary folk called it the **Twelve Days of Christmas**.

As Christianity became more firmly rooted in Europe, political leaders declared the Twelve Days to be legal holidays. Near the end of the ninth century King Alfred the Great of England mandated that his subjects observe the Twelve Days of Christmas, outlawing all legal proceedings, work, and fighting during that time. The Norwegian King Haakon the Good established the Christian observance of the festival in Norway in the middle of the tenth century.

## Entertainments

Medieval Europeans celebrated throughout the Twelve Days of Christmas. They might attend religious services or watch mystery plays that retold biblical stories pertinent to the season (*see* **Feast of the Ass; Nativity Plays**). In addition, the well-to-do made music, played games, danced, told stories, hunted, jousted, and feasted. In late medieval times the elite of some European countries began to celebrate the season with roving, costumed events known as masques. In a more homemade version of this custom, ordinary folk dressed as mummers (*see* **Mumming**) or received a band of mummers into their home or tavern. In England, peasants who worked on large estates rested from their customary chores during the Twelve Days. Moreover, they partook of a communal feast provided to them by the lord of the estate, offering him in return a gift of farm produce. Christmas festivities in England ended on Plough Monday, when farm laborers went back to work.

## Christmas Feasts in Medieval Europe

In the late Middle Ages, the typical English Christmas dinner probably included roast meat, chicken, or wild fowl, white bread (a medieval luxury), and ale or cider. The rich, of course, fared somewhat better. When the Bishop of Hereford hosted a Christmas feast for his household and 41 guests in the year 1289, his kitchens sizzled with a wide variety of roasted meats. The bishop's hard-working chefs butchered and cooked two oxen, four pigs, four deer, two calves, sixty fowls, eight partridges, and two geese. In addition, they brewed beer, baked bread, and prepared cheese for all. The assembled company washed down their meal with forty gallons of red wine and four gallons of white wine, as well as an "unscored" amount of beer.

A wide variety of what we might consider unusual fowl could appear on a medieval Christmas menu, such as swans and peacocks. The chefs of the well-to-do strove to present these beautiful birds in artful ways. For example, they might decorate the roasted carcass, often enclosed in pastry, with the bird's plucked feathers and place a lighted wick in the bird's beak. In addition to peacock and swan, medieval diners also relished heron, crane, bittern, plover, snipe, and woodcock. Chefs searching for a make-ahead dish that would resist spoilage often created large fruit, meat, and butter pies for the Christmas table. These pies later evolved into the dish we know as **mincemeat pie**.

The wealthy and noble often served wild boar for Christmas, commanding their pages to bring the roasted boar's head to the table with great ceremony. Indeed, boar's flesh

(known as "brawn"), as well as pork, were favorite Christmas meats. The English often accompanied these roasted meats with Christmas ale and wassail. Lastly, like their counterparts in the rest of Europe, medieval Britons celebrated throughout the Twelve Days of Christmas. The largest and most festive meal was often served on **Twelfth Night**, or on Epiphany.

The French also celebrated the Christmas season with lavish feasts and openhanded hospitality. Castle doors were thrown open and wayfarers welcomed to feast at the lord and lady's table. When poor folk appeared at the door they were given food and, sometimes, clothing as well. Like their English counterparts, cooks in French castles served swan, peacock, and, occasionally, even stork to their guests. These guests might number into the hundreds. After they had sated their appetites, the guests could relax and enjoy entertainments provided by storytellers, jugglers, dancers, magicians, or traveling musicians.

## Famous English Christmas Feasts

In the Middle Ages, English monarchs sometimes threw Christmas feasts of legendary proportions. Often these feasts doubled as affairs of state, with the king hosting foreign dignitaries, local nobility, visiting knights, and other important guests. The assembled company might easily number well into the hundreds; some records declare the thousands. Moreover, this legion of hungry guests might stay for some or all of the Twelve Days of Christmas.

Knowing the scale of these dinner parties helps to put some of the royal menus in perspective. For example, in 1213 King John of England provided his guests with one of the largest and most sumptuous Christmas banquets on record. The shopping list for this gargantuan feast included 200 pigs, 1,000 hens, 15,000 herrings, 10,000 salt eels, scores of pheasants, partridges, and other birds, 27 hogsheads of wine, 100 pounds of almonds, 50 pounds of pepper, and 2 pounds of saffron, as well as other spices. At some point in the preparations, the cooks feared they were running short and sent for an additional 2,000 hens and 200 head of pork. King Henry III is reported to have entertained 1,000 noblemen and knights at York one Christmas. His cooks slaughtered 600 oxen for the feasts, and accompanied the resulting roast beef with salmon pie, roast peacock, and wine.

Needless to say, with such long guest lists, royal cooks could prepare quite a wide variety of dishes for the Christmas feast. Although most of the surviving menus seem to focus on roast meat and fowl, King Henry V treated his court one year to a diverse Christmas banquet featuring a wide variety of seafood in addition to the traditional brawn and mustard. The assembled company sampled herbed pike, powdered lamprey, salmon, bream, roach, conger, halibut, crayfish, sturgeon, lobster, whelks, porpoise, carp, tench, perch, turbot, and more. Altogether the king's cooks prepared over forty species of fish. Afterwards the royal chefs presented the king's guests with a dessert of marchpane (a forerunner of marzipan).

## Adapting Pagan Customs

Many researchers believe that medieval Christmas celebrations absorbed a number of pre-existing pagan customs. Church policy itself may have had something to do with this. In the early Middle Ages missionaries found many recent converts unwilling to give up elements of their former celebrations. In the year 601 Pope Gregory the Great wrote a letter to St. Augustine, missionary to Britain, advising him on how to deal with this problem. The letter reveals that missionaries were often encouraged to suggest a Christian significance to old pagan customs, rather than try to abolish them. According to Pope Gregory:

> Because they [the Anglo-Saxons] are wont to slay many oxen in sacrifices to demons, some solemnity should be put in the place of this, so that on the day of the dedication of the churches, or the nativities of the holy martyrs whose relics are placed there, they may make for themselves tabernacles of branches of trees around those churches which have been changed from heathen temples, and may celebrate the solemnity with religious feasting. Nor let them now sacrifice animals to the Devil, but to the praise of God kill animals for their own eating, and render thanks to the Giver of all for their abundance; so that while some outward joys are retained for them, they may more readily respond to inward joys. For from obdurate minds it is undoubtedly impossible to cut off everything at once, because he who strives to ascend to the highest place rises by degrees or steps and not by leaps. [Miles, 1990, 179]

Indeed, the ancient custom of decking homes with **greenery** may have infiltrated medieval Christmas celebrations in just this manner. According to some writers, the roots of this custom lie in the Roman practice of celebrating their midwinter festivals by decorating homes and temples with greenery. Moreover, the Romans celebrated Saturnalia by electing a mock king to preside over the customary feasts. Many mock kings sprouted up during the medieval Christmas season, perhaps as echoes of this ancient custom. They included the Bishop of Fools, who presided over the **Feast of Fools**, the **King of the Bean**, the **Lord of Misrule**, and the **boy bishop**. The old pagan beliefs of the north may also have contributed a few items to medieval Christmas lore. Some writers suspect that **Berchta**, the female spirit that haunted the Twelve Days of Christmas in German-speaking lands, may have evolved from an old Germanic goddess. They attribute the same origin to the band of spirits known as the **Wild Hunt**. Finally, medieval Germans honored Christmas by burning a **Yule log**, another custom that may date back to ancient times.

### Creating Christian Customs

On the other hand, a good number of medieval Christmas customs grew out of Church practices or Christian folklore and legends. For example, the customs and festivities associated with the many saints' days scattered throughout the Christmas season blossomed during the Middle Ages. So did the observance of **Advent**, Epiphany, the **Feast of the Circumcision**, and **Midnight Mass**. Nativity plays, the **Nativity scene**, and **Christmas carols** also became popular during this era. The **paradise tree**, a possible forerunner of the Christmas tree, accompanied one of these medieval Nativity plays.

### Surviving Medieval Customs

Many of these medieval customs and observances have now faded away. Nevertheless, we still celebrate Christmas by feasting, resting, decking our homes and churches with greenery, and partaking in popular forms of entertainment. Christmas carols remain with us, as do Nativity plays, although we know them today as Christmas pageants or as the Hispanic folk dramas of Las **Posadas** and Los **Pastores**.

# Merry Christmas

In contemporary English the word "merry" means "jolly," "cheerful," "lively," or "happy." Few people realize, however, that it once meant something slightly different. At the time the English coined the phrase "Merry Christmas," merry meant "pleasant," "delightful," or "joyful." When used to describe a holiday, the word "merry" signaled that it was a time of festivity or rejoicing. In greeting one another with the phrase "Merry Christmas," the English were wishing each other a festive and joyful holiday.

Here's how to say "Merry Christmas" in languages from around the world.

| | |
|---|---|
| Afrikaans | Geseknde Kersfees |
| Albanian | gëzuar Krishtlindja |
| Alsauldatian | gleckika Wïanachta |
| Arabic | miilaad majiid |
| Armenian | Shnorhavor Surb tsnund |
| Belarusian | Z Bozym naradzenniem |
| Bohemian | Vesele Vanoce |
| Bosnian | sretan Božić |
| Brazilian Portuguese | Boas Festas |
| Bulgarian | Vesela Koleda |
| Burmese | Christmas nay hma mue pyaw pa |
| Catalan | Bon Nadal |
| Chinese (Cantonese) | Sin Dan Fae Lok |
| Chinese (Mandarin) | shèng dàn kuài lè |
| Croatian | sretan Božić |
| Czech | Stastne a Vesele Vanoce |
| Danish | Glaedig Jul |
| Dutch | Vrolik Kerstfeest |
| Esperanto | Felican Kirstnaskon |
| Estonian | Rõõmusaid Jõulupuhi |
| Faeroese | Gledhilig Jol |
| Finnish | Hyvaa Joulua |
| Flemish | Zalig Kerstfeest |
| French | Joyeux Nöel |
| Gaelic (Irish) | Nollaig Shona |
| Gaelic (Scots) | Nollaig Chridheil |
| Georgian | Gilotsavt Shobas |
| German | Fröhliche Weihnachten |
| Greek | Kala Christougenna |
| Hawaiian | Mele Kalikimaka |
| Hebrew | Hag ha-Molad Sameah |
| Hindi | Krismas ki subhkamna |

| | |
|---|---|
| Hungarian | Boldog Karácsonyi |
| Icelandic | Gledhileg Jol |
| Indonesian | Selemat Hari Natal |
| Inupik (Eskimo) | Jutdlime Pivdluarit |
| Italian | Buon Natale |
| Japanese | Meri Kurisumasu |
| Javanese | sugeng Natal |
| Korean | Sungtanul Chukaheyo |
| Kurdish | Noela we pîroz be |
| Lao | souksan van Christmas |
| Latin | Natale Hilare |
| Latvian | Priecigus Ziemsvetkus |
| Lithuanian | Linksmu kaledugnenna |
| Macedonian | srećen Božić |
| Norwegian | God Jul |
| Pennsylvania German | Frehlicher Grischtdaag |
| Persian | Krismas-e Shoma Mubarak |
| Polish | Wesolych Swiat |
| Portuguese | Feliz Natal |
| Romanian | Craciun Fericit |
| Russian | Vesëlogo Rozhdestva |
| Serbian | Hristos se Rodi |
| Slovak | Vesele Vianoce |
| Slovenian | Vesele Bozicne |
| Spanish | Feliz Navidad |
| Swedish | God Jul |
| Tagalog | Maligayang Paskó |
| Tahitian | 'ia 'oa'oa e teie Noera |
| Thai | Suk san wan Christmas |
| Turkish | Neseli Noel |
| Ukranian | Srozhdestvom Kristovym |
| Vietnamese | Chuc Mung Giang Sinh |
| Welsh | Nadolig llawen |
| Yiddish | Fraylekhn Krimes |
| Yoruba | E Ku Odun |
| Zulu | UKhisimusi omuhle |

# *Messiah*

*Messiah* by George Frideric Handel is perhaps the most popular piece of classical music associated with the Christmas season. Two common misconceptions have spread along with its fame. Although many call the work *"The Messiah,"* Handel named his oratorio simply *"Messiah."* These days most performances of the piece take place around Christmas. Nevertheless, Handel never intended Messiah to be connected with the Christmas season. In fact, he wrote the oratorio in the late summer of 1741 and premiered it around Easter of the following year. Subsequent performances during Handel's lifetime also took place around Easter.

### Composition of Messiah

Although he composed the music for *Messiah,* Handel did not select the biblical texts that make up the libretto. His friend Charles Jennens compiled a collection of biblical verses outlining the birth and death of Jesus and the redemption of humankind. Jennens's compilation delighted and inspired Handel. He sat down to write the music for these texts on August 22, 1741. Composing with lightning speed, he completed the oratorio about three weeks later, on September 14. Some say that Handel once remarked about the work's creation, "I did think I did see all Heaven before me, and the great God himself." The approximately two and one-half hours of music is divided into three parts, often referred to as the "Nativity," "Passion," and "Redemption" sections because of the themes developed in each.

Handel scored *Messiah* as an oratorio. An oratorio is a long choral work made up of arias, duets, trios, and choruses. Oratorios attempt to tell a story, usually a religious one. The music must convey all, since no dialogue, scenery, or costumes are used. Some experts believe that oratorios evolved out of the medieval mystery plays (*see also* **Nativity Plays**). Indeed, early oratorios included dance and dramatic representations, as well as church hymns, and were usually performed in churches. Handel's *Messiah* differed significantly from the first oratorios written in the early 1600s. *Messiah* consists of nothing other than music, beautiful and sometimes difficult music. Handel often employed opera singers to perform the challenging solo parts of his oratorios and staged the performances in theaters rather than churches.

## *First Performance of* Messiah

Although the German-born Handel was living and working in London at the time he composed *Messiah,* the first public performance of the oratorio took place in Dublin, Ireland. Handel brought several principal singers over from England, including noted operatic soprano Signora Avoglio and singer-actress Susannah Cibber, who sang the alto parts. He engaged Dublin musicians to present the other solo parts. The choir consisted of singers from both Dublin cathedrals, although the premiere performance took place in a music hall on Fishamble Street. The cantankerous dean of St. Patrick's Cathedral, who was none other than Jonathan Swift, the author of *Gulliver's Travels*, at first refused to permit his choristers to participate in an event held in such a secular setting. Luckily for the audience, and for the history of music, he eventually relented.

In order to increase the number of people who would fit in the available seating, newspaper advertisements kindly requested that ladies who planned to attend refrain from wearing hoops under their skirts. Gentlemen were asked to leave their swords at home.

Handel's *Messiah* premiered on April 13, 1742, and was warmly received. Cibber's rendition of "He Was Despised" so moved one member of the audience, Dr. Patrick Delaney, a friend of Jonathan Swift's, that he cried out, "Woman, for this thy sins be forgiven thee!" Delaney may have had some very specific sins in mind, since rumors concerning Susannah Cibber's amorous affairs had made her the talk of London. In the days that followed, several Dublin newspapers printed the following review:

> On Tuesday last Mr. Handel's Sacred Grand Oratorio, the *Messiah,* was performed in the New Musick Hall in Fishamble-street; the best Judges allowed it to be the most finished piece of Musick. Words are wanting to express the exquisite Delight it afforded to the admiring crowded Audience. The Sublime, the Grand, and the Tender, adapted to the most elevated, majestick and moving Words, conspired to transport and charm the ravished Heart and Ear.

The review also praised Handel for donating the proceeds from this performance to three Dublin charities.

### *Later Performances of* Messiah

Encouraged by Dublin's warm reception, Handel returned home to London and arranged for performances to take place in that city. London rewarded his best efforts with rejection. Church officials objected to staging a work on a sacred theme in the profane space of a public theater. In spite of these objections, Covent Garden Theater hosted the first London performance of *Messiah* on March 23, 1743. The audience and the critics responded with indifference. In addition, Handel's friend Jennens, who had supplied the libretto for *Messiah*, faulted the composer in a letter to a friend. With blind conceit, Jennens wrote, "His *Messiah* has disappointed me, being set in great hast, tho' he said he would be a year about it, & make it the best of all his Compositions. I shall put no more Sacred Works into his hands thus to be abused" (Jacobi, 1982, 41-42).

Apparently, King George II attended one of the early performances of *Messiah*. Some writers believe this occasion gave birth to the tradition whereby the audience stands during the "Hallelujah" chorus. (Others believe that King George III started this tradition). In any case, one of these kings rose from his seat at this point in the piece. Whether he was reacting to the exuberance of the music or simply attempting to stretch his legs cannot now be determined. In those days etiquette demanded that no one remain seated when the king stood up. As a result, the entire audience rose to its feet, creating a tradition still observed today.

During the decade of the 1740s, Handel aired *Messiah* only a few more times. The work teetered on the edge of obscurity until 1750, when Handel began to perform it in a series of annual concerts to benefit charity. Over the next nine years the work achieved widespread popularity.

## Handel's Death

On April 6, 1759, two days before Palm Sunday, Handel conducted what was to be the last performance of his life, a presentation of *Messiah* at Covent Garden. He collapsed upon leaving the theater and had to be carried home. In the days that followed, Handel passed in and out of consciousness. The elderly composer recognized the seriousness of his condition. In one of his clear moments he expressed his wish to die on Good Friday, as did Jesus, "in the hope of rejoining the good God, my sweet Lord and Savior, on the day of his Resurrection." On Good Friday, April 13, 1759, seventeen years to the day from the premiere performance of *Messiah* in Dublin, Handel lay dying at his home in London. He passed away quietly sometime between that evening and the following morning.

A few days before his death, Handel requested that he be buried in Westminster Abbey and set aside money to pay for his funeral monument. The artist who created the monument depicted the composer at work on one of the arias from Messiah. Visitors to Westminster Abbey may note that the monument dedicated to the composer's memory misspells the word "messiah."

## Handel's Personality and Legacy

Although later generations attributed a kind of milquetoast piety to the famed composer of *Messiah,* Handel's friends and contemporaries described him as a somewhat gruff yet amiable man. He rejoiced in the consumption of large quantities of food and drink, earning himself a reputation for gluttony. Stubborn, arrogant, and irritable when it came to the correct interpretation of music, he acquainted many musicians with the rough edge of his tongue. He could, and often did, swear fluently in four languages. On the other hand, Handel possessed an excellent sense of humor combined with a flair for telling funny stories. He won a reputation for honesty in financial dealings, so much so that musicians accepted his occasional IOUs without a qualm. Finally, friends, family, musicians in his employ, and charities all benefited from his generosity.

Although *Messiah* stands as perhaps the composer's best-known work, Handel himself did not count it as his greatest achievement. He judged the chorus "He Saw the Lovely Youth" from his oratorio *Theodora* to be far superior to the "Hallelujah" chorus from *Messiah*. Neither proud nor self-effacing, Handel evaluated his own accomplishments fairly and was capable on occasion of belittling some of his less-distinguished pieces of music. Later composers paid tribute to his brilliance. Ludwig von Beethoven once exclaimed "He was the greatest composer that ever lived. I would uncover my head and kneel before his tomb." Franz Joseph Haydn, after hearing *Messiah* for the first time, reportedly exclaimed of Handel, "He was the master of us all."

# Midnight Mass

The Roman Catholic Church honors Christmas with three separate masses, each with its own distinctive liturgy. The first of these masses takes place in the middle of the night on Christmas Eve and is called Midnight Mass. In Spanish-speaking countries, Midnight Mass is known as the Misa de Gallo, or the rooster's mass.

The first Christmas masses were celebrated at St. Peter's Basilica in Rome on Christmas morning. In the fifth century Roman officials added another mass to be celebrated in the middle of the night. Rules in effect from about 400 to 1200 A.D. prescribed that this mass be held ad galli cantum; that is, when the rooster crows. Roosters begin to crow at about three in the morning. Eventually, however, the scheduling of the mass shifted to midnight. Perhaps the popular belief that Jesus was born at midnight influenced this shift. A fourth-century Latin hymn expresses this belief:

When the midnight, dark and still,
Wrapped in silence vale and hill:
God the Son, through Virgin's birth,
Following the Father's will,
Started life as Man on earth. [Weiser, 1990, 52]

In the fifth century a third mass, held at daybreak, was added to the first two. Each of the three masses, however, emphasized a different aspect of the Nativity. The first mass at midnight celebrated the mystery of the relationship between the Father and the Son, the second rejoiced at the birth of the Son on earth, and the third commemorated the birth of the Son in human hearts. Folk tradition translated these three themes into descriptive names for each of the masses. Thus, the Midnight Mass was known as the "Angels Mass," the dawn mass became the "Shepherds Mass," and the morning mass was called the "Mass of the Divine Word."

Until the eleventh century, the pope alone held the privilege of conducting three masses in honor of Christmas. After that time, the custom spread throughout the Church. Today Roman Catholic churches and cathedrals throughout the world offer Midnight Mass on Christmas Eve. In addition, television stations in seventy nations transmit live broadcasts of the pope's Midnight Mass from St. Peter's Basilica in Rome.

# Mincemeat Pies

## Christmas Pie

The name "mincemeat" may puzzle many of those who have come across a meatless recipe for this dish in their cookbooks. Mincemeat pies are an old English Christmas favorite. The dish got its name from what used to be its main ingredient, minced meat. Over the centuries, however, meat gradually dropped out of many recipes. Today the dish gets most of its flavor from fresh and dried fruits, spices, and sugar.

### Medieval Christmas Cookery

In pre-industrial times people slaughtered the animals that were to provide them with their winter meats in late autumn. At this time of the year domesticated animals could no longer find enough to eat by grazing. Since most of the family's grain was needed for feeding human beings throughout the lean winter months, the animals that were not kept for breeding purposes were killed (*see also* **Martinmas**). In medieval times this meant that cooks could expect a large quantity of meat to prepare for the feasting that took place during the **Twelve Days of Christmas**.

Food preservation, however, challenged medieval cooks, since they did not have access to preservatives or reliable refrigeration. Instead, people employed sugars and spices to preserve meats and fish. Fresh and dried fruits were less expensive and easier to obtain than sugar or honey, so they were often used to flavor dishes. In England, medieval cooks prepared large fruit, meat, and butter pies for wealthy families entertaining many guests at Christmas. Some researchers believe that the sugary fruit helped to preserve the meat; others contend that its function was to cover the flavor of the aging meat. Enclosing the ingredients in a tough, airtight crust also helped to preserve them. Medieval diners apparently possessed a rather blunt sense of humor about their foods. They sometimes called these sturdy enclosures "coffins." Not only could these hard-crusted meat pies be prepared well ahead of time, but also their rich ingredients served as a special Christmas treat.

The dish we know today as mincemeat pie was so popular during the **Christmas season** that, in earlier times, it was also called Christmas pie. During the Middle Ages, the presentation of the Christmas pie was just as important as its ingredients, since medieval feasts aimed at offering diners a spectacle as well as a meal. A late fourteenth-century recipe for Christmas pie describes a manner of both preparation and presentation:

> Take a Pheasant, a Hare, a Capon, two Partridges, two pigeons, and two Conies; chop them up, take out as many bones as you can, and add the livers and hearts, two kidneys of sheep, forcemeat made into balls with eggs, pickled mushrooms, salt, pepper, spice, and vinegar. Boil the bones in a pot to make a good broth; put the meat into a crust of good paste "made craftily into the likeness of a bird's body"; pour in the liquor, close it up, and bake well; "and so serve it forth with the head of one of the birds at one end and a great tail at the other, and divers of his long feathers set cunningly all about him." [Crippen, 1990, 122-23]

Another popular way of presenting the Christmas pie required the cook to mold the pie into the shape of a manger and place a dough image of the baby **Jesus** on top.

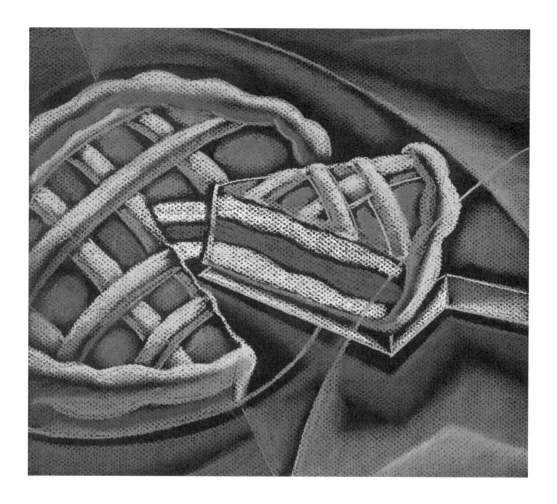

## Jack Horner's Christmas Pie

Mincemeat pies have played a prominent role in several episodes of English political and religious history. In 1532 King Henry VIII began a campaign to reduce the political and economic power of the Roman Catholic Church in England. He started to dissolve England's monasteries and to claim their wealth for the crown. Some say that Richard Whiting, the last abbot of Glastonbury, tried to protect his abbey from this fate by freely offering the monarch the deeds to twelve of the abbey's richest estates (*see also* Glastonbury Thorn). He attempted to tickle the king's fancy as well as satisfy his greed by inserting the deeds into the crust of a Christmas pie that was to be presented to the king as a Christmas gift. The abbot asked one of his trusted agents, Thomas Horner, to deliver the pie to the king. Along the way, however, Horner reportedly pulled out the deeds for himself. Some writers claim that an old English nursery rhyme commemorates this Christmas theft in what are now veiled images:

> Little Jack Horner
> Sat in a corner
> Eating a Christmas pie
> He put in his thumb
> And pulled out a plum
> And said, "What a good boy am I!"

In this instance, crime did pay. Henry VIII dissolved Glastonbury Abbey and seized its possessions, Horner took possession of Mells Manor, and Abbot Richard Whiting was brutally executed on a trumped-up charge of treason. It is only fair to add that Horner's descendants, still living at Mells Manor, deny much of this story. They claim that Thomas Horner bought Mells from the king and that the rhyme has nothing to do with their ancestor. The full truth of the matter may never be known.

## Puritan Opposition to Mincemeat

In the following century Christmas pie once again landed in the middle of England's political and religious controversies. In the seventeenth century, mincemeat pie, along with plum pudding, raised the ire of an increasingly powerful Protestant sect known as the **Puritans**. Some writers claim that the manger-shaped pies and dough images of Jesus scandalized the Puritans' sense of religious decorum. Others suggest that the Puritans viewed the consumption of mincemeat pie as an act of gluttony that did not befit the season of the Nativity. An anonymous writer of the time parodied the Puritans' objection to traditional English Christmas fare in the following lines of verse:

> The high-shoe lords of Cromwell's making
> Were not for dainties—roasting, baking;
> The chiefest food they found most good in,
> Was rusty bacon and bag pudding;
> Plum-broth was popish, and mince-pie—
> O that was flat idolatry! [Chambers, 1990, 2: 755]

The Puritans condemned mincemeat pie and those who feasted on it at Christmas time. Another writer mimicked their thundering denunciations of the dish in the following lines:

Idolatrie in crust! Babylon's whore
Rak'd from the grave, and bak'd by hanches, then
Sew'd up in Coffins to unholy men;
Defil'd, with superstition, like the Gentiles
Of old, that worship'd onions, roots, and lentiles! [Pimlott, 1978, 46]

Catholics and Anglicans defended the traditional Christmas pie against Puritan attackers. As Protestants and Catholics strove with one another to dominate England's political life, the consumption or avoidance of mincemeat pie at Christmas time became a sign of religious and political loyalties. One writer mocked the views of his more extreme Puritan contemporaries in the following lines of verse:

All plums the prophet's sons deny,
And spice-broths are too hot;
Treason's in a December pie,
And death within the pot. [Chambers, 1990, 2: 755]

In spite of this controversy, both plum pudding and mincemeat pie survived the brief period of Puritan rule in the seventeenth century. They emerged once again in the following centuries as English Christmas favorites. In 1728 one foreigner who had experienced an English Christmas noted that at this time of year, "Everyone from the King to the artisan eats [plum] soup and Christmas pies."

## Changing Recipes

Over the years mincemeat pie recipes began to call for less meat and more fruit and sugar. A sixteenth-century pie described by English poet Robert Herrick contained beef tongues, chicken, eggs, orange and lemon peel, sugar, and various spices. As sugar became more affordable and, therefore, more widely available, a division between sweet and savory dishes arose in English cooking. Mincemeat pie gravitated towards the galaxy of sweet foods. In fact, many later recipes for mincemeat pie omit meat entirely. Nevertheless, most of these meatless pies still call for suet, or beef fat.

Today's Christmas baker can choose between meat and meatless recipes. For example, one recipe calls for sliced apples, chopped lean beef or ox hearts, suet, sugar, cider, sour cherries, raisins, citron, candied orange and lemon peel, mace, cinnamon, cloves, nutmeg, salt, pepper, and nuts. More common, however, are recipes that omit the meat and add additional fruits to the mixture, such as figs, prunes, cherries, pears, dried apricots, raisins, or currants. Sherry, brandy, or molasses may be added as well. Mincemeat ages well and may be made several weeks in advance in order to allow the flavors to blend and mature.

# Miracle on 34th Street

*Miracle on 34th Street* (1947) has become one of America's best-loved Christmas movies. Based on a book of the same name, it tells the story of Susan Walker (a little girl who doesn't believe in **Santa Claus**), her mother Doris Walker (an independent career woman), neighbor Fred Gailey (a lawyer who has fallen in love with Doris), and an elderly gentleman who calls himself Kris Kringle. Doris Walker works at Macy's in **New York City**. She hires Kris Kringle to play Santa Claus for **Macy's Thanksgiving Day Parade**. Seeing that he is a natural in the role, she convinces him also to work as a store Santa. Kringle's unconventional philosophy of sending customers to rival stores if Macy's does not carry the item they're looking for boosts Macy's sales. Nevertheless, his belief that he really is Santa Claus raises difficulties. Kringle remains unaware of these difficulties for quite a while, as he works on inspiring Susan's belief in Santa Claus and aiding Doris's handsome neighbor in his campaign to win her heart. By the end of the movie, the girl has found faith in Santa, her mother has fallen in love with the neighbor, and Kris Kringle has returned home.

## The Author of the Book

Valentine Davies grew up in New York City. He attended the University of Michigan and Yale Drama School and went on to write plays, novels, and, eventually, screenplays. He and director George Seaton became pals and, during a vacation that the two of them took with their wives in Nevada, he shared with Seaton his idea for *Miracle on 34th Street*. Seaton set to work on creating a screenplay and finished his first draft about a year and a half later. Davies's short novel was published in the same year that the film was released. For his part in the film, Davies won an Academy Award for best original story. Davies and Seaton worked together on other projects, including the films *Chicken Every Sunday* (1949) and *The Bridges at Toko-Ri* (1955).

## The Director and Screenwriter

George Seaton began his theatrical career as a stage actor and producer. In 1933 he began to write screenplays. He did double duty on *Miracle on 34th Street*, both writing the script and directing the film. His ability to translate Davies's novel into the more visual medium of a movie script garnered him an Academy Award for best screenplay. Though it did not win, the movie also received an Academy Award nomination for best picture of the year.

## The Actors

Little Natalie Wood, who played Susan Walker, made her motion picture debut in 1943 at the age of five. She had appeared in three other movies before *Miracle on 34th Street*. Her naturalness on camera adds much appeal to the film and made her a child star. She continued her career on into adulthood and picked up three Academy Award nominations along the way for her roles in *Rebel Without a Cause* (1955), *Splendor in the Grass* (1961), and *Love With a Proper Stranger* (1963). She is also remembered for her tragic death in a drowning accident off the California coast in 1981.

*Miracle on 34th Street* charms audiences by pairing 8-year-old Natalie Wood with 72-year-old Edmund Gwen, who played Kris Kringle. While Wood was a relative newcomer, both to life and to the world of film, the elderly Gwen had achieved the status of veteran in the world of the dramatic arts. Born in Wales in 1875, he appeared in his first movie in 1916, after a successful London stage career. *Miracle on 34th Street* won him the acclaim of his peers. He received an Academy Award for best supporting actor for his portrayal of Kris Kringle.

The film's romantic angle often takes a back seat to its comedic bits and its touching treatment of a mother and child's journey towards the capacity to imagine, hope, and trust. Maureen O'Hara, who plays Doris Walker, and John Payne, who plays her boyfriend Fred Gailey, were well paired as a subdued romantic couple. Just as she did in *Miracle on 34th Street,* O'Hara often played independent, strong-willed women who go it alone in a world where men have the upper hand. John Payne played many romantic leads in the 1940s. In the 1950s his career turned towards action and western films. He also starred in the western-themed television show, "The Restless Gun."

### Facts about the Film

Seaton had originally planned to use the false names "Tracy's" and "Trimballs" for the two famous New York stores that appear in the film. After both stores gave permission to use their proper names, however, he changed them back to Macy's and Gimbel's. A good portion of the movie was shot on location in New York City. Seaton was even permitted to range freely about the 34th Street store during the Christmas season, in order to film Macy's real holiday rush. During the movie's opening scenes, viewers are treated to actual shots of Macy's famous Thanksgiving Day Parade.

Although *Miracle on 34th Street* appears incredibly sweet to today's audiences, the Roman Catholic Church voiced moral objections to the film at the time of its debut. Church officials disapproved of the movie because the leading lady plays a divorced woman.

When the film first came out, publicity experts played up the romantic aspects of the film rather than its connection to Christmas. In fact, instead of opening during the holiday season, the film premiered in June 1947.

### Remakes

The enduring popularity of the 1947 film inspired Twentieth-Century Fox to authorize a remake in 1994. The new, color version of the film stars child actress Mara

Wilson as Susan Walker and Richard Attenborough as Kris Kringle. This time around, however, Macy's refused to let the filmmakers use its name. After shooting a few parade shots in New York City—not Macy's real parade, but rather a movie version of the yearly event—production moved to Chicago. In this version of the story, Susan's mother works for a fictional department store called Cole's, which faces stiff competition from its arch-rival, Shopper's Express.

The story was also adapted as a made-for-television movie in 1973. Barely remembered television versions of the story aired in 1955, 1956, and 1959, the first two airing under the title *Meet Mr. Kringle*.

# Mistletoe

The parasitic plant known as Viscum album to botanists has attached itself in a mysterious way to the celebration of Christmas. More commonly known as mistletoe, this plant frequently makes its home on the branches of apple trees, but may also be found on poplars, hawthorns, limes, maples, and even, occasionally, on oak trees. According to an old English custom, sprigs of mistletoe may be hung over doorways and from ceilings around Christmas time; anyone may kiss a person who passes beneath the mistletoe. How did this plant and this custom come to be associated with Christmas? Perhaps no definitive answer to this question can be given, but we can review the history of the plant from ancient times to the present. Over the centuries a variety of European beliefs and customs have linked mistletoe to the winter season, magic, good will, and flirtation.

### Evergreens in Ancient Times

Mistletoe is an evergreen, a plant that stays green throughout the winter. Like **holly** and **ivy**, mistletoe even bears fruit during this cold, dark season. The ancient Romans as well as the pagan peoples of northern Europe adorned their homes with evergreen boughs for their winter festivals (*see also* **Kalends**; **Yule**). These plants, which continue to thrive as others around them appear to wither and die, may have symbolized the promise of new life or of eternal life to these ancient peoples. The custom of decking homes and temples with greenery during the heart of winter passed on into later northern European Christmas celebrations.

## Celtic Customs and Beliefs

Over a century ago, the famous anthropologist and classics scholar Sir George Frazer suggested that mistletoe was an especially sacred plant to both the ancient Romans and the ancient peoples of northwestern Europe (sometimes referred to as the Celts). He proposed that the mistletoe plant, which not only lives without roots in the ground but also stays green in winter, baffled these ancient peoples. Therefore, they assigned mistletoe a special role in their religious beliefs.

Frazer claimed that the pagan peoples of ancient France, Britain, and Ireland held mistletoe to be sacred, and they harvested it in special ceremonial ways. These peoples believed that mistletoe possessed magical powers and that the rare plants that grew on oak trees were the most powerful of all. Mistletoe gained its power in part from its ability to live halfway between heaven and earth. Therefore, when the Druids, or pagan priests, harvested the plant, they cut it with golden sickles and were careful never to let it touch the ground. The Druids called the plant "all-healer" and thought it had the power to cure many ills, including infertility, nervous diseases, and toothaches. (Today we know that mistletoe berries are highly poisonous, however). Mistletoe was also thought to attract good luck and to ward off witchcraft. Frazer asserted that the European folklore of his day still contained traces of these ancient beliefs. He noted that in some modern Celtic languages the word for mistletoe translates to "all-healer."

## Norse Mythology

The ancient Norse also reserved a special place for mistletoe in their mythology. Balder, the Norse god of sun and summer, was beloved in heaven and on earth. His mother, Frigga, the queen of the Norse gods, loved Balder so much she set about extracting a promise from every thing on the earth to refrain from harming her son. She disregarded the puny mistletoe, however, thinking it powerless to damage the sun god.

This omission provided an opportunity for the evil god Loki to scheme against Balder. Loki obtained some mistletoe and fashioned it into a spear. Then he brought it to Hodur, Balder's blind brother, the god of night. The other gods were amusing themselves by tossing all sorts of objects at Balder and watching them turn aside at the

last minute, bound by their promise not to harm the god. Loki offered Hodur the spear, assuring him that it, too, would turn aside before it could hurt the sun god. Hodur threw the mistletoe spear at his brother. It pierced Balder's chest and killed him. According to one version of the myth, the father of these two brothers, Odin, eventually sent someone to kill Hodur, thus avenging Balder's death.

At least one writer has suggested that the Norse attached this myth to the turning of the seasons, viewing the summer solstice as the time of Balder the sun god's death, and the winter solstice as the time of Hodur the night god's death.

## Mistletoe as an Emblem of Good Will

This Norse myth suggests that the ancient Scandinavians believed that mistletoe possessed unseen powers—in this case, put to evil purposes. At some point, though, mistletoe became a symbol of peace and good will in pagan Scandinavia. Enemies who happened to meet beneath it in the forest declared a day's truce from fighting. In Scandinavia, a branch of mistletoe hung above a threshold thus came to signify the offer of hospitality and friendship within. Some claim that, after the coming of Christianity, mistletoe was seldom incorporated into church Christmas decorations, due to its strong association with the pagan past. Others disagree with this claim. If such a ban did exist, then York Cathedral in England defied it. During medieval times, Church officials placed a branch of mistletoe upon the high altar on Christmas Eve, signaling a general pardon for all wrongdoers for as long as it remained there.

## Kissing under the Mistletoe

The custom of kissing under the mistletoe appears to be of English origin. Although in recent centuries the British have earned a reputation for being physically reserved, this was not always the case. In the sixteenth century the visiting Dutch scholar Erasmus wrote that the English were so fond of kissing at meeting and parting that it was impossible to avoid being constantly kissed. It is difficult to say with certainty when the British adopted the custom of kissing under the mistletoe at Christmas time. A seventeenth-century document speaks of the transport and sale of mistletoe at Christmas, but none mentions the custom of kissing under the mistletoe until the eighteenth century, when some writers suggest that it became a common practice.

The custom attracted a number of somewhat contradictory folk beliefs. According to one belief, each time a boy kissed a girl under the mistletoe, he must pluck one of the berries. When no berries remained, no more kissing could occur under that branch. Some claimed that to refuse a kiss under the mistletoe meant that one would not marry in the next twelve months. Others claimed that no marriage was possible after such an offense. Another folk belief advised householders to burn their mistletoe branches after **Twelfth Night** in case the boys and girls who kissed under them never married. Still another recommended that a sprig of mistletoe be kept in order to drive evil away from the house during the coming year. The sprig might also be used to light the fire under next year's Christmas pudding, or plum pudding. Finally, some thought it unlucky to cut mistletoe at any other time than Christmas.

The English often displayed mistletoe in the form of a kissing bough, a circular, or even spherical, configuration of greenery woven around hoops of wire or wood. One expert claims that the kissing bough reached the peak of its popularity in the eighteenth century and began to decline in the nineteenth century. In *The Pickwick Papers*, British writer Charles Dickens offers a charming description of the fun and flirtation that occurred under the mistletoe in his day:

> From the centre of the ceiling of this kitchen, old Wardle had just suspended with his own hand a huge branch of mistletoe, and this same branch of mistletoe instantaneously gave rise to a scene of general and most delightful struggling and confusion; in the midst of which, Mr. Pickwick, with a gallantry that would have done honour to a descendent of Lady Tollimglower herself, took the old lady by the hand, led her beneath the mystic branch, and saluted her in all courtesy and decorum. The old lady submitted to this piece of practical politeness with all the dignity which befitted so important and serious a solemnity, but the younger ladies, not being so thoroughly imbued with a superstitious veneration for the custom—or imagining that the value of a salute is very much enhanced if it cost a little trouble to obtain it—screamed and struggled, and ran into corners, and threatened and remonstrated, and did everything but leave the room until some of the less adventurous gentlemen were on the point of desisting when they all at once found it useless to resist any longer and submitted to be kissed with a good grace. Mr. Winkle kissed the young lady with the black eyes, and Mr. Snodgrass kissed Emily, and Mr. Weller, not being particular about the form of being under the mistletoe, kissed Emma and the other female servants just as he caught them. As to

the poor relations, they kissed everybody, not even excepting the plainer portions of the young-lady visitors, who, in their excessive confusion, ran right under the mistletoe as soon as it was hung up, without knowing it! Wardle stood with his back to the fire, surveying the whole scene with the utmost satisfaction; and the fat boy took the opportunity of appropriating to his own use, and summarily devouring, a particularly fine mince-pie that had been put carefully by for someone else.

Today, many people still enhance their Christmas festivities with mischievous sprigs of mistletoe. The custom is typically found in Britain, France, or countries where the British have settled, such as Canada and the United States.

# Mumming

## Geese Dancing, Guising, Masking, Mummering

Mumming is a form of folk entertainment in which bands of masked and costumed merrymakers roam the streets singing, dancing, acting out stories, or simply engaging in horseplay. In past centuries people throughout Europe celebrated the **Christmas season** by mumming or by hosting bands of mummers in their homes. In the United States today, children practice a similar form of seasonal masquerading at Halloween.

Since mumming began as a folk rather than elite tradition, mummers usually wore simple, homemade costumes, often accompanied by masks or blackening of the face. Indeed, some scholars trace the origins of the English word "mumming" back to the ancient Greek term for "mask," mommo. In some cases, the mummer's costume represented a mythical figure whose character or behavior the mummer enacted in a kind of folk drama called a mummers' play. In other cases, mummers simply cavorted under the cover of disguise, engaging in playful but sometimes rather unruly behavior to the amusement or irritation of their neighbors. Christmas time mumming was particularly common in the British Isles, where it survived as a popular folk custom until the mid-nineteenth century.

## Ancient Precedents

How did this custom attach itself to the Christmas season? Some would answer this question by pointing to the revels that took place during the ancient Roman feast of **Kalends**. During this midwinter new year festival, groups of young men ran through the streets dressed as women or animals and, under the cover of disguise, engaged in many behaviors that would normally have been frowned upon.

Although Christian authorities condemned these activities, they proved difficult to stamp out, even after Christianity became the dominant religion and Christmas an important winter holiday. One researcher has counted at least forty separate Church documents containing official denunciations of these kinds of midwinter masquerades. These documents range from the fourth to the eleventh centuries and come from authorities in many European lands as well as north Africa and the Near East.

## Mumming in Britain

Some researchers believe that these ancient customs lingered on in a few places, eventually giving rise to Christmas time mumming practices. Others disagree, arguing that these ancient practices died out in all but a few places hundreds of years before medieval mumming customs were established. In any case, Christmas time mumming can be traced back to the late Middle Ages. The earliest documents referring to it date back to the thirteenth century. Although mumming sprang from the lower classes, by the fourteenth century King Edward III adopted an elaborate rendition of this practice as a Christmas season entertainment at court. Among the elite, these costumed Christmas revels eventually developed into masques or masquerades.

In some areas mumming was known as "masking" or "guising" (from the word "disguise"). In other areas the word "guising" eventually became "geese dancing." In fifteenth- and sixteenth-century England bands of mummers, also called "maskers" or "guisers," frequently appeared on the streets during the **Twelve Days of Christmas**. For the most part, people engaged in mumming and welcomed mummers into their homes because it was fun. Mummers relished parading in costume and appreciated the protection it gave them to praise or tease their neighbors as they saw fit. The less well-off might also avail themselves of this opportunity to exact hospitality from their more prosperous neighbors. Indeed, mummers usually demanded and received

317

food or drink from each household or locale they visited. No doubt many people liked the lively atmosphere created by the mummers and enjoyed their entertaining antics. Others probably resented being pestered for **gifts** of food and drink.

## Mummer's Plays

In Great Britain and Ireland some mummers eventually began to entertain their hosts with short folk dramas called mummers' plays. Since mummers' plays were often passed down through oral traditions, they varied in many details. Nevertheless, three main story lines have emerged, which experts have dubbed the hero-combat, the sword play, and the wooing ceremony. The hero-combat was the most popular of these stories. Some of the characters likely to appear in this play include St. George, Father Christmas, the king of Egypt or England, the king's daughter, a pompous doctor, and a Turkish knight. The story revolves around a fight between the hero, St. George, and the Turkish knight. One combatant kills the other. Afterwards, the bumbling doctor miraculously manages to revive the dead soldier. All of this takes place amidst a great deal of silly or garbled dialogue in which characters flatly announce their identities and narrate their actions. Father Christmas often serves as a kind of announcer for the play. In England women did not usually take part in mumming, so all the roles were played by men.

After presenting their play, the mummers collected coins from the audience in return for their dramatic efforts. Mummers performed these plays most frequently at Christmas time, but in some areas they were presented around Easter and All Souls' Day (November 2). Although some writers believe these plays, or at least the themes they touch on, to be ancient, others point out that the earliest written records of the plays date back to the eighteenth century.

## Mumming in Europe

British and Irish mumming traditions have been well documented by generations of historians and folklorists. Although Christmas mumming was practiced in many parts of Europe, it is somewhat more difficult to find descriptions of the custom from other European countries. One of the best portraits of the practice outside of Great Britain and Ireland comes from the pen of Leo Tolstoy, the great Russian writer. The following excerpt from his novel *War and Peace* (1865-69) describes Christmas festivities in a well-to-do Russian household:

The mummers (some of the house-serfs) dressed up as bears, Turks, inn-keepers and ladies—frightening and funny —bringing with them the cold from the outside and a feeling of gaiety, crowded, at first timidly, into the anteroom, then hiding behind one another they pushed into the ballroom where shyly at first and then more and more merrily and heartily, they started singing, dancing, and playing Christmas games. The countess, when she had identified them and laughed at their costumes, went into the drawing-room…. Half an hour later there appeared among the other mummers in the ballroom an old lady in a hooped skirt—this was Nicholas. A Turkish girl was Petya. A clown was Dimmler. An hussar was Natasha, and a Circassian was Sonya with burnt-cork mustache and eye-brows. After the condescending surprise, non-recognition, and praise from those who were not themselves dressed up, the young people decided that their costumes were so good that they ought to be shown elsewhere.

## Mumming in North America

Mumming remained a popular Christmas season pastime in England until the mid-nineteenth century. After that time it faded away almost completely, being kept alive in only a few places by local enthusiasts. Long before its decline, however, English emigrants had carried this custom to the New World. In the seventeenth century the English established themselves in Newfoundland (now part of Canada). Local inhabitants there carried on a tradition of Christmas mumming, or "mummering," as they called it, until the 1960s.

In the United States, English settlers introduced mumming to an ethnically diverse population. In Pennsylvania, English Christmas time mumming traditions combined with the German folk figure Belsnickel to create the custom of belsnickeling (*see* **Knecht Ruprecht**). When these influences collided with the holiday season noisemaking traditions of Scandinavians and the musical and dance heritage of African Americans, new traditions were born.

Although Philadelphia city officials periodically attempted to disband the noisy holiday revelers, they finally accepted these customs in an organized format, issuing the first official permit for the Philadelphia Mummers Parade in 1901. Philadelphians continue to stage this extravagant event every year on New Year's Day. Squads of elaborately costumed mummers, magnificent floats, and lively string bands all march through the city streets, and judges select the winning entries. In spite of its name, the parade bears little resemblance to its ancestral English mumming traditions, except that participants wear costumes and, often, masks.

### Related Customs

Mumming was only one of a number of old Christmas customs that authorized revelry, including unruly or forbidden behavior, under the cover of masks and disguises. These practices span many centuries and come from different lands. Examples include belsnickeling, the ceremonies surrounding the **boy bishop**, the customs associated with **Berchta**, Black Peter, Germany's Knocking Nights, the **Feast of Fools**, masques, pantomimes, Los **Pastores**, Las **Posadas**, Plough Monday, St. Sylvester's Day, and **Twelfth Night** celebrations. Although their historical and cultural roots vary, some authors identify in these customs a perennial return to the ancient theme of celebrating midwinter with costumed merrymaking.

### Controversies

Although Christmas mumming no doubt entertained many participants and onlookers, mummers also caused many disturbances. Complaints against mummers ranged from excessive noisiness to malicious mischief and even criminal acts. Perhaps the excitement of shedding one's usual social role with the aid of a disguise, combined with a good deal to drink, tilted some mummers towards raucous behavior. In other cases, some who set out to steal, incite political disturbances, or simply settle old scores with a neighbor found it convenient to disguise themselves as mummers. This tendency toward disorder caused local authorities throughout the centuries to attempt to eradicate the practice. Indeed, the oldest document known to mention Christmas mumming records that it was forbidden in the French town of Troyes in 1263. In 1405 the practice was outlawed in London. In the seventeenth century the **Puritans** railed against it. Throughout the nineteenth century Pennsylvania legislators attempted to abolish it. Ironically, legislators were never able to kill this form of folk entertainment. Mumming finally died a natural death at a ripe old age when the societies that gave birth to it had changed so much that ordinary people simply abandoned the practice.

# Myrrh

The sap of the myrrh tree (*Commiphora myrrha*) dries into hard, reddish brown lumps of gum resin known as myrrh. Although unfamiliar to us today, in ancient times myrrh was a precious and much-sought-after substance. The **Magi**, or Wise Men from the East, brought the baby **Jesus** a **gift** of myrrh.

### History and Significance

In order to understand the significance of this gift, we must explore the uses of myrrh in biblical times. Ancient records tell us that it was perhaps most commonly employed as a medicine. The Romans, Greeks, Assyrians, and other peoples of the ancient Mediterranean and Near East prescribed myrrh in treatments for a wide variety of afflictions, including sores in the mouth, infections, coughs, and worms. It was also burned to fumigate the rooms of the sick. Myrrh appears at the beginning of Jesus' life as a gift and at the end of his life as a medicine. Shortly before his crucifixion, Jesus is offered a cup of wine mixed with myrrh (Mark 15:23). This suggests that myrrh was used as a painkiller. The ancient Egyptians used myrrh in the process of embalming corpses. The ancient Hebrews also treated the dead with myrrh; according to the Gospel of John, Jesus' body was treated with myrrh and aloes before being wrapped in cloth for burial (John 19:39).

Myrrh was also highly valued as a component of perfume and incense. Although myrrh has a pleasant smell, like many more familiar perfume products, it has a bitter taste. In fact, the English word "myrrh" comes from the Hebrew and Arabic terms for "bitter." Myrrh was especially prized as an ingredient in perfumed oils and lotions because of its enduring fragrance and long shelf life. The Hebrews made myrrh one of the primary ingredients of the holy oil with which they anointed their high priests and the sacred objects of their temples. It was also used to make incense, which many ancient peoples, such as the Egyptians, Greeks, Romans, Hebrews, Persians, and Babylonians, burned in home and temple worship. Frankincense was preferred over myrrh in the making of incense, however.

In ancient times, Arabia supplied the Mediterranean and Asia with most of their myrrh and frankincense. These products were so highly valued and so difficult to obtain outside of Arabia that they became a luxury affordable only by the rich.

The Magi's gifts of **gold, frankincense,** and myrrh each have been assigned a special significance in Christian lore and legend. Due to its bitterness, the gift of myrrh has often been interpreted as a symbol of the hardships that Jesus would suffer in his adult life: persecution and early death. The fact that myrrh was used in embalming has led some to assert that myrrh represents Jesus' humanity. Like us, he would die. Another interpretation suggests that because myrrh had many medicinal uses in biblical times, it must represent Jesus' role as a healer of body and spirit. Finally, it might be argued that the gift of myrrh symbolizes Jesus' role as a Jewish religious leader, since myrrh was a main ingredient in the holy oil used to anoint Jewish high priests.

### Customs

Until the mid-1700s, tradition dictated that the British monarch offer a gift of frankincense, gold, and myrrh at the Chapel Royal on Epiphany. Heralds and knights of the Garter, Thistle, and Bath accompanied the king on this reenactment of the Magi's royal pilgrimage. The procession was abandoned under the unstable King George III, although a proxy continues to deliver the monarch's gift of gold, frankincense, and myrrh to the Chapel Royal on Epiphany. A similar royal offering was at one time customary in Spain.

## *Myrrh Today*

Today myrrh trees can be found in Saudi Arabia, Ethiopia, and Somalia. Myrrh is still used as a component of incense and perfume. It is also found in mouthwashes, gargles, and toothpastes. Interest in the medicinal properties of myrrh has been increasing in recent years. Herbalists recognize its antiseptic, antifungal and astringent qualities. Moreover, a recent scientific study has found that myrrh indeed does reduce pain, affirming ancient uses of the drug.

# National Christmas Tree

The National Christmas Tree stands on the lawn of the President's Park South—or Ellipse, as it is more commonly called—in Washington, D.C. Its ceremonial illumination each year in early December kicks off a festival called the Pageant of Peace. The pageant was established in order to "foster friendship and understanding among all peoples" and "to reflect the unity of purpose that emanates from the diversity of traditions and backgrounds of mankind." The festival lasts until January 6, **Epiphany**. Over the years, radio and then television coverage has made the National Christmas Tree an increasingly important symbol of Christmas celebrations in the United States.

## *The Early Years*

Community trees illuminated with electric lights date back to the first years of the twentieth century. From California the idea spread to **New York City**, resulting in a tree-lighting ceremony in Madison Park (now known as Madison Square Park). In 1913 the first community tree in Washington, D.C., was erected on the East Plaza of the Capitol Building. Lighting ceremonies took place in 1913 and 1914, but folded due to lack of funds. The event resumed at the end of World War I.

In 1923 the Capitol tree was eclipsed by another community tree, however, this one standing on the Ellipse south of the White House and lit by the president himself (*see also* **White House, Christmas in the**). That year President Calvin Coolidge agreed to flip the switch that illuminated the 60-foot fir tree's electric lights. He did so at sundown on Christmas Eve, but showed little interest in the proceedings. The evening's activities also included a free concert at the tree by the Marine Band quartet, an evening carol sing on the North Lawn, and a midnight reenactment of the journey of the **Magi** at the Washington Monument.

President Coolidge later designated the General Grant tree, located in California's King's Canyon National Park, the **Nation's Christmas Tree**. Although this 267-foot-tall tree is never decorated with lights and **ornaments**, Christmas ceremonies have taken place at the foot of the tree since 1925.

Washington's first National Christmas Tree had come from Coolidge's home state of Vermont, a donation from Middlebury College. Between the years 1924 and 1933 the ceremony took place in Sherman Plaza using a living **Christmas tree**. During these years the event became increasingly popular. Radio announcers broadcast the ceremony in 1925. In 1926, a flare was sent up at the moment of the illumination. This signal alerted buglers dispersed throughout the city to proclaim the lighting of the tree in song. By 1929 the hot lights and heavy ornaments had so damaged the tree that it had to be replaced.

Between the years 1934 and 1938, the renovation of Sherman Plaza forced the lighting ceremony to move to Lafayette Park. Two living Christmas trees were used in alternate years, in order to avoid permanently harming either one.

## World War II

In 1939 the tree-lighting ceremony returned to the Ellipse, but in 1941 President Franklin D. Roosevelt ordered it moved to the South Lawn of the White House, a decision he felt would make the proceedings "more homey." The United States entered World War II in December of that year. On Christmas Eve the British Prime Minister Winston Churchill, who was in Washington to confer with Roosevelt about the war, appeared alongside President Roosevelt at the tree-lighting ceremony. Both gave brief speeches about the war and Christmas. In 1942 wartime blackout requirements led to the cancellation of the tree's illumination. Nevertheless, First Lady Eleanor Roosevelt insisted on an alternate ceremony. Schoolchildren collected ornaments for the tree, and a ceremony featuring the ringing of chimes was substituted for the usual illumination. The blackouts continued in 1943 and 1944. In these years, tags bearing the names of men serving in the military were attached to each ornament.

## Post-War Years

By Christmas of 1945, World War II was over and Washingtonians rejoiced anew as President Harry S. Truman pushed the button that illuminated the National Christmas Tree for the first time since 1942. Truman preferred to spend Christmas at home in Missouri and so missed a number of illumination ceremonies. Without an appearance by the President, the event's glamour and popularity sagged.

President Dwight D. Eisenhower and his wife Mamie breathed new life into the illumination ceremony, however. In 1954 they moved it back to the Ellipse, which permitted larger crowds to gather. In that same year, the date of the ceremony was moved back to December 17 and a series of related activities lasting from December 17 to January 6 was added. This program of activities, named the "Christmas Pageant of Peace," was concocted by local businessmen to attract more tourists to the area at Christmas time. Performers from twenty-seven foreign embassies participated in the pageant that year, demonstrating the Christmas songs, dances, and traditions of their countries. A full-scale **Nativity scene**, featuring live animals, was also erected as part of the pageant. In addition, during the Eisenhower years the tree-lighting ceremony was televised to ever-expanding TV audiences, which helped make the tree a national icon of the holiday season.

Between the years 1954 and 1972, festival organizers scouted out beautiful, tall trees from various parts of the country, bought them, cut them down, and imported them to Washington to serve as the National Christmas Tree. In that era festival organizers thought that planting a living Christmas tree on the Ellipse would interrupt the area's usage during the rest of the year. As the festival became a more important part of the nation's Christmas celebrations, various states began to send smaller Christmas trees to stand alongside the "pathway of peace" that leads to the National Christmas Tree. Eventually all fifty states were represented.

## Problems and Protests

Over the years there have been problems with some of the ceremonies. In 1963, the illumination ceremony was postponed until December 22. President John F. Kennedy

had been shot and killed on November 22, and the nation observed a thirty-day mourning period for him in which it was deemed inappropriate to light the tree.

The illumination ceremony became the site of political protests during Richard M. Nixon's presidency. Citizens who opposed American involvement in Vietnam used the occasion to voice their objections to the war, heckling the president during his speech. One year the police arrested nine people, charging them with disorderly conduct.

Another kind of objection was raised by the American Civil Liberties Union. On behalf of several plaintiffs, they charged that the Nativity scene that had become part of the display violated the constitutional guarantee against the government establishing or promoting a particular religion. The courts decided in their favor in 1973, and the Nativity scene was eliminated.

At the same time, the White House received numerous letters that criticized the continuing practice of cutting down a magnificent tree each year for the ceremony. In response to these concerns President Nixon requested that a living tree be planted on the Ellipse. In 1973 the National Arborist Association contributed a forty-two-foot Colorado blue spruce from Pennsylvania, which was uprooted and transplanted to Washington, D.C., to serve as the National Christmas Tree. The tree lasted only four years. In 1977 it was replaced with another Colorado Blue Spruce, which was knocked over by strong winds in January 1978. The following year it was replaced by yet another Colorado Blue Spruce, almost forty feet high, which was uprooted from the home of the Myers family of York, Pennsylvania, in exchange for $1,500.

In December 1978, a new ritual was added to the illumination ceremony. Amy Carter, the daughter of President Jimmy Carter, was lifted to the top of the Christmas tree by a cherry picker to place the last, topmost ornament on the tree. In the years that followed, this honor was generally reserved for a member of the president's or vice-president's family. In 1980 Penne Langdon, the wife of one of the American hostages being held in Iran, performed this task.

As a means of expressing America's solidarity with the hostages, President Carter ordered that the National Christmas Tree remain unlit in 1979 and 1980. The hostages were released on January 20, 1980, President Ronald Reagan's Inauguration Day. Even though Christmas had passed, Reagan had the tree decorated and illuminated in celebration of both events.

## The Eighties and Beyond

The Reagans often invited children to assist them in the tree-lighting ceremony. One year a boy scout and a girl scout attended the ceremonies. Another year a child selected by the Make-a-Wish Foundation helped light the tree. During the Reagan years, the president lit the Christmas tree by remote control from inside the White House. An assassination attempt on Reagan's life in 1981 in combination with other death threats led security advisors to insist on this change.

Reagan's successor, President George H. W. Bush, once again strolled out to the Ellipse to light the tree. During Bush's presidency, his wife, Barbara Bush, placed the topmost ornament on the Christmas tree four years in a row. As the wife of Reagan's vice-president, she had also performed this task, and so holds the national record for most cherry picker rides (twelve) to the top of the National Christmas Tree.

Over the years the Pageant of Peace expanded, thereby pushing the date of the illumination ceremony back into the early part of December. During the Clinton presidency it took place on various dates between December 5 and December 11.

In 2002, President George W. Bush and First Lady Laura Bush were assisted by two local schoolchildren in lighting the tree. In 2007, at the request of the White House, energy-efficient LED Christmas lights were used for the first time on the National Christmas Tree. Improvements in LED lighting technology made the 2008 tree much more energy efficient than the previous year. By 2010, the total electrical power consumption used to light the National Christmas Tree was only about 7,000 watts. In previous years, when traditional incandescent lights were used on the tree, the total power consumption was more than 50,000 watts.

In 2010, President Barack Obama, First Lady Michelle Obama, and their daughters Sasha and Malia lit the National Christmas Tree together. The ceremony was broadcast on national television and also streamed live on the National Christmas Tree web site. This would prove to be the last lighting ceremony for that particular tree. On the morning of February 19, 2011, the forty-eight-year-old, forty-two-foot-tall Colorado blue spruce was destroyed by high winds gusting at speeds up to fifty miles per hour. The tree's trunk snapped about four feet above ground level. The National Park Service later announced that a successor tree had already been located and would be brought to the Ellipse in preparation for Christmas 2011.

# Nation's Christmas Tree

King's Canyon National Park, located in east central California, is home to some of the largest trees in the world. These enormous redwood trees, called giant sequoias, or *Sequoiadendron giganteum*, can live for over 3,000 years. One of these behemoths, named the General Grant tree, serves as the Nation's Christmas Tree.

The General Grant tree is only the third largest sequoia in the park. Nevertheless, its dimensions impress. The tree reaches over 267 feet in height. It measures 40 feet in diameter and 107 feet in circumference around the base. The first branch extending off the trunk does so at about 100 feet from the ground. A sturdy young adult, the tree is estimated to be between 1,500 and 2,000 years old.

President Calvin Coolidge declared the General Grant tree to be the Nation's Christmas Tree in 1926. He did so at the request of Charles E. Lee of Sanger, California. Lee visited King's Canyon in 1924, and as he gazed up at the General Grant tree, he overheard a little girl next to him say that it would make a marvelous **Christmas tree**. Inspired by this chance remark, he led a **December 25** Christmas program at the foot of the tree in 1925. He also wrote to the President, requesting that the chief executive officially designate the General Grant as the Nation's Christmas Tree. Coolidge did so on April 28, 1926. President Dwight D. Eisenhower established the tree as a national shrine in 1956, dedicating it to those who died while serving their country.

The yearly Christmas ceremony at the foot of the tree has continued since 1925. The event has been nicknamed the "trek to the tree." It attracted 450 celebrants in 2001. In addition to visitors from across the nation and around the world, many residents of nearby Sanger, California, make the yearly pilgrimage, led by members of the town's chamber of commerce. Park rangers traditionally place a large Christmas **wreath** at the base of the tree. The "trek" takes place on the second Sunday in December.

Alternative ceremonies take place all the way across the country in Washington, D.C. There a rival tree, located on the Ellipse (or President's Park South), serves as the **National Christmas Tree**.

# Nativity Legends

Folklorists define a legend as a short, oral narrative about a person, place, or incident. Legends purport to be true, which generally means that they stay within the boundaries of what's considered possible within the shared cultural assumptions of the tale tellers and their audience.

The English word "legend" comes from the Latin word *legere*, which means "to read." The term originated in the early Middle Ages in reference to accounts of the lives of the saints read aloud at religious services held on their feast days. As the Middle Ages wore on, these saints' tales became more and more numerous, and more and more fantastic. Gradually, the word legend came to mean an untrue or improbable story. Medieval people not only told legends about saints, but also about biblical events and characters. Indeed, scriptural texts gave so little information concerning important events like the Nativity that much room remained for ordinary people to embroider their fanciful designs around the bare outlines of the story.

### Legends Concerning Jesus' Birth

The **Gospel according to Matthew** tells of a miraculous star that appeared in the heavens to herald the birth of **Jesus** (*see* **Jesus, Year of Birth; Star of Bethlehem**). Old European legends expanded on this theme, inventing other miraculous signs that occurred on the day of Jesus' birth. For example, many tales proclaimed that on the day Jesus was born, plants burst into bloom and rivers ran with wine.

Although the **Gospel accounts of Christmas** do not mention any animals at the scene of Jesus' birth, medieval legends not only declared their presence at the manger in **Bethlehem**, but also told of their marvelous deeds. According to one tale, the rooster was the first animal to respond to the miraculous birth. He fluttered up to the roof of the stable and cried in Latin, *"Christus natus est,"* which means "Christ is born." It probably did not seem too odd to western European Christians in the Middle Ages to imagine a rooster in ancient Judea crowing in Latin to honor Christ's birth, since Latin was the official language of the Western Church. When the raven heard the rooster's declaration, he rasped the question, *"quando,"* or when? The rook replied, *"hac nocte,"* this night. The ox murmured, *"ubi,"* where? The sheep bleated, "Beth-

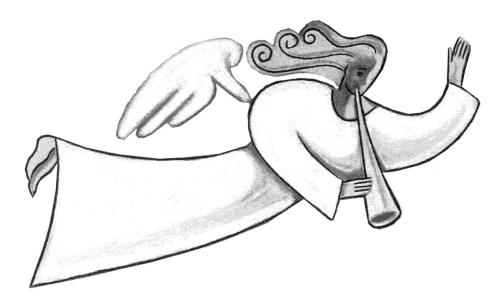

lehem," and the ass bellowed, "*eamus*," let's go! This clever tale assigns each of the animals a Latin phrase that mimics the sound of its own voice.

Other legends recounted the ways in which various animals paid tribute to the Christ child on the night of his birth. According to one such story, the **robin** stood near the flames of the Holy Family's meager fire, beating its wings all night to keep the fire alive and, as a result, singeing its breast red from the flames. The stork tore feathers from her own chest to make a downy bed for the newborn Jesus, and ever since has been honored as the patron of new births. The nightingale nestled near the manger and caroled along with the **angels**. As a result, her song still remains sweeter and more musical than that of other birds. The owl did not follow the other animals to the stable at Bethlehem. Shamed by its own irreverence, the owl has ever since hidden from the sight of other animals, appearing only by night to cry in a soft voice: "Who? Who? Who will lead me to the Christ child?"

Even plants honored and aided the newborn Jesus and his mother, **Mary**. Yellow bedstraw and sweet woodruff offered themselves as bedding for Mary and the baby, thereby earning the folk name "Our Lady's Bedstraw." Some tales assigned creeping thyme the same modest role and a similar folk name, "Mary's Bedstraw." When the Holy Family fled into Egypt (*see also* **Flight into Egypt**), the **rosemary** plant provided Mary with a clean place on which to hang Jesus' baby clothes after she had washed them. For rendering this small service to Jesus and his mother, the plant was blessed ever after with beautiful blue flowers and a sweet fragrance. In other versions of this tale, Mary hung Jesus' clothes on a lavender bush, which afterwards produced delightfully fragrant flowers. She hung her own blue cloak on the rosemary plant, whose previously plain white flowers remained forever imprinted with its color and soothing fragrance.

## Christmas Legends

Over the centuries Christmas and the customs connected with it have inspired a multitude of legends. Many related folk beliefs accompanied these legends. These folk beliefs frequently echoed the underlying premise of the Nativity legends recounted above—that is, that the whole of creation responds to the Savior's birth by acts of praise, adoration, and service.

One popular European legend declared that oxen knelt in their stables at midnight each year on Christmas Eve to honor the moment of Jesus' birth. Often animals were granted powers far beyond their normal capacities on Christmas Eve. English, French, and German folklore maintained that barnyard animals whispered among themselves in human language at that moment. The tales cautioned that these animals often spoke of the faults of their human masters or of impending deaths in the community, making it perhaps unwise to try to overhear them. The daring listener would probably find greater delight in creeping up to a beehive on Christmas Eve, since English folklore insisted that bees sang psalms, hymns, or symphonies in glorious harmonies to commemorate the Nativity.

Among Middle Eastern Christians, stories circulated about trees and plants, especially those growing along the banks of the Jordan River, that bowed towards Bethlehem at that same moment. Many European legends marveled at trees and plants that momentarily burst into fruit and flower on Christmas Eve. An old Russian folk belief hinted that water briefly turns into wine in honor of the occasion. French and German folklore declared that hidden treasures revealed themselves at midnight on Christmas Eve, and that mountains split open to display their hidden veins of precious metals and stones. Other tales told of buried or sunken **bells** that somehow tolled mysteriously at midnight on Christmas Eve. (For other Christmas legends, *see* **La Befana; Berchta; Cherry Trees; Christmas Trees; Flight into Egypt; Frau Gaude; Glastonbury Thorn; Jultomten; Kallikantzari; Poinsettias; Snow Maiden; Twelve Days of Christmas; Urban Legends; Wenceslas, King; Wild Hunt.**)

# Nativity Plays

Throughout the centuries people have celebrated Christmas in folk dramas known as Nativity plays that reenact the story of the birth of **Jesus**. This tradition can be traced back to the liturgical dramas of the European Middle Ages. Today the Christmas pageant, the Hispanic customs of Las **Posadas** and Los **Pastores**, the star boys, and various living **Nativity scene** customs carry on this tradition.

## *Liturgical Dramas*

The liturgical dramas of the Middle Ages provide us with the earliest documented examples of Nativity plays. These dramas began as simple reenactments of biblical stories, spoken in Latin and performed by members of the clergy and choir during religious services.

One of the earliest recorded versions of a play of this sort was performed at the cathedral in Rouen, France, in the twelfth century. In this brief representation of the Nativity, a choirboy, playing the part of an **angel**, announced the birth of Christ from on high. The choir sang, "Glory to God in the highest," and the priests below answered, "and on earth peace to men of good will." Several of the cathedral's canons (clerical staff), dressed as **shepherds**, drew near the altar. Two priests, acting as midwives, stopped them and asked whom they sought. The shepherds replied, "Our Savior, who is Christ the Lord." The priests then pulled back a curtain revealing a stable that contained a statue of the Virgin and Child. The shepherds bowed and worshiped, then returned to their places singing, "Alleluia."

The clergy used liturgical dramas to introduce a mostly illiterate population to a range of biblical stories. These simple dramas proved quite popular and began to be embellished. Humorously exaggerated and outlandish events eventually slipped in. These innovations entertained the audience and were not, in those times, seen as inappropriate by the ordinary person. Church authorities disagreed, however. Some scholars believe that this controversy, plus the need for greater space to accommodate the growing audiences, nudged these brief dramas out onto the church steps and other public arenas in the eleventh and twelfth centuries.

By the thirteenth century these dramas developed into "mystery" or "miracle" plays performed by lay actors. Mystery plays presented biblical stories concerning God's or Christ's intercession in the world, while miracle plays presented religious stories not found in the Bible—for example, dramas concerning the lives of the saints. Some scholars argue that these plays developed from secular dramatic traditions that evolved alongside, and not from, liturgical traditions. Whatever their origins, the mystery plays took many of the same biblical stories and greatly expanded them so that the plots now included numerous legendary or fanciful events and characters. In addition, actors recited the often humorous and sometimes even ribald dialogue in the local language rather than in Church Latin.

## Mystery Plays

From the thirteenth to the sixteenth centuries, mystery plays were performed in public plazas and other open-air settings across Europe. Ordinary citizens not only enjoyed these public performances, but also acted in them and financed them. In England various guilds produced the mystery plays most closely related to their trade. The goldsmiths, for example, took responsibility for the adoration of the **Magi**, one of the most popular Christmas plays. Other Christmas themes represented in these plays included the slaughter of the innocents (*see* **Holy Innocents' Day**), the **Flight into Egypt**, and the shepherds' pilgrimage to **Bethlehem**.

In the meantime, Church authorities continued to disapprove of the coarse and humorous elements that had crept into the liturgical dramas and mystery plays. Roman Catholic authorities finally forbade churches from presenting the dramas in the fourteenth and fifteenth centuries. The secular versions of the plays began to die out in the sixteenth century due to opposition by the Church as well as the influence of new religious perspectives brought about by the Reformation. In England, the **Puritans** opposed the plays as sacrilegious and worked towards their eradication.

## Folk Dramas in the New World

Even as Europeans were abandoning the mystery and miracle plays, Spanish missionaries were introducing them in the New World. Once again the clergy found that simple, dramatic representations of Bible stories could teach elements of the Christian religion to the illiterate. In this instance the plays also helped to bridge the gap in language and culture between the Spanish missionaries and the native peoples.

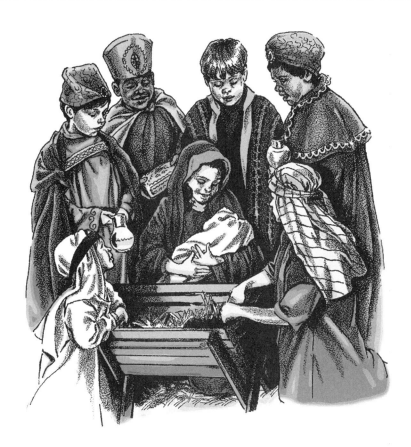

Two of these religious plays survive today in the form of folk dramas that have become Christmas traditions in Mexico and other Central American countries as well as the American Southwest. Los Pastores tells the story of the shepherds' pilgrimage to the Christ child, while Las Posadas tells the story of **Mary** and **Joseph** searching for shelter in Bethlehem.

## Folk Dramas in Europe

In spite of the waning of Nativity plays in Europe, the tradition of **Christmas season** folk dramas continued in other guises. Many writers credit St. Francis of Assisi with creating the first Nativity scene in the early thirteenth century. Using real people and animals, he recreated the scene at the manger in Bethlehem in a cave near the Italian village of Greccio. The custom of staging living Nativity scenes soon spread throughout Europe. It survives today as a Christmas Eve custom in southern France and an **Epiphany** custom in parts of Italy.

Medieval Europeans also donned costumes for another Christmas tradition, **mumming**. Although the masked merrymaking carried out by mummers may not qualify as a form of drama, in some areas mummers presented folk plays as well as simply cavorting under the cover of a disguise. Christmas season mumming practices survived until recent times in Europe and North America. Several Epiphany customs also contain dramatic elements. In many Spanish-speaking countries, people reenact the arrival of the Three Kings at Bethlehem with parades featuring costumed Wise Men riding through the streets on horseback. In central Europe, Epiphany triggers the appearance of the star boys, local lads who carol from house to house dressed as the Three Kings.

### The American Christmas Pageant

Of all the Christmas customs involving elements of folk drama, the contemporary American Christmas pageant bears perhaps the closest resemblance to the early medieval Nativity plays. These pageants are usually performed by children or teens with the aid of adults. They frequently take the form of a simple drama depicting the events surrounding the birth of Jesus. Christmas legends or the "holiday spirit" provide alternative themes. Christmas pageants often include music, especially **Christmas carols**, and various kinds of recitations. One writer traces the history of the American Christmas pageant back to mid-nineteenth-century Boston. Parishioners of a German Catholic church sponsored a pageant in which the parish children, dressed as shepherds and singing Christmas carols, dramatized the shepherds' pilgrimage to Bethlehem. The pageant attracted the attention of people throughout the city. The custom eventually spread across the country to Catholic and Protestant churches alike.

# Nativity Scenes
## Crèche, Manger Scene, Putz

Against the backdrop of a stable complete with straw and farm animals, figurines representing **Mary** and **Joseph** peer with wonder into the cradle where the newborn **Jesus** lies. Dolls representing the Three Kings, or **Magi**, approach with **gifts**, while **shepherds** kneel in adoration of the child. This recreation of the Gospel accounts of

Jesus' birth is called a Nativity scene. Placed in churches, homes, or outdoor locations, Nativity scenes enhance worship or simply delight onlookers with beautiful representations of Christ's birth.

## Origins

The earliest uses of a crib in worship date back to fourth-century Rome. Of the three masses observed at Christmas, one was called *Ad Praesepe* (meaning "to the crib"). This mass took place in the basilica of Santa Maria Maggiore, at a shrine built from boards believed to have come from the original stable of the Nativity in Bethlehem. Churches throughout Italy and Europe gradually adopted the custom of saying mass over a crib at Christmas time.

St. Francis of Assisi generally receives the credit for popularizing the Nativity scene as we know it. It is said that at Christmas time in 1224 he recreated the manger scene using real people and animals in a cave near the Italian village of Greccio. Mass was said in this novel setting, and St. Francis preached about the humble birth of the newborn King. Onlookers enjoyed this reenactment of Christ's birth so much that the custom soon spread throughout Italy and Europe.

Reenactments of this sort still take place on Christmas Eve in some villages in the French region of Provence. Lengthy processions of costumed villagers solemnly file through the streets, arriving finally at the manger of Christ's birth, where a living Mary, Joseph, and baby Jesus await them. In the towns of Les Baux and Séguret, hundreds of people walk in candlelit Christmas Eve processions that end in the local church, where a mass is said.

Living Nativity scenes are also reenacted yearly in Italy. In Abruzzi, Italy, on the night before **Epiphany**, the village of Rivisondoli sponsors a procession and living Nativity scene that involves up to 600 people. Many wear traditional regional costumes and are accompanied by animals as they make their pilgrimage to the manger. Worshipers may also bring gifts for the Holy Child, such as fruit, lambs, chickens, or pigs. The Magi, played by local officials, ride horses. The Virgin Mary rides a donkey and Joseph walks by her side. The procession ends at a manger within a cave and is followed by singing.

## Early Nativity Scenes

The popularity of these living Nativity scenes gave rise to another custom: recreating the birth scene with figurines. By the sixteenth century many churches throughout Italy and Germany presented a Nativity scene of this type at Christmas time. Some French churches adopted the custom as well.

In the seventeenth century families began to create their own Nativity scenes. These became more elaborate with time. The art form reached spectacular heights in eighteenth-century Naples, Italy. Families competed with each other to produce the most elegant and elaborate crib scenes. These scenes expanded far beyond the manger to include village backdrops, ordinary villagers, ruined Roman temples, **angels**, and even foreigners whom the families thought might have rushed to Bethlehem had they known of the miraculous birth.

Rich and noble Italian families employed established artists and sculptors to create clay or wood heads and shoulders. The artists then attached these heads to flexible bodies fashioned out of cloth, string, and wire. Costumes cut of rich fabrics, some embellished with jewels, adorned each figure. The splendor of the backdrops, however, vied with the exquisitely detailed props and figurines for the viewer's attention. Some settings included real waterfalls, while others featured gushing fountains or even an erupting Mount Vesuvius. Today many of these marvelous works are preserved and displayed in Italy's museums and churches.

The Nativity scene also rooted itself firmly in French soil, especially in the southern region of Provence. The first manger scenes included only those figures most related to the story of the Nativity: Mary, Joseph, the baby Jesus, the shepherds, and so on. In the eighteenth century, however, people began to display a multitude of characters in their home Nativity scenes. Some historians claim that Italian peddlers introduced these new figurines to southern France.

In 1803 small clay statuettes from Provence, called *santons* (or "little saints"), appeared at the Christmas fair in Marseille. These santons became an essential element of the French Nativity scene. In addition to characters mentioned in the biblical accounts of the Nativity, the Provençal santons represented a wide variety of ordinary French townspeople, such as the baker, the mayor, the fishmonger, the village idiot, and others. One historian has identified many of these figures as stock characters in folk **Nativity plays** that circulated throughout the region as early as the Middle Ages. Like their Italian counterparts, French Nativity scenes depicted the birth of Christ taking place in a local setting, such as a village in Provence. French settlers brought the Christmas crib with them to Canada where another innovation occurred. The French Canadians of Quebec often set up their Nativity scenes under the **Christmas tree**.

## Southern Europe

In southern Europe, where the Christmas tree never found much favor, home Christmas decoration focuses around the Nativity scene. The Spanish call the scene a nacimiento (meaning "birth") or a belén (meaning "Bethlehem"), the Italians call it a presépio (meaning "crib"), and the French call it a crèche (meaning "crib"). In the same way that many North Americans collect Christmas tree **ornaments**, many southern European families slowly build a treasured collection of Nativity figurines. Though the scene itself may be assembled beforehand, many await Christmas Eve or Christmas morning to place the baby Jesus in his crib. Some civic and church celebrations also center on manger scenes. In Spain, Nativity scenes may be found in public plazas. On Epiphany, several local men dressed as the Three Kings may visit the public Nativity scene, reenacting the adoration of the Magi.

In Italy, Nativity scenes can be found everywhere in the weeks before Christmas. Shop windows display manger scenes made out of pastry, bread, fruit, seeds, shells, and even butter. Children make Nativity scenes out of cardboard or papier mâché. Many churches present crib scenes as well. The Basilica of Saints Cosmos and Damian in Rome houses one of the most famous. Measuring twenty-seven feet high, forty-five feet long, and twenty-one feet wide, it contains several hundred hand-sculpted wooden statues. Rome's Church of Santa Maria in Ara Coeli exhibits the most famous Christ child, however. An old custom encourages children to recite carefully memorized sermons in front of his crib. Folk beliefs credit the jewel-studded golden infant, known as "Santo Bambino," with the power to heal.

## Central Europe

In Germany, Switzerland, Austria, and other central European countries, the preparation of Nativity scenes still provides a delightful occupation for children and adults during **Advent**. The German Nativity scene, called a Krippe (meaning "crib"), may contain hundreds of figurines and many lovely details. In the Czech Republic and Slovakia, people call their manger scenes "Bethlehems." In some areas the figures may be constructed from bread dough and later painted.

## *Latin America*

Spanish colonizers brought the Nativity scene with them to the Americas. The Nativity scene enjoys widespread popularity throughout Latin America today, where it is known as a *nacimiento, pesebre, portale,* or in Portuguese-speaking Brazil, as a *presepio* or *lapinha*. Latin American manger scenes range from simple representations of the Holy Family to elaborate depictions of the manger, village, and surrounding countryside. This countryside may host characters more likely to be found in rural South America than in ancient Judea, including women making tortillas, Indians selling tropical fruit, and peasants leading heavily laden burros. The figurines themselves range from relatively crude clay representations to delicate antique figurines passed down from previous generations. In Mexico many families set up their Nativity scenes on December 16, a date that corresponds with the beginning of the nine-day Christmas novena.

Many Latin American families place the Jesus figurine in his cradle on Christmas Eve. The Magi, on the other hand, inch forward daily towards the manger, arriving on January 6, Epiphany. Throughout Latin America Nativity scenes may also be found in churches and public squares. Many of these traditions can also be found throughout the American Southwest, a region of the United States with a long history of Spanish and Mexican settlement.

### The United States

In the eighteenth century, German Moravian immigrants brought this custom with them to the United States. The Moravian Nativity scenes, called putz (from the German word for "decorate"), spread out in extravagant detail. Dozens or hundreds of figurines might be placed amidst gardens, fountains, arbors, villages, streams, bridges, waterfalls, and other delightful scenery. Noah's ark and the pairs of attendant animals often made their appearance in the putz as well. These elaborate designs might take up an entire room. People who built putzes invested a lot of time and energy into giving their landscapes a life-like appearance. They gathered real moss and other greenery to cover the hills and fields, sprinkled sand along their lakefronts to create beaches, and illuminated their buildings from within with tiny candles. Some devotees created miniature mechanical devices to turn mill wheels and make water flow in streams. In Pennsylvania many German Americans, particularly those in areas settled by Moravians, maintain the custom of "putzing" and "putz-visiting." The town of **Bethlehem, Pennsylvania**, founded by Moravians, builds a community putz every year. On one occasion, the builders used eight hundred pounds of sand, sixty-four tree stumps, twelve bushels of moss, forty evergreen trees, and forty-eight angels in the creation of the community putz.

In the early twentieth century it was customary for many cities and towns throughout the United States to set up public Nativity scenes at Christmas time, often on the grounds of city hall or other government land. In the early 1970s, these displays became the focus of controversy. Questions were raised about the separation of church and state, and the appearance of the local government promoting one particular religion over others. In 1973, the American Civil Liberties Union won a landmark lawsuit that ruled Nativity scenes on government land to be in violation of the U.S. Constitution. As a result, many cities and towns have discontinued the practice of displaying public Nativity scenes. However, many families and churches continue to enjoy this Christmas tradition, and outdoor Nativity scenes can often be found displayed on privately owned land.

# New York City, Christmas in

A number of New Yorkers and New York City customs have played an important role in the development of the American Christmas. Several nineteenth-century New Yorkers helped to bring **Santa Claus** into being. In more recent times New York City has become an important destination for Christmas shoppers and tourists. Finally, at least one of the city's Christmas traditions, **Macy's Thanksgiving Day Parade**, has become a nationally televised event announcing the start of the Christmas season.

### Birth of Santa Claus

Most historians agree that Santa Claus bears a suspicious resemblance to the European **gift** bringer **St. Nicholas**. This resemblance is no coincidence, in spite of the fact that Dutch and German immigrants to the American colonies don't appear to have brought with them much of their St. Nicholas folklore. The early American writer Washington Irving gave St. Nicholas an important position in New York's Dutch community in his satirical book *A History of New York* (1809). In 1822 one of Irving's friends, Clement C. Moore, a languages professor at New York's General Theological Seminary, used elements of Irving's portrayal of St. Nicholas in a poem of his own. Entitled "'Twas the Night Before Christmas" ("A Visit from St. Nicholas"), the poem describes a Christmas gift bringer who rides through the night skies on Christmas Eve in a magic sleigh pulled by flying **reindeer** and enters homes via the chimney. Though Moore called the gift bringer "St. Nicholas," the American public soon dubbed the pot-bellied, pipe-smoking man "Santa Claus." Moore's description suggests that St. Nicholas was smaller than life-sized, in fact, an elf. In the latter part of the nineteenth century, *Harper's Weekly* illustrator Thomas Nast published a series of prints depicting Santa Claus. Nast settled on depicting him as a life-sized, portly old man with a long white beard and a pipe. This description seized the public's imagination and became part of Santa's official image.

In 1897, yet another New Yorker, this time an eight-year-old girl named **Virginia O'Hanlon,** helped Americans to settle some of their metaphysical questions concerning the national gift bringer. She wrote a letter to a local newspaper called the *New York Sun* asking the newspaper editor to tell her whether or not Santa Claus was real. Virginia's letter and the newspaper's response have become beloved bits of American Christmas lore. The often-quoted phrase, "Yes, Virginia, there is a Santa Claus," comes from the paper's editorial response, written by reporter Francis P. Church.

## Macy's Parade

As Santa Claus became an important part of American Christmas folklore, he was drafted into the service of many commercial ventures. For example, he plays an important role in Macy's Thanksgiving Day Parade, begun in 1924. Macy's started the parade as a means of attracting shoppers to its stores and extending the Christmas **shopping** season as far back as Thanksgiving. The classic Christmas movie *Miracle on 34th Street* (1947) boosted the parade's fame by showing shots of the parade during the movie's opening scenes. Nationwide television coverage followed. In this manner the parade worked its way from an event of local importance to a national icon of the start of the holiday season. The parade's trademark feature consists of a series of enormous balloons in a wide variety of fun shapes, including those of cartoon characters and animals. Traditionally, Santa Claus brings up the rear of the parade. For New Yorkers, Santa's arrival kicks off the start of the holiday shopping season.

## Window Displays

In addition to their reputation for quantity and quality of goods, a number of New York stores are famous for their Christmas **store window displays.** The more well-known department stores announce opening dates for their windows, which often pre-date Thanksgiving, and people trying to get the first glimpses of these magnificent tableaux may crowd the pavement outside the stores on these days. Indeed, thousands line up to see the windows at Lord and Taylor—located on Fifth Avenue at 38th Street—which often feature mechanized, moving displays.

## Rockefeller Center

Other New York City Christmas sites and decorations that have become familiar to the public at large include the **Christmas tree** and skating rink at Rockefeller Center. Over the years Rockefeller Center has become an important destination for the city's Christmas tourists.

The first Rockefeller Center Christmas tree, erected in 1931, measured only twelve feet high. It was put up on the empty lot by the men at work constructing the new complex of buildings, some say out of gratitude for having a job during the Depression. In 1933, the owners of the completed Rockefeller Center decided to carry on the tradition of the yearly tree. The tradition has been going strong since then. The first few Christmas trees at Rockefeller Center were erected in the middle of the sunken plaza. In 1936, the plaza was transformed into a winter ice-skating rink. Nowadays the tree is set up next to the skating rink, at 50th Street and Fifth Avenue.

Designers have tried various tree-decorating schemes over the years. In 1933, strings of blue and white lights ornamented the tree. Another year only floodlights were used. During World War II, **ornaments** took the place of the lights that were eliminated in order to meet wartime blackout requirements. The use of ornaments was discontinued, however, when it was discovered that high winds, enhanced by the wind tunnel effect created by the surrounding tall buildings, could easily dislodge them from the tree. Decorators realized the danger posed by ornaments the year they festooned the tree with aluminum icicles. During strong winds the tree menaced people passing below by discharging volleys of the spear-like icicles.

In recent years, the tree has been decorated with 30,000 multi-colored, energy-efficient LED lights strung on more than five miles of wire. The lights are powered in part by hundreds of solar panels located on the roof of one of the Rockefeller Center buildings. The tree is topped with a giant crystal star made by Swarovski. The star measures 9 1/2 feet in diameter and is 1 1/2 feet deep. It contains 25,000 individual crystals with a total of one million facets. The star is lit by 720 LED bulbs that are controlled by a special computerized light sequencing program to produce a twinkling effect. Each year, the Rockefeller Center Christmas Tree is viewed by more than 2.5 million people.

Rockefeller Center's landscape and garden team search New York and New England for potential Christmas trees throughout the year. In order to find a Norway Spruce—the preferred variety—that has grown to about seventy or eighty feet, the team may employ the services of a helicopter. The trees usually come from privately owned properties rather than forests, as this variety is not native to the region. Once the ideal tree is spotted, the owners are approached with an offer to sell their tree. Many feel it an honor to have their tree selected for Rockefeller Center. The final selection is made by mid-summer. At the end of the Christmas season, the tree is recycled. In 2010, the seventy-four-foot tall, forty-foot diameter Norway Spruce was milled into lumber and donated to Habitat for Humanity.

### Other Decorations

A number of the city's well-known buildings and institutions decorate for the holidays. The corporation that owns the Empire State Building illuminates the upper floors of the building with red and green lights during the month of December. The Humanities and Social Sciences Library of the New York City public library system—located at Fifth Avenue between 41st and 42nd Streets—shows its holiday spirit by placing two 60-pound **wreaths** around the necks of the magnificent stone lions that adorn the steps to the building. New Yorkers have become accustomed to the giant snowflake that dangles above the intersection of Fifth Avenue and 57th Street. The snowflake stands approximately two-and-one-half stories high and contains 6,000 light bulbs. This seasonal decoration first appeared in 1984. Ritzy Park Avenue puts on its own show for Christmas, decking the trees planted in the Avenue's meridians with white and gold lights. The display stretches for about two miles, beginning around 48th Street and ending at 96th Street.

### Events

Each Christmas season the Rockettes, a troupe of female dancers, put on a special Christmas show at Radio City Music Hall. This tradition dates back to 1933. Each year the Rockettes perform the dance of the toy soldiers, which ends with the toy soldiers, all in a row, falling over backwards like a set of dominoes. Since 1954 New Yorkers have also enjoyed yearly performances of *The Nutcracker* by the New York City Ballet Company. Those who prefer song to dance may attend the *Messiah* Sing-In at Avery Fisher Hall. At this event the audience takes a stab at singing Handel's oratorio themselves. This tradition dates back to the 1960s. Many New Yorkers and out-of-towners celebrate Christmas by taking in a Broadway show. Indeed, New York's justly famous theater district sells more tickets at Christmas time than at any other time of year.

## New Year's Eve

Finally, many Americans close out the holiday season by tuning in to another New York City event: the large street party at Times Square on New Year's Eve. The climax of the party comes at midnight, when a large, illuminated ball atop a pole standing on the roof of the former Times Building begins to drop. The fall lasts sixty seconds and marks the last minute of the old year and the exact beginning of the new year. This event has been broadcast on television since 1943. In recent years, an estimated one million people have gathered in Times Square on New Year's Eve to wait for the magic moment when the ball drops. Millions more in the U.S. and around the world watch the festivities on television.

## Heightened Security

After the tragic terrorist attacks of September 11, 2001, security in New York City has been heightened, particularly during any events that draw large crowds of people. The New York Police Department has instituted anti-terrorism countermeasures and exercises an abundance of caution when dealing with large-scale events such as the Macy's Thanksgiving Day Parade, Christmas at Rockefeller Center, and New Year's Eve at Times Square. Among other measures that go unpublicized, the city typically deploys a larger number of both uniformed and plainclothes police officers to patrol events. In recent years, police have blocked or restricted access to a greater number of streets and access points in areas surrounding large events. Event attendees are not allowed to carry or wear backpacks, and special technologies such as radiation detectors may also be used for screening purposes.

# Noel

## Noël, Nowel, Nowell

Contemporary English dictionaries define the word "noel" (also spelled "noël," "nowel," or "nowell") as a cry of joy associated with the celebration of Christmas. In past eras English speakers also used the word to refer to the feast of Christmas itself. This usage never faded in the French language, where the word *Noël* still means Christmas, or, when spelled without a capital "n," means **Christmas carol.** Although the English word "noel" is now considered somewhat obsolete, a number of traditional Christmas carols retain this old expression.

Researchers differ in their explanations of the origin of the word "noel." Most trace it back to the Latin word for birthday, *natalis*. Indeed, in the fourth century Church authorities in Rome introduced Christmas as *Dies Natalis Domini*, the "Birthday of the Lord" (*see also* **December 25**). The more formal name for the holiday was *Festum Nativitatis Domini Nostri Jesu Christi*, the "Feast of the Nativity of Our Lord Jesus Christ." Over the centuries the Latin words *Natalis* and *Nativitatis* passed into local languages across western Europe, giving birth to vernacular words for Christmas. For example, the Portuguese call Christmas *Natal*, the Italians refer to it as *Natale*, and the Spanish call it *Navidad*. Other modern words for Christmas that probably evolved from the Latin *natalis* include the Gaelic *Nollaig*, the Welsh *Nadolig*, and the Provençal *Nadal*. Most scholars also trace the English "noel" and the French "Noël" back to the Latin word *natalis*.

In contrast, other writers suggest that the English word "noel" evolved from the Latin word for "news," *novella*. They believe that this Latin term was used to tell the joyous news of the birth of **Jesus**, and so became the jubilant cry of those celebrating the feast of Christmas, or even another term for the feast itself. One researcher who supports this theory notes that in the Middle Ages people greeted news of especially happy events with cries of "noel." Finally, another scholar has suggested that "noel" comes from the Hebrew word *Immanuel* (or Emmanuel). This word—which, in Christian scripture is used to refer to Jesus (Matthew 1:23)—means "God with us."

# North Pole

How did **Santa Claus** come to choose the North Pole as his home? He didn't. This address was chosen for him by American cartoonist Thomas Nast. In 1882 Nast depicted Santa perched on top of a crate bearing the label "Christmas box 1882, St. Nicholas, North Pole." Nast's vision apparently caught on. Several years later, another artist portrayed Santa returning to his North Pole home. Soon, it became standard lore that the jolly **gift** giver inhabited the polar north.

What inspired Nast to give Santa such a remote residence? The influential portrait of the Christmas gift giver, painted decades earlier by Clement C. Moore in "'Twas

the Night Before Christmas" ("A Visit from St. Nicholas"), described him wearing fur robes. This made it likely that he came from a cold climate. Nast may also have read Horatio Alger's 1875 poem entitled "St. Nicholas," in which Alger declared that this "patron saint of Christmas night" lived beyond the "polar seas." At the time when Nast was conjuring up his images of Santa, no explorer had yet reached the North Pole, although several expeditions had begun the perilous journey. This remote and mysterious place, which no human being had yet seen, must have seemed the perfect abode for that elusive and magical creature, Santa Claus (*see also* Children's Letters).

# The Nutcracker

One of the best-loved and most widely known ballets of our time, *The Nutcracker*, tells the story of a young girl's enchanted Christmas Eve. German writer, illustrator, and composer E. T. A. Hoffmann wrote the original story on which the ballet is based. Russian composer Pyotr Ilich Tchaikovsky set the tale to music in the early 1890s. Some ballet companies present *The Nutcracker* every year at Christmas time. In addition, Tchaikovsky's "The Nutcracker Suite," a shorter, orchestral work that summarizes the music presented at length in the ballet, appears on many Christmas concert programs.

## The Tales and the Making of the Ballet

Hoffmann would have been delighted to discover that his stories lived on to inspire the works of great composers. Hoffmann himself found tremendous inspiration in the works of Austrian composer Wolfgang Amadeus Mozart, so much so that he changed his own middle name to Amadeus. Years after Hoffmann's death, his life as a teller of tales fueled the musical imagination of French composer Jacques Offenbach. Offenbach's opera *The Tales of Hoffmann* spins a fantasy around the writer and a number of his works.

One of Hoffmann's stories, "The Nutcracker and the Mouse King" (1819), intrigued French writer Alexandre Dumas. Dumas published a translated and freely adapted version of this story in French. Dumas's "The Story of a Nutcracker" (1844) charmed the director of Russia's Imperial Ballet, who decided to commission a work based on the story. He hired the French choreographer Marius Petipa and his Russian colleague Lev Ivanov to choreograph the dancing. Petipa and Ivanov outlined the stage action needed to tell the story. Then they handed over a specific set of instructions to the composer who had been commissioned to write the music for the ballet. Luckily for future ballet lovers they selected Pyotr Tchaikovsky, who at that time was already considered a rising star among Russia's composers.

Hoffmann's complicated and somewhat frightening tale can hardly be recognized in today's productions of *The Nutcracker*. Petipa and Ivanov presented *The Nutcracker* as a delightful children's fantasy. The ballet companies that have performed *The Nutcracker* since then have adjusted the story here and there as well.

### The Story as Told in the Ballet

Basically, the tale unfolds as follows. The first act takes place at a Christmas Eve party in Nuremberg, Germany. Many guests and their children arrive at the home of the Stahlbaum family. While the adults decorate the **Christmas tree**, the children play with toys. The mysterious Drosselmeyer arrives, bringing **gifts** for his godchildren, Clara and Fritz Stahlbaum. Clara immediately falls in love with one of the toys, a wooden nutcracker. Careless Fritz takes possession of the toy and breaks it, upsetting Clara greatly. The guests depart and the children are sent to bed.

Shortly thereafter, Clara comes back to the drawing room to visit her nutcracker. Clara finds herself reduced to the same size as the nutcracker and her brother's toy soldiers. Dozens of mice come out of their holes and, led by their king, attack the soldiers. The nutcracker rallies the toy soldiers against the mice. As the mouse king and the nutcracker fight one another, Clara throws her shoe at the mouse king, giving the nutcracker the chance to defeat him. The soldiers win, and the nutcracker turns into a prince. Out of gratitude for her help, the nutcracker prince takes Clara on a journey to the Kingdom of Sweets. They pass through a flurry of dancing snowflakes as they enter the magic kingdom.

In act two the citizens of the Kingdom of Sweets entertain Clara and the nutcracker prince. Exotic foodstuffs, such as Arabian coffee and Spanish hot chocolate, dance for them. Even flowers come to life and begin to waltz. Finally, the queen of this enchanted kingdom, the Sugarplum Fairy, dances with the nutcracker prince (*see also*

Sugarplums). Most versions of the ballet end with Clara returning to her own world, while in others she remains in the Kingdom of the Sweets.

## Tchaikovsky's Score

Although Tchaikovsky accepted the job of producing the musical score for *The Nutcracker*, the task proved somewhat troublesome for him. He began working on the score in winter 1891. His personality and life circumstances may have contributed to the difficulty he experienced in composing the lighthearted music for the ballet. Extremely sensitive by nature, he often fell into periods of deep gloom. Several months before he began work on *The Nutcracker*, his close friend and patron, Nadezhda von Meck, abruptly severed both their financial and personal relationships for no apparent reason. This abandonment plunged Tchaikovsky into depression and deeply shook his faith in human relationships. This recent event may explain why the composer found himself uninspired by the task of setting the sweet, simple fairy tale to music. Moreover, the rigid framework given him by the choreographers, which specified the character and exact length of many musical passages, restricted the degree of creativity he could bring to the work.

Nevertheless, Tchaikovsky labored away at the project until two great life events interrupted his progress. In March he left Russia for the United States, where he had been engaged to conduct the concert that was to open New York City's new music hall, known today as Carnegie Hall. His journey to the United States took him through Paris, France. There he learned that his sister Alexandra had died. In a letter to his brother Modest, the composer confessed, "Today even more than yesterday I feel the absolute impossibility of portraying the 'sugar-plum fairy' in music."

After a successful sojourn in the United States, his return trip to Russia again took him through France. There he bought a newly invented musical instrument called a celesta to take back with him to Russia. Tchaikovsky would introduce Russian audiences to its haunting xylophone-like tones in "The Dance of the Sugarplum Fairy," one of the most famous passages from *The Nutcracker*. When Tchaikovsky arrived in Russia in June, he once again took up his work on the score. In spite of all his efforts, he confided in a letter to a friend that he thought *The Nutcracker* music far inferior to the music he had composed for the ballet *Sleeping Beauty*.

Tchaikovsky's estimation of the value of *The Nutcracker* music gradually increased. He decided to write an orchestral suite based on the ballet music. This time it took

him only twelve days to complete the work. "The Nutcracker Suite" premiered in March 1892, before the ballet had ever been performed. The audience loved the evocative melodies and requested several encores. Even today, "The Nutcracker Suite" stands as one of Tchaikovsky's best-loved works.

## First Performances

The first performance of *The Nutcracker* ballet took place on December 17, 1892, in St. Petersburg, Russia. The audience and critics reacted without enthusiasm. Some writers point out that audiences of Tchaikovsky's time were not used to the idea of ballets being performed to high-quality symphonic music. In fact, Tchaikovsky's three great ballet scores—*Swan Lake*, *Sleeping Beauty*, and *The Nutcracker*—raised the standard for ballet music and opened the door for other important composers to enter the field. Early audiences of *The Nutcracker* may also have disliked the fact that children occupy center stage for most of the first act and that the serious dancing does not really begin until the second act. Luckily for Tchaikovsky, however, Tsar Alexander III of Russia liked the ballet. With the Tsar's nod of approval, *The Nutcracker* became a standard work in the world of Russian ballet. Outside of Russia, however, the ballet remained unknown for many years.

At the height of his career, less than a year after the premiere of *The Nutcracker*, Tchaikovsky was dead. In fall 1893, a Russian nobleman discovered that his nephew had an affair with the composer and threatened to expose Tchaikovsky as a homosexual. Alarmed by this development, a number of Tchaikovsky's associates and former college classmates met to decide the composer's fate. This so-called "court of honor" ruled that Tchaikovsky should commit suicide in order to protect his, and, by extension, their reputations. Tchaikovsky had long feared the scandal and complete social shunning that would engulf him and his family if the public discovered his sexual orientation. When the great composer was found dead two days later, his associates circulated the story that during a cholera epidemic, he had contracted the disease from drinking a glass of unboiled water at a restaurant.

## International Fame

The first performance of *The Nutcracker* in the West took place in London in 1934. In 1944 the San Francisco Ballet became the first American company to present the ballet. In 1954 the New York City Ballet added the work to their repertoire. Since that time *The Nutcracker* has become a December favorite for many dance companies. The work naturally attached itself to the **Christmas season**, since all the action in the story takes place on Christmas Eve. The story's magical elements offer ballet companies the opportunity to entertain their audiences not only with wonderful music and dancing, but also with fabulous costumes and fantastic special effects. The razzle-dazzle appeals to children as well as adults. In fact, many parents bring children to see *The Nutcracker* as a special holiday treat. Due to its popularity with audiences, the ballet has become a relied-upon money-maker for many ballet companies. Box-office receipts from its performances must often finance a good portion of a company's season.

# Old Christmas Day

When Pope Gregory XIII established the Gregorian calendar in 1582, he ushered in an era in which the people of Europe disagreed on what day it was. As a result, various groups celebrated Christmas on different days. Before the Gregorian reform, Europe had adhered to the Julian calendar, which was a full ten days behind the newly instituted Gregorian calendar. Some nations and churches refused to adopt the Gregorian reforms. In these lands people continued to celebrate Christmas on **December 25**, but did so according to the Julian calendar. Their celebrations fell on January 5 according to the new Gregorian calendar. In past eras the English sometimes referred to January 5 or 6 as "Old Christmas Day."

## Calendar Confusion

By the sixteenth century many learned Europeans realized that there was something seriously wrong with their calendar system. The calendar in use at that time was called the Julian calendar, named after the Roman emperor Julius Caesar, who authorized its adoption in 46 B.C. A small but important error marred this calendar system. The astronomers who designed the Julian calendar calculated the solar year to be 365.25 days long. In fact, it takes the earth 365.2422 days to complete its orbit around the sun. While this difference only amounts to 11 minutes and 14 seconds every year, each passing year compounded the error, increasing the gap between the dates on the Julian calendar and the astronomical events and seasonal changes of the solar year. For example, in 45 B.C. spring equinox fell on March 25. By the time the Council of Nicea met in 325 A.D. to determine the date of Easter, spring equinox was falling on March 21.

As the centuries passed, scholars debated the calendar problem, although nothing was done to correct it until the sixteenth century. In 1545 the Council of Trent empowered Pope Paul III to propose a solution to the dilemma. Investigators labored on the problem for forty years, until a Jesuit astronomer named Christoph Clavius submitted a viable program of calendar reform to Pope Gregory XIII. In 1582 Pope Gregory XIII officially adopted Clavius's proposed reforms, resulting in a new calendar system known as the Gregorian calendar.

The researchers who devised the Gregorian calendar knew the true length of the solar year and based the new calendar around it. In order to correct the errors that had compounded over the years from the use of the Julian calendar system, Pope Gregory XIII decreed that ten days be eliminated from the calendar year of 1582. Thus, in that year October 5 was followed by October 15 in all lands that had adopted the new calendar. This brought the spring equinox back to March 21, the date on which it had occurred at the time of the Council of Nicea. Medieval calendar systems had also been plagued by the fact that the nations of Europe began their new year on different dates. The Gregorian calendar also declared January 1 to be New Year's Day in an attempt to standardize the beginning of the European year.

## Resistance to Reform

Although scholars agreed that the Julian calendar system was flawed, many European nations resisted the changes proposed by the Gregorian calendar. Religious controversies fueled this resistance. The Roman Catholic nations of Italy, France, Luxembourg, Spain, and Portugal switched to the new calendar system in the same year it was announced. Many Protestant nations hesitated to adopt the calendar for fear of seeming to accept the authority of the Pope. In addition, much of Orthodox eastern Europe viewed the proposed changes as out of step with their religious traditions. This meant that at the close of the sixteenth century, the nations that did adopt the Gregorian reforms were fully ten days ahead of those that did not.

## Europe Adopts the New Calendar

By 1584 most of the Roman Catholic German states had adopted the calendar, along with Belgium and parts of the Netherlands. Hungary switched to the new calendar in 1587. Switzerland began making the changes in 1583 and completed them 229 years later, in 1812. More than one hundred years passed before the Protestant nations began to adopt the Gregorian calendar. Denmark and the German Protestant states did so around the year 1700. In 1752 Great Britain and its colonies converted to the Gregorian calendar system. Sweden followed suit in 1753. Japan joined the Gregorian system in 1873, and Egypt in 1875. Between the years 1912 and 1917, many of the eastern European states switched to the Gregorian calendar system, including Albania, Bulgaria, Estonia, Latvia, Lithuania, Romania, and the former Yugoslavia. China also embraced the Gregorian system during those years. Russia joined the club in 1918, just after the Revolution. Greece held out until the early 1920s, the last major European nation to adopt the sixteenth-century reforms.

## Christmas Controversy

At the time of its creation, the ten-day gap between the new Gregorian calendar and the old Julian calendar created a situation in which the peoples of Europe celebrated Christmas on different days. By the time England adopted the Gregorian calendar in 1752, the gap had crept up to eleven days. With the stroke of a pen, English legislators ordered that September 2, 1752, be followed by September 14, 1752.

Many ordinary people defied this change, fearful that it would adversely affect their livelihood in some way. Although many writers have reported that resistance to the new calendar took the form of riots and slogans, such as "Give us back our eleven days," recent research has failed to find convincing evidence of these events. Instead, it appears that people resisted the change in less dramatic, more personal ways. Some refused to celebrate the feast days on the new Gregorian schedule and clung instead to the old dates, now known by different names (*see also* **Glastonbury Thorn**). For example, under the Gregorian reform the day that had been December 25 instantly became January 5. Many called January 5 "Old Christmas Day" or Christmas Day "Old Style." Correspondingly, December 25 was known as Christmas Day "New Style." By the nineteenth century Old Christmas Day had crept a day further away from the Gregorian calendar, falling on January 6, **Epiphany**. As the Julian calendar continued to drift away from the Gregorian calendar throughout the twentieth century, Old Christmas Day shifted yet another day forward in the Gregorian calendar, falling on January 7.

Some branches of the Orthodox Church have never accepted the Gregorian calendar. Their festival dates are still set according to the Julian calendar. Therefore, they observe Christian festivals on different dates than do most Western Christians. In Russia, for example, Orthodox believers celebrate Christmas on January 7. Orthodox Ethiopians and Egyptians also observe Christmas on January 7.

# Ornaments

Snow-covered evergreens standing in the woods are merely trees. Once decorated, they become **Christmas trees**. Over the centuries people have adorned their Christmas trees with many different kinds of objects. The very earliest ornaments tended to recall the religious significance of the holiday. At one point people decorated their Christmas trees with good things to eat and **gifts** for one another. In more recent times Christmas ornaments have served primarily as pretty decorations for the tree.

### Earliest Ornaments

The earliest known Christmas tree ornaments were apples. Medieval actors used them to decorate the **paradise tree**, the central prop of the paradise play, a medieval European mystery play often performed on December 24 (*see also* **Nativity Plays**). The apples represented the temptation of Adam and Eve in the Garden of Eden. Later, unconsecrated communion wafers were added to the tree, representing the salvation offered to humankind by **Jesus**. Cherries might also hang from the tree in honor of the Virgin **Mary** (*see also* **Cherry Trees**). Although these town-square dramas eventually fell out of favor with the populace, some historians suspect that people in parts of France and Germany kept the custom of celebrating Christmas with a decorated fir tree, which eventually became known as a Christmas tree.

The first detailed description of a decorated Christmas tree in someone's home dates back to 1605 and comes from Strasbourg, Germany. According to this account, early seventeenth-century Germans festooned their Christmas trees with roses made out of colored paper, apples, wafers, and decorations made of shiny bits of gold foil or sugar. Indeed, a wide variety of ornaments made from food dangled from early German Christmas trees. The Germans hung gilded nuts on their trees, and later, cookies. They shaped these cookies in the form of **angels, bells, hearts, and stars** (*see also* **Star of Bethlehem**). Fruits and vegetables molded out of marzipan and colored with vegetable dyes soon followed. Some people made ornaments out of eggshells, transforming them, for example, into tiny baskets which could be filled with candy. In fact, the traditional German Christmas tree was covered with so many good things to eat that it was nicknamed a "sugar tree." Children looked forward to dismantling the tree on January 6, **Epiphany**, because they were then allowed to gobble up all the treats that had tempted them throughout the Christmas season.

### Early Nineteenth-Century Ornaments

German immigrants brought their tree-decorating ideas with them to the United States. Like their ancestors in the old country, the Pennsylvania Dutch covered their Christmas trees with apples, nuts, and cookies. Some of them had brought elaborately carved wooden cookie molds with them from Germany. Others devised new tin cookie cutters to transform their dough into birds, animals, flowers, and other fanciful shapes.

As more Americans adopted the Christmas tree in the nineteenth century, they continued the German tradition of decorating it with good things to eat (*see also* **America, Christmas in Nineteenth-Century**). With a needle and thread they created long strings of cranberries and popcorn to drape over its branches, thereby adding two native American plant products to the decorated tree. They also created cornucopias, small cone- or horn-shaped containers filled with hard candies, and dangled them from the tree. Some stuffed lace bags with tiny treats and hung these as ornaments. Lucky children might also find **sugarplums** tucked among the branches of the tree. Candy canes, too, whose shape recalled **shepherds**' crooks, might swing from the branches of the nineteenth-century tree. Inventive women also fashioned ornaments out of strings of beads, ribbons, gilt paper, and lace.

In addition, many Americans adopted the German custom of hanging gifts for children on the branches of the Christmas tree. This worked because parents gave their children lightweight, unwrapped trinkets rather than heavy, boxed gifts throughout most of the nineteenth-century (*see also* **Shopping; Wrapping Paper**). Some families, however, preferred to hang **stockings** by the fireplace as receptacles for gifts. As people began to give each other heavier gifts, the placement of gifts shifted to the space beneath the Christmas tree.

Covered with cookies and candies, studded with nuts, gilded with glittering candles, and trimmed with trinkets of all sorts, the nineteenth-century Christmas tree dazzled children and adults alike. In his short story "A Christmas Tree" (1850), English author Charles Dickens captured the allure of the bountifully decorated tree of his era in the following lines:

> I have been looking, this evening, at a merry company of children assembled round that pretty German toy, a Christmas tree. The tree was planted in the middle of a great round table, and towered high above their heads. It was brilliantly lighted by a multitude of little tapers; and everywhere sparkled and glittered with bright objects. There were rosy-cheeked dolls, hiding behind green leaves; and there were real watches (with movable hands, at least, and an endless capacity of being wound up) dangling from innumerable twigs; there were French polished tables, chairs, bedsteads, wardrobes, eight-day clocks, and various other articles of domestic furniture (wonderfully made, in tin, at Wolverhampton), perched among the boughs, as if in preparation for some fairy housekeeping; there

were jolly, broad-faced little men, much more agreeable in appearance than many real men—and no wonder, for their head took off, and showed them to be full of sugarplums; there were fiddles and drums; there were tambourines, books, work-boxes, paint-boxes, sweetmeat-boxes, peepshow-boxes, and all kinds of boxes; there were trinkets for the elder girls, far brighter than any grown-up gold and jewels; there were baskets and pin cushions in all devices; there were guns, swords and banners; there were witches standing in enchanted rings of pasteboard, to tell fortunes; there were teetotums, humming-tops, needle-cases, pen-wipers, smelling-bottles, conversation-cards, bouquet-holders; real fruit, made artificially dazzling with gold leaf; imitation apples, pears, walnuts, crammed with surprises; in short, as a pretty child, before me, delightedly whispered to another pretty child, her bosom friend, "There was everything, and more."

Dickens's enticing description leaves little room to wonder why the decorated Christmas tree soon became the focus of family Christmas celebrations.

## Commercial Ornaments

Sometime around 1870 a new fad in Christmas tree decorations began. Instead of decorating the tree with gifts and things to eat, people began to buy commercially made decorations designed solely for use as ornaments. Most of these early commercial ornaments came from Germany.

Early German designers fashioned novel ornaments out of tin and wax. In the city of Dresden, artisans specialized in making ornaments out of embossed and painted cardboard. Only some of their designs featured Christmas symbols. They also crafted numerous ornaments shaped like fish, birds, ordinary and exotic animals, or recent inventions, such as the steamship and the motor car. In 1878 artisans from Nuremberg devised thin strips of silver foil that could be strewn over the tree's branches like icicles. They called the thin strips *engelshaar*, which means "angels' hair," but we know them today as "tinsel." German printers also adopted recently invented color-printing techniques to turn out thousands of color illustrations of Christmas themes. Popular designs included angels and **St. Nicholas**. People collected especially pretty images and began to use them to ornament their Christmas trees and, sometimes, even to decorate their **Christmas cookies**.

## Glass Ornaments

The blown-glass ornaments that began to pour out of Lauscha, Germany, in the 1870s really caught the public's fancy. Lauscha had been a center of German glass-making for centuries. In the second half of the nineteenth century, some of its artisans discovered that they could blow decorative shapes out of glass to adorn Christmas trees. Demand was so high that the entire town was quickly drawn into the ornament industry. Whole families worked side by side, with the adult men molding the glass, the adult women silvering and painting the ornaments, and children breaking the glass stems and attaching metal caps. Soon, buyers representing major American stores, such as F. W. Woolworth, were making trips to Lauscha to snap up these unique Christmas decorations.

These early buyers chose their stock from a profusion of glass apples, pears, pinecones, and icicles. As the market for their products expanded, the glassblowers began to diversify their output into a dizzying range of shapes. Soon buyers could choose between a myriad of vegetable shapes, including pickles, carrots and corn, angels, St. Nicholas, cartoon characters, hot air balloons, zeppelins, fish, dogs, clowns, birds, trumpets, drums, violins, bells, hearts, houses, churches, and more. A great deal of handcrafting went into many of these early glass ornaments. Some artisans, for example, took the trouble to insert tiny whistles into the stems of their trumpet ornaments, so that they could sound a single note. Americans could not get enough of these German novelties.

Although World War I disrupted production in Germany and cut off America's supply, the ornament trade resumed in the post-war years. World War II, however, struck the German industry a blow from which it would never recover. Not only was Germany devastated by the war, but the town of Lauscha fell within the territory turned over to the Soviets afterwards, becoming part of East Germany. The Communist government frowned upon trade with the United States and the other Western nations. This policy severely limited the artisans' access to the once-worldwide market for Lauscha's goods. In addition, many children of glassblowers abandoned this sweaty, labor-intensive trade after the war.

During World War II the Corning Glass Company began to produce ornaments in the United States. Corning replaced the glassblowers with glass-blowing machines, however. Although the machines turned out uniform, round balls rather than the dazzling variety of shapes produced by the German artisans, a machine could pro-

duce in a minute the same number of ornaments it took a German glassblower all day to produce.

Contemporary Americans decorate their Christmas trees with a wide variety of ornaments. A dizzying number of commercially made ornaments are available for purchase. Many people enjoy collecting ornament sets, adding new pieces as they are produced each year. Some ornaments are reminiscent of the decorations used in bygone times, some are inspired by religious or cultural heritage, and some are family heirlooms that have been passed down through generations. Families often decorate their Christmas trees with homemade items crafted by their children or other relatives. Many Americans choose to decorate their Christmas trees according to a theme—for example, using ornaments and other decorations of specific colors, or displaying items that represent a favorite hobby or particular interest. Imagination seems to be the only limit in devising ornaments for contemporary American Christmas trees.

## Lighting the Tree

The earliest description of an illuminated tree comes from southern Germany in the year 1660. The light was provided by candles. Since candles were relatively expensive in those days, humble folk often had to make do with devices such as miniature wicks floating in walnut shells filled with oil.

Most of our early accounts of illuminated trees date from the nineteenth century, when the Christmas tree was becoming popular in Britain and the United States. By the second half of the nineteenth century, candles had become an expected ornament on the American Christmas tree. People found the spell of the candle-covered tree nearly irresistible, in spite of the dangers it posed. The candles not only threatened to set the tree itself on fire, but also could consume flammable ornaments or ignite the clothing of anyone who brushed by them. Newspaper advice columns cautioned families to designate at least one person to keep a watchful eye on the lit tree at all times and to have a bucket or wet sponge handy to extinguish any accidental fire. Often the tree was lit for the first time on Christmas Eve. Excited children fidgeted outside the parlor doors while their parents painstakingly placed and lit the candles. Some were told that **Santa Claus** not only left the gifts but also decorated the tree. The magical sight of the glowing, gift-bestrewn tree enchanted children and adults alike.

In spite of the yearly newspaper reports of Christmas tree fire tragedies, people continued to illuminate their trees with candles. So great was the desire for a safe, illuminated tree that in 1882, only three years after inventor Thomas Edison gave the world the first electric light, one of his associates figured out how to use the new invention to light up a Christmas tree. The new electric tree soon became a fashionable Christmas toy for the rich, who could afford to hire an electrician to come to their homes and wire the tree by hand. In 1895 electric lights appeared on the **White House** Christmas tree at the request of President Grover Cleveland.

In 1903 the Ever-Ready Company of New York brought electric Christmas tree lights nearer the reach of ordinary people by devising the first string of ready-made lights. Problems remained, however. Not only were these strings heavier than today's lights, but each light was connected to the next by "series" wiring. This meant that when one bulb burned out, the whole string refused to light. In addition, during the first decades of the twentieth century, many American homes still did not have electricity. Gradually, electricity spread throughout the country and the price of the strings of electric lights came down. Only after World War II did "parallel" wiring come into widespread use. In this wiring system the failure of one bulb did not affect the others.

Christmas tree lights are now available in a seemingly endless array of colors, shapes, and sizes. The most significant recent innovation in Christmas light technology occurred in the 1990s with the development of LED (light-emitting diode) light strings. LED lights typically cost more than traditional incandescent Christmas lights, but the benefits of the newer technology helped propel their popularity. LED lights generate far less heat and generally have a significantly longer operating life. These energy-efficient lights also consume approximately 90 percent less power than traditional Christmas lights. In 2007, the **National Christmas Tree** in Washington, D.C., was converted to all-LED Christmas lights. This change reduced the total electricity required to light the tree from more than 50,000 watts to about 7,000 watts.

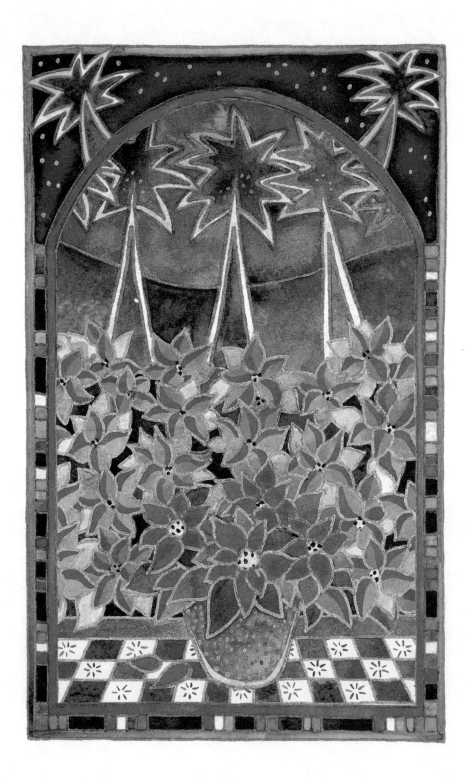

# Paradise Trees

## Christbaum

Few people today would recognize fir trees decorated only with red apples and white, circular wafers as paradise trees. The paradise tree developed as a prop for the paradise play, a medieval European mystery play performed around Christmas time. Indeed, with its early historical connection to the **Christmas season**, the paradise tree may well have been the forerunner of the **Christmas tree**.

### Mystery Plays

In medieval western Europe, mystery or miracle plays taught biblical stories and Christian ideas to a largely illiterate populace (*see also* **Nativity Plays**). At first, only clergy acted in these plays, which were spoken in Latin and presented inside churches. As audiences grew, performances were moved to the front steps of the church or to large open plazas. With this movement out of sacred space, lay people began to take part in the plays, and the dialogue slipped into local languages. What's more, frivolous, humorous, and ribald incidents were added to the basic plot. Church officials frowned on these changes, but the plays only increased in popularity. Small groups of actors traveled from town to town satisfying the popular demand for this form of entertainment.

## *Paradise Plays*

Mystery plays often rooted themselves in the seasons and feast days of the Church calendar. The paradise play, which recounted the story of **Adam and Eve**, attached itself to the **Advent** season. Although the play featured the story of the Creation and the disobedience of Adam and Eve, it closed with the promise of the coming of a Savior. This made it appropriate for the celebration of Advent and Christmas. Moreover, the medieval Church declared December 24 the feast day of Adam and Eve. Around the twelfth century this date became the traditional one for the performance of the paradise play.

## *Paradise Trees*

The paradise tree served as the central prop for the paradise play. It represented the two important trees of the Garden of Eden: the Tree of the Knowledge of Good and Evil and the Tree of Life. Originally, only apples adorned the paradise tree. These symbolized the fall of humanity described in the Adam and Eve story. Perhaps because most other trees were barren and lifeless during December, the actors chose to hang the apples from an evergreen tree rather than from an apple tree. In the fifteenth century, round, white communion wafers were added to the paradise tree. These wafers stood for the promise of reconciliation with God made possible through **Jesus** Christ. Sometimes cherries also served as tree **ornaments**, symbolizing faith and reminding audiences of **Mary** and the Annunciation (*see also* **Cherry Trees**). A circle of lit candles usually surrounded the paradise tree during performances. The play was performed within this circle.

Church authorities banned miracle plays in the fifteenth century, but these popular plays continued to be performed for at least another century. Before disappearing completely, they bequeathed the custom of the paradise tree to the peoples of France and the Rhine River region of Germany. Some Germans adopted a new name for the tree, calling it a *Christbaum*, or "Christ tree." Over time, white pastry dough ornaments cut into the shape of hearts, **angels**, stars, and **bells** replaced the communion wafers. Ornaments representing humans, lions, dogs, birds, and other animals were made out of brown dough. Blooming paper roses might also embellish the tree, a symbol of the birth of Jesus. During the nineteenth century, some German people still put figurines representing Adam, Eve, and the serpent under their trees at Christmas time. In some sections of Bavaria the Christmas evergreen, decorated with lights, apples and tinsel, is still called a paradise tree.

# Los Pastores

## La Pastorela

*Los pastores* (pronounced lohs pah-STOH-rays) means "the shepherds" in Spanish. This is the name given to a Mexican folk drama that tells the story of the pilgrimage of the **shepherds** to the newborn Christ child. The play is also referred to as *La Pastorela*, which means "the pastoral" or "the country story" in Spanish. Performances of this play usually take place in mid- to late December.

The **Gospel according to Luke** (2:8-20) states that an **angel** announced the birth of **Jesus** to a group of shepherds and encouraged them to make a pilgrimage to

**Bethlehem.** The shepherds went to Bethlehem and found the Christ child, confirming the words of the angel. The story told in *Los Pastores* is loosely based on this Bible passage.

## History

The roots of The Shepherds' Play can be traced back to the mystery or miracle plays of medieval Europe (*see also* **Nativity Plays**). These plays began as brief interludes during church services in which the clergy enacted simple versions of Bible stories and religious doctrines. These liturgical dramas began sometime around the tenth and eleventh centuries. The clergy used them to teach elements of the Christian religion to a largely illiterate population. The plays proved popular, and eventually folk performers began to stage them in public arenas. Many changes accompanied this shift. The new folk dramas embroidered the original plots, adding humorous and racy dialogue, characters, and events. These innovations caused the Church to ban these performances in the fifteenth century.

Many of these plays dealt with the stories behind the Christian holidays and were performed on those days. The Shepherds' Play was one of a number of stories enacted at Christmas time. During the fifteenth century, several Spanish authors developed elaborate written versions of The Shepherds' Play, or *Los Pastores*. These plays featured coarse and comical shepherds who entertained audiences by responding to the great events surrounding the Nativity with fear, greed, and confusion. In fact, the amusing antics of the shepherds nearly eclipsed the solemn story of the Nativity.

In the sixteenth century, Spanish missionaries came to Mexico to convert the native peoples to Christianity. The Native Americans not only came from very different cultural backgrounds than did the Spanish, but also spoke very different languages. In order to bridge this gap, the missionaries decided to use mystery plays to teach them Bible stories. They introduced *Los Pastores* sometime during the sixteenth century.

Like the mystery plays of medieval Europe, *Los Pastores* eventually passed from the hands of the clergy and the church grounds to the hands of the people and the public plaza. This transition produced similar results. Although the basic outline of the story remained the same, the play continued to evolve along the same lines it had followed in Europe. Over time new characters and events were added to the play. The drama evolved into a comedy in which the Devil tries to distract the dull-witted shepherds from their quest and heaven's angels intercede to keep the oafish pilgrims on course.

## Plot and Characters

Although the plots may vary somewhat according to local traditions, a number of main characters appear in every version of the play. The starring roles go to the shepherds. They are portrayed as lazy, thick-headed, and easily distracted from their quest by opportunities to eat, sleep, or flirt. In fact, these less-than-heroic shepherds must be coaxed and even argued into setting out on their pilgrimage. At some point they encounter an elderly though spunky hermit. The hermit helps keep the shepherds on their course and entertains the audience with his sharp tongue. A scheming Devil appears throughout the play, sometimes disguised to fool the shepherds and sometimes in a traditional red costume complete with horns and a tail. He and his minions attempt to lure the shepherds away from their pilgrimage by appealing to all their weaknesses.

Often, the play also includes the angel **Gabriel**, who announces Jesus' birth to the shepherds, and the archangel Michael, who descends from heaven to protect the shepherds from the Devil's temptations. Sometimes a host of angels must battle a squadron of devils in order to protect the boorish travelers. At last, however, the shepherds arrive in Bethlehem and present their **gifts** to the Holy Family. The play ends with the Devil conceding defeat.

## Performances

Local townspeople, schools, and even semi-professional acting groups present versions of *Los Pastores*. The drama is usually staged in some public place, like a plaza or a church, but may also be presented at someone's home. It may last anywhere from half an hour to several hours. Actors use dialogue, song, dance, verse, costume, and melodramatics to convey the story.

This Mexican folk drama may be found in numerous towns and cities in the United States, especially in areas where many Mexican Americans live, such as the southwestern states. Some American folklorists point out, however, that fewer and fewer folk performances are given each year. Instead, the tradition is being carried on by professional and semi-professional actors. The city of San Antonio, Texas, at one point hosted dozens of amateur troupes dedicated to the presentation of *Los Pastores*. Today only one amateur group remains, bringing about twenty performances a year to churches, missions, or people's backyards between Christmas Eve and **Candlemas**, February 2. In addition, the San Antonio Missions National Historic Park presents the public with a more formal, professional version of the play each year.

# Poinsettias

## Flor de la Nochebuena

Poinsettias originated in Mexico. The leaves that crown the end of each poinsettia stalk undergo a seasonal color change in December, turning from green to red. As Christianity spread across Mexico during the colonial era, this color change turned poinsettias into a popular Christmas decoration. The Mexicans call the plant *flor de la Nochebuena*, or "Christmas Eve flower."

A Mexican folktale explains this name. Many years ago on Christmas Eve a poor girl sought a gift to offer to the Christ child. She realized, however, that she owned nothing beautiful enough to give the infant. She began to cry, but eventually her desire to pay tribute to the child overcame her shame. She plucked a branch of an ordinary green plant that grew beside the road and humbly brought it to the manger. As she laid it beside the crib the leaves of the plant burst into a brilliant red in recognition of the child's humility and Jesus' pleasure with the gift.

The popularity of poinsettias in the United States can be traced back to the initial interest of one man, Dr. Joel Roberts Poinsett. Appointed the first U.S. ambassador to Mexico, Poinsett also maintained an interest in botany. While stationed in Mexico in 1825, he noticed a plant whose ordinary green leaves turned a brilliant red in December. Intrigued by these tongues of fire, he sent samples home to South Carolina, where he maintained a greenhouse. Other horticulturists soon adopted the plant. Botanists named the plant *Euphorbia pulcherrima*, but the public called it "poinsettia" in honor of the man who first imported it to the United States. By the last quarter of the nineteenth century New York shopkeepers were offering poinsettias at Christmas time. By the twentieth century Americans had fully adopted the plant as a Christmas symbol. The current popularity of the poinsettia as a Christmas decoration can be measured in numbers. In 2000 Americans bought more than 65 million of these potted plants.

The leaves of the poinsettia are very sensitive to light. During the darkest weeks of the year the leaves at the end of each stalk react to the shortage of sunlight by changing color. Although people commonly refer to the poinsettia's scarlet blooms as "flowers," in fact only the yellow buds at their centers are flowers. The red halos that surround them are composed of a special kind of leaf known as a bract.

Americans seem to favor red poinsettias as Christmas decorations, but other less well known varieties of the plant sport leaves that change from green to white, yellow, or pink. A number of these varieties were developed by the Ecke family. In the early part of this century Paul Ecke, a flower farmer located near Los Angeles, California, played a major role in developing new varieties of poinsettias and championing these hardier and more attractive plants as Christmas decorations. His cross-country promotional tours eventually paid off. Not only has the poinsettia become a Christmas symbol, but also the Ecke family farm, now located in Encinitas, California, continues to supply a large percentage of America's demand for the potted plants and the cuttings from which they grow (*see also* **Urban Legends**).

# *The Polar Express*

*The Polar Express* is a children's book written and illustrated by Chris Van Allsburg. Published in 1985, *The Polar Express* has sold more than seven million copies worldwide. It has been listed as a *New York Times* Bestseller and a Best Illustrated Book, and won the Caldecott Medal in 1986. *The Polar Express* has become a beloved holiday classic that takes its place among cherished Christmas traditions in America.

The story focuses on a young boy who has just been told by his friends that **Santa Claus** is not real. Struggling to continue believing in Santa, the boy waits to hear the bells of Santa's sleigh on Christmas Eve. Instead, he hears a strange different sound outside his bedroom window. The boy discovers that an old-fashioned steam engine called the Polar Express has stopped in front of his home, and the conductor invites him aboard. On the train, the boy joins a group of children on their way to the **North Pole**. They arrive just in time for the first gift of Christmas. The boy is chosen to receive the first gift, which can be anything he wishes. He chooses a single silver bell from Santa's sleigh. Santa cuts a bell from the **reindeer** harness, and gives it to the boy before taking flight in his sleigh for the Christmas Eve journey around the world. On the train ride home, the boy discovers the bell seems to have fallen through a hole in his pocket, and is lost. In despair, he returns home and goes to sleep. On Christmas morning, among all the presents is a tiny box with the boy's name on it. Inside is the silver bell from Santa's sleigh. The beautiful chiming sound of the bell delights the boy and his young sister, but their parents think the bell is broken because they cannot hear it ring. Only those who truly believe in Santa can hear it. The boy finds his belief in Santa restored, and continues to believe in the spirit of Christmas. As he grows to adulthood, he never loses the ability to hear the sound of Santa's sleigh bell ringing.

A movie version of *The Polar Express* was produced in 2004. This computer-animated feature-length film closely follows the story of the book, bringing to life the magic of the tale. It was the first feature film ever to be shot using advanced motion capture technology. This technique allows the actions of live actors to drive the facial expressions, emotions, and movements of the digital characters. Technological innovations made during the creation of *The Polar Express* were groundbreaking achievements that influenced future computer-animated productions. The movie was a tremendous success in theaters, grossing nearly $182 million. *The Polar Express* was nominated for three Academy Awards in 2004, for Sound, Sound Editing, and Original Song for "Believe."

The enduring popularity of *The Polar Express* story has resulted in numerous live Polar Express events throughout the country. These events typically offer children and adults the opportunity to take a themed train ride to the "North Pole," including activities such as live performances of key scenes in the story, a chance to meet Santa and his elves, or a reading of the book.

# Las Posadas

During the nine days before Christmas, many Hispanic communities host a nightly procession known as Las Posadas. In Spanish *las posadas* means "the inns" or "the lodgings." According to this old Mexican custom, groups of children and adults reenact **Mary** and **Joseph** searching for shelter in **Bethlehem**. Staging Las Posadas requires the coordination of many people. The event may be organized by a group of neighbors, families and friends, churches, or community organizations.

## *The Procession and Celebration*

Las Posadas begins on the evening of December 16. Participants gather at a pre-arranged time and place, sometimes offering prayers before the event begins. Two youngsters are selected to play the roles of Joseph and Mary. These roles may be carried out in a variety of ways. In many places they hold images of Joseph and Mary before them as they lead the procession out into the street. These images are called *misterios*, or "mysteries." In other places the children acting as Joseph and Mary dress the part, donning robes that evoke the biblical era. In rural villages, Mary may ride upon a donkey. In some locales a child dressed as an **angel** clears the way for the Holy Couple. Participants file out in procession behind Mary and Joseph, carrying candles and singing Christmas songs.

The procession dramatizes Joseph and Mary's search for a place to spend the night in Bethlehem, an event suggested in chapter two of the **Gospel according to Luke**. In Las Posadas the couple must be refused shelter at least once before a kind innkeeper finally takes them in. Joseph and Mary lead the procession through the streets to the first house. Joseph knocks on the door and begs shelter for the night. He often chants this request in rhymed verse. The homeowner has agreed in advance to participate in the event, playing the role of the innkeeper. He or she comes to the door, but refuses Joseph's request. Joseph and Mary turn away into the night, leading the procession to another house. The organizers may arrange many refusals or only one. Sometimes the first innkeeper experiences a change of heart after Joseph explains their situation and reveals their identities. In any case, Joseph and Mary finally encounter a family that graciously welcomes them, and their entourage, into the house. This family will host the evening's entertainment.

Before the arrival of the procession, the hosts prepare a **Nativity scene** or altar with room for the images that the children carry. When the entire procession has entered the house, Mary and Joseph come forward, putting the statues in the places reserved for them. This act, and the accompanying prayer, concludes the procession and the party begins. The hosts offer traditional Mexican sweets, such as tamales, *bizcochitos* (sugar cookies) and such beverages as spiced hot chocolate to their guests. The evening's entertainments usually include music, dancing, a candy-filled *piñata* for the children, and sometimes fireworks.

Las Posadas may be enacted in a variety of ways, depending on local traditions as well as on limitations of time, space, money, and personnel. In the old days, processions took place on each of the nine nights preceding Christmas. Today, many groups stage only one procession on the last of the nine nights, Christmas Eve. Although traditionally the pilgrims marched through the streets, Las Posadas has been adapted to fit new living situations. In some areas, Mary and Joseph wend their way down the halls of apartment buildings. In others they graciously include the corridors of nursing homes in their trek.

### History

In many ways Las Posadas resembles the old European custom of Christmas time **mumming**. Most writers trace its historical roots back to the medieval European mystery or miracle plays, however (*see also* **Nativity Plays**). These plays taught Bible stories and religious doctrine to a largely illiterate people. They began sometime around the tenth and eleventh centuries as simple enactments of the liturgy performed in churches by the clergy. As the plays became more complex and entertaining, audiences grew. Eventually, folk performers began to stage them in public arenas. Many changes deemed undesirable by the clergy accompanied this shift. These innovations caused the Church to ban these performances in the fifteenth century.

Nevertheless, dramatizing biblical stories had proved an effective means of communicating religious ideas. In the sixteenth century two Spanish saints created a new kind of religious ceremony to accompany the Christmas holiday. St. Ignatius Loyola proposed that special prayers be offered on each of the nine days before Christmas. This type of religious observance, known as a novena, found favor with St. John of

the Cross, who added a religious pageant to the event. Spanish missionaries brought this custom to Mexico in the sixteenth century, where they used it to teach the story of the birth of **Jesus** to the native people they found there. As these ceremonies were organized by Church officials, they were at first very religious and quite somber. Gradually, the people themselves began to organize the event, and a lighter, more festive mood began to emerge.

### Observances in U.S. Cities

From Mexico Las Posadas spread south to El Salvador, Guatemala, Honduras, and Nicaragua, and north to the United States. In the latter, many impressive observances of Las Posadas can be found throughout the southwestern states. In Albuquerque, New Mexico, a number of Roman Catholic churches organize traditional nine-night Posadas. Different families host the celebrations during the first eight nights, then the churches themselves hold the party on Christmas Eve. In Santa Fe, New Mexico, the Posadas re-enactment includes costumed devils playing the roles of the people who refuse lodging to the couple. The devils taunt the Holy Family, while the crowd boos the devils. In San Antonio, Texas, a Posadas procession along the river attracts thousands of people. Mariachi musicians, choral ensembles, and ordinary citizens follow behind Mary and Joseph. **Luminarias**, or small bonfires, light the parade route. The crowd rejoices when the Holy Family finally finds lodging. Afterwards the city hosts a party for children in a nearby plaza. On Olvera Street in Los Angeles, the event starts at the historic Avila Adobe, where the merchants create candlelit processions led by Mary and Joseph, who are followed by children, adults, and animals. Singing hymns and holiday songs, they stop at individual stores, asking for shelter, until finally they are invited in. Then the celebration begins, with piñatas for the children, hot chocolate and treats, and music and entertainment for all.

# Puritans

In the sixteenth century a religious reform movement surged across Europe. The leaders of this movement, known as the Reformation, sought to abolish Church practices they deemed inconsistent with scripture. The Reformation gave birth to Protestant Christianity and to the many different sects and denominations that fall under that heading. In Britain it inspired the formation of a number of sects, one of which was known as the Puritans.

The Puritans advocated a "purified" form of worship, stripped of traditional embellishments such as organ music, choir singing, ecclesiastical robes, and church decorations. Puritan ministers wore street clothes while presiding over simplified services in plain churches.

Throughout the sixteenth century British Puritans lobbied for Church reform. The majority of high-ranking officials in the Church of England opposed them, however, as did Queen Elizabeth I and her Stuart successors. In the early seventeenth century, small groups of English Puritans sought religious freedom by immigrating to America. There they founded Plymouth Colony and, later, Massachusetts Bay Colony (*see also* **America, Christmas in Colonial**; Victorian Era, **Christmas in**).

By the mid-seventeenth century, Puritan forces had gained the upper hand in British politics and succeeded in ousting the king. During the years in which they dominated the political scene, the Puritans legislated a number of religious and social reforms forcing English society to conform to their beliefs. They directed some of these reforms toward the celebration of Christmas.

## *Campaign against Christmas*

Before coming to power Puritan leaders had preached against what they viewed as irreverent and excessive Christmas customs. For example, in 1583 Philip Stubbes published a pamphlet titled *Anatomie of Abuses*, detailing what he viewed as the offensive behaviors with which the English celebrated Christmas. To his mind, a season marked by masking, **mumming**, theater-going, games, gambling, feasting, and dancing, as well as by an increased number of sexual encounters and robberies, could hardly be said to honor Christ.

By the mid-1600s, however, Puritan critics had gone from attacking excesses associated with Christmas to attacking the holiday itself. Between 1644 and 1659 the Puritan majority in Parliament attempted to abolish the celebration of Christmas. They pointed out that the Bible neither gives the date of the birth of **Jesus** nor requests that people honor it (*see also* **Jesus, Year of Birth**). According to their way of thinking, this meant that Christmas should be eliminated. Many Puritan leaders condemned those who disagreed with them as enemies of the Christian religion.

Puritan leaders in Parliament did more than just speak out against Christmas. In 1642 they banned the performance of plays at Christmas. In the year 1644 Christmas fell on the last Wednesday in December. The law ordered that people fast and do penance on the last Wednesday in the month. The Puritans saw to it that no exception would be made for Christmas. In London people ignored the edict, and shops closed as usual for Christmas Day. The following year the Puritan Parliament outlawed the religious observance of Christmas altogether, forbidding special church services in honor of the day. Handfuls of the traditionally devout defied the ban and sought out priests who quietly continued to offer services on Christmas Day. Yet even such sober celebrations could involve the risk of arrest.

## Active and Passive Resistance

In 1647 Parliament took the final step and outlawed the secular celebration of Christmas and many other Christian feast days. The edict met with active resistance, leading in some instances to violent clashes with officers of the law. Throughout the country, people responded with anger and violence: angry crowds flocked to shops that followed the new law and remained open on Christmas, and riots broke out in several cities. Some threatened that if they could not observe Christmas Day under the current government, then they would see the king put back on his throne.

In spite of this outburst of opposition, subsequent Christmases saw few open confrontations. Historians believe, however, that behind closed doors many English families continued to celebrate a private Christmas, consisting of a day's rest, a festive meal, and family merriment. Indeed, throughout the period in which both the religious and secular observance of the day were banned, many London shops continued to close on Christmas Day.

Even these private, home celebrations did not escape Puritan criticism. Not only did Puritans object to those who observed Christmas by not working, attending religious services, and enjoying traditional entertainments, some strongly disapproved of traditional Christmas foods as well. To extremists, such foods as **mincemeat pie** and plum pudding took on political connotations. Resisting them signified one's loyalty to the current regime; indulging in them revealed royalist or Roman Catholic sympathies.

## *Scotland*

In Scotland Puritanism took greater hold of both the laity and clergy. John Knox, leader of the Scottish Reformation and founder of the Presbyterian Church, opposed all church festivals. In 1561 the Scottish national assembly eliminated Christmas along with many other Christian feast days. In the years that followed, local authorities attempted to enforce this law. People were arrested for dancing and singing Christmas carols, for throwing parties, and for not working on Christmas Day. Nevertheless, thirty years later, shortly after the turn of the seventeenth century, some people still resisted the elimination of the old festivities.

Religious authorities repeatedly condemned the little bursts of midwinter revelry that took place in their towns. In 1606 clergymen in Aberdeen again felt compelled to denounce those who at Christmas or New Year's donned costumes, wore the clothing of the opposite sex, or danced with bells, whether in the streets or in private homes. By the 1640s authorities began to turn their attention towards quelling home celebrations of the holiday. In 1659 one especially severe minister went to extreme lengths to enforce this ban. He undertook a house to house search on Christmas Day to make sure that none of his parishioners were enjoying a private Christmas goose.

### The Return of the Monarchy

In 1660 Parliament restored the monarchy and King Charles II assumed the British throne. King Charles restored all the old holidays, including Christmas. Many historians believe, however, that English Christmas celebrations never quite recovered their former luster. Indeed, the British never revived a number of old Christmas traditions, such as masques and the raucous revelry associated with the **Lord of Misrule**. In Scotland, the Puritan attempt to abolish Christmas succeeded more completely. New Year's Day replaced Christmas as the principal winter holiday in that region.

### Conclusion

The Puritans' approach to Christmas might surprise people today, but Puritan leaders sincerely believed that they were restoring their country to the true Christian faith. In Reformation Europe, politics and religion fused together to form a single system of rule. Each country's leader chose that nation's religion, making religious dissent equivalent to political rebellion. Political authorities could, and did, imprison, persecute, and execute citizens for their religious beliefs. Over time, both Protestants and Catholics suffered from this climate of intolerance, depending on who was in power. Puritanism was once defined by the American journalist H. L. Mencken as "the haunting fear that someone, somehow, may be happy." After reviewing the history of the Puritan campaign against Christmas, many contemporary Americans might agree with him.

# Reindeer

The natural habitat of the reindeer, or Arctic deer, spans the northernmost reaches of Russia, Siberia, and the Scandinavian countries. Reindeer also roam across Canada and Alaska, where they are sometimes known as caribou. Reindeer differ from other deer not only in their capacity to withstand cold, but also in the ability of both male and female animals to grow antlers. Until the twentieth century, an indigenous people of northern Scandinavia called the Sami made their living primarily as reindeer herders. These reindeer facts, however, cannot by themselves explain how these unfamiliar animals were drafted into contemporary American Christmas lore.

## *Santa's Reindeer*

The idea that **Santa Claus** drives a sleigh pulled by flying reindeer is usually credited to one man's flight of fancy. In 1822 Clement C. Moore, a classics professor at General Theological Seminary, wrote a poem for children entitled "'Twas the Night Before Christmas" ("A Visit from St. Nicholas"). This poem, officially published in 1844, did much to establish the legend and lore of Santa Claus in the United States (*see also* **Elves**, **North Pole**, and **Sugarplums**). In it Moore assigns eight flying reindeer the task of pulling Santa's toy-laden sleigh. Moreover, he gave these animals names: Dasher,

Dancer, Prancer, Vixen, Comet, Cupid, Donder, and Blitzen. Moore encoded his own private joke in these last two names. In the original poem, the names were Dunder and Blixem, which mean "thunder" and "lightning" in Dutch.

How did Moore come up with this unusual reindeer imagery? Certainly **St. Nicholas,** who might be considered Santa's European predecessor, never resorted to such an unusual mode of conveyance (*see also* **St. Nicholas's Day**). No definitive answer can be given to this question, although researchers have made a number of speculations. One writer points out that the year before Moore wrote "A Visit from St. Nicholas," William Gilley published a poem that depicts "santeclause" driving a sleigh pulled by flying reindeer. Moore may have read this poem and simply borrowed the idea from this little-known work. Others have suggested that Moore was inspired by an image from old Norse mythology in which Thor, the thunder god, rides a flying chariot pulled by the magical goats, Gnasher and Cracker. It may also be that Moore paired Santa with the exotic reindeer in order to suggest that he came from a remote land in the far northern reaches of the world.

In 1939, a new reindeer was added to Santa's team. Rudolph made his debut in a poem that was created as part of a Montgomery Ward department store advertising campaign (*see also* **"Rudolph the Red-Nosed Reindeer"**). Written for children, the poem describes a young reindeer that was rejected by his playmates for being different. Rudolph had a large, shiny red nose instead of a small black nose like the other reindeer. But Rudolph saved the day with his unusual nose on one particular Christmas Eve when the weather was so misty that Santa could not see to fly his sleigh. Rudolph's glowing red nose lights the way, saving Christmas for everyone. The poem became extremely popular and was eventually developed into a children's story book, a song, and an animated television special.

# Réveillon

The French celebrate Christmas Eve with an elaborate meal called *réveillon* (pronounced ray-veh-YON). *Réveillon* means "awakening" in French. This banquet usually takes place after attending **Midnight Mass** on Christmas Eve. In past times people

may have savored réveillon even more than they do today because it signaled the end of the four-week **Advent** fast.

## *Réveillon in France*

Although in France some people choose to celebrate réveillon in restaurants, most opt to feast at home. Many invite extended family members and guests to their table. To sustain themselves through the long church services, the family often takes a light snack in the early evening. Small children may be put to bed for a few hours before the evening's activities begin. When families dine at home, the women usually cook and serve the food. This may include washing dishes between courses in order to serve each on a clean plate.

Special preparations set the tone for an elegant celebration. The table sparkles with candles, polished silverware, and a Christmas centerpiece. The family's best table-cloth lies underneath. Much work in the kitchen must take place before the diners sit down, since the meal may consist of up to fifteen courses. Several wines accompany the meal, and toasts are offered throughout. The feast often begins with oysters or other shellfish. In Paris, common réveillon dishes include goose liver pâté, roast turkey or roast goose stuffed with prunes and pâté, special preparations of potatoes and vegetables, cheese, fruit, nuts, and for dessert, *bûche de Noël* (Christmas log), a special chocolate, cream-filled cake shaped like a log.

Other regions maintain their own traditional Christmas Eve menus. In the southern region of Provence a choice of thirteen desserts greets diners at the end of the meal, one for **Jesus** and each of the twelve apostles. Typical desserts include marzipan, sweet bread, cookies, and such fresh and dried fruits as figs, dates, pears, and oranges.

### *Réveillon in the United States and Canada*

The tradition of the réveillon supper traveled with French colonists to the Americas. In the nineteenth century the French population in New Orleans continued to celebrate Christmas Eve with attendance at Midnight Mass followed by réveillon dinners at home. Today many prominent New Orleans restaurants attract diners with sumptuous réveillon menus. The French Canadians of Quebec also inherited the tradition of coming home to réveillon supper after Midnight Mass. A traditional réveillon menu in Quebec consists of *la tourtière* (a meat pie), a stew of meat balls and pork, minced pork pie, oyster or pea soup, a variety of sauces and relishes, and several desserts. Traditional réveillon desserts include pastries, candies, fruitcake, sugar pie, cornmeal cake, doughnuts, ice cream, and bûche de Noël.

# Robins

Robins appear on **Christmas cards, ornaments,** and other Christmas decorations. No one seems to know, however, just how the birds became a Christmas symbol. British and Irish folklore links the robin with the wren, another Christmas bird. Past folk beliefs assigned magical qualities and near sacred status to both birds.

## Folklore

British and Irish folklore often paired the robin and the wren. Some folk verses painted the two as sweethearts, in spite of the fact that they represent different species. These verses always cast the robin as male and the wren as female. The following lines describe their romance:

Cock robin got up early
At the break of day,
And went to Jenny's window
To sing a roundelay.
He sang cock robin's love
To little Jenny Wren,
And when he got unto the end,
Then he began again. [Lawrence, 1997, 38]

Traditional lore also paired robins and wrens according to their shared qualities. Several English and Irish folk verses express the following sentiment:

The robin and the wren
Are God Almighty's cock and hen. [Armstrong, 1970, 168]

Perhaps the assumption that the birds were especially beloved by God gave rise to folk beliefs warning against harming robins or wrens. As the following folk verses teach, bad luck inevitably followed:

Cursed is the man
Who kills a robin or a wren.
Kill a robin or a wren
Never prosper, boy or man.
The robin and the redbreast
The robin and the wren
If ye tak' out of the nest
Ye'll never thrive again. [Lawrence, 1997, 40]

According to various legends, one of these sacred birds once performed a heroic feat for humankind. Old tales from various parts of Europe lauded either the wren or the robin as the original fire-fetcher, the creature who delivered the first flames to humankind. In addition, English folklore assigned supernatural abilities to the robin.

A fairly widespread belief credited the robin with a foreknowledge of death and illness. According to these beliefs, a robin tapping on the window or flying in or about the house meant that death, disease, or some other misfortune would visit the family. Along similar lines, English folklore also claimed that both the robin and wren pitied the dead. According to this belief, the two birds often covered the lifeless bodies of whatever dead creatures they encountered in the woods with moss or leaves. These gestures of compassion supported their reputation as kindly, holy creatures.

### Christmas Symbol

Very little in the above account makes the robin a natural choice for a Christmas symbol. Nevertheless, in Victorian times the robin appeared frequently on Christmas cards as an emblem of the season (*see also* **Victorian Era, Christmas in**). Perhaps the popularity of this image grew out of a general affection for this non-migratory bird, remembered especially at the time of year when nature presented the robin with its harshest conditions.

In addition, some connection can be drawn between the bird images printed on some nineteenth-century Christmas cards and elements of the folk beliefs explained above. For example, one illustration depicts a smartly dressed robin in top hat, jacket, and vest courting a wren in bonnet and shawl. Another shows a winter woodland scene in which a robin and wren drape moss and leaves over a doll (whose body resembles that of a dead child partially covered with snow). Other Victorian Christmas cards cast the robin as a symbol of the new year and the wren as a symbol of the old year.

Far more difficult to understand, however, is the popularity of Christmas cards depicting dead birds, especially robins, which peaked during the 1880s. Such sentiments as "Sweet messenger of calm decay" and "Peace divine" accompanied these perplexing pictures. Nowadays most people would agree that neither the sentiments nor the images evoke the spirit of Christmas. The Victorian fondness for that which evoked tender emotions, especially pity, may explain the popularity of these kinds of cards.

Few people today associate the robin with death. Instead, the image of the robin at Christmas time probably triggers kindly thoughts about animals enduring the cold of winter or about the promise of spring to come.

# Rosemary

Seasonal decorations of **greenery** have embellished European Christmas celebrations for centuries. Rosemary was at one time a popular element in these decorations. Between the fourteenth and the mid-nineteenth centuries, rosemary reigned as a favorite item in English Christmas garlands. In the seventeenth century the English poet Robert Herrick noted that, according to local custom, "Rosemary and baies [bays] that are most faire were stuck about the houses and the churches as Christmas decorations" (*see also* **Laurel**).

Folk belief attributed a number of positive qualities to the plant, qualities that might be thought to justify its association with the season. Rosemary signified remembrance, as attested to by Ophelia in Shakespeare's play, *Hamlet*. In addition, evil spirits fled in the presence of rosemary. Finally, its name echoed that of **Mary**, mother of **Jesus**, one of whose symbols was the rose. Should these explanations be found wanting, many legends developed to offer a Christian explanation of the herb's connection with Christmas (*see also* **Nativity Legends**). Rosemary's popularity has since declined, however. Today we seldom include this fragrant herb in our Christmas decorations.

# "Rudolph the Red-Nosed Reindeer"

In the early twentieth century an ordinary department store worker added a new **reindeer** to Santa's team. Robert L. May, an employee at Montgomery Ward, wrote a poem entitled "Rudolph the Red-Nosed Reindeer" in 1939. The store printed the poem and distributed it to children as a sales gimmick.

Written to appeal to children, the poem tells the story of a young reindeer who was rejected by his playmates for being different. The rejected youth, named Rudolph, had a large, shiny, red nose while all the other reindeers had small black noses. One very misty Christmas Eve, however, **Santa Claus** discovers that the shiny red nose gives off enough light to help him sail safely through the murky night skies. Once the other reindeer realize Rudolph's nose is a valuable asset, they befriend the once lonely youngster.

Almost two and one-half million copies of the poem were sent home with shoppers in 1939, and more than three and one-half million in 1946, when Montgomery Ward reprinted May's work. The store then released the copyright on the poem back to the author, who published it in a book for children.

In 1949 a friend of May's named Johnny Marks composed a song based on the story told in the poem. In its first year on the market, Rudolph fans bought two million copies of the song. Entitled, like the poem, "Rudolph the Red-Nosed Reindeer," it remains a popular, contemporary Christmas tune, which has now been recorded hundreds of times.

In the decades following publication of the poem and the song, Rudolph's fame continued to spread. His story has been told in twenty-five different languages, and hundreds of Christmas knickknacks now bear his image. Rudolph has also appeared in numerous television specials and movies.

The 1964 Christmas television special "Rudolph the Red-Nosed Reindeer" introduced Rudolph's story to a new generation. In this expanded version of the tale, Rudolph sets out on an adventurous journey to find his place in the world. Along the way, he meets a motley cast of characters, including a young doe named Clarice who has a crush on Rudolph. Hermey, an elf who really wants to be a dentist, joins up with the pair and they travel on to meet the gold-obsessed miner Yukon Cornelius. Together, the group convinces an Abominable Snowman named Bumble to join them. When they find an island full of forgotten misfit toys, Rudolph decides to get Santa involved in rescuing the toys. A terrible blizzard hits the North Pole on Christmas Eve, and when Rudolph finally makes it back to Santa's workshop, he finds that Christmas has been cancelled because of the bad weather. But all is not lost—Rudolph uses his shiny red nose to guide Santa's sleigh and Christmas is saved for everyone. The story is enhanced by numerous musical numbers, such as "Silver and Gold" and "A Holly Jolly Christmas," some of which later became popular Christmas songs in their own right. The innovative stop-motion animation technique used by American production company Rankin-Bass to create the movie became the standard against which future animations were measured. The movie became an enduring success, and continues to be broadcast every year.

In 1976, the animated television special "Rudolph's Shiny New Year" was created as a sequel to the original 1964 movie. In this story, Baby New Year goes missing and Father Time needs Rudolph's help to find him before New Year's Eve. Another sequel, the animated "Rudolph and Frosty's Christmas in July," was released in 1979. In this outing, Rudolph and Frosty must escape the clutches of the evil wizard Winterbolt, who wants to steal Rudolph's famous nose and Frosty's magic top hat (*see also* **"Frosty the Snowman"**). The 1998 animated special "Rudolph the Red-Nosed Reindeer" featured a slightly different story line, including a different cast of characters, but shared the same overall themes as the original. In the 2001 animated special "Rudolph the Red-Nosed Reindeer & the Island of Misfit Toys," a mysterious Toy-Taker is gobbling up toys around the world. Rudolph and characters from the original 1964 story must find the stolen toys in time to save Christmas.

These sequels and remakes enjoyed varying degrees of success, but none became as much a part of American Christmas traditions as the original. The 1964 television special remains the most popular version of Rudolph's story. Over the years, the original "Rudolph the Red-Nosed Reindeer" cartoon has become a beloved cultural phenomenon. A seemingly endless variety of Rudolph merchandise is now available, including books, movies, cartoons, music, video games, board games, action figures, Christmas ornaments and other decorations, and all manner of stuffed toys and dolls. In 2005, the Rudolph and Santa puppets used to create the 1964 stop-motion animation were discovered in the attic of a former Rankin-Bass employee. Prior to restoration, the two puppets were valued at approximately $8,000-$10,000 for the pair. They were purchased at an undisclosed price by a collector, who also paid to have them fully restored. When they were put on public display in 2006, thousands of people came to the Center for Puppetry Arts in New York to get a glimpse of the famous icons.

# Salvation Army Kettles

The sight of a man or woman bundled up against the cold, standing next to a red kettle and shaking a hand-held bell greets many an American shopper entering or leaving a department store at Christmas time. For more than 100 years, the Salvation Army has stationed these bell-ringers on street corners and at shopping malls, to collect money to help those in need. For many, the red kettle and tinkling bell have become a holiday symbol and a reminder that the Christmas season is upon us.

The Salvation Army is a non-profit, religious organization dedicated to spreading the Christian faith and aiding the poor. It began in 1865 in London, England, when Methodist minister William Booth decided that in order to reach social outcasts and poor people with the Christian message, he would have to leave his church and preach in the streets. Booth and his followers overcame early opposition and achieved a degree of success. In 1878, Booth changed his organization's name from the Christian Mission to the Salvation Army. In 1880 some of his followers immigrated to the United States, founding a branch of the Salvation Army in New York City. The organization is now active in 115 countries and claims over four million members worldwide.

The first Salvation Army Christmas kettle appeared in San Francisco in 1891. In that year Joseph McFee, who had achieved the rank of captain within the Salvation Army, resolved to raise funds to provide Christmas dinners for those in need. The Englishman remembered having seen people with big pots collecting coins for charity back home in his native Liverpool. He decided the same strategy could work in the U.S. McFee obtained a kettle and permission to set it up at the foot of Market Street, where the Oakland ferry landed. His campaign was a success, and by 1895 thirty Salvation Army divisions in various towns and cities were using the Christmas kettles. The use of kettles to collect coins reminded donors that their money would be used to prepare meals for the poor. Indeed, in the early days the slogan "Keep the pot boiling" often appeared on the Salvation Army signs posted above the kettles. In 1897 the Salvation Army declared that donations made to kettles nationwide had provided 150,000 Christmas dinners for poor people. By 1898 the New York chapter of the Salvation Army was providing an enormous, sit-down Christmas dinner for the poor in Madison Square Garden.

The vision of Christmas as a season especially appropriate for charitable giving gained in popularity in the second half of the nineteenth century (*see also* **America, Christmas in Nineteenth-Century;** *A Christmas Carol*). By the last decade of the nineteenth century, the idea of funding Christmas dinners for the poor had become particularly fashionable among the middle and upper classes. Rich donors often attended the dinners as well, which were held in arenas or theaters. The well-to-do were required to buy a ticket to the event, which entitled them to a spectator's seat inside the arena. There they witnessed first-hand masses of poor people sating their hunger, and, hopefully, expressing their gratitude to their benefactors. These trends in charitable giving may have contributed to the Salvation Army's sweeping success in their Christmas kettle campaign.

The Salvation Army still provides sit-down Christmas dinners for those in need, but today's kettle donations may also go towards providing the means for poor families to celebrate Christmas dinner at home or towards other social services. Through its many programs, the Salvation Army served 30 million Americans in 2009. The Salvation Army maintains more than 7,800 centers in communities across the country, and 55 percent of its annual funding comes from direct public support, such as kettle donations. In recent years, the Salvation Army has extended its red kettle campaign through the use of technology. Donations can now be made by credit card to online kettles via the Salvation Army's web site or through the use of an iPhone app.

# Santa Claus

## Kriss Kringle, St. Nick

Born in the United States of mixed ethnic and religious heritage, Santa Claus became an important folk figure in the second half of the nineteenth century, about the time when Americans were beginning to celebrate Christmas in large numbers (*see also* **America, Christmas in Nineteenth-Century**). Santa Claus bears a good deal of resemblance to his closest relative, the old European gift bringer **St. Nicholas**. Indeed "St. Nick" serves as one of Santa's nicknames.

While the origins of many legendary figures remain obscure, historians have traced the basic framework of the Santa Claus myth back to the creative works of three individuals: author Washington Irving, scholar and author Clement C. Moore, and illustrator Thomas Nast. These men, in turn, drew on elements of European and Euro-American Christmas folklore in their portrayals of the Christmas gift bringer. Interestingly enough, Americans embraced this "ready-made" folklore in the late nineteenth century, a time when ready-made goods of all kinds became widely available due to the rise of industrial manufacturing.

Today Santa Claus reigns as an icon of American Christmas celebrations. Many Christmas decorations bear his image, and popular songs tell of his home at the **North Pole** and his Christmas Eve activities. Nearly every American child can tell you that Santa is a plump old man with a white beard who wears a baggy red suit and cap trimmed with white fur. Many send letters to his North Pole workshop describing the **gifts** they would like to receive for Christmas (*see also* **Children's Letters**). They eagerly await Christmas Eve, when he loads his sled with toys for good girls and boys and flies around the world, sliding down chimneys to place the presents under decorated **Christmas trees**. As if to confirm this Christmas story, men in Santa suits regularly appear on street corners, at office parties, and in department and toy stores around Christmas time.

### Before Santa Claus

In spite of its contemporary popularity, Christmas was not widely celebrated in the United States at the turn of the nineteenth century (*see also* **America, Christmas in**

Colonial). A few ethnic groups, however, clung to the Christmas customs inherited from their European ancestors. Before Santa Claus became a familiar gift bringer to most Americans, the Pennsylvania Dutch received Christmas gifts from the Christ Child, whom they called *Christkindel*, *Christ-kindlein*, or *Christkindchen*.

The Pennsylvania Dutch were Swiss and German immigrants who settled in Pennsylvania during the eighteenth and nineteenth centuries. These German-speaking immigrants called themselves *Deutsche*, which means "German." Eventually, Americans turned "*Deutsche*" into "Dutch." Some elements of German Christmas folklore came with these groups to the United States. This folklore included two Christmas gift bringers, the Christ Child and Belsnickel (*see* **Knecht Ruprecht**).

### The Christ Child in America

Unlike Santa Claus, who rides in a magical flying sleigh, the early American Christ Child traveled from house to house on a humble donkey. Children left out plates or baskets filled with hay for the Child's donkey. The Christ Child exchanged the hay for nuts, candy, and cookies.

By the early 1800s, however, the image of the Christ Child began to blur together with that of another European gift giver, the elderly St. Nicholas. Moreover, the German words for Christ Child, *Christ-Kindel* or *Christ-Kindlein*, began to slur as more non-German speakers attempted to pronounce these words. "*Christkindel*" turned into "Krist Kingle," and later, into "Kriss Kringle." In 1842 the publication of *The Kriss Kringle Book* cemented this pronunciation error and compounded it by using the name to describe a gift giver who seemed suspiciously like Santa Claus. Eventually, all that remained of the German Christ Child was the Americanized name "Kriss Kringle." And even that was transformed into a nickname for Santa Claus.

### Belsnickel in America

Belsnickel may have contributed to the image of Santa Claus in a more direct way. In Germany, Belsnickel, or Knecht Ruprecht, accompanied St. Nicholas on his gift-giving rounds. Germans pictured him as a shaggy, soot-covered man who carried a whip, a bell, and a sack of treats. In Pennsylvania Dutch country, however, Belsnickel made his rounds without St. Nicholas. He brought nuts, candies, and cookies to children daring enough to brave a possible smack of the whip as they scrambled for the treats he tossed on the floor. Since Belsnickel often dressed in furs, some historians have speculated that his image may have inspired the fur-trimmed suit worn by Santa Claus. In the United States, beliefs and customs surrounding Belsnickel survived somewhat longer than those surrounding the Christ Child, but died out in the early twentieth century.

### St. Nicholas in America

Whereas Belsnickel and the Christ Child appeared around Christmas, St. Nicholas traditionally brought his gifts on the eve of his feast day, December 6 (*see also* **St. Nicholas's Day**). Historical evidence suggests that the gift-giving customs surrounding the saint were well known in the Netherlands during the eighteenth century. By contrast, only a few scattered references to beliefs and customs surrounding St. Nicholas can be found among Dutch and German immigrants to the United States during this same era. Apparently, folk traditions concerning St. Nicholas as a winter season gift giver did not cross the Atlantic with Dutch and German immigrants in any great force.

### Washington Irving and St. Nicholas

The St. Nicholas we know today needed the help of writer Washington Irving to establish a toehold in this country. In 1809, Irving's satirical *A History of New York* raised St. Nicholas to a position of importance in New York's Dutch-American community, primarily as a symbol of ethnic identity. In doing so, he made a few changes to the traditional European image of the saint. Irving replaced the tall, somber, and commanding man in a red bishop's robe with a short, round, jolly Dutchman who smoked a long-stemmed pipe and dressed in colonial garb.

### Clement C. Moore and St. Nicholas

Clement C. Moore, a professor at New York's General Theological Seminary, was a friend of Washington Irving's. In 1822 Moore wrote a poem about St. Nicholas that was destined to shape the American image of Santa Claus: "'Twas the Night Before Christmas" ("A Visit from St. Nicholas"). There are various explanations of how Moore developed the appearance of St. Nicholas. Some say he based it partly on the image of him presented in Irving's *A History of New York* and partly on a plump Dutch man who lived near Moore's house. Moore's St. Nicholas also bears some resemblance to Irving's portrait of Wouter Van Twiller, the first governor of the New

Netherlands colony in what is now New York. He may also have based the character on a sleigh driver he met in New York City.

Although the poem is about St. Nicholas, Moore shifted the traditional date of Nicholas's visit from the eve of the saint's feast day to Christmas Eve. In this way Moore transformed the saint into a Christmas gift bringer. In addition, Moore's poem promoted the European St. Nicholas's Day custom of using **stockings** as convenient receptacles for gifts. Moore also retained the old European idea that St. Nicholas enters homes through the chimney, an idea some writers ultimately trace back to the belief that pagan deities spiraled downwards into homes on the smoke of hearth fires (*see also* Berchta).

In spite of his reliance on Dutch folklore in portraying the image and activities of St. Nicholas, Moore eliminated **Black Peter,** St. Nicholas's faithful companion in the Netherlands. According to Dutch tradition, Black Peter usually did the dirty work of climbing down the chimney and so acquired a grimy appearance. In Moore's poem, St. Nicholas himself descends the chimney and thus appears all "tarnished with ashes and soot." Moore may also have been patterning this aspect of St. Nicholas's appearance after Belsnickel, whom nineteenth-century German-American youth would impersonate by coating their faces and hands with soot.

Although Moore is sometimes credited with the invention of Santa's flying **reindeer,** historians note that the image actually appeared in a little-known children's poem published a year before Moore wrote "A Visit from St. Nicholas." Moore did, however, assign the reindeer the names by which we still know them today: Dasher, Dancer, Prancer, Vixen, Comet, Cupid, Donder, and Blitzen (originally Dunder and Blixem, from the Dutch for thunder and lightning). Moore's poem was first published under his own name in 1844.

## More Confusion Over Names

By the time the next major contributor to the gift bringer's mythology came upon the scene, the St. Nicholas figure popularized by Moore and Irving had become known as Santa Claus. The Dutch phrase for St. Nicholas is *Sinterklaas.* Apparently, American English speakers found this word troublesome. Scholars have uncovered a number of early American renditions of the good saint's name, including "St. Aclaus," "St. Iclaus," "Santeclaw," "Sancte Klaas," "St. Claas," and "St. a claus." Eventually, Americans settled on "Santa Claus," a name which, for most English speakers, obscured the gift giver's link back to one of Europe's most popular saints.

## Thomas Nast and Santa Claus

Nineteenth-century illustrations depicting Santa Claus reveal that people held widely varying views as to what the gift bringer looked like. Some imagined him as fat, others as thin. Some saw him as gnome-like, others as an adult human being. One magazine illustration even depicted him as a little girl, perhaps confusing him with another gift bringer, *Christkindel.* In the late 1800s illustrator Thomas Nast, a German-born immigrant, published a series of Santa Claus drawings that captured the public imagination and settled the issue of Santa's appearance.

In embellishing the mythic figure outlined by Moore and Irving, Nast may well have drawn on his knowledge of northern European customs surrounding Christmas gift givers. In a series of drawings published over the course of thirty years, Nast created the Santa Claus costume with which we are so familiar today: a long, white beard, black boots, and a red suit trimmed with white fur. At least one writer has speculated that Nast drew on popular German conceptions of a fur-clad gift giver, such as Belsnickel, in designing the costume. The fact that the costume was primarily red, however, suggests that Nast had the European St. Nicholas in mind, since the saint was traditionally depicted wearing the red robes of a bishop.

Nast expanded the Santa lore of his time by giving the gift bringer a home address, the North Pole, and some new helpers, **elves**. Furthermore, although Moore's poem suggested that Santa was an elf himself, Nast settled on portraying him as a fat, jolly, elderly man. Some speculate that Nast knew of the Scandinavian tradition whereby elves deliver Christmas gifts. They suggest that knowledge of this folk custom may have inspired him to add elves to Santa's household.

## Nineteenth-Century Developments

Although the folklore surrounding Santa Claus has for the most part remained remarkably stable since its creation, a few changes occurred over the course of the nineteenth century. The original Dutch St. Nicholas punished misbehaving children by leaving them only a rod or stick, which symbolized a beating. So did Knecht Ruprecht, Belsnickel, and, by some reports, *Christkindel*. As the century rolled by, however, Americans placed less and less emphasis on the punitive aspect of Santa's mission. Some researchers attribute this development to changing concepts of childhood and child rearing. By the late nineteenth century many Americans began to view children less as unruly creatures who needed to be controlled by threat of punishment and more as ignorant and innocent souls who needed to be taught through nurturance and good example. Apparently, Santa Claus changed his attitudes towards children along with the rest of the country.

Moore's poem makes no mention of a Christmas tree and has the jolly gift giver fill the children's stockings instead. Nevertheless, Santa eventually adopted the old German custom of placing gifts under the Christmas tree. In 1845, a children's book titled *Kriss Kringle's Christmas Tree* presented American audiences with the idea that the Christmas gift bringer hangs his gifts on the Christmas tree. Throughout the nineteenth century the association between the tree and the gifts grew stronger as the custom of installing a decorated tree in one's house at Christmas time gained in popularity. As Americans began to give one another more and heavier gifts, they began to place them beneath the tree rather than hang them on the tree. And while stockings hung by the fireplace never completely disappeared from the American Christmas scene, they became a much less important component of the gift-giving ritual when Santa began to place gifts under the tree.

## Father Christmas

Father Christmas is an English folk figure who personified the Christmas season for centuries. Unlike Santa Claus, Father Christmas originally did not distribute gifts. Instead, he represented the mirth, generosity, and abundance associated with the celebration of Christmas. Father Christmas always took on the form of an adult male. Some portrayed him as hale and hearty, while others depicted him as gray and wizened. Popular images of Father Christmas usually showed him wearing a red or green robe with fur trimming and a crown of holly, ivy, or mistletoe.

During the nineteenth century, the imported American Santa Claus began to appear in England. Unlike Father Christmas, Santa Claus brought gifts to children rather than personifying the Christmas season. Moreover, he was vaguely related to the old, European St. Nicholas. As Santa Claus became popular in England, his identity began to merge with that of Father Christmas. Eventually, Santa Claus all but erased the identity of Father Christmas as a separate and distinct folk figure. Father Christmas retained only his name, while his image and activities all but mirrored those of Santa Claus.

## Promoting the Santa Claus Myth

At the turn of the twentieth century, the Santa Claus myth had become so well established that retailers, advertisers, and charities began to use it to promote their interests (*see also* Shopping). Hired Santas began to appear on street corners and in department stores. In 1937, the first training school for professional Santas was established in Albion, New York. Its classes taught potential Santas how to act and dress the role and coached them in Santa mythology. By the mid-1950s **New York City** alone could boast of at least three such Santa schools.

In the first half of the twentieth century, however, some people worried whether the sudden proliferation of street-corner Santas would cause children to question the

Santa Claus story. In 1914 a group of concerned citizens in New York City formed the Santa Claus Association, a group whose self-appointed mission was to safeguard children's belief in Santa Claus. At Christmas time they busied themselves with collecting children's letters to Santa Claus from the post office and responding to the requests they contained. Other groups did their part to limit the overbooking of Santas. In 1937, the Salvation Army stopped hiring Santas to promote their cause. In 1948, the Boston city council recommended that the city host only one Santa per season to be headquartered on Boston Common.

While some worked to protect children's belief in Santa Claus, others wondered whether children should be taught the story at all. Some religious parents expressed concern that children would confuse Santa Claus with **Jesus**. Their concern echoed that of German Protestant reformers from centuries past who eventually succeeded in replacing St. Nicholas as the holiday season gift bringer with *Christkindel*.

## More Recent Developments

Santa has become such a popular American institution that a multitude of training courses are now available for the thousands of people who portray Santa Claus each year at public events. Most of the training for professional Santas focuses on how to maintain their jolly manner and appearance while under pressure from the public. Practical advice, such as how to calm crying children, blends with bits of Santa etiquette, such as not accepting money from a parent, and how to avoid promising children something that their parents might not be able to deliver.

The twentieth century witnessed only a few refinements to the basic Santa Claus myth. The most important of these was the addition of a new member to Santa's team of flying reindeer, a gawky, young, red-nosed creature named Rudolph. **Rudolph the Red-Nosed Reindeer** enjoyed instant popularity with the American public, inspiring both a popular song and a children's television program. In addition, beginning in the 1920s the Coca-Cola Company commissioned artist Haddon Sunblom to draw a series of color illustrations of Santa Claus for an advertising campaign. Like Nast's earlier illustrations, these drawings helped to define the image of Santa Claus in the minds of many Americans.

In recent years, American pop culture has spread to almost every part of the globe. People from all over the world can now identify the jolly, chubby, white-bearded man in the red suit as Santa Claus. He competes with traditional Christmas gift bringers in other countries, such as Italy's La Befana and Russia's Grandfather Frost.

# Saturnalia

The ancient Romans honored the god Saturn in a midwinter festival known as Saturnalia. Many of the customs associated with Saturnalia reversed ordinary social rules and roles. Early Christian writers disapproved of this rowdy Roman revelry. Nevertheless, some of the customs associated with Saturnalia later attached themselves to the celebration of Christmas (*see also* **Kalends**).

## Saturn and His Festival

Some scholars believe that the Romans borrowed Saturn from the Greeks by simply exchanging the deity's Greek name, *Kronos*, for the Roman name, *Saturn*. In addition, they assigned him a new, Roman history. Others believe that he evolved from a minor Etruscan god of agriculture. Scholars debate the meaning of the Roman god's name. Some believe the word "saturn" comes from the Latin verb for "to sow," whose root is *sat*. Others, however, think it evolved from *saturo*, which means "to fill" or "to satisfy." According to Roman mythology, Saturn ruled over the kingdom of Latium, the region surrounding Rome, as its first king during its golden age. He established the first laws and taught human beings agriculture. In this era of joy and plenty, people lived together in harmony and shared equally in the earth's bounty.

The Romans honored Saturn as the patron of agriculture and of civilized life. They held his festival at the end of the autumn sowing season when cold weather arrived in earnest. In the early years of the Roman Republic, Saturnalia took place on December 17. At the close of the first century A.D., however, the celebrations had stretched into a full week of fun ending around December 23. Many of the customs associated with Saturnalia recalled the equality and abundance that characterized Saturn's reign on earth.

## Equality

Lucian, a second-century Greco-Roman writer, drew up a set of rules summarizing proper conduct during Saturnalia. Chief among these rules was the decree that "all men shall be equal, slave and free, rich and poor, one with another." This temporary

equality was especially apparent at the banquets characteristic of this Roman holiday. During the rest of the year, the seating arrangements, portions, and service offered at Roman feasts reflected differences in wealth and social rank among the guests. Lucian's rules for Saturnalian banquets, however, neatly erased these inequalities. At a Saturnalian feast:

> Every man shall take place as chance may direct; dignities and birth and wealth shall give no precedence. All shall be served with the same wine.... Every man's portion of meat shall be alike. When the rich man shall feast his slaves, let his friends serve with him. [Miles, 1990, 166-67]

Perhaps the slaves enjoyed the festival more than anyone else. They were exempted from their usual duties and from all forms of punishment. Furthermore, during the time of the festival they wore the felt cap given to freed slaves and could criticize and mock their masters without fear of reprisal. Moreover, at the feast held in honor of the holiday slaves sat down to eat first and were waited on by their masters.

## Mock Kings

The mock kings who presided over the Saturnalian feasts offered one humorous exception to the general rule of equality. As these monarchs were chosen by lot, anyone might become king for the evening, even a slave. The king's commands had to be obeyed, no matter how outrageous. According to one observer, the king's orders might require "one to shout out a libel on himself, another to dance naked, or pick up the flute-girl and carry her thrice around the room." Christmas celebrations in medieval Europe also elevated a variety of mock authorities into temporary positions of power (*see also* **Boy Bishop; Feast of Fools; King of the Bean; Lord of Misrule**). Many researchers trace the origins of these figures back to the mock kings who presided over the Saturnalian banquets.

### Leisure and Merrymaking

Slaves were not the only people enjoying free time during Saturnalia. Schools, stores, and courts of law closed their doors for the duration of the festival. No one worked during Saturnalia except those who provided the food that fueled the feasts. In fact, Lucian's rules mandated that people put all serious business aside and devote themselves to enjoyment:

> All business, be it public or private, is forbidden during the feast days, save such as tends to sport and solace and delight. Let none follow their avocations saving cooks and bakers. Anger, resentment, threats, are contrary to law. No discourse shall be either composed or delivered, except it be witty and lusty, conducing to mirth and jollity. [Miles, 1990, 166]

In addition to feasting and drinking, the Romans enjoyed public gambling during Saturnalia, an activity that was against the law during the rest of the year. They expressed good will towards one another by exchanging small **gifts**, especially wax candles called *cerei*, wax fruit, and clay dolls called *signillaria*. Other popular customs included various kinds of informal masquerades in which men and women cavorted in the clothing of the opposite sex. More serious-minded Romans disapproved of the drunken excesses and the noisy, carousing crowds that wandered through the streets during the festival.

Echoes of this ancient Roman holiday remain in the English language. Today we use the word "Saturnalian" to refer to celebrations characterized by excess and abandon.

# Shepherds

The Bible tells multiple stories about the birth of **Jesus** (*see also* **Gospel Accounts of Christmas**). The **Gospel according to Luke** tells that an **angel** announced the birth of Jesus to some humble shepherds who were spending the night in a nearby field. Many Bible commentators have remarked that this incident shows that God's favor rests with the poor, since they were the first to receive news of Christ's birth.

After receiving the angel's visit, the shepherds journey to **Bethlehem** in order to pay homage to Jesus, the newborn king. They find the Holy Family lodged in a stable. Since **Mary** had no crib, she laid the baby Jesus in a manger, or trough used to feed animals. Thus in Luke's account of Jesus' birth, the Holy Family lodges with the animals and is visited by shepherds.

The **Gospel according to Matthew** offers a different version of events. In that account, educated and well-to-do men from the East, the **Magi**, are the first to learn of Jesus' birth. Matthew's story implies that the Holy Family lives in Bethlehem. No shepherds appear in Matthew's account, just as no Magi appear in Luke's account.

### Sheep and Shepherds in the Bible

In biblical times people relied on sheep and goats more than any other kind of domestic animal. Important figures from the Hebrew scriptures, or Old Testament, were shepherds—such as Abraham, Moses, and David. Nevertheless, shepherds were considered very humble folk and were thus looked down on by some.

The Bible mentions sheep and shepherds hundreds of times. Most of these references are metaphorical rather than literal, however. Sheep require a good deal of care and the expert guidance of a shepherd to flourish. In order to illustrate God's care for his people, biblical writers sometimes described God as a shepherd and God's people as sheep. The Bible also compares good leaders to shepherds.

Jesus, who began his life among animals and those who care for them, would later be described as both lamb and shepherd. In explaining his mission as a teacher, healer, and leader, Jesus refers to himself as a shepherd (Luke 15:4-7, Matthew 15:24, John 10:3-30). The early Christians pictured Jesus in this way as well (Hebrews 13:20,

1 Peter 2:25). The Bible also portrays Jesus as a lamb (John 1:29). The ancient Jews sacrificed lambs as a means of reconciling themselves to God after having sinned. The first Christians came to see Jesus as a kind of sacrificial lamb, whose willing death for their sakes released them from the consequences of sin.

## Christmas Customs

The shepherds' pilgrimage to Bethlehem has been reenacted in countless **Nativity plays,** including the Hispanic folk play known as *Los Pastores*. In some predominantly Catholic countries, people refer to the dawn mass on Christmas Day as the "Shepherds' Mass," in honor of their journey to visit the newborn Jesus. Pilgrims to Jesus' birthplace in Bethlehem can visit various "Shepherds Fields," sites promoted as the place where the shepherds received the angelic announcement of Jesus' birth.

# Shoes

## Boots

Most Americans are familiar with the Christmas custom of hanging up a **stocking** by the fireplace for **Santa Claus** to fill with **gifts**. In some countries, however, people use shoes or boots rather than stockings as gift receptacles.

In Sicily, children leave their shoes outdoors on the eve of St. Lucy's Day, December 13. When the kindly saint passes by during the night, she deposits treats in the shoes, which the children discover the next morning.

In the Netherlands, children put shoes by the fireplace on the eve of **St. Nicholas's Day**, December 6. Dutch children sometimes also leave hay, carrots, or sugar for St. Nicholas's horse. In the morning they find their shoes filled with presents. German children also receive gifts from **St. Nicholas** on his feast day. They place their boots by the fireplace, a window, or the bedroom door on the evening of December 5. In the morning they feast on the sweets tucked inside the boots.

In Iceland the **Christmas Lads** fill children's shoes with candy. Youngsters help the Lads find the shoes by positioning them on a windowsill in the days preceding Christmas. A similar custom takes place in Estonia, where young people leave shoes out on a windowsill in the weeks before Christmas and wait for **elves** to come fill them with treats.

In France children set their shoes before the fireplace, underneath the **Christmas tree**, or near the **Nativity scene** on Christmas Eve. The French gift bringer, Père Noël, fills them with sweets and toys before morning comes.

In Spain the Three Kings, or **Magi**, stuff children's shoes with trinkets and sweets on **Epiphany**, which the Spanish also refer to as Three Kings Day. Spanish children deposit their shoes on the balcony, outside their front door, or near a fireplace on the evening of January 5. Many considerately leave straw for the Magi's camels as well. The next morning they race to recover trinkets and sweets left inside the shoes. The Three Kings also fill the shoes of Mexican, Brazilian, and Filipino children on Epiphany. Filipino and Brazilian youngsters put their shoes near a window or door on Epiphany eve and in the morning find them overflowing with sweets and trinkets.

In Mexico children place their shoes near the Nativity scene, or just outside a door or window that they might serve as handy baskets for gifts. They often offer water and straw for the Kings' camels as well.

# Shooting in Christmas

In some areas of Europe, the United States, and Lebanon people celebrate Christmas Eve by making noise. One especially noisy custom comes from central and northern Europe and is called "shooting in Christmas." In Germany some people still follow this old folk tradition. Several hundred marksmen gather in Berchtesgaden, Germany, each year on Christmas Eve. As midnight approaches, they fire rifles and mortars for nearly an hour to usher in Christmas. Folklorists suspect that in past times people hoped that the sudden bangs produced by noisemaking customs such as these would frighten off evil spirits (*see also* Ghosts; Twelve Days of Christmas).

Emigrants brought this custom with them to the United States, where it sometimes migrated from Christmas Eve to New Year's Eve. In the eighteenth century bands of men tramped from house to house between midnight and dawn on New Year's Eve in Pennsylvania's German communities. They shot off their guns, recited folk rhymes, and partook of each household's hospitality. This noisy habit irritated some of their neighbors. In 1774 the Pennsylvania Assembly attempted to preserve the general peace by passing an act prohibiting any random firing of guns on or around New Year's Day.

In spite of this opposition, the custom of shooting in the new year lingered on in some German-American communities until well into the twentieth century. In the nineteenth century many southerners and westerners shot off guns to welcome in Christmas Eve and Christmas Day (*see also* America, Christmas in Nineteenth-Century; Williamsburg, Virginia, Christmas in Colonial). Southerners added to the din by setting off firecrackers as well.

# Shopping

Over the past century Americans have turned Christmas into a very expensive holiday. The average American Christmas celebration requires a variety of purchases that are considered mandatory for a happy holiday. These typically include **gifts** for family members, friends, co-workers, neighbors, children's teachers, service providers such as hairdressers or housekeepers, and many others, often including the family pets. Beyond all of the gifts that need to be purchased, there are also expenses for holiday treats such as candy and cookies, menu items for holiday meals, and food and beverages for holiday parties. Additional expenses can include decorations for inside and outside the home, ornaments, lights and other accessories for **Christmas trees**, and the tree itself. Paper goods that usually need to be bought include **wrapping paper**, gift tags, **Christmas cards**, postage stamps, and party supplies. On top of all of this, many Americans also have the travel expenses associated with visiting faraway relatives at Christmas time.

All of this Christmas shopping takes a significant amount of time. Many Americans complain that the pressure of shopping for and wrapping a heap of Christmas gifts exhausts them, especially when added to the extra cooking, entertaining, and decorating that takes place around Christmas (*see also* **Depression**). Others protest that the yearly tidal wave of spending has all but drowned the religious or spiritual meaning of the holiday. Still others worry about the waste of environmental resources. They point out that our current Christmas consumption habits produce five million extra tons of garbage between Thanksgiving, the kick-off of the Christmas shopping season, and Christmas Day. Finally, many Americans may simply be spending more than they can afford to on maintaining their material Christmas celebrations. How did Americans come to celebrate Christmas by focusing on such commercial consumption of material goods?

## Christmas in Nineteenth-Century America

Christmas was not always an important holiday in America. It was not even a legal holiday in many colonial American communities (*see also* **America, Christmas in Colonial**). Early Americans did not typically exchange personal Christmas gifts, and

most Christmas spending was focused instead on food and drink. During the second half of the nineteenth century, Christmas gifts became increasingly more common. During this time, many people preferred to give homemade rather than store-bought items (*see also* **America, Christmas in Nineteenth-Century**).

In the decade following the Civil War, American retailers began to cash in on the increasing popularity of Christmas. After 1870, newspaper advertisements promoting various products as potential Christmas gifts appeared in New York and Philadelphia papers with increasing frequency. In 1874, Macy's department store in New York promoted the purchase of Christmas gifts to passersby with magnificent **store window displays** featuring $10,000 worth of imported dolls. Other department stores soon followed suit with lavish Christmas displays. But some Americans still felt that store-bought goods were too impersonal and too commercial to give as Christmas gifts.

### Increasing Commercialism

Retailers, manufacturers, and advertisers employed several devices to break down consumer resistance to manufactured goods. Retailers began to package Christmas purchases in special Christmas wrapping paper as a way of increasing the festivity of store-bought items. The special wrapping paper lifted the item out the realm of ordinary purchases and identified it specifically as a Christmas gift. Manufacturers chimed in by shipping all sorts of ordinary goods in special Christmas packaging. Advertisers ran campaigns suggesting that mass-produced items, such as handkerchiefs, umbrellas, and socks, would make ideal Christmas presents.

In the early twentieth century, retailers and advertisers put **Santa Claus** to work for them. He appeared in many advertisements, endorsing all manner of ordinary household items as perfect Christmas gifts. Moreover, around 1900 he began to appear at department stores and on street corners in business districts throughout the country. These hired Santas attracted customers to stores and collected donations for charitable causes.

As Christmas sales increased, retailers began to rely upon them for a high percentage of their yearly revenues. In order to lengthen this very profitable time of year, some stores began to promote the idea that the Christmas shopping season began on the day after Thanksgiving. In 1920, Gimbel's department store of Philadelphia sponsored the first Thanksgiving parade. The parade alerted Philadelphians to the start of the Christmas shopping season and quite naturally featured the American Christmas gift bringer, Santa Claus. Hudson's department store in Detroit and Macy's in New York soon adopted this festive advertising gimmick, planning their first Thanksgiving parades in 1924 (*see also* **Macy's Thanksgiving Day Parade**).

So profitable was the Christmas shopping season that retailers lobbied President Franklin Roosevelt to prolong it from three weeks to four weeks. In 1939, after a decade of slow sales caused by the Depression, the head of Ohio's Federated Department Stores caught Roosevelt's ear with the argument that a longer Christmas shopping season would boost Christmas sales. Roosevelt acted on this advice, shifting the date of Thanksgiving from November 30 to November 23. In 1941 Congress changed the date of Thanksgiving again, decreeing that it fall on the fourth Thursday in November. A four-week Christmas shopping season was firmly established.

### Changing Consumer Preferences

Shifts in the American economy also aided retailers in the quest for Christmas customers. As the United States shifted from an agricultural to an industrial economy in the late nineteenth century, many people lost both the leisure and the necessary raw materials to make homemade gifts. They turned instead to the marketplace for their Christmas presents. Furthermore, most Americans seemed to find the new industrially manufactured items highly desirable, and many now had the cash to buy them. The great shift from homemade to manufactured Christmas gifts took place between 1880 and 1920. After 1920 Americans relied almost exclusively on store-bought Christmas gifts.

Before 1910 people who purchased Christmas gifts often gave cheap, decorative items, such as ceramic knickknacks, to friends and family. These frivolous novelty gifts soon fell out of favor. People began to send Christmas cards to their friends, distant relatives, and business associates in lieu of these gimmick gifts. Family members and close friends received gifts that were more useful, though more expensive, than the old gimcracks had been. These included such items as tools and household appliances.

By the late 1920s, buyers' preferences began to shift again, this time towards luxury items such as jewelry and fine clothing. The homemade Christmas gifts of the mid-nineteenth century had satisfied people's basic needs. Now, consumers were expected to familiarize themselves with the individual tastes and secret desires of each person for whom they bought gifts. In order to aid shoppers in this stressful mental exercise, retailers came up with a new idea: gift certificates.

## Black Friday

Modern commercial advertising for the Christmas shopping season often begins in earnest for Black Friday. Black Friday is the name given to the day after Thanksgiving, when most American retailers offer special sale prices to kick off the Christmas shopping season. The term Black Friday originally referred to the stock market panic that occurred on September 24, 1864. In the late 1960s, a Philadelphia newspaper used the phrase to describe the rush of large crowds of shoppers on the Friday after Thanksgiving. Some stores reported that day as the first time they had made a profit all year, and so the Black Friday name also became linked to accounting balance sheets, where black ink is used to represent profits. The name stuck, although it did not become widely used until the 1990s. By that time, Black Friday had become an unofficial retail holiday in the U.S.

Thanksgiving weekend, including Black Friday, is now the biggest shopping day of the Christmas season, accounting for some $45 billion in sales nationwide. Stores often open much earlier than normal on Black Friday. Some stores open at two or three in the morning, and some open at midnight. In a 2010 Black Friday survey, nearly ten percent of people began their shopping at midnight. By four in the morning, 24 percent of Black Friday shoppers were at stores. Stores that opened on Thanksgiving Day or evening served 22.3 million shoppers in 2010. The National

Retail Federation estimates that in 2010 more than 212 million people shopped in stores on Thanksgiving weekend.

Retailers take advantage of the opportunity to boost profits on that day by holding special promotions called "doorbuster" sales. A doorbuster sale typically involves popular or high-demand items that are offered at a very low price. Sometimes the number of items available at the sale price is very limited, or the sale price is only valid for a short time. Because of these limitations, shoppers often line up outside the store hours before opening time, waiting for the doors to open so that they can rush in to try and claim one of the doorbuster sale items.

Crowds of impatient shoppers rushing in all at once, with everyone trying to get the same sale items, have produced tragic results. There have been many incidents of people being injured or even killed by the trampling crowd. For example, in 2008 a worker at a Wal-Mart store in New York was trampled to death when the store opened its doors. That same year, two people were shot in a dispute at a Toys R Us store in California.

In the wake of these tragedies, concerns over the safety of shoppers and store employees have caused some changes in the Black Friday policies of many retailers. Many stores now hire safety consultants to develop plans for crowd control. Some stores began to issue tickets or wristbands to people waiting in line outside, allocating the limited number of sale items to those who arrived earliest. With this system, only those with a ticket or a wristband are allowed to purchase the designated item. This has been effective in limiting the rush of the crowd when the store opens its doors.

A dizzying array of Black Friday resources is available to help shoppers plan their one-day spending spree. Blogs, web sites, newspapers, and online shopping forums often chart the deals, including store hours, doorbuster sales, and even store floor plans and display maps. Some people shop Black Friday sales in teams, dividing up their collective shopping list so that they can all get the most benefit from price discounts.

## Cyber Monday

Cyber Monday is the name given to the first Monday after Thanksgiving. The term was coined in 2005, as online shopping was becoming a popular alternative to fighting the Christmas shopping crowds in stores. Web site retailers typically offer their

best deals on Cyber Monday. These sales are similar in nature to Black Friday promotions, but without the hassle of going shopping in the middle of the night and dealing with large crowds of people seeking the same bargains. In 2010, online shoppers spent an estimated $1 billion, breaking all records for online shopping and making it the biggest online shopping day in history.

### Financing Christmas

The increasing commercialization of Christmas has affected American saving and spending habits. By the early twentieth century, many employers gave their workers special **Christmas bonuses.** This token addition to their regular wages helped workers to participate in the new, materialistic Christmas. As this participation still strained the budgets of many working people, **Christmas club accounts** sprang up to help them save money throughout the year in order to finance a December spending spree.

A survey of American shoppers in November 2010 revealed that spending plans for gifts had increased 58 percent over the previous year. Americans polled for this survey indicated that they planned to spend in the range of $650-$1,100 on Christmas gifts. When asked about the importance of prices for individual gifts, 55 percent said they would wait for items to go on sale. About 19 percent said they would pay full price for gifts, while 26 percent said it would depend on the gift item. In a separate survey, 58 percent of respondents described their overall Christmas gift spending in 2010 as about the same as in 2009. In addition to the amount spent on Christmas necessities and gifts for others, the average American shopper spends just over $100 buying impulsive unplanned gifts for themselves.

# Slaves' Christmas

Slavery in the United States can be traced back to the early seventeenth century. Although some of these colonial era slaves included Native Americans and poor Europeans, the vast majority of people subjected to slavery in America were of African descent. Slavery never became as popular in the Northern states as it did in the Southern states. By the 1830s the Northern states had all but eliminated slavery, though it was still legal throughout the South. Slavery in the Southern United States ended with the close of the American Civil War in 1865.

How did the slaves celebrate Christmas? Though many belonged to well-to-do families, they themselves were poor and shared only a small fraction of the families' lavish festivities. Many, but not all, slaveowners granted their slaves a day or more of rest at Christmas time. Some also provided them with ample amounts of food, including the better cuts of meat, a form of nourishment that some scholars believe they rarely enjoyed during the rest of the year. Some also distributed passes to certain slaves, permitting them to visit relatives who lived in different places. Slaves relished these Christmas pleasures, activities that many slaveowners took for granted the year round. (*See also* **America, Christmas in Nineteenth-Century.**)

## *Leisure*

Many slaveowners gave their slaves three days off at Christmas time. Some permitted fewer or no days of rest, and others allowed more than three days. On some plantations slaves were authorized to select a **Yule log** to burn in the main fireplace of the manor house. The slaves' holiday lasted as long as the log burned. Naturally, the slave sent to fetch the Yule log from the woods exercised a great deal of care in choosing what he hoped would be a very slow-burning log. In this way the Christmas holiday could be extended to New Year's Day.

Not every slave got to rest at Christmas time. Since slaveowning families sometimes hosted elaborate Christmas dinners and parties, slaves who worked as household servants often found their workload increased at Christmas time. What's more, slaves could not count on time off at Christmas, since the master could always cancel their holiday. Indeed, some slaveowners withheld the privilege of celebrating Christmas from slaves who had displeased them during the year.

Most plantation slaves passed their Christmas holiday by taking part in some or all of the feasting, singing, dancing, music making, and storytelling that characterized Christmas in the slaves' quarters. Some slaves took advantage of the time off to hold quilting bees. Many of the quilts they made featured the color red, a favorite shade with many slaves. Both slave men and women participated in the craft of quilting. Other handicrafts were also produced and sold at Christmas time, because in many areas custom permitted slaves to keep all the money they earned during the Christmas holiday. (The rest of the year any money they earned belonged to their mas-

ters.) Some slaves may have devoted time to a more dangerous holiday hobby: studying. Studying was dangerous because many Southern states had strict laws forbidding the education of slaves.

## Food and Drink

Some slaves never quite got enough to eat throughout the year. Rich, sustaining, and especially tasty foods, like choice cuts of meat, butter, eggs, and sugar, almost never appeared on slaves' tables. Since most masters gave their slaves extra rations of high-quality food at Christmas time, the holiday not only represented a mouth-watering chance for slaves to eat their fill, but also afforded them an opportunity to savor some of the tasty foods that their masters enjoyed year round. At Christmas time, slaves might dine on a combination of meats, including roast chicken, ham, pickled pigs' feet, squirrel, or possum. Side dishes might include squash, greens cooked with ham hocks, salad greens and eggs, or ashcakes (boiled cornmeal sweetened with molasses and wrapped in cabbage leaves to bake). For dessert some slaves baked a cake or made sweet potato pie. On some plantations the mistress prepared a large Christmas banquet, which the master and mistress served to their slaves.

Many of these Christmas feasts included homemade wine or generous servings of the masters' own liquor. This policy often resulted in drunkenness, as slaves were not permitted to drink at any other time of the year and thus were unaccustomed to the effects of alcohol. Former slave and abolitionist Frederick Douglass believed that many slaveowners promoted this drunkenness as a means of discouraging slaves from seeking their own freedom. After the holidays were over, slaveowners suggested to the slaves that if freed they would quickly slip into a life of laziness and alcoholic overindulgence. They pointed to the slaves' recent excesses as evidence for their argument.

## Visits and Marriages

Slaves could never count on keeping their families together. Sometimes the master would sell a husband away from a wife, or a child away from his or her parents. Nevertheless, some slaveowners permitted slaves to visit nearby relatives at Christmas time. On Christmas Eve the master distributed passes permitting certain individuals to travel. Slaves welcomed the visitors warmly. Even if not a relative, the visitor would bring news from another part of the county and, perhaps, greetings from a relative. Slaves looked forward to these Christmas visits all year long. Nevertheless, this privilege could be withheld from slaves who displeased their masters.

Christmas was a popular time for slaves to marry. The joyous family reunions and rowdy revelry that characterized the "Big Times," as slaves sometimes referred to the Christmas holiday, inspired an increased number of romantic encounters leading to marriage.

## Gifts

Many slaveowners gave **gifts** to their slaves at Christmas time. Typical gifts included hats, hair ribbons, tobacco, sugar, bandanas, collars, or coins. In addition, the master often offered as Christmas gifts the things he would have to supply for the slave anyway, such as warm clothing and shoes. Some wealthy plantation owners furnished slaves with gifts of money at Christmas time. They might also present them with the means to prepare a sumptuous banquet, offering them such luxury foodstuffs as beef, chicken, turkey, pork, duck, apples, oranges, cakes, pies, and biscuits.

Plantation slaves sometimes had to make a formal visit to the "big house" (the manor house) to receive these gifts. Many never entered the mansion during the rest of the year. They arrived dressed in their best clothing to perform the little ritual surrounding Christmas gift giving. Along with his gifts, the master offered Christmas greetings to the slaves, wishing each of them a happy holiday. Sometimes he gave them a glass of **eggnog** and proposed a toast. Upon receiving his or her gift the slave would extend Christmas greetings and good wishes to the master and his family. Sometimes the slaves would collectively present the master or mistress with a token gift, such as a homemade basket or a clutch of eggs.

At other plantations, the slaves did not receive their gifts in the big house. Instead, the master and mistress visited the slaves in their quarters to watch them sing and dance and to present them with gifts. Sometimes the white folks joined for a while in the slaves' festivities.

On Christmas Day, custom permitted slaves to ask a Christmas gift of any white person they saw. All they had to do was to approach them and shout out, "Christmas gift!" before the white person could speak to them. Slaveowners who considered themselves good-natured let themselves be bested, and stocked up on coins, sweets, and trinkets to give away in this little **game**.

In spite of their poverty, slave parents often gave their children a modest Christmas gift. These gifts consisted of things like homemade baskets, hats, aprons, or strip quilts.

## Song and Dance

Temporarily relieved from the daily routine of hard work, plantation slaves celebrated by music making and dancing. Some records indicate that these Christmas

Eve and Christmas Day revels lasted most of the night. Slave musicians played music with any kind of instrument they could get their hands on, including home-made drums, pipes, fiddles, and banjos. Those who could not find or play musical instruments could still sing songs to entertain one another and to accompany in-strumental music.

In some parts of the South slaves practiced a Christmas masquerade known as **Jonkonnu**. Men dressed in tattered, makeshift costumes and masks. Thus attired they rambled from house to house playing music and dancing. Householders gave them coins or trinkets in exchange for their entertainment.

Slaves also sang religious music at Christmas time. In fact, African-American slaves developed their own style of religious songs known as "spirituals." Some well-known spirituals retell elements of the Christmas story. These include "Mary Had a Baby," "Go Tell It on the Mountain," "Rise up Shepherd and Follow," "Sister Mary Had-a But One Child," and "Behold That Star."

## Religion

Slaves attended religious services and gathered together to pray at Christmas time. Some slaves belonged to conservative Christian denominations, such as the Baptists and Methodists, which forbade dancing. These people would avoid the Christmas parties and instead organize prayer meetings. Some of the meetings lasted for hours; others lasted all night.

## Running Away and Rebelling

Christmas was a popular time of year to run away from one's master and to seek freedom in the North. Slaves reasoned that they were less likely to be missed at home or apprehended on the roads at Christmas time than at any other time of the year. They would not be expected to show up for their daily chores until after the holiday. Furthermore, whites were accustomed to seeing many black wayfarers on the streets and byways during the holiday season. The liberties allowed slaves at Christmas time may also have inspired a number of slave revolts. One historian has estimated that approximately one third of both documented and rumored slave rebellions occurred around Christmas. In the year 1856, slave revolts occurred in nearly every slave-holding state at Christmas time.

### Christmas Legends, Lore, and Superstition

Throughout the South, both white and black children were told that **Gabriel** the **angel** sprinkled stardust on the earth in early winter. It turned into the first frost of the season as it hit the ground. Its sparkling beauty served to remind children of the coming of the Christ Child. Slaves also passed along bits of old European Christmas lore, such as the belief that animals gain the power of human speech on Christmas Eve (*see also* **Nativity Legends**). If one crept quietly into the barn at just the right moment, one might overhear them murmur praises to God and the baby **Jesus**. Nevertheless, to do so would bring a mountain of bad luck down on one's head.

## Psychological Pressures

In addition to all the other deprivations experienced year-round by American slaves, they were also subjected to unusual kinds of psychological pressures at Christmas time. These pressures resulted from the role that Christmas played in justifying the institution of human slavery to slaveowners. For example, the slaves' own joy could be used against them, since some slaveowners pointed to the happy Christmas celebrations of their slaves to justify the institution of slavery. Others harped on their slaves' enjoyment of leisure and alcoholic beverages at Christmas time, suggesting to them that they had a natural inclination towards idleness and drunkenness and thus were better off as slaves. While slaves ran the risk of inspiring these thoughts in their masters if they indulged in Christmas pleasures, they skirted other dangers if they refused. The master might view those who grumbled at Christmas time as potential troublemakers (who would be watched closely and subjected to possible future punishments). As a result, slaves may have felt obligated to appear pleased with the Christmas celebrations allotted to them, even when they were in fact unhappy.

Some masters cynically promoted slave Christmas celebrations, believing that this once-yearly binge relieved just enough suffering and want to prevent slaves from openly rebelling against their inferior status. Others may have been less aware of the possibility that the simple pleasures they afforded their slaves at Christmas time played a role in the preservation of slavery.

## Conclusion

In spite of all the pressures and deprivations they were subjected to, African-American slaves wrested some degree of holiday happiness out of the foods and freedoms allowed them at this time of year. Rising above their circumstances, they contributed a number of beautiful spirituals to the American repertoire of **Christmas carols**. Our Christmas celebrations today are still the richer for them.

# Snow Maiden

## Snegurochka

The Snow Maiden is a figure from traditional Russian folkore. She is usually represented as a beautiful little girl or teenager with long blond braids. She dresses in a light blue robe and cap trimmed with white fur. She may wear a modern, knee-length robe and white boots or a more traditional ankle-length robe. In the original legend, she was not related to Christmas. In the twentieth century, Communist officials linked the legend of the Snow Maiden with their chosen gift bringer, **Grandfather Frost**. Contemporary Russian folklore declares that the Snow Maiden is Grandfather Frost's grandchild and assigns her the role of helping him distribute **gifts** to Russia's children on New Year's Eve.

### *Legend of the Snow Maiden*

*Snegurochka* is the Russian word for "Snow Maiden." Many different versions of her tale can be heard across Russia. The outlines of the story remain the same, however.

Once upon a time an old, peasant couple were watching their neighbors' children romp in the snow. The couple had always wanted children of their own but had reached old age without having any. As they watched the youngsters play, their longing inspired them to build a little girl out of snow. They rolled, patted, and shaped the snow, creating the image of a beautiful little girl with long braids. She was so lifelike that they spoke to her, beseeching her to come to life and live in their house as their own daughter. Moments later the snow girl seemed to breathe, then her lips and cheeks blushed pink, and her braids turned from white to golden blond. Their wish had come true! The girl told them that she had come from the land of winter to be their daughter. The astonished couple hugged the girl and took her home with them.

The Snow Maiden was cheerful and good as well as beautiful. Everyone loved her. The old couple took great joy in making a home for her and in watching her frolic with the other children. But as spring approached, the Snow Maiden began to change. Little by little, she lost her good spirits and seemed to grow tired or ill. One day she announced that the time had come for her to return to the far north, to the land of winter. The couple begged her not to go. The old woman hugged her daughter tightly and felt drops of water on the surface of the girl's skin and clothes. This alarmed the old couple, but neither knew what to do. In a few minutes the Snow Maiden had melted away completely.

Her disappearance broke their hearts. They mourned for her throughout the spring and summer. They tried to shut their ears to the laughter of children playing in the sunshine, since it only reminded them of the sweet Snow Maiden. The old couple passed a gloomy autumn, and, soon, winter returned to the land. One evening, as the snow swirled around the eaves of their house, they heard a knock at the door. The sound struck fear into their hearts because they could not imagine who would visit them on such an evening. Soon they heard a familiar high-pitched voice cry, "Mama, Papa, open the door! The winter snows have returned your daughter to you!" The old man flung open the door and there stood the smiling Snow Maiden. The old couple wept and embraced her. Just as before, the three of them passed a joyful winter together. As spring approached, the old couple resigned themselves to the Snow Maiden's disappearance. They did not grieve for her when she melted, though. They knew that the winter snow would return their Snegurochka to them next year.

# St. John's Day

On December 27 the Christian calendar commemorates St. John the Evangelist, also called St. John the Divine. One of the twelve apostles of **Jesus**, John is known as "the disciple whom Jesus loved." Perhaps this explains why he was honored with a feast day that falls just two days after Christmas. Germans and Austrians observed the day with the blessing and drinking of wine. At an old ceremony known as the *Johannissegen*, Roman Catholic priests blessed wine brought in by parishioners. The people then took the wine home and toasted one another with it, saying, "Drink the love of St. John." According to folklore, the blessed wine also bestowed health on all who drank it. For this reason even babies were encouraged to take a sip of the holy liquid on St. John's Day. Folklore also claimed that the blessed wine warded off lightning, attracted a bountiful harvest, kept other wines from going sour, and banished many diseases.

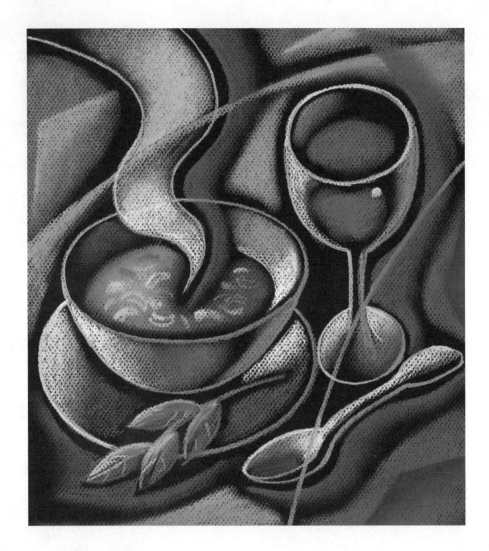

### History and Legends

St. John's Day is one of three Christian festivals that follow in close succession after Christmas. St. Stephen's Day occurs on December 26, St. John's Day on December 27, and Holy Innocents' Day on December 28. These commemorative days were established by the late fifth century. The figures they honor share two things in common. Stephen, John, and the Innocents all lived during the time of Christ and were martyred for him. In addition, Stephen, John, and the Innocents represent all the possible combinations of the distinction between martyrs of will and martyrs of deed. The children slaughtered at the command of King **Herod** in **Bethlehem** did not choose their fate, but suffered it nonetheless, and so were considered martyrs in deed. St. John willingly risked death in his defense of the Christian faith, but did not suffer death, and so was considered a martyr of will. St. Stephen risked and suffered death for his faith, and thus became a martyr of will and deed.

By the sixteenth and seventeenth centuries Europeans were celebrating St. John's Day with the consumption of large quantities of wine, blessed and otherwise. These celebrations may have been inspired by a legend in which John was offered a cup of poisoned wine by a pagan priest. In some versions of the story John drinks the wine with no effect; in others he detects the poison before drinking it.

# St. Nicholas

St. Nicholas lived in the late third and early fourth centuries. Very little is known about his life. By the Middle Ages, however, he had become one of Europe's most venerated non-biblical saints. In France and Germany more than two thousand churches carry the saint's name, bearing silent testimony to the intensity of past devotions. St. Nicholas was the **Christmas season** gift bringer in parts of northern Europe. His legend and the customs surrounding it traveled to America with European immigrants. In the United States St. Nicholas was transformed into **Santa Claus.** His new American name evolved from his old Dutch name, *Sinterklass*. Although Nicholas's popularity has declined considerably since medieval times, some Europeans still celebrate his feast day, which falls on December 6 (*see* **St. Nicholas's Day**).

### Life of St. Nicholas

Nicholas was born in Asia Minor, a region that later became the nation of Turkey. Most scholars believe he was born around 280 A.D. and died around 343. He pursued a religious career and eventually became bishop of Myra, a town in Asia Minor now called Demre. Some believe that he attended the Council of Nicea in 325 A.D. This important meeting of the leaders of the early Christian Church produced the Nicene Creed, a fundamental statement of the Christian faith. Other researchers point out that his name does not appear on the roster of those in attendance until the Middle Ages, when his cult was at the height of its popularity. Although next to nothing is known for certain about the saint's life, many legends credit him with miraculous deeds.

### St. Nicholas and the Three Maidens

One of the oldest and most popular of these legends tells how young Nicholas saved three sisters from an evil fate. The sisters had all reached the age at which young women marry. Unfortunately, their father could not provide any of them with a dowry, so he planned to sell them into prostitution. When Nicholas found out about this, he took a small bag of **gold** to the family's house after it got dark and threw it in an open window (some say he threw it down the chimney). The father gratefully seized the gold and used it to pay for the dowry of the eldest girl. Nicholas provided dowries for the second and third daughters in the same fashion. The third time Nicholas pulled this trick, the girls' father was waiting for him. When the bag of gold came flying into the house, he ran outside, discovered Nicholas, and thanked him for his generosity. Nicholas asked the man not to tell others of his good deed.

Some writers believe this legend eventually gave rise to several Christmas season customs, including the tradition whereby St. Nicholas distributes **gifts** on his feast day. In addition, the custom of putting out **shoes** or hanging **stockings** by the fireplace to receive gifts from the saint, and later Santa, might also have been inspired by this story. This legend achieved such widespread fame and popularity that the three bags of gold became an emblem of the saint. Sometimes artists simplified their images of the saint by depicting the bags of gold as three gold balls. Eventually, the three gold balls became the symbol for a pawnbroker's shop, perhaps because to those who knew the legend, the gold balls recalled the act of reclaiming something of worth.

### St. Nicholas and the Three Students

While the above story tells of a good deed the saint did during his lifetime, other tales recount the miracles he worked after his death. One of the most popular of these sprouted up in twelfth-century France and describes how St. Nicholas aided three traveling students who fell into the hands of an evil innkeeper. While the students slept, the innkeeper searched their bags and stole all their money. In an attempt to cover up his crime, he not only killed the sleeping students but also cut them up and hid the pieces of their bodies in his pickle barrels. The saint, outraged at this crime, caused the pieces of their bodies to come together again and restored the students to life. This story depicts Nicholas once again coming to the rescue of young people. Perhaps this inclination to aid the young explains why later traditions identified Nicholas as a bringer of gifts to children.

### St. Nicholas and the Unpaid Loan

Another medieval tale describing a miracle performed by the dead saint tells how he prevented an unscrupulous Christian from cheating a Jewish moneylender. The saint caused the Christian's death in such a way as to reveal the hiding place of the money he owed to the moneylender. Uncomfortable with this solution to his problem, the moneylender remarked that if the saint were truly good he wouldn't have let the guilty man die. Thereupon St. Nicholas brought the Christian back to life. The Christian then repented his attempt to cheat the moneylender and paid his debt. These events impressed the moneylender so much that he converted to Christianity. Thus, St. Nicholas acquired a reputation for imposing scrupulous honesty in financial transactions.

In Italy, around the time of the Renaissance, the Medici family, a wealthy and influential clan of bankers and politicians, placed three gold balls on their coat of arms. They probably hoped that this symbol of St. Nicholas would inspire confidence in the integrity of their financial dealings. Eventually, others in the financial trades began to use the gold balls as a symbol of their profession.

### Patronages

Many other tales tell how the saint rescued sailors from storms at sea, returned the kidnapped, defended those falsely accused of crimes, and fought against evil spirits associated with such pagan deities as Artemis. Along with the story of the three dowryless maidens, these tales circulated with greater frequency in southern and eastern Europe. There Christians recognized Nicholas first and foremost as the patron of seafarers. Belief in the saint's concern for those at sea spread throughout Europe. Evidence of this belief can be found in the many churches in European port towns dedicated to the saint.

In northern and central Europe, however, where the tale of the three students achieved widespread popularity, people venerated St. Nicholas primarily as the patron of children. Indeed, over time illustrations depicting the story of the three students reduced their ages so that they began to appear as children rather than as young men. This trend can also be detected in northern European depictions of the three dowryless maidens. Furthermore, in northern Europe St. Nicholas acquired the reputation of being sympathetic to the prayers of those looking for marriage partners and those hoping for children. His association with fertility further supported his identity as a patron of children.

By the late Middle Ages people living in different regions of Europe held somewhat different images of the saint's concerns. These differences explain why Nicholas eventually became a bringer of gifts to children in northern and central Europe and not in southern and eastern Europe. As the popularity of his cult grew, Nicholas acquired many patronages. He became the patron saint of children, students, bankers, pawnbrokers, sailors, dock workers, brewers, coopers (barrel makers), travelers, pilgrims, thieves, undeserving losers of lawsuits, and the nations of Greece and Russia.

## Bones of St. Nicholas

For centuries the Church of St. Nicholas in Myra guarded what were believed to be the saint's remains in a stone sarcophagus. Around the year 1000, some of the saint's relics were donated to the city of Kiev, an act that planted the saint's cult in Russia. In the eleventh century another, more dramatic move took place. In the year 1087 a ship from Bari, Italy, arrived at Myra. The men on board seized the remains of the saint and carried them back to Bari. It is unclear whether or not the custodians of the saint's relics in Myra consented to their removal. The Italians may have been motivated by fear that the Muslim Turks, who had invaded Asia Minor from the east, would desecrate the saint's tomb; or the citizens of Bari may simply have coveted the privilege of housing the saint's relics, since in those days people held the bodily remains of saints in great honor.

Soon after Nicholas's bones were established in Bari, a steady train of pilgrims began to visit the town, no doubt bringing new wealth and prestige to the city. To accommodate the bones as well as the tourists, the archbishop commissioned the building of a glorious new basilica in Bari. It was completed in 1108. Only afterwards did anyone recognize that the Muslim workmen who had built and decorated much of the church had incorporated an assertion of the Islamic faith onto the church walls. The phrase "There is no God but Allah, and Mohammed is His Prophet," written in Arabic calligraphy, was woven into the designs decorating the walls. Given the beauty of these designs, church officials decided not to remove them.

## St. Nicholas in the Twentieth Century

The cult of St. Nicholas in western Europe reached its height during the Middle Ages. In the centuries that followed, interest in the saint slowly diminished, reflecting an overall decline in the veneration of saints. In 1969 the Vatican itself struck a blow at the saint's status when it removed Nicholas from the universal calendar of saints, making his veneration optional, rather than obligatory, for all Roman Catholics.

Perhaps this demotion explains why in 1972 the Roman Catholic Church willingly donated some of the saint's long-coveted bones and relics to the Greek Orthodox Church of New York City. One might also recall that the Orthodox and Roman Catholic churches split apart from one another in 1054, shortly before the seizure of St. Nicholas's bones from their tomb in Orthodox Asia Minor by sailors from Roman Catholic western Europe. Viewed in this light, the transfer of a portion of St. Nicholas relics back to the Orthodox Church appears as something of a belated apology for this questionable act. In any case, the gift was presented as a token of the growing good will between the Roman Catholic and Orthodox churches. The Greek

Orthodox Cathedral in New York kept some of the relics, but the majority of them are now housed in the Shrine of St. Nicholas in Flushing, New York.

In recent years the citizens of Demre, Turkey, have begun to lobby for the return of the bones to their original resting place. Their group, called the "Santa Claus Foundation," sent a letter to the archbishop of Bari requesting the return of the relics. Since Turkey is a predominantly Muslim country, some grumble that the group is not motivated by religious beliefs, but rather by the desire to secure a lucrative tourist attraction for their town. Demre already hosts a yearly celebration on St. Nicholas's Day. The sixteen-year-old event, which began as a religious symposium, now includes a festival featuring the awarding of a "Father Christmas Peace Prize."

# St. Nicholas's Day

During the Middle Ages St. **Nicholas** was one of the most venerated saints in western Europe. Although his popularity has since declined, his feast day, December 6, is still celebrated in the Netherlands and other European countries. Immigrants brought the legends and customs surrounding St. Nicholas with them to the United States. There the saint was transformed into the American **Christmas** season gift bringer called **Santa Claus**.

### Shoes, Stockings, and Gifts

In Austria, the Netherlands, Belgium, the Czech Republic, Slovakia, and parts of Germany, folk tradition cast St. Nicholas in the role of a Christmas season gift bringer. Folk representations of St. Nicholas usually portray him as an elderly, white-bearded man who carries a bishop's staff and dresses in a red bishop's robe and miter. This kindly saint distributes presents to others in honor of his feast day. On the night of December 5 he brings fruit, nuts, cookies, candy, and other small **gifts** to well-behaved children. Those who have misbehaved too often during the year might receive a stick, warning them of punishment to come.

Children expecting presents on St. Nicholas's Eve helpfully provide small receptacles in which the saint may deposit his gifts. In the Netherlands children leave their **shoes** by the fireplace. In the Czech Republic and Slovakia children attract the saint's attention with **stockings** hanging on the window frame. In Austria Nicholas knows to look for children's shoes on the windowsill. Perhaps inspired by legends of pagan spirits descending into homes via the smoke from the hearth, St. Nicholas often enters homes through the chimney (*see also* **Berchta**).

### St. Nicholas's Helpers

The powerful saint does not have to carry out his gift-giving activities alone. According to some folk traditions, he can compel a minor demon to aid him in his mission. In the Czech Republic and Slovakia this devil is known as a **cert**. In parts of Germany, Austria, and Switzerland a shaggy demon called Klaubauf, or Krampus, serves St. Nicholas. He frightens children with his blackened face, scarlet eyes, horns, and clanking chains. Incidentally, the name "Klaubauf" is a contraction of the German phrase *Klaub auf!*, which means "pick 'em up." This is an especially appropriate name, since St. Nicholas and his helper often toss their goodies on the floor. In other parts of Germany a rough fellow named **Knecht Ruprecht**, or "Knight Ruprecht," sometimes aids the saint. In the Netherlands a menacing character called **Black Peter** tags along behind Nicholas. These sinister figures often carry a heavy sack of gifts, the book in which the saint has recorded the children's behavior, and a stick with which to smack misbehavers.

### History

As early as the tenth century, St. Nicholas's Day was observed with liturgical dramas retelling the story of the saint. By the twelfth century these dramas had evolved into "St. Nicholas Plays," which were usually produced by choirboys in honor of the saint's feast day (*see also* **Nativity Plays**). These plays retold some of the most widely known legends concerning St. Nicholas and were quite popular during the late Middle Ages, when the cult of St. Nicholas reached its zenith in western Europe. They present us with some of the earliest surviving European plays that take as their subject matter something other than Christian scripture.

Some researchers think that the custom of giving gifts to children on St. Nicholas's Day started in the twelfth century. At that time nuns from central France started to leave gifts on the doorsteps of poor families with children on St. Nicholas's Eve. These packages contained nuts and oranges and other good things to eat. Some researchers believe that ordinary people adopted the custom, spreading it from France to other parts of northern Europe. Other writers suppose that the folklore surrounding St. Martin may have inspired the traditions that turned St. Nicholas into a gift giver. In past centuries St. Martin, another bishop-saint, was said to ride through the countryside delivering treats to children on the eve of his feast day (*see* **Martinmas**). In the Netherlands, Nicholas's helper, Black Peter, wears sixteenth-century clothing, which may indicate that St. Nicholas was bringing gifts to Dutch children at least as far back as that era.

Western Europeans honored Nicholas as the patron saint of children. Some of the customs associated with his feast day gave children the opportunity to reign over adults. For example, in medieval times the festivities surrounding the **boy bishop** often began on St. Nicholas's Day. The boy bishop, a boy who assumed the rank of bishop for a short while, was one of the mock rulers who presided over Christmas season merrymaking in the Middle Ages (*see also* **King of the Bean; Lord of Misrule**). In the sixteenth century, schoolboys in the British Isles hit upon the idea of **barring out the schoolmaster** in order to gain a few days' vacation. This custom, which continued for several centuries, was often practiced on St. Nicholas's Day.

An early seventeenth-century document records a German Protestant minister's displeasure with the myth that St. Nicholas brings gifts for children. His sentiments echoed the concerns of many Protestant leaders of that era who wished to do away with the veneration of saints. In the centuries that followed, the **Christkindel,** or "Christ Child," became the Christmas season gift bringer in most of Germany. This change indicates that Protestant leaders had achieved some success in their campaign against the saint.

### St. Nicholas's Day in the Netherlands

The Netherlands hosts Europe's most extensive St. Nicholas Day celebrations. They begin with the official arrival of St. Nicholas in the Netherlands, weeks before his feast day. Each year the arrival of St. Nicholas and Black Peter from their home in far-off Spain is reenacted in Amsterdam, the capital of the Netherlands. A great crowd gathers to witness the arrival of the ship bearing the saint and his helper. A white horse, St. Nicholas's traditional mode of transport, stands ready to serve the saint. As the gift bringers descend from the ship, the crowd easily identifies Nicholas by his red bishop's robe, miter, crook, and long white beard. After greeting the mayor, the saint

and his helper lead a parade to Amsterdam's central plaza. There the royal family officially welcomes Holland's Christmas season gift bringers. This event is broadcast on Dutch television.

In the weeks that follow, **store window displays** show treats and gifts appropriate for St. Nicholas's Day. Meanwhile, children dream of the evening when they will put their shoes by the hearth to receive gifts from the kindly saint. Dutch folklore asserts that Nicholas and Black Peter, mounted on the saint's magical white horse, fly across Holland on St. Nicholas's Eve, distributing gifts to children. Black Peter does the dirty work of slipping down the chimneys to deposit the children's gifts. He also collects the carrots, hay, and sugar that thoughtful children have left there for St. Nicholas's horse. If the two should find any children who misbehave frequently, they leave a rod or switch, warning of punishment to come.

Families begin celebrating St. Nicholas's Day on the evening of December 5, when they enjoy a special meal together. A traditional St. Nicholas's Day dinner features roast chicken or duck. In addition, many special sweets are served at this meal. Some cooks mark each person's place at the table with *letterbankets*, large, marzipan-filled pastries shaped like letters of the alphabet. Other St. Nicholas's Day treats include *speculaas*, spicy butter cookies, *oliebollen*, doughnuts with raisins in them, and *taai-taai*, honey cookies.

It is not unusual for St. Nicholas and his helper, Black Peter, to visit these parties. Sometimes they just open the door, throw candies into the room, and dash away. Other times they enter and deliver these treats to the children in person, along with advice and admonitions concerning future behavior. Adults know that friends or family members are impersonating these figures, but children are often astonished by the pair's detailed knowledge of their good and bad deeds during the past year.

Family members also exchange presents with one another at this time. In fact, St. Nicholas's Eve, *Sinterklaas-Avond* in Dutch, is sometimes called *Pakjes-Avond*, or "Parcel Evening." Attention falls less on the simple gifts themselves, however, than on the tricky way in which they are delivered and the rhyming verses that accompany them. Sometimes the package only contains a clue as to where the real gift is hidden. Other times small gifts are wrapped in a succession of much larger boxes. The Dutch take great care in composing humorous lines of verse to accompany these gifts. Everyone looks forward to hearing these short poems read out loud. Those who can't come up with something clever can hire one of the professional verse writers who ply their trade at department stores around St. Nicholas's Day. Indeed, rhyming verses can be found throughout Dutch society at this time of year. Visitors to the Dutch parliament may be surprised to find the nation's politicians occasionally delivering a short rhyming speech in honor of the holiday.

# St. Stephen's Day

St. Stephen lived during the time of the Apostles and the founding of the Christian Church. The Book of Acts (chapters 6 and 7) describes Stephen as a man "full of grace and power," as well as a skilled speaker. He was stoned to death around 35 A.D. for his religious beliefs, becoming the first Christian martyr. His feast day falls on December 26, the second of the **Twelve Days of Christmas**.

### History and Legend

Three Christian festivals follow in close succession after Christmas Day. St. Stephen's Day occurs on December 26, **St. John's Day** on December 27, and **Holy Innocents' Day** on December 28. These commemorative days were established by the late fifth century. The figures they honor share two characteristics in common. These characteristics motivated Church authorities to schedule their commemorative days close together in the **Christmas season**. Stephen, John, and the Innocents all lived during the time of Christ, and each was connected in a special way to his life and teachings. In addition, all became martyrs for him. In fact, Stephen, John, and the Innocents represent all the possible combinations of the distinction between martyrs in will and martyrs in deed. The children slaughtered on the orders of King **Herod** in **Bethlehem** did not choose their fate, but suffered it nonetheless, and so were considered martyrs in deed. St. John willingly risked death in defense of the Christian faith, but did not suffer death, and so was considered a martyr in will. St. Stephen risked and suffered death for his faith, thus becoming a martyr in will and deed.

During the Middle Ages many legends arose about beloved saints, especially when biblical or historical accounts of their lives failed to provide sufficient details. An old

English **Christmas carol** about St. Stephen illustrates this tendency. The carol dates back to the year 1400 and depicts the saint as a kitchen servant in King Herod's castle at the time of the birth of **Jesus**:

> Stephen out of the kitchen came, with boar's head on hand,
> He saw a star was fair and bright over Bedlem stand.
> He cast down the boar's head and went into the hall,
> I forsake thee, King Herod, and thy works all.
> I forsake thee, King Herod, and thy works all.
> There is a child in Bedlem born is better than we all.  [Duncan, 1992, 63-64]

With his great hall and boar's head supper, the King Herod of this writer's imagination resembles a medieval English lord more closely than he does a king of ancient Judea.

### European Customs

Perhaps Stephen's death at the hands of a stone-throwing mob explains how he later became the patron saint of stonecutters and bricklayers. It is somewhat more difficult to explain how he became the patron saint of horses in many European countries, since they play no role in the story of his life or death. Nevertheless, throughout central and northern Europe many old folk customs associated with St. Stephen's Day feature horses. In rural Austria people decked their horses with ribbons and brought them to the local priest to receive a blessing. Afterwards the horses fed on blessed oats in order to insure their health and well-being in the coming year. In past centuries English and Welsh folklore recommended the running, and then bleeding, of horses on St. Stephen's Day. In those days people believed that this practice, which consisted of making a small cut in the horse's skin and letting some blood drain out, promoted good health. Horses were also bled in parts of Austria and Germany on St. Stephen's Day. Various German folk customs also advocated the riding or racing of horses on St. Stephen's Day. In Munich men on horseback entered the church during St. Stephen's Day services and rode three times around the sanctuary. Hundreds of riders and their beribboned horses participated in this custom, which was not abandoned until 1876.

Other customs at one time associated with St. Stephen's Day include the wren hunt in Ireland, Wales, and England, and the blessing of fields and straw in southern France, where the day was also known as "Straw Day." In past centuries the Welsh celebrated December 26 as "Holming Day." On this day men and boys struck each other on the

legs with **holly** branches. In some areas men thrashed women and girls about the arms with the branches. The spiny holly leaves quickly drew blood. Although some people interpreted the custom as a reminder of the bloody death of St. Stephen, it may also have originated from the belief that periodic blood-letting ensured good health.

A few final customs associated with St. Stephen's Day reflect a somewhat closer connection to the saint. In Poland people confer St. Stephen's Day blessings by throwing handfuls of rice, oats, or walnuts at one another. This act symbolizes the stoning of St. Stephen. In past centuries the English gave small **gifts** of money to all those who provided them with services during the year. These tips were called "boxes," and thus St. Stephen's Day became known as Boxing Day. In a small way this practice served to redistribute wealth in the community. Since St. Stephen's role in the Christian community of which he was a member was to ensure the fair distribution of goods, perhaps this custom can be said to reflect the saint's earthly vocation.

### Swedish Customs and Lore

Old Swedish traditions also encouraged the racing of horses on St. Stephen's Day. In past centuries, horse races sometimes followed St. Stephen's Day church services. Folk belief suggested that the man who won the race would be the first to harvest his crops. The Swedish historian Olaus Magnus mentioned these races in his writings, and they are believed to date back to medieval times. In rural areas, mounted men raced each other to the nearest north-flowing stream or ice-free spring in the early morning hours, believing that the horse that drank first would stay healthy throughout the year.

The most noted Swedish St. Stephen's Day custom, however, involved bands of men on horseback called "Stephen's men" or "Stephen's riders." On St. Stephen's Day they rose before dawn and galloped from village to village singing folk songs about the saint. These robust performances awakened householders, who then refreshed Stephen's men with ale or other alcoholic beverages. Today one can still see bands of young men, often in traditional costumes, singing folk songs from door to door on St. Stephen's Day.

Swedish folklore implies that the country's St. Stephen's Day customs do not honor the St. Stephen of the New Testament, but rather a medieval saint of the same name who spread Christianity in Sweden. According to legend, the medieval Stephen loved horses and owned five of them. When one tired, he mounted another in order to spare the beasts without interrupting his tireless missionary efforts. The Stephen riders are thus thought by some scholars to represent the saint and his devoted followers.

Other scholars, however, doubt the existence of the medieval St. Stephen. They propose instead that legends concerning the medieval saint arose to explain persistent pre-Christian customs associated with the day. These researchers note that horses were sacred to the cult of Frey, the Scandinavian god of sunlight, fertility, peace, and plenty (*see also* Yule). Other experts trace the origin of St. Stephen's Day horse riding back to the ancient Roman custom of racing horses around the time of the **winter solstice**.

# Star of Bethlehem

## Christmas Star

In the **Gospel according to Matthew** (2:2-14), we learn that the rising of an unusual star guided the **Magi** to Jerusalem. The Magi interpreted this star as a sign that a great person was about to be born. They treated the star as a beacon, following it to the place directly above which it shone. There, in **Bethlehem**, they recognized **Jesus** as the newborn king whose birth was foretold by the star.

### *Astrology in Biblical Times*

The **Gospel according to Luke**, which also tells the story of Jesus' birth, says nothing of the Star of Bethlehem, yet the miraculous star plays an important role in Matthew's account (*see also* **Gospel Accounts of Christmas**). What could explain this difference? Perhaps it has something to do with beliefs the ancient Hebrews held about astrology.

Many peoples of the ancient Near East, such as the Greeks, Romans, and Mesopotamians, thought that the stars influenced human behavior. Furthermore, unusual stellar events were widely believed to announce the birth of great individuals. Astrologers, therefore, cultivated knowledge of the stars in order to predict human events.

The ancient Hebrews seemed to be influenced by these beliefs, although for the most part their leaders rejected astrology. The Hebrew Bible (the Christian Old Testament) reflects this ambivalence. On the one hand, certain passages denounce astrology as foreign and wrong. On the other hand, some passages suggest that unusual human events could be accompanied by the movement of heavenly bodies. One prophecy links the coming of the Messiah with the rising of a new star. It proclaims that "a star shall come forth out of Jacob, and a scepter shall rise out of Israel" (Numbers 24-17). In another prophecy, a rising star stands for the coming of the Messiah. The prophecy declares that "nations shall come to your light and kings to the brightness of your rising" (Isaiah 60:3).

The difference between Matthew's and Luke's accounts of Jesus' birth may reflect this same ambivalence towards astrology. Matthew wrote of the rising of an unusual star, implying that the birth of Jesus fulfilled certain Old Testament prophecies about the coming of the Messiah. Luke's exclusion of the story of the star is consistent with the strand of Jewish belief that rejected astrology as a foreign religious doctrine.

### Scientific Explanations for the Star

Did a strange star appear in the heavens at the time of Christ's birth? The question intrigues many scholars, from Bible experts to astronomers. A definitive answer still eludes them, however, because the two most important pieces of information necessary to solve the mystery are themselves unclear. First, Matthew's gospel provides only a vague mention of the star. Second, the exact year of Jesus' birth remains in doubt (*see* **Jesus, Year of Birth**), so researchers scan astronomical records from the years around 1 B.C. searching for unusual happenings in the sky.

Matthew's description could fit any bright, irregularly occurring celestial phenomena. For instance, he might have been referring to a comet. Comets, however, were generally thought to herald disaster in ancient times, so it is unlikely that the appearance of a comet could have inspired the Magi to search for a newborn messiah. The Magi might have been spurred into action by a conjunction, which occurs when two or more planets appear to draw very near each other in the sky. Finally, they might have witnessed an exploding star, or nova.

The first European person to seek a scientific explanation of the Star was Johannes Kepler, the famous German astronomer and mathematician. He speculated that the Christmas Star might in fact have been a conjunction. By calculating the movements of the planets backwards in time, he determined that there had been a conjunction of Mars, Jupiter, and Saturn in 7-6 B.C. Since that time a variety of astronomical explanations for the Star have been proposed. Until recently, most scholars agreed that the triple conjunctions of 7-6 B.C. presented themselves as the best candidates for the Christmas Star. Jupiter and Saturn drew near to each other on three occasions in that year, very spectacularly on May 22, and again on October 5 and December 1. Triple conjunctions of this sort are very rare, and the Magi, wise men who watched the stars, would have known that.

In recent years, another set of conjunctions has also begun to interest the experts. On August 12 in the year 3 B.C., Jupiter and Venus approached each other in the sky. The Magi might also have noted that this unusually close conjunction took place in the constellation of Leo. Leo, the lion, symbolized the people of Judah. This close

conjunction was surpassed less than a year later when the two stars appeared to over-lap each other in the early evening sky on June 17, 2 B.C. This extremely rare event, called an occultation, would certainly have attracted the attention of the Magi. No living person has ever witnessed an occultation, since the last one occurred in 1818 and the next will take place in 2065. What's more, between the dates of these two conjunctions, another set of three conjunctions occurred. The planet Jupiter and the star Regulus passed close by one another on September 14, 3 B.C., again on February 17, 2 B.C., and yet again on May 8, 2 B.C. This triple conjunction may have had special significance to the Magi as well. Both Jupiter and Regulus were associated with kingship by ancient Babylonian astrologers.

How do researchers decide which of these known astronomical events comes closest to fitting the description of the Christmas Star? They attempt to reconcile the dates of these events with other events that were supposed to have happened near the time of Christ's birth. For example, both Gospel accounts of Christmas agree that Jesus was born during the reign of **Herod** the Great. Most historians believe that Herod died in 4 B.C. Therefore, Jesus must have been born during or before 4 B.C., an assumption that rules out the possibility that the conjunctions of 3-2 B.C. could have been the star observed by the Magi. Yet other scholars contest the arguments offered by these historians and claim instead that Herod probably died in 1 B.C. In that case, the conjunctions of 3-2 B.C. become the best candidate for the Christmas Star.

### Religious Perspectives

Finally, many religious people feel that a scientific explanation for the Star of Bethlehem is not needed. Some feel that the story of the Star is a symbolic, rather than a historical, account, attempting to convey spiritual truths rather than material facts. Others believe that the Christmas Star really did rise over Bethlehem when Jesus was born. Some people who hold this opinion think that it was a naturally occurring phenomenon of some kind. Others believe that God caused this miraculous star to appear in order to proclaim the birth of the Savior. They do not expect anyone to find a logical, scientific explanation for the star.

### Folklore

Centuries of fascination with the Star of Bethlehem have made stars an important Christmas symbol. They often top our decorated **Christmas trees** and appear in other Christmas decorations. Old Christmas customs, such as the cavorting of the star boys, also make use of this symbol. Finally, many planetariums present special programs exploring the many theories about the Star of Bethlehem around Christmas time. These programs offer a new, scientific way to celebrate this ancient Christmas symbol.

# Stockings

The early nineteenth-century poem by Clement C. Moore, "'Twas the Night Before Christmas" ("A Visit from St. Nicholas"), describes an old Christmas custom concerning stockings. The poem's narrator notes that his children's stockings "were hung by the chimney with care, in hopes that **St. Nicholas** soon would be there." Many American homes today present a similar scene on Christmas Eve. Children leave stockings near the fireplace expecting that **Santa Claus** will come and fill them with candy and toys during the night.

Some writers trace the roots of this stocking custom back to an ancient legend concerning St. Nicholas (*see also* **St. Nicholas's Day**). The legend tells of an anonymous act of kindness performed by the saint. Nicholas knew of a man who had three daughters of marriageable age for whom he could not afford dowries. Since the girls could not get married without dowries, their father was considering selling them into prostitution. One evening Nicholas came by their house and threw a small sack of **gold** through the window, thereby providing a dowry for the eldest girl. He donated dowries for the other two girls in the same manner. On the evening of the last gift, the man raced outside, caught Nicholas in the act, and thanked him for his generosity. In some versions of this story, Nicholas throws the sack of gold down the chimney and it lands in one of the daughter's stockings, which had been hung there to dry.

In medieval times people across Europe celebrated St. Nicholas's Day on December 6. In a number of northern European countries, folk traditions developed around the idea of St. Nicholas bringing treats to children on St. Nicholas's Eve. Adults instructed children to leave their **shoes** by the fire that evening so that the saint could pop down the chimney and fill them up with fruit, nuts, and cookies. In some parts of Europe families substituted stockings for shoes.

Eventually, the tradition of giving **gifts** to children began to gravitate towards Christmas. In Germany children began to hang stockings by the end of their beds on Christmas Eve so that the Christ Child (*see* **Christkindel**) could fill them with treats as she voyaged from house to house. This stocking custom migrated to the United States, England, France, and Italy during the nineteenth century (*see also* **America, Christmas in Nineteenth-Century**). In the twentieth century Santa Claus replaced both the Christ Child and the saint, emerging as the dominant winter holiday gift giver. Some believe that the stockings children hang up today ultimately hark back to St. Nicholas's good deed. These days, however, Santa, not the saint, is expected to perform this Christmas miracle.

# Store Window Displays

Department stores present window displays to the public all year round. But the scenes displayed at Christmas time are different. More imaginative, more opulent, and tinged with fantasy or nostalgia, these scenes add to the enjoyment of many holiday shoppers. The enticing Christmas window display is as old as the contemporary Christmas, having established itself as an important seasonal tradition in the late nineteenth century.

## Nineteenth-Century Beginnings

Historians trace Christmas window displays back to the 1820s. These first few displays featured nothing more than merchandise surrounded by a few flowers, some **greenery**, and patriotic symbols. Still, during the 1820s and 1830s many inhabitants of New York City spent some part of Christmas Eve making the rounds of the better toy and candy stores, admiring the modest displays of shop wares nestled among evergreens and lit by gaslights (*see also* **New York City, Christmas in**).

Christmas shop windows quickly evolved beyond serving as mere functional displays of goods and became a form of commercial entertainment. By the 1870s New York shop window displays had reached such artistic heights that they were being reported in the newspapers. In 1872 a toyshop called L. P. Tibbals tickled the public's fancy with a large display of toy trains and other moving mechanical toys. Macy's became famous for its yearly display of dolls. In 1874 its designers created a miniature croquet party populated by $10,000 worth of dolls imported from Europe (*for more on Macy's, see* **Macy's Thanksgiving Day Parade**). In the same year Lord and Taylor was praised for their fine display of **Christmas trees** and garlands.

Each year window dressers at rival stores vied with one another to produce the most eye-catching and talked-about Christmas displays of the season. By the 1880s New York window dressers were treating the public to a series of mechanized, moving displays. When one store mounted a tableaux featuring scenes from Montreal's winter carnival—complete with sledders sliding down an icy hill—Macy's countered by creating a miniature reproduction of a scene from the popular novel *Uncle Tom's Cabin* (1851-52)—the one in which the character Eliza is chased by bloodhounds.

Displays such as these tended to sacrifice the capacity of the store window to advertise goods for sale in favor of attracting attention by means of novelty. Nevertheless, such lavish and artistic displays offered a form of free holiday entertainment to the public and thereby added to the store's prestige.

Though people thought the store windows entertaining, storeowners were well aware of the commercial value of these displays. In 1895, the *Dry Goods Chronicle* gave the following advice to businesses gearing up for the Christmas **shopping** season:

> Fit up your place as it was never fitted before. Dress it in evergreens and bright colors. Make your store such an inviting bower of Christmas loveliness that people cannot stay away.

These extravagant Christmas fantasies invited shoppers to treat the holiday as a season of material abundance and wish fulfillment. Shop owners hoped that this attitude would inspire purchases.

## Twentieth-Century Trends

In the twentieth century, store window displays continued to serve as a form of Christmas season entertainment. In many large cities, stores unveiled their holiday displays the day before Thanksgiving or on Thanksgiving Day itself. These "openings" sometimes attracted large crowds. Families often made special trips downtown or to nearby big cities during the holiday season, specifically to admire the Christmas windows. In many cities, there would be one store that emerged as the perennial favorite in the unofficial yearly competition of Christmas window dressing. In Chicago, Marshall Fields grabbed the spotlight. In Cleveland, Higbees and the May Company split the honors. In New York City, Macy's, with its seventy-five feet of display windows along 34th Street, established a solid reputation for outstanding Christmas windows. In Minneapolis, Dayton's won rave reviews, while in Philadelphia Wanamaker's wowed the public with its yearly Christmas extravaganzas.

Display designers at Dayton's and Wanamaker's hit upon the strategy of moving their displays inside the building, so that customers would actually have to enter and walk past merchandise for sale in order to view the decorations. Wanamaker's offered the public religious displays, while Dayton's specialized in the secular aspects of Christmas. The "Grand Court" in Wanamaker's interior held what was at one time the largest pipe organ in the world, making it easy for window dressers to turn the court into an elegant "cathedral" at Christmas time. The store played up this theme by hiring its own musical director, who led sing-alongs of **Christmas carols** for shoppers and organized Christmas concerts in the court. In 1966, Dayton's recreated an entire "Dickens Village" in the interior of the store (*for more on Charles Dickens, see A Christmas Carol*). The "village" contained thirty-four buildings, one hundred fifty characters (automatons and humans), and twenty-five vignettes, all built at three-quarters life size. The attraction took up 12,000 square feet of floor space and cost about a quarter of a million dollars. The village was a hit with the public. It drew 110,000 people into the store in its first week alone, and 20,000 a day thereafter. To defray the tremendous cost of the exhibit, the store decided to use it again the following two years.

In recent years, the number of special holiday window displays has been reduced partly by the shift in retailers moving from centralized downtown shopping areas to other locations such as suburban malls. While lavish Christmas window displays have been discontinued in some places, the tradition is still going strong in many cities. In 2008, cable television channel HGTV produced a special program taking viewers behind the scenes of some of the most popular department store Christmas window displays. Some larger cities have begun to take advantage of the public's interest in these holiday window displays by creating special travel tours to entice out-of-town visitors. For example, New York City sightseers can find walking tour maps to help plan visits to all of the major department store Christmas window displays. Meanwhile, smaller communities have begun encouraging stores to create special Christmas windows, some for the very first time, by holding annual window display competitions.

Many professional window dressers working for big city department stores begin planning their next Christmas display as soon as the current holiday season ends. Though store windows change year round, many designers consider their Christmas windows to be their most important effort of the year, a chance to show off their skills and to make a reputation for themselves in the world of window dressing.

# Sugarplums

In Clement C. Moore's famous poem, "'Twas the Night Before Christmas" ("A Visit from St. Nicholas"), the children lie "nestled all snug in their beds, while visions of sugar-plums danced through their heads." Although today's children crave candy canes and chocolates at Christmas time, Moore's poem reminds us that over one hundred years ago children longed for sugarplums. In fact, sugarplums symbolized a child's Christmas joys to such an extent that Pyotr Ilich Tchaikovsky's late nineteenth-century Christmas ballet, *The Nutcracker*, features a character called the "Sugarplum Fairy," who rules over the Kingdom of Sweets.

What exactly are sugarplums, anyway? In past centuries people might call any kind of candied fruit a sugarplum. In addition, confectioners used the term to refer to candied spices. Thus, dried and sugared plums, apricots, cherries, ginger, aniseeds, and caraway seeds might all go by the name "sugarplum." Traditional recipes suggest various preparations for this confection. Some sugarplum recipes called for coating dried fruit in sugar or sugary icing. Others recommend cooking it in sugar syrup. Nineteenth-century American cooks occasionally stewed greengage plums in a sugar and cornstarch syrup, calling the resulting sweets "sugarplums."

Today's cooks might find it confusing to lump so many different confections together under the name "sugarplum." In earlier times, however, the word "plum" served as a generic term for any kind of dried fruit. Given this definition, the term "sugarplum" might be said to offer an accurate description of these candies. Sugarplums, or "comfits" as confectioners sometimes called them, not only delighted children as special Christmas treats, but also enriched a variety of cakes and puddings during the seventeenth through nineteenth centuries.

# "'Twas the Night Before Christmas" ("A Visit from St. Nicholas")

Many of the images that we envision when thinking about **Santa Claus** and Christmas derive from a nineteenth-century poem, "A Visit from St. Nicholas," by Clement C. Moore. The poem begins with the line "'Twas the night before Christmas," which has become the title by which it's best known. A theologian and professor of Oriental and Greek literature at the General Theological Seminary in New York, Moore was also an author who wrote poems, biographies, and scholarly works on a variety of subjects.

Today, "'Twas the Night Before Christmas" is one of the most widely read poems in the world. Considered the classic American Christmas poem, it has shaped the modern view of Santa Claus and the Christmas holiday. Indeed, the images from the poem, which helped establish the legend of Santa Claus in the United States, have since taken on a life of their own. Moore called his gift bringer **St. Nicholas** but moved the date of his visit from the eve of his feast day to Christmas Eve. But the St. Nicholas he described is the Santa we know today—dressed in fur, twinkling eyes, merry dimples, and a little round belly that shook when he laughed like a bowlful of jelly. He drives a sleigh full of toys pulled by flying **reindeer** that land on the roof. Then he comes down the chimney with a pack full of toys and fills all the children's

stockings—an idea derived from the European view that St. Nicholas enters homes through the chimney and leaves gifts in stockings.

Moore's vision of Santa Claus was further refined by those who followed. In the latter part of the nineteenth century, *Harper's Weekly* illustrator Thomas Nast published a series of prints depicting Santa Claus. Nast depicted him as a life-sized, portly old man with a long white beard and a pipe. He gave him a home, the North Pole, and added the elves as his labor force. This description seized the public's imagination and became part of Santa's official image, solidifying the image from Moore's poem.

The story of the origin of the poem is as charming as the poem itself. In 1822, Moore told his children a Christmas story. Legend says that he composed the poem while taking a sleigh ride home with his family on Christmas Eve and that he was inspired in his depiction of Santa by the roly-poly Dutchman who drove the sleigh. Others with a more prosaic approach have suggested that he was inspired by one of his neighbors or by the American writer Washington Irving and his satirical book *A History of New York*.

In 1823, the poem was titled "A Visit from St. Nicholas" and published anonymously in the *Troy (NY) Sentinel*. Some reports suggest that a houseguest or relative transcribed it when Moore recited it in 1822, then sent it anonymously to the newspaper the following year. In 1844, he published a collection entitled *Poems* that included the piece, thereby establishing his authorship. He later said that he had delayed claiming authorship for the poem because he was embarrassed about writing what he called "a mere trifle."

Some reports—then and now—have credited Henry Livingston Jr., a poet living in New York, as the author of "'Twas the Night Before Christmas." Livingston died during the period between when the poem was published anonymously and when Moore published it in his book, so he never commented on the fact that Moore took credit for its authorship. A recent scholar has bolstered the argument that Livingston may be the poem's author. Don Foster, an English professor at Vassar College, has accused Moore of literary fraud and has marshaled an argument that some other scholars have found compelling.

Yet no matter who wrote the poem, "'Twas the Night Before Christmas" continues to live on as one of our favorite works of literature, as each year brings new interpretations of this enduring classic.

# Twelfth Night

## Epiphany Eve, Old Christmas Eve

According to an old European form of reckoning, the **Christmas season** ended on the twelfth day after Christmas. People relaxed and celebrated during these dozen days known as the **Twelve Days of Christmas**. Twelfth Night marked the last evening of the Twelve Days of Christmas. Twelfth Night customs called for one final burst of feasting and revelry to commemorate the close of the Christmas season. Church custom, and some ethnic traditions, placed Twelfth Night on the evening of January 5. In certain places, however, people celebrated Twelfth Night on January 6.

### Feasts, Cakes, and Kings

In past eras the English, French, Spanish, German, and Dutch commemorated Twelfth Night with feasts, special cakes, and a kind of masquerade presided over by the **King of the Bean**. This mock king may have evolved from a similar figure popular during the Roman midwinter festival of **Saturnalia**. In medieval courts, mock kings, like jesters, served to entertain the assembled company during the Christmas season. Records from some English households indicate that they were chosen from among those with musical or other skills that lent themselves to entertainment. Moreover, they took charge of organizing the holiday season festivities. These mock kings acquired many other names, including the **Lord of Misrule**, the Master of Merry Disports, and the Abbot of Unreason. Records from late medieval France indicate that one method of choosing this mock ruler was to serve out pieces of cake into which a single bean had been baked. The one whose piece of cake contained the bean got the job. His title, *Rex Fabarum*, or King of the Bean, may have referred back to this manner of selection or to his lack of real power.

During the Renaissance, this particular title and custom appear to have gravitated towards Twelfth Night. Ordinary people began celebrating Twelfth Night with feasts, cakes, and bean kings. These kings, along with their queens, directed the remainder of the feast. The rest of those attending the feast took up the role of courtiers. The following day, **Epiphany**, introduced the image of a different kind of king. Starting in the Middle Ages, western European Epiphany customs began to revolve around commemorations of the arrival of the Three Kings, or **Magi**, in Bethlehem.

### Shakespeare's Twelfth Night

In or around the year 1600 William Shakespeare wrote the play *Twelfth Night, Or What You Will*. Although the play does not refer to the holiday per se, it does weave a comedy around the actions of characters in disguise. Some literary researchers think that Shakespeare put the words "Twelfth Night" into the play's title in order to suggest a particularly appropriate time of year for the play's performance. Indeed, playgoing was a popular activity during the Twelve Days of Christmas.

### Masques

During the Renaissance, some of the most splendid feasts of the Christmas season occurred at the homes of the wealthy on Twelfth Night. In England King Henry VIII appears to have introduced the Italian custom of celebrating Twelfth Night with masques. These elaborate costumed events featured the enactment of some simple scenes or tableaux using song, dance, flowery speeches, and fancy scenery. The custom might be thought of as an elite version of the **mumming** practices already established among the common people. The masques performed at court were short, simple, and sometimes frivolous works designed to raise as much laughter as possible while providing a colorful spectacle. These productions were very popular during the Christmas season, but were also performed at other times of year. The famous writer Ben Jonson raised the artistic level of these works somewhat when he offered a Christmas masque—*Christmas His Masque*—to be performed at court in the year 1616. In England the Twelfth Night masque reached its zenith in the early seventeenth century and afterwards began to decline.

### Characters

In the late seventeenth century the English diarist Samuel Pepys described his enjoyment of a new custom whereby Twelfth Night merrymakers drew slips of paper from a hat on which were written the names of characters found at the bean king's court. They were expected to impersonate this character for the rest of the evening. In this way everyone present at the celebration, not just the king and queen, got into the act. By the end of the eighteenth century this innovation had almost completely

replaced the earlier custom of planting a bean and a pea inside the Twelfth Night cake. In fact, it became so popular with ordinary folk that, by the end of the eighteenth century, shops sold packets of cards with names and drawings of characters printed on them. The absurd names given to these characters served to describe their exaggerated personalities. Examples include Sir Tunbelly Clumsy, Sir Gregory Goose, and Miss Fanny Fanciful.

In the early part of the nineteenth century, the English still celebrated Twelfth Night with parties, cakes, mock kings, and characters. The English writer Leigh Hunt described the Twelfth Night festivities of his era in the following way:

> Christmas goes out in fine style,—with Twelfth Night. It is a finish worthy of the time. Christmas Day was the morning of the season; New Year's Day the middle of it, or noon; Twelfth Night is the night, brilliant with innumerable planets of Twelfth-cakes. The whole island keeps court; nay all Christendom. All the world are kings and queens. Everybody is somebody else, and learns at once to laugh at, and to tolerate, characters different from his own, by enacting them. Cakes, characters, forfeits, lights, theatres, merry rooms, little holiday-faces, and, last not least, the painted sugar on the cakes, so bad to eat but so fine to look at, useful because it is perfectly useless except for a sight and a moral—all conspire to throw a

giddy splendour over the last night of the season, and to send it to bed in pomp and colours, like a Prince. [Miles, 1990, 337-38]

## Pranks

By the early nineteenth century, the Twelfth Night cake had evolved into a large and complicated display of cake, icing, and other embellishments. Bakeries displayed these models of the confectioner's art in their windows, and people gathered outside to admire them. The playful atmosphere of Twelfth Night may have encouraged schoolboys to carry out the following Twelfth Night prank. Unnoticed among the throng of cake-admirers, they pinned the clothing of two adults together or nailed a gentleman's coattails to the windowsill. Then they stood back and enjoyed the confusion that arose when the pinned and nailed individuals attempted to leave the bakery window.

## Last of the Twelve Days of Christmas

Some Twelfth Night customs appear to have sprung from its position as the last night of the Twelve Days of Christmas. Old folk customs in France and the German-speaking countries encouraged noisemaking processions on Twelfth Night, designed to drive out the spirits that prowled the dark evenings of the Twelve Days of Christmas. Old German folk beliefs also suggested that **Berchta**, a frightening figure associated with the Twelve Days, appeared to people most often on Twelfth Night. In fact, the day took on her name in some German-speaking areas, becoming *Perchtennacht*, or "Berchta Night." Finally, other Twelfth Night customs arose from its status as the evening before Epiphany. On this evening Italian children expect La **Befana** to arrive bearing their Christmas season **gifts**. Likewise, children in the Spanish-speaking world await the arrival of the gift-bearing Three Kings (*see also* **Epiphany**).

## Decline of Twelfth Night

The importance of Twelfth Night as a holiday declined throughout the second part of the century. Some writers blame this on rapid industrialization, which in general resulted in the increase of the number of workdays and the decrease in the number of holidays. As Twelfth Night began to wane, so did its customs. One of them, however, the Twelfth Night cake, was kept alive in at least one place by a curious bequest. In the late eighteenth century an actor by the name of Robert Baddeley achieved some success playing at London's Drury Lane Theatre. In his will he left a sum of one hundred pounds to be invested in such a way as to provide the actors playing at Drury Lane Theatre on January 5 with wine and a Twelfth Night cake every year. The will also stipulates that in return for the feast the company drink to his health.

### Twelfth Night in Colonial America and the Early United States

When the British settled in colonial America, they brought their Twelfth Night celebrations with them. In the eighteenth century, Twelfth Night parties frequently took place in regions where large numbers of English colonists had settled, such as Virginia, Maryland, Delaware, and Pennsylvania. They were especially popular with members of the Church of England (later the Episcopal Church) and among the wealthy, who celebrated Twelfth Night with formal balls. These balls featured a bountiful buffet table, loaded with such delicacies as Twelfth Night Cake (a kind of fruit cake), roasted meats, candied fruit, cookies, fritters, and New Year's pie. This last item was an elaborate dish prepared by placing a beef tongue into a boned chicken, wedging the chicken into a boned duck, stuffing the duck into a boned turkey, cramming the turkey into a boned goose and then roasting the stuffed goose in an oven. Just as in Europe, colonial and early American cooks placed a bean and a pea inside their Twelfth Night cakes as a means of selecting a Twelfth Night king and queen.

In colonial and early American times, the Christmas season, capped by the celebration of Twelfth Night, was associated with romance and served as a favorite time of year for weddings (*see also* Twelve Days of Christmas). Twelfth Night balls offered young, single people the chance to meet and to interact freely, and perhaps to find a mate. This goal was facilitated by the fact that the parties usually featured dancing and some form of masking, as well as card and dice games. Indeed, some balls were designed exclusively as affairs for the young. One very famous colonial romance led to a marriage scheduled for Epiphany, the day after Twelfth Night. Future president George Washington and his bride, Martha Dandridge Custis, married on January 6, 1759.

Needless to say, those who did not celebrate Christmas deplored the idea of a Twelfth Night ball (*see* **America, Christmas in Colonial; Puritans**). One man, Mordecai Noah, who published a book on home economics in the year 1820, had this to say about the wasteful custom of Twelfth Night feasting:

> What a sum to be destroyed in one short hour! The *substantials* on this table, consisting of a few turkeys, tongues, hams, fowls, rounds of beef and game, all cold, could have been purchased for *fifty dollars*; the residue of

this immense sum was expended for whips, creams, floating islands, pyramids of kisses, temples of sugarplumbs, ices, *blanc manges*, macaroons and plumb cake; and ladies of delicacy, of refined habits, of soft and amiable manners, were *at midnight*, cloying their stomachs, after exercise in dancing, with this trash. [Weaver, 1990, 13-14]

# Twelve Days of Christmas

## Christmastide, The Days of Fate, The Nights of Mystery
## Smoke Nights, The Twelve Quiet Days

The Twelve Days of Christmas fall between **December 25** and January 6, that is, between Christmas and **Epiphany**. Church customs, as well as some folk traditions, reckon the twelve-day period as beginning on Christmas and ending on the day before Epiphany. Other traditions recognize the day after Christmas as the first of the Twelve Days and Epiphany as the last. In past centuries Europeans experienced the Twelve Days as both a festive and fearful time of year.

### Establishment of the Holiday

By the fourth century most western European Christians celebrated Epiphany on January 6. In the same century Western Church officials declared December 25 to be the Feast of the Nativity. In establishing these dates for the two festivals, the Church bracketed a twelve-day period during which a number of non-Christian celebrations were already taking place. For example, the Roman new year festival of **Kalends** as well as the Mithraic festival commemorating the **Birth of the Invincible Sun** occurred during this period. What's more, the raucous Roman holiday of **Saturnalia** was just drawing to a close as this period began. Further to the north, some researchers speculate that the Teutonic peoples may have been observing a midwinter festival called **Yule** at about this time of year. The establishment of Christmas and Epiphany during this cold, dark season provided further occasions for midwinter celebrations. In 567 the Council of Tours declared the days that fall between Christmas and Epiphany to be a festal tide. This decision expanded Christmas into a

Church season stretching from December 25 to January 5. In English this period is known as Christmastide.

Early Church authorities condemned the riotous festivities that characterized the pagan holidays celebrated during this period, especially Kalends, which fell on January 1. Eventually, they declared January 1 to be a Christian holiday, the **Feast of the Circumcision**. They urged their followers to observe this and the other Christian festivals that took place at this time of year with a joyful sobriety rather than drunken gaming, masking, dancing, and revelry.

As Christianity became more firmly rooted in Europe, political leaders declared the Twelve Days to be legal holidays. Near the end of the ninth century, King Alfred the Great of England mandated that his subjects observe the Twelve Days of Christmas, outlawing all legal proceedings, work, and fighting during that time. The Norwegian King Haakon the Good established the Christian observance of the festival in Norway in the middle of the tenth century.

### Feasting, Resting, Revelry, and Charity

In late medieval England, manor house records indicate that the gentry indeed exempted the peasants who worked their lands from labor during these days. Of course, the weather also cooperated, late December presenting the farmer with little to do in the fields or barns. Custom also dictated that the lord provide a feast for all those working on his lands. In exchange, the workers, or villeins, were expected to bring gifts of farm produce to the manor house.

The well-to-do enjoyed a variety of diversions during the Twelve Days, including feasting, storytelling, hunting, playing and listening to music, and watching and participating in dances and tournaments. King Richard II of England organized a Christmas tournament that drew knights from all over Europe. The jousting matches lasted nearly two weeks and were followed each evening by feasting and dancing. The late medieval tale *Sir Gawain and the Green Knight*, set in England during the **Christmas season**, offers a marvelous description of how the well-to-do entertained themselves during these festival days.

By the end of the Middle Ages, both jousting and the manorial feast for those who worked on large estates disappeared as ways of celebrating the Twelve Days. Although some landowners continued to entertain the poor at this time of year, most preferred

to feast with family and friends. Records from the time of the Renaissance indicate that the English continued to enjoy feasting, dancing, music-making, and performances of various kinds during the Twelve Days (*see also* **Christmas Carols and Other Music; Lord of Misrule; Nativity Plays**). Playgoing was another popular holiday diversion around the time of the Renaissance. Lastly, the courtly masque evolved out of the **mumming** and disguising practices already common at this time of year during this era.

The idea that the wealthy should make some special provision for the poor during the Twelve Days of Christmas lingered throughout the following centuries. As late as the nineteenth century some English farm laborers felt entitled to claim Christmas hospitality from the local landlord. The customs associated with Boxing Day also reflected the notion that the well-to-do should give generously around Christmas time. This noble ideal inspired the American writer Washington Irving to write a story about an English squire who tried to maintain old-fashioned Christmas hospitality by keeping an open house during the Twelve Days. Irving's work influenced the English writer Charles Dickens. Dickens's famous work *A Christmas Carol* tells the story of a rich and greedy old man who learns compassion and charity one Christmas Eve.

Wealthy colonial Americans who celebrated Christmas observed the Twelve Days as a period of festivity, relaxation, and romance. Many parties took place during the twelve days. Young, single people found these occasions ideal for light-hearted flirting or serious scouting for a possible mate. Many weddings also took place during this period.

### Other Holidays

A variety of holidays punctuate the Twelve Days of Christmas. The customs, stories, and festivities associated with these observances add additional color to the celebration of the Twelve Days. These holidays include **St. Stephen's Day** on December 26, which later became Boxing Day in England, **St. John's Day** on December 27, **Holy Innocents' Day** on December 28, New Year's Day and the Feast of the Circumcision on January 1, and **Twelfth Night** on January 5 or 6. These celebrations, along with the festivities associated with the Twelve Days themselves, declined as European societies became increasingly industrialized.

### Ghosts and Spirits

Much of the lore and many of the customs associated with the Twelve Days suggest that ordinary people viewed the time as one in which supernatural forces and spirits roamed the earth. Indeed, in ancient times the pagan observers of the Yule festival believed that the spirits of the dead returned to earth during these few days.

Perhaps this belief eventually gave rise to the lore surrounding the **Wild Hunt**. In much of northern Europe this band of fierce spirits was believed to ride the stormy night skies during the Twelve Days of Christmas. In the German-speaking lands the witch-like figure of **Berchta** haunted the Twelve Days. In Scandinavia the mischievous **Jultomten** lurked about the house during this season. In Iceland the prankster spirits known as the **Christmas Lads** annoyed householders while keeping just out of sight. Greek folk beliefs suggested that small goblins known as the **kallikantzari** caused many a mishap during the Twelve Days. In parts of northern Europe, folk beliefs warned that bears, werewolves, and trolls wandered about preying on the unwary. British folklore suggested that fairies and the Will o' the Wisp, a magical creature who appeared as a light or flame in the darkness, hindered those who traveled abroad on these dark nights (*see also* **Elves**). Perhaps the English custom of telling **ghost** stories at Christmas time can be traced back to the widespread European folk belief that ghosts and spirits are especially active at this time of year.

Folklore suggested many remedies for this situation. In Germany and Austria people burned incense in their homes and churches throughout the Twelve Days. They believed that the smoke drove out evil influences and spirits. In fact, some Germans referred to the Twelve Days as the "Smoke Nights," *Rauchnächte* in German, in reference to this custom. Moreover, German speakers sometimes referred to the Twelve Days as the "Nights of Mystery," perhaps in reference to the religious significance of the season as well as the heightened activity of the spirit world during these days. Other German folk customs associated with the Twelve Days included making loud noises, crossing oneself, wearing frightening masks and costumes, and burning bonfires as ways of scaring off harmful spirits. In spite of all this noise and activity, people from the German region of Bavaria called this period the "Twelve Quiet Days." This name reflects old folk beliefs found in parts of England, Denmark, and Germany prohibiting spinning, washing, cleaning, and baking during this time.

While Germans and Austrians tried to scare off the Christmas season goblins, the Scandinavians tried to appease their relatively harmless visitors. Scandinavian folk custom advised householders that supplying the Jultomten with a nightly bowl of porridge would put these household sprites in a better mood. The Greeks, on the other hand, approached the problem in much the same way as did the Germans.

Greek lore warned householders to keep a fire burning in the hearth during the Twelve Days to ward off the kallikantzari.

## *Fortune-Telling*

In some parts of central Europe, events that transpired during the Twelve Days were taken as omens of what would happen in the coming twelve months. For example, the weather that occurred during the Twelve Days foretold the year's weather patterns, according to folk belief. In German-speaking lands the Twelve Days were sometimes called the "Days of Fate," perhaps in reference to these kinds of beliefs. Folklore also suggested that dreams occurring during these days predicted coming events. In past eras girls employed magical formulas at this time of year to discover who their future husbands would be. One such silly exercise recommended throwing a shoe into a pear tree twelve times in a row. If the shoe stuck in the tree on any of these attempts, one could rest assured of marrying the man of one's dreams.

# Urban Legends

In addition to traditional **Nativity legends**, Christmas has inspired a number of urban legends over the years. An urban legend is a story about some mundane aspect of contemporary life that is usually believed by its teller to be true even though it is, in fact, false. While traditional legends often concern magical or supernatural creatures and events, urban legends generally involve everyday situations and events familiar to both listener and teller. They often contain an implied warning or commentary on some aspect of contemporary life. Urban legends spread primarily by word of mouth and email, publication on web sites, and media coverage.

## Poisonous Poinsettias

One urban legend concerning an everyday aspect of the Christmas holiday takes the form of a dire warning about the leaves of **poinsettias**. It claims that they contain a deadly poison. Each year, it declares, small tots die from sampling the enticing, bright red leaves. Apparently, this legend took shape in 1919 when a child in Hawaii died suddenly, and people simply assumed that the culprit was a poinsettia leaf. This myth acquired so much power that in 1975 a petition was submitted to the Consumer Products Safety Commission requesting that poinsettias be sold with a warning label. After looking into the facts of the matter, the Commission denied the request.

According to the POISINDEX(r), a reference source used at most poison control centers, poinsettia leaves are not poisonous to humans. The national Animal Poison Control Center advises that poinsettia leaves are only mildly toxic to cats and dogs. The U.S. Department of Agriculture agrees, although some researchers suspect that consuming sufficient quantities of the plant's milky sap may cause abdominal pain, diarrhea, and vomiting. Poinsettia leaves taste terrible, however, making it extremely unlikely that anyone would consume enough to get sick. The myth of the poisonous poinsettia persists in spite of the evidence against it.

### Crucified Santa Claus

Another urban legend concerning Christmas tells of a tasteless holiday store window display in Japan. According to the legend, the personnel at a Japanese department store attempted to boost Christmas sales by setting up a cheery, crucified **Santa Claus** in their display window. One version of this legend claims that this event took place in 1945, others claim it happened in the 1990s. One variant describes the Santa as a billboard image, another claims that the department store in question prepared a number of doll-sized, crucified Santas. The location at which this event supposedly took place also varies from story to story.

This legend uses cultural differences to play on the fears of those who suspect that non-Christian foreigners cannot or will not understand traditions that are cherished by many Americans. While Christians make up less than one percent of Japan's population, the Japanese have adopted many secular aspects of the Christmas holiday. In Japan, *Kurisumasu* is an opportunity to enjoy **Christmas trees**, poinsettias, twinkle lights and other decorations, festive music, and special foods. Some people exchange gifts, and stores often have special *Kurisumasu* sales. Although some of the customs associated with Christmas may have been adapted differently in Japan, there is no evidence that suggests there is any truth to the legend of the crucified Santa.

### Candy Cane Symbolism

One persistent urban legend suggests that hundreds of years ago, candy makers encoded Christian symbols into the red-and-white design of candy canes. The story asserts that the red stripes represent the blood of Christ, and the white background his purity. Some versions of the legend assert that the three thin red stripes on some candy canes stand for the Holy Trinity. Other versions of the tale add that the J-shape of the candy cane stands for Jesus, and that the hardness of the candy cane stands for the idea that Jesus' church is founded on a rock.

In fact, the history of the candy cane is uncertain. Some researchers believe that the candy cane was invented in Europe in the seventeenth century, and that the shape was intended to resemble a shepherd's crook rather than the letter "j." One tradition maintains that it was invented by clerics from the cathedral in Cologne, Germany, as a treat for children attending Christmas services held around the **Nativity scene**. The original candy cane was pure white. American candy manufacturers added the red stripes in the early twentieth century.

## *"Santa" Dies in Chimney*

Another gruesome urban legend tells of a family's Christmas tragedy. A man regretfully informs his wife and children that he must go out of town on a business trip over the Christmas holiday. The wife and children resign themselves to celebrating Christmas without him. He finishes his business earlier than expected, however, and returns home on Christmas Eve. He decides to surprise his children by dressing up as Santa Claus and coming down the chimney with a sack of toys. He gets stuck in the chimney and suffocates to death. Meanwhile, his wife and children decide to celebrate Christmas Eve by lighting a fire in the fireplace. The smoke refuses to be drawn up the chimney and pours into the living room, accompanied by a funny smell. The children investigate what is blocking the chimney and find the lifeless body of their father, dressed as Santa Claus.

The impact of this tale hinges on the contrast between the wholesome, family Christmas celebration and the macabre discovery of the father's dead body. Like other urban legends, many variations of this morbid tale circulate throughout the population. The exact reason for the man's return, the cause of his death, and clues that led his family to investigate what's blocking the chimney may vary, but the outline of the story remains the same. No verified account of any such event exists. Nevertheless, there have been several documented instances of burglars and would-be Santas getting stuck in chimneys and having to be rescued by police and fire departments. The legend of the dead, smoked Santa lives on, however.

# Victorian Era, Christmas in

The Victorian Era refers to the period when Queen Victoria ruled the British Empire, from 1837 to 1901. Although she played little part in it herself, she presided over the revival of English Christmas celebrations. At the turn of the nineteenth century, many English Christmas customs had disappeared or were in decline. By the 1840s, however, the English had begun to revive the splendor of the **Christmas season.** The Victorian Christmas mixed new customs, such as the **Christmas tree**, with old ones, such as the singing of **Christmas carols**. In this way the Victorians recreated the English Christmas as a festival of good will, charity, and domestic harmony.

## *Decline*

By the early 1800s Christmas had fallen out of fashion in England. Historians find few mentions of Christmas in newspaper articles or advertisements from the early decades of the nineteenth century. Moreover, folklorists of the era lamented the decline of many old Christmas customs. Indeed, Christmas withered along with the entire calendar of saints' days and feast days inherited from earlier times. Changes in the British economy severely curtailed the observance of these holidays in the late eighteenth and early nineteenth centuries. For example, in the year 1761 the Bank of England closed its doors for 47 holidays. By 1825 the number of observed holidays had declined to 40, and in 1830 it dropped to 18. By 1834 the number of holidays honored by the Bank of England had plummeted to four. Some of the holidays eliminated were those that fell in or around the **Twelve Days of Christmas**, including **Holy Innocents' Day** and **Epiphany**. In 1833 the Factory Act ruled that British workers had a legal right to only two holidays besides Sunday: Christmas and Good Friday.

## Revival

During the second half of the nineteenth century the English reclaimed and transformed Christmas. What caused the turnaround in attitude? Some historians believe that the Oxford movement, a campaign for religious reform within the Church of England, generated renewed appreciation of Christmas traditions through its promotion of ritual, decoration, and the old holy days. In addition, images of Prince Albert and Queen Victoria celebrating Christmas with a decorated Christmas tree kindled widespread interest in this new Christmas custom. Finally, some writers credit Charles Dickens's influential portraits of Christmas charity in *A Christmas Carol* (1843) and Christmas cheer in *The Pickwick Papers* (1837) with inspiring Victorian appreciation of the Christmas season. Others disagree, arguing that Dickens captured the emerging Victorian attitude towards Christmas, rather than inspired it. Whatever his place in the chain of cause and effect, both British and American audiences hailed *A Christmas Carol*, and the tale became a cherished element of Victorian Christmas lore.

## Christmas Dinner

Christmas dinner was one of the few English Christmas customs that had never really gone out of fashion. The Victorians relished their holiday feast, contributing two new dishes to the traditional Christmas dinner. Plum pudding, a dessert, replaced plum porridge as a first course. The Victorians also adopted roast turkey as a possible main course, in addition to the more traditional roast beef or roast goose. The renewed emphasis on the pleasures of the table, so ably promoted by Dickens, elevated the Christmas dinner into a centerpiece of the Victorian festival.

## Christmas Charity

Changes in the treatment of the poor at Christmas time reveal the importance of Christmas charity in Victorian times. In 1847 a new law allowed Christmas dinners to be served in all workhouses for the poor. Charitable donations supplied much of the food for these dinners. During the Victorian era, performing acts of charity became an important part of the observance of Christmas for many middle-class people. Some visited workhouses on Christmas Day. Others distributed **gifts** of food and money, known as "boxes," among the poor of their parish on the day after Christmas. In Victorian times people called the twenty-sixth Boxing Day in reference to this custom. In past eras the English had observed December 26 as **St. Stephen's Day**. Parliament declared Boxing Day a public holiday in 1871.

## Protestants Embrace Christmas

As the themes of charity and domestic harmony became dominant in Victorian Christmas celebrations and the disorderly, public revelry of past eras faded, those Protestant denominations that had once opposed the celebration of Christmas softened their attitudes toward it. This opposition dated from the time of the Reformation and found its strongest advocates in the **Puritans**. In late nineteenth-century America a similar process of reincorporation was underway as many Protestant churches in the United States also accepted Christmas back into the fold of legitimate observances (*see also* **America, Christmas in Nineteenth-Century**).

## Christmas Trees and Gifts

At the beginning of the nineteenth century the English gave Christmas gifts, or boxes, to servants, the poor, and those who provided them with services during the year. Those who gave holiday season gifts to family and friends did so on New Year's Day. In the early part of the nineteenth century, however, New Year's gift giving appeared to be dying out. Two English folklorists writing in the 1830s remarked upon the ominous decline of the practice. In the Victorian era, the English revived winter season gift giving, transferring the custom from New Year's Day to Christmas. The Christmas tree played an important role in this transfer and revival.

Historians credit German-born Prince Albert for importing this German custom to Great Britain. A well-known 1840s illustration depicting Queen Victoria, Prince Albert, and their children gathered around the Christmas tree motivated middle-class families to adopt this custom. (Fashionable Victorians often sought to imitate royal tastes.) Like the Germans, English families covered their Christmas trees with good things to eat and small gifts. Hence, the tree focused everyone's attention on giving and receiving. In addition, because it stood at the center of the household, the tree drew the exchange of Christmas gifts into the family circle. By the end of the century, Victorians customarily gave Christmas gifts to friends and family. New Year's gifts had become the exception rather than the rule. Queen Victoria remained loyal to the old custom, though, still sending New Year's, rather than Christmas, gifts as late as 1900.

While the Christmas tree grew in popularity among middle-class Victorians, many working-class families adopted the more affordable and convenient Christmas **stocking**. This custom, too, encouraged the exchange of small gifts within the family.

By the 1880s **Santa Claus** had arrived in England. Unlike the English Father Christmas, Santa Claus brought gifts to children at Christmas time. By the end of the century the popularity of this American gift bringer prompted retailers to begin using his image to boost Christmas sales.

## Christmas Carols

In the early years of the nineteenth century several English folklorists predicted the approaching demise of the Christmas carol. Observers of English folk customs mourned that only a scattered handful of old people knew and sang the traditional songs. This timely handwringing may have inspired several important collections of Christmas carols, which were published in the early part of the century. With their renewed interest in Christmas and its traditions, middle-class Victorians welcomed these traditional songs back into their Christmas festivities. By the 1870s churches began to incorporate these almost-forgotten Christmas songs into their holiday services. In 1880 an Anglican bishop, Edward W. Benson, later archbishop of Canterbury, first devised the Ceremony of Lessons and Carols, a special Christmas service blending Bible readings with carol singing.

## Christmas Greetings and Entertainments

By the 1860s Victorians had come to cherish seasonal greeting cards (*see also* **Christmas Cards; Robins**). Many of these cards wished the recipient "Happy New Year" rather than "**Merry Christmas**," but by the 1870s the increasing importance of Christmas led card makers to include Christmas greetings as well. Victorian Christmas card designers created colorful and elaborate cards, often enhanced with silk, cords, and tassels. The ingenious cards so enchanted the public that newspapers reviewed new designs and people carefully collected and displayed the cards they received.

At about mid-century Christmas crackers emerged as another Victorian Christmas novelty. These cardboard tubes, wrapped in decorative papers, contained a variety of tiny trinkets. When pulled on both ends, the party favors burst with a loud popping sound.

Other Christmas entertainments included parlor games. In the game called "Snapdragon," the hostess filled a bowl with currants (a raisin-like dried fruit), poured spirits on top of them, and set a lighted match to the mixture. Players dared one another to grab a currant out of the flaming bowl. When the family tired of Snapdragon they might move on to other parlor games, such as Blind Man's Bluff or charades, or they might entertain one another with recitations, magic tricks, or Christmas carols.

The kissing bough offered a different kind of entertainment to the lovelorn or to the adventurous who lingered nearby. According to custom, one could steal a kiss from anyone who passed beneath its branches of **mistletoe**. Victorian tastes in Christmas decorations called for plenty of **greenery** in addition to the kissing bough, usually displayed in the form of ropes, **wreaths**, and sprays.

Victorians continued their Christmas fun on Boxing Day. On this day many families crowded into theaters to view a pantomime, a circus-like presentation of a folk or fairy tale.

## Customs in Decline

Although many of the more boisterous English Christmas customs, such as **mumming**, had already deteriorated by Victorian times, a few more withered away under the spell of the new Victorian Christmas. **Twelfth Night**, which had been celebrated in the past with sumptuous cakes, costumed balls, and charades, faded throughout the Victorian period as Christmas Day grew in importance. In addition, the waits, bands of nighttime musicians who serenaded householders at Christmas time in exchange for food, drink, or tips, also fell out of favor during this era. Nevertheless, by the end of the nineteenth century, the Victorians celebrated Christmas more vigorously than their ancestors had at the beginning of the century.

# Virginia O'Hanlon

In 1897 an eight-year-old girl named Virginia O'Hanlon wrote a letter to a newspaper called the *New York Sun*. The letter asked the newspaper editor to tell her whether or not Santa Claus was real. Virginia's letter, and the newspaper's response, have become beloved bits of American Christmas lore. The often-quoted phrase, "Yes, Virginia, there is a Santa Claus," comes from the paper's editorial response, written by reporter Francis P. Church and published on September 21, 1897.

### *Virginia's Letter and the* Sun's *Response*

Dear Editor:

I am 8 years old. Some of my little friends say there is no Santa Claus. Papa says "If you see it in The Sun it's so." Please tell me the truth, is there a Santa Claus?

Virginia O' Hanlon
115 West 95th Street
New York City

Virginia, your little friends are *wrong*. They have been affected by the skepticism of a skeptical age. They do not *believe* except they *see*. They think that nothing can be which is not comprehensible by their little minds. All minds, Virginia, whether they be men's or children's are little. In this great universe of ours man is a mere insect, an ant, in his intellect, as compared with the boundless world about him, as measured by the intelligence capable of grasping the whole of truth and knowledge.

Yes, Virginia, there *is* a Santa Claus. He exists as certainly as love, and generosity and devotion exist, and you know that they abound and give to your life its highest beauty and joy. Alas! how dreary would be the world if there were no Santa Claus! It would be as dreary as if there were no Virginias. There would be no childlike faith, then, no poetry, no romance to make tolerable this existence. We should have no enjoyment, except in sense and sight. The eternal light with which childhood fills the world would be extinguished.

Not believe in *Santa Claus*! You might as well not believe in fairies! You might get your papa to hire men to watch in all the chimneys on Christmas Eve to

catch Santa Claus, but even if they did not see Santa Claus coming down what would that prove? Nobody sees Santa Claus. The most real things in the world are those that neither children nor men can see. Did you ever see fairies dancing on the lawn? Of course not, but that's no proof that they are not there. Nobody can conceive or imagine all the wonders there are unseen and unseeable in the world.

You tear apart the baby's rattle and see what makes the noise inside, but there is a veil covering the unseen world which not the strongest man, nor even the united strength of all the strongest men that ever lived, could tear apart. Only faith, fancy, poetry, love, romance, can push aside that curtain and view—and picture the supernal beauty and glory beyond. Is it all real? Ah, Virginia, in all this world there is nothing else real and abiding.

No Santa Claus? Thank God he lives, and he lives forever! A thousand years from now, Virginia, nay ten times ten thousand years from now, he will continue to make glad the heart of childhood.

### Who Was Francis P. Church?

Francis Church, the child of a Baptist minister, was born in 1839. He graduated from Columbia College in 1859 and went on to cover the Civil War as a reporter for the *New York Times*. Some time after that he joined the staff of the *New York Sun*, where he covered religious matters.

When Virginia's letter arrived at the offices of the *Sun* in 1897, the editorial page chief assigned Church the chore of writing a response. Church, known for his bitter, sarcastic wit, was none too pleased with the assignment, but resigned himself to crafting a suitable reply. His response surpassed everyone's expectations. It was so popular that the *Sun* reprinted it every year at Christmas time, until the paper went out of business about fifty years later. Church died in 1906.

### Whatever Happened to Virginia?

Virginia's early thirst for knowledge continued as she matured into adulthood. She graduated from New York's Hunter College in 1910 with a B.A., and went on to acquire an M.A. at Columbia University. She completed her studies with a Ph.D. from Fordham University. Dr. O'Hanlon served as an educator in New York City's public school system, ending her career as principal of P.S. 401 in Brooklyn. She retired in 1959 and died in 1971.

# Wenceslas, King

## St. Wenceslaus, Vaceslav, Vaclav

The familiar **Christmas carol**, "Good King Wenceslas," tells of a virtuous deed performed by the noble King Wenceslas on the day after Christmas, **St. Stephen's Day.** Is King Wenceslas a historical or a legendary character? If historical, did he ever perform a deed similar to that described in the carol?

According to the carol, King Wenceslas spied a poor man scavenging wood outside his castle on St. Stephen's Day. Moved by the needy man's plight, King Wenceslas found out where he lived and set forth with his page to bring the man food, drink, and fuel. The wind and cold nearly overcame the king's page but, with Wenceslas's encouragement, the page stumbled forward, treading in his master's footprints. Heat rose from the tracks of the saintly king, a sign of heaven's approval of his act of charity.

The story told in the song combines historical fact with pious speculation. The song's lyrics describe a tenth-century Bohemian duke who later became a saint. Known as St. Vaceslav or St. Vaclav, his name is usually rendered as "Wenceslas" or "Wenceslaus" in English. He was born to a Christian father, Wratislaw, and a pagan mother, Drahomira, around the year 903. His grandmother, St. Ludmilla, educated him in the Christian faith.

When his father died, his mother became the duchess of Bohemia. Drahomira resented the influence of Ludmilla over the young Wenceslas, and so arranged to have the older woman murdered. Horrified by this act and by her unscrupulous political dealings, Wenceslas eventually wrested power away from his mother and assumed the title of duke. Drahomira had hindered the spread of Christianity, but Wenceslas supported the new religion. Furthermore, Duke Wenceslas acquired a reputation for personal piety and charity to the poor. Drahomira still opposed him, however, and soon convinced Wenceslas's brother Boleslaw to murder the young Duke and take his place on the throne. Wenceslas died at the hands of his brother on September 28 in the year 935. Although he may have been deprived of earthly power at a young age, Wenceslas was elevated to sainthood after his death. He became the patron saint of Bohemia by the eleventh century. His feast day is September 28.

In the nineteenth century an Englishman named John Mason Neele wrote the lyrics to "Good King Wenceslas." He based the story on legends concerning the saint's good deeds as duke of Bohemia. He paired these lyrics with a thirteenth-century tune he found in an obscure book of early songs. Although the sturdy melody may now automatically evoke images of the noble king trudging through the snow, the tune had earlier been used as a spring carol titled "Spring Has Now Unwrapped the Flowers." Neele's winning combination of words and music spread the legend of Wenceslas to listeners who otherwise would never have known of the saint.

# "White Christmas"

"White Christmas" is the most popular Christmas song ever recorded. Written by Irving Berlin and featured in the 1942 movie *Holiday Inn*, it soon inspired a large and loyal following. Bing Crosby, one of America's most popular mid-century crooners, sang the tune in the motion picture and also recorded it as a single. It sold so many copies that the die press used to imprint the records literally wore out. Crosby recorded the song again in 1947, once more in 1952—as part of the sound track for the movie *White Christmas*—and yet again in 1955. By 1968 listeners had snapped up 30 million copies of the song. For decades "White Christmas" reigned not only as the best-selling Christmas song ever recorded, but also as the best-selling single ever recorded. In 1997, pop star Elton John finally toppled this achievement with his musical tribute to Princess Diana, "Candle in the Wind."

## The Composer

Irving Berlin was the stage name of Israel Baline, the youngest child of a Russian Jewish family that immigrated to the United States in 1893 and settled in New York City's Lower East Side. Although his own family did not celebrate Christmas, the composer later fondly recalled childhood memories of scampering over to his neighbors, the O'Hara's, to enjoy their Christmas tree and share in their Christmas goodies. Perhaps he called on some of these memories when he composed his nostalgic, best-selling Christmas song. Musical success was no stranger to Irving Berlin, however. He published 800 songs in his lifetime, many of them hits, and wrote hundreds more. Berlin possessed a knack for capturing in song the spirit of the times, an event, or a holiday, even one that he didn't himself celebrate. In addition to "White Christmas," some of his timeless tunes include "Oh How I Hate to Get Up in the Morning," "(There's No Business Like) Show Business," and "God Bless America."

## "White Christmas," the Song

In 1940 Berlin began work on a series of songs for a musical comedy about a man who retires from show business to run a country inn open only on holidays. While working on the show's Christmas song, he remembered a winter spent in sunny Hollywood, where it never quite felt "like Christmas." He realized that the very difficulties he recalled formed the basis of a song. He fixed in his mind an image of jaded Hollywoodites sitting around a southern California swimming pool at Christmas time, reminiscing about the Christmases of their childhoods, and then put pencil to paper. The song as originally composed includes a first verse that speaks of palm trees and mild weather. Later renditions of the song usually skip this verse.

Although it generally took Berlin days, weeks, or months to write a song, he completed "White Christmas" in a single, all-night work session. Berlin, never afraid to sing his own praises, was so pleased with "White Christmas" that the morning after he completed the song he told his transcriber, "It is not only the best song I ever wrote, it's the best song anybody ever wrote" (Glancy, 2000, 65).

## Holiday Inn

Berlin succeeded in selling his songs and story idea to Paramount Pictures, which turned them into the 1942 musical *Holiday Inn*. The movie gave "White Christmas" the public exposure it needed to become a hit. It featured Bing Crosby, who played a singer and dancer who moves to the country to run an inn open only on holidays. He falls in love with an up-and-coming singer, played by Marjorie Reynolds, who must choose between the retiring innkeeper and a flashy Hollywood-bound dancer played by Fred Astaire. Berlin composed a song for each holiday featured in the movie. As he liked to exercise a great deal of control over the presentation of his songs, he worked closely with the director, technicians, and actors, advising the singers on appropriate phrasing and execution for each song. Perhaps irritated with this constant stream of advice, the director asked Berlin to leave the set while they filmed Bing Crosby singing "White Christmas." Berlin agreed, but then found that he couldn't resist hanging around. He hid himself behind some flats (panels used to dampen sound), but was discovered during the filming by a technician.

Although the cast predicted that the film's Valentine's Day song, "Be Careful, It's My Heart," would become the most beloved song from the show, "White Christmas" soon entranced audiences. It spoke powerfully to American soldiers fighting in World War II, who were also dreaming of other, happier times. They swamped their radio stations with calls requesting the song. Back home, "White Christmas" won the Academy Award for the best song in a motion picture released in 1942.

While the American public dreamed along with "White Christmas," the idea behind the story for *Holiday Inn* fueled the business imagination of Kemmons Wilson. When he opened a chain of family motels in the 1950s he named it after one of his favorite movies, "Holiday Inn."

## White Christmas, *the Movie*

Meanwhile, back in Hollywood movie producers decided to capitalize on the popularity of "White Christmas" by filming a remake of *Holiday Inn* that would again feature the song. In order to make sure the public knew that the movie revolved around the tune, they named the film *White Christmas* (1954). Bing Crosby once more played the lead role, this time with actor Danny Kaye as his sidekick. The two play old army buddies who are also song and dance men. They meet and fall in love with two singing and dancing sisters, played by Rosemary Clooney and Vera Ellen. The foursome prepare a Christmas show for a rural Vermont inn run by a retired army general, Crosby and Kaye's former commander. Like *Holiday Inn*, *White Christmas* gives Crosby two opportunities to sing "White Christmas," one at the beginning and the other at the end of the story.

### *A Personal Tribute*

In 1967 New York City composer and singer John Wallowitch and a group of his friends gathered on the sidewalk outside Irving Berlin's house to celebrate Christmas by serenading the retired composer with his famous holiday song, "White Christmas," and a love song called "Always." These devoted fans kept up this yearly Christmas time tribute until Berlin's death in 1989. In 1983, the singers actually rang the doorbell and were invited in. Berlin graciously told them that their visit and performance was the nicest Christmas present he had ever had.

# White House, Christmas in the

The White House became the official residence of the president of the United States in 1800. Throughout the nineteenth century, it was referred to as the President's House, the President's Palace, or the Executive Mansion. President Theodore Roosevelt dubbed it the White House in 1901. As Christmas became a more important holiday in the United States, White House Christmas celebrations expanded beyond family festivities to include **charitable giving**, political functions, activities dedicated to enhancing public relations, and special observances, such as the lighting of the National Christmas Tree.

## White House Christmas Parties

President John Adams and First Lady Abigail Adams were the first to occupy the White House upon its completion in November 1800. They hosted the first White House Christmas party that year. This party included special festivities for children, although the celebration did not end on a happy note. Susanna, the Adams's grandchild, showed the other children the miniature dish set she had received for Christmas. One little girl became so envious that she broke the tiny dishes into pieces. At this provocation, Susanna flew into a rage and bit the nose and cheeks off her companion's doll. The president himself had to exercise his diplomatic skills and executive authority to break up the fight and restore order. Meanwhile, the newly constructed White House proved difficult to heat no matter how much wood was burned in the fireplaces. Shivering guests left the party as early as they could.

Future White House Christmas parties proved better than the first one. In 1805, Thomas Jefferson threw a Christmas party for his six grandchildren. One hundred children attended and were entertained by the president himself, who played rollicking tunes on the violin. In 1811, President James Madison and First Lady Dolley Madison gave a sumptuous Christmas dinner party for family members and other guests. The Virginia-style feast featured turkeys, chickens, ducks, wild game, vegetables, and puddings. After dinner, guests and hosts entertained each other with games, singing, and dancing. In 1835, President Andrew Jackson invited a large number of Washington children to a Christmas Day party in the White House. He treated them to a feast prepared by his French chef and served in the formal dining room. After dinner he supplied the children with cotton snowballs and permitted them to have a snowball fight in the East Room. First Lady Edith Roosevelt, wife of President Theodore "Teddy" Roosevelt, once threw a Christmas party for 600 children, the sons and daughters of administration officials. It included a special dinner in the state dining room, at which the President helped serve the children their food.

Some White House Christmas parties were social events with diplomatic overtones. In 1860, President James Buchanan hosted a delegation of Pawnee Indians at a White

House Christmas party. In 1874, President Ulysses S. Grant and First Lady Julia Grant welcomed the King of Hawaii to their Christmas party. When a fire struck the White House on Christmas Eve of 1929, First Lady Lou Hoover skillfully managed to keep the party going while President Herbert Hoover rushed to the site of the fire in the West Wing. Although sixteen fire engines answered the alarm, some of the president's guests stayed through the entire party without ever realizing that the building was on fire.

By the late twentieth century, Christmas parties hosted at the White House were growing in both size and number. Some parties reflected the personal tastes of the president or first lady. For example, in 1957 First Lady Mamie Eisenhower threw a Christmas tea party for women reporters. Some parties, once instituted, were continued by succeeding administrations. President John F. Kennedy and First Lady Jacqueline Kennedy threw a variety of specialized Christmas parties, including one for diplomats and another for diplomats' children. President Lyndon Johnson continued both of these events.

In 1979, President Jimmy Carter and First Lady Rosalynn Carter gave a Christmas ball for 1,000 people, including members of Congress, their spouses, and other guests. The very next night the Carters threw another Christmas party for 500 members of the Washington press corps. First Lady Nancy Reagan, wife of President Ronald Reagan, threw a Christmas party for 178 hearing-impaired children in 1981. She hired professional entertainers, also hearing-impaired, to lead the festivities and presented each child with a Christmas gift. President George H.W. Bush and First Lady Barbara Bush hosted numerous Christmas parties over a busy two-week period each year. The 1994 Christmas party for the White House press corps, hosted by President Bill Clinton and First Lady Hillary Clinton, included 2,000 guests.

In 2005, President George W. Bush hosted twenty-six parties between December 4 and December 20, often with multiple events on the same day. Different parties were held for various groups of diplomats, members of Congress, Secret Service agents, high-ranking military officers, children of deployed military service men and women, important political donors and supporters, political journalists, and White House staff. At these parties, President Bush and First Lady Laura Bush spent hours posing for individual photos with guests. That year, more than 9,500 guests enjoyed elaborate candlelit buffets of ham, turkey, lamb, cheeses, and more. By the end of the final party, the White House kitchens had produced more than 30,000 Christmas cookies, 10,000 petit fours, and 1,100 truffles.

Christmas parties hosted by President Barack Obama and First Lady Michelle Obama became known as slightly more relaxed affairs, with jazz music and expanded menus including less traditional dishes, such as sushi. In 2009, the Obama's hosted twenty-eight Christmas parties, entertaining more than 50,000 guests in three weeks.

### White House Christmas Decorations

In 1889, President Benjamin Harrison set up the first indoor **Christmas tree** in the Oval Room of the White House. First Lady Caroline Harrison supervised the trimming of the tree with lit candles and other ornaments. Over the next forty years, some White House families chose to have a Christmas tree and some did not. In 1901, President Teddy Roosevelt famously tried to ban live Christmas trees in the White House out of concern for conserving America's forests. However, he was persuaded by his children to overturn the short-lived ban. The decorating of an official White House Christmas Tree became an annual tradition in 1929 during President Hoover's term. Since then, America's first ladies have supervised Christmas decorating at the White House.

The tradition of choosing a theme for the official White House Christmas Tree was started in 1961 by First Lady Jacqueline Kennedy. The theme she chose for that year was Tchaikovsky's *The Nutcracker* ballet. This tree was set up in the Blue Room and was decorated with toys, birds, angels and other figures inspired by the story of *The Nutcracker*. In 1962, she expanded the decorating scheme with a second themed tree located in the North Entrance of the White House.

Subsequent themes for the main White House Christmas Tree have included Early Americana, American Flowers, American Folk Art, Antique Toys, Children's Nursery Rhymes, Angels, St. Nicholas, Christmas Carols, Animals, Reading, Patriotism, and Music. In some years the decorating theme incorporated additional features such as specific colors, the use of only natural materials, or all handmade ornaments. For the 1985 White House Christmas Tree, volunteers created 1,500 ornaments by recycling all of the **Christmas cards** that were received by President Reagan the previous year.

Over the years, Christmas decorations at the White House have grown to include elaborate displays in most public areas. First ladies often begin thinking about the year's decorating theme as early as March in order to allow enough time for plans to

be made. Hundreds of White House staff and volunteers work countless hours to create, install, and maintain the decorations, many of which are reused each year. In 2010, First Lady Michelle Obama chose the theme Simple Gifts for all of the White House Christmas decorations. Many public rooms and corridors were decorated to illustrate different aspects of that theme. For example, the East Wing Lobby celebrated gifts of the American outdoors, while the Library highlighted the gifts of hearth and home. The Vermeil Room showcased the gifts of music. Other spaces were dedicated to the gifts of abundance, conservation, and tradition. A special Military Appreciation Tree was set up in the East Entrance of the White House to honor the contributions and sacrifices of America's service men and women. Another highlight of that year's decorations was a detailed model of the White House made of gingerbread and chocolate, weighing more than 350 pounds.

Public interest in Christmas at the White House has also grown over time. Each year, a special reception and preview of the decorated rooms is given for members of the media and is typically attended by journalists from around the world. More than 50,000 visitors pass through the White House during the Christmas season each year. Nationally broadcast television programs and photos on the White House web site provide an insider's glimpse of the holiday splendor.

### White House Charity

Giving to charity became an important aspect of nineteenth-century Christmas celebrations (*see also* **America, Christmas in Nineteenth-Century**). According to popular stories, the generosity of some of the nineteenth century presidents and their families reflected this trend. According to one account, President Andrew Jackson once brought sweets and toys to a local orphanage at Christmas time. The orphans' plight moved him, as his parents had both died by the time he was fourteen, leaving him without a home. When asked by the children about Santa Claus, he said that as a child he had not known of him, nor had he celebrated Christmas.

Abraham Lincoln's son Tad was reported to have a generous heart at Christmas time. According to one story, in 1863 he insisted on shipping the books his parents bought him for Christmas to soldiers fighting the Civil War. His father agreed with the plan, requesting that food and blankets also be added to the box. On Christmas Day in 1864, Tad brought some poor children to the White House. The cook refused to feed them, but Tad went over her head and appealed to his father, who, pleased with his son's generosity, ordered that each be fed a turkey dinner.

Presidential Christmas charity continued throughout the twentieth century. First Lady Grace Coolidge, wife of President Calvin Coolidge, handed out gifts at the offices of the Salvation Army. First Lady Lou Hoover also gave to the needy, as did Eleanor Roosevelt, who personally visited poor neighborhoods on Christmas Day, bearing food and gifts. President Harry S. Truman provided two needy families— one white and the other black—with Christmas gifts and dinner, a custom which he preferred not to publicize. In 1961, Jacqueline Kennedy brought gifts to 200 children at the District of Columbia's Children's Hospital. Nancy Reagan visited the same hospital at Christmas time twenty years later. During the holiday season, the Obama family volunteered at food banks and soup kitchens, personally serving meals to the hungry. The Obamas also prepared holiday care packages that were shipped to members of the military serving overseas.

## Greetings from the White House

Franklin D. Roosevelt and Eleanor Roosevelt were the first presidential couple to send large numbers of cards at Christmas time. These cards were specially prepared by the White House engraver. During the time of the Eisenhower presidency, it became customary for the president to send an official Christmas card to heads of state, members of the cabinet, senators, congressional representatives, and other government workers. Dwight D. Eisenhower was an amateur artist, and during his administration some of his own paintings were featured on the White House Christmas card. His portrait of Abraham Lincoln, executed from a black-and-white photograph, appeared on the White House card one year. In another year the White House Christmas card featured one of his landscape paintings.

Since Eisenhower's time, White House Christmas cards have usually depicted the president and first lady, or offered views of the White House at Christmas time. Subsequent presidents often commissioned painters or photographers to produce images especially for the White House Christmas card.

During the late twentieth century, the number of Christmas cards sent from the White House each year began to grow. In 1969, President Richard Nixon sent 37,000 Christmas cards. In 1980, the Carters sent more than 100,000 cards. During the

1990s, the Clintons customarily sent out 300,000 cards. President George W. Bush is reported to have sent out close to 1.5 million cards each year.

### White House Christmas Firsts

President Benjamin Harrison set up the first indoor Christmas tree at the White House in 1889. Grace Coolidge organized the first Christmas carol sing in 1923, with the help of choristers from the First Congregational Church. The ceremonies surrounding the lighting of the National Christmas Tree got their start in 1923 under President Calvin Coolidge. Coolidge also composed the first presidential Christmas message to the American people. The first official White House Christmas card dates back to the Eisenhower administration. Jimmy Carter was the first president to participate in a public menorah-lighting ceremony, held in 1979 in Lafayette Park in Washington, D.C. (*see* **Hanukkah**). Subsequent presidents also participated in menorah-lighting ceremonies. In a 1997 Oval Office ceremony, President Clinton became the first president to light a menorah inside the White House. In 2010, President Obama hosted a dinner marking the second night of Hanukkah.

# Wild Hunt

### Asgardsreid, Furious Host, Furious Hunt, Gabriel's Hounds, Gandreid, Jolerei, Julereien, Raging Host, Yuletide Host

Since ancient times, legends have told of supernatural forces that roam the earth around the time of Christmas. If one listens closely to the swirling winds of a stormy winter night, eerie voices seem to howl in the darkness. In past centuries much folklore from northwestern Europe interpreted these sounds as a sign that the Wild Hunt was abroad. People invented many names for this unruly procession of ghosts, goblins, and deities that stormed across the night skies. For the most part, the wailing spirits frightened listeners, but in some places they also aided human beings.

Belief in the Wild Hunt was especially strong between the ninth and fourteenth centuries. Historical records indicate that some medieval Europeans believed the Wild

Hunt capable of rampaging through their dreams, carrying their spirits off on unwholesome adventures while their bodies slumbered. Folkloric records indicate that the Wild Hunt might appear in the skies at any time of year. Nevertheless, in many locales the ghostly riders were thought to be most active during the **Twelve Days of Christmas**, especially **Twelfth Night**.

The leaders, members, and purpose of the Wild Hunt varied somewhat from region to region. In Wales, Gwyn ap Nudd, king of the Underworld, led the hunt. In England some believed the Wild Hunt was led by King Arthur. Others referred to the noises on the wind as the baying of Gabriel's Hounds. The phantom hounds represented the souls of unbaptized infants, and their passing signified a death to come. In Norway the Hunt was known as the *Gandreid*, which means "spirits' ride." According to Norwegian folklore, the spirits of those who had died during the past year charged across the night skies during the Gandreid, increasing the fertility of all the fields they passed over. The Gandreid was most active around **Epiphany**, or Twelfth Night.

In German-speaking and Scandinavian lands the Hunt was known as *Asgardsreid*, literally "Asgard's Ride," and was thought to occur most often during **Yule** or the Twelve Days of Christmas. Asgard was the home of the Scandinavian gods. Many believed that the fearsome, one-eyed king of the Scandinavian gods, Odin, led the wild ride across the skies to Asgard, mounted on his eight-legged steed. He and his riotous following were sometimes called the Wild Hunt, the Raging Host, the *Jolerei* or the *Julereien* (the Yuletide Host), and it was believed dangerous for Christians to see them. Nevertheless, some peasants left the last sheaf of grain in their fields as an offering for Odin's horse. In some locales Odin's wife Frigga headed the throng of spirits.

In other German-speaking areas the noises on the wind meant that the goddess **Berchta** and her following of wraiths, fairies, and the souls of small children rode abroad. Berchta roamed the world during the Twelve Days of Christmas, but was especially active on Twelfth Night. She rewarded the industrious and punished the lazy. In northern German lands the Furious Hunt or Furious Host was led by a similar goddess, Holde, who commanded a similar band of followers. The passing of Holde and her followers blessed the lands below, ensuring that crops would double during the coming year.

# Williamsburg, Virginia, Christmas in Colonial

The town of Williamsburg became the capital of colonial Virginia in 1699. In colonial times the town was the site of important political, social, and cultural events. When Richmond became the capital of Virginia in 1780, Williamsburg's importance declined. In 1926 John D. Rockefeller (1839-1937), a wealthy philanthropist, decided to renovate or rebuild many of the town's eighteenth-century buildings. The result was a historic zone of 120 colonial-style buildings that has become a major tourist attraction. Visitors during the **Christmas season** can enjoy many elements of a colonial Christmas in Virginia, including accommodations furnished in the style of the eighteenth century, special concerts, colonial-style Christmas feasts, bonfires, fireworks, and tours of the Christmas decorations of the historic district.

### Christmas in Colonial Virginia

In colonial times, American Christmas celebrations varied considerably from region to region (*see also* **America, Christmas in Colonial**). These differences stemmed from the religious affiliation of the foremost religious or ethnic group in the region. While the stern **Puritans** who dominated much of New England frowned on the celebration of Christmas, the many Christmas-loving Anglicans who made their homes in Virginia relished the holiday. In Puritan-governed communities, Christmas was treated like any other work day, but in Williamsburg and much of the rest of Virginia, Christmas kicked off the start of a merry season of feasts, parties, weddings, and relaxation (*see also* Twelve Days of Christmas).

Devout Anglicans observed **Advent**, a period of spiritual preparation for the coming of Christ, in the weeks preceding Christmas. The very observant among them fasted, consuming only one full meal a day. They also meditated on their own shortcomings and on the biblical passages concerning the birth of **Jesus** and the second coming of Christ. The less observant found their thoughts drifting to the coming pleasures of Christmas.

For well-to-do Virginians, the holiday season revolved around festive meals and parties. Foods available to colonial Virginians at Christmas time included turkeys and other wild game, ham and other kinds of farm-raised meat, oysters, bread, corn, winter vegetables like potatoes and turnips, dried fruit, and preserved fruits and summer vegetables. Fresh and candied fruit, puddings, and cakes were favorite holiday desserts. Virginians washed down these foods with wine, liquor, beer, or other alcoholic beverages like hard cider, rum punch, and **eggnog**.

Perhaps more important than the food was the opportunity to socialize. Family reunions, visits with friends and relatives, and parties both large and small were the hallmarks of the season. Perhaps because newcomers often brought word of new ideas and events in far-off places, hostesses were eager for strangers to join friends and family members in their celebrations. In 1746 the *London Magazine* applauded the open-handed Christmas celebrations of colonial Virginians:

> All over the Colony, an universal Hospitality reigns, full Tables and open Doors, the kind Salute, the generous detention.... Strangers are fought after with Greediness, as they pass the Country, to be invited. [*Christmas in Colonial and Early America*, 1996, 12]

Music making and dancing were important activities at these holiday get-togethers. Christmas parties might include the singing of **Christmas carols** as well as instrumental music for dancing. People welcomed Christmas morning with all sorts of noisemaking activities. Virginians, like many other southerners, shot off guns and banged on pots and pans to usher in the holiday (*see also* **Shooting in Christmas**).

### Marriage and Romance

The Christmas season, especially the period between Christmas Day and **Twelfth Night,** was a time associated with weddings and romance. Several famous early American couples from Virginia wed at this time of year. Future first president George Washington and his bride, Martha Dandridge Custis, married on January 6, 1759. In 1782 Thomas Jefferson, who later became the third president of the United States, married Martha Wayles Skelton on New Year's Day.

### Slaves and Free Blacks

Slaveowners generally gave their slaves a few days off at Christmas time (*see also* **Slaves' Christmas**). In addition to the slaves, Williamsburg was home to many free blacks who worked in the skilled trades or as laborers. Indeed, historical research suggests that African Americans, both slave and free, comprised over half the population of Williamsburg.

## Men, Women, Children, and Gifts

Well-to-do men often rode out to hunt on Christmas morning while women supervised the preparation of the Christmas feast. In colonial Virginia, Christmas was more of an adult holiday than a children's festival. No special activities were planned to entertain children, and few parents gave their offspring **gifts**. Instead, as was the custom in that age, gifts were given to social inferiors to thank them for their service over the past year. Some tradesmen observed the custom of Christmas boxing, and most slave masters gave gifts to their slaves. Some people gave small gifts to family members and close friends on New Year's Day. George Washington, one of the colony's wealthiest men, proved an exception to these gift-giving rules. In 1759 he recorded the fact that he bought the following items as presents for his stepchildren: a bird on bellows, a cuckoo, a turnabout parrot, a grocers shop, an aviary, a Prussian dragoon, a man smoking, six small books for children, six pocket handkerchiefs, and other toys.

## Christmas Decorations

In colonial times, Virginians decked the insides of their homes and churches with **greenery**. They made garlands of evergreens, which they strung along banisters and railings and wrapped around pillars. At home, ropes of greenery might dangle from the fireplace mantel. In addition, some pressed sprigs of **holly** against their window panes or displayed bouquets of holly and other winter greenery on their tables. They might also strew their homes with herbs, such as **rosemary**, bay (or **laurel**), lavender, and rose petals, in order to give rooms a fresh scent. Boys often shot down boughs of **mistletoe** from high tree branches so that it could be fashioned into kissing boughs and other **ornaments**. The making of these decorations was usually women's work.

## Christmas in Contemporary Williamsburg

In 1934, after the partial restoration of colonial Williamsburg had been completed, some residents of the historic district began to decorate their homes, inside and out. The practice grew and flourished year after year. Now tourists have become accustomed to seeing **wreaths** featuring fresh fruit and other colorful, natural materials on the front doors of Williamsburg homes and shops. The first wreaths of this kind were created by historical researcher Louise Fisher, who was inspired by the designs of Italian Renaissance sculptor Luca della Robbia (1400-1482) and also by the work of English artist Grinling Gibbons (1648-1721). Della Robbia's garlands and wreaths included natural garnishes, such as lemons, apples, and pine cones. Fisher knew these natural materials to be available in the eighteenth century and began to produce front door wreaths along these designs. Soon all Williamsburg followed suit, and from there this style of wreath began to spread across the country. Some people know them as Williamsburg-style wreaths, while others call them Della Robbia wreaths.

In 1937 the first contest for front door wreaths and decorations took place. Soon homeowners began to vie for the prestigious blue ribbon affixed to the most charming Williamsburg-style doorway decorations. The cash prize donated by the Colonial Williamsburg Foundation also tempted homeowners to participate. In response to interest from tourists, a popular Christmas decorations tour of the historic district was launched in 1969.

In recent years, concerned that contemporary doorway decorations may be giving tourists the wrong impression, colonial Williamsburg officials have begun to publicize the fact that there is no historical evidence that colonial Virginians decorated the outside of their homes at all at Christmas time. Moreover, historians agree that they would never have wasted fruit, a relatively rare and precious item, especially in the winter, on outdoor or indoor decorations of any kind. Sometimes colonial hostesses arranged fruit into a pyramid and set it at the center of their buffet table, where it served both as a colorful table decoration and as dessert.

Residents of colonial Williamsburg also developed the tradition of placing a lighted candle in their window during the Christmas season (*see also* **Bethlehem, Pennsylvania, Christmas in; Candles**). Historians give a cool nod of approval to this custom, since colonists did put candles in their windows to honor a royal anniversary of some kind or a military victory. They didn't, however, light these candles at Christmas time. Nevertheless, contemporary residents of the town see the practice as a compromise between the demands of historical accuracy and their own desire to observe the modern custom of lighting up one's home for Christmas. Nowadays a ceremony called the Grand Illumination, which takes place in early December, kicks off the season of candlelit windows in Williamsburg. In the past the ceremony has included the singing of Christmas carols and a procession through the historical district led by a fife and drum corps, as well as a group of men in colonial costumes representing the night watch. As the procession passes each home, family members light their candles. The procession continues until the windows of the historical district twinkle with candles.

Beginning in 1957, Christmas celebrations in colonial Williamsburg have also included fireworks displays. Although colonists exploded fireworks in celebration of successful military campaigns and in honor of a monarch's birthday, they did not use them at Christmas time. Again, the use of Christmas fireworks in colonial Williamsburg represents a compromise between historical accuracy and the desire to celebrate. Special bonfires, another authentic colonial custom, also light up the night skies at Christmas time.

# Winter Solstice

Winter solstice, the shortest day of the year, falls on December 21 or 22 in the Northern Hemisphere. Winter solstice marks that turning point in the year after which the days begin to lengthen and the nights begin to shorten. In the Northern Hemisphere the longest day of the year, summer solstice, falls on June 21 or 22. In the Southern Hemisphere this same day is observed as winter solstice. In the course of human history many peoples have honored the solstices with ceremonies and festivals. Early Christian authorities placed Christmas near the winter solstice in the hopes of replacing pagan holidays clustered on and around that date (*see also* **December 25**).

## Solstice Astronomy

The word "solstice" comes from the Latin phrase *sol stitium*, which means "the sun stands still." A daily observer of the sunrise will notice that the sun comes up at a slightly different position along the horizon each day. In the Northern Hemisphere, as summer turns to winter, the sun rises a bit further to the south each day. The days grow shorter and the nights longer. Finally, the sun appears to rise over the same point on the horizon for several days in a row. This is the time of the winter solstice, the time when the sun appears to "stand still" along the horizon. In reality, the sunrise still moves on those days, but only very slightly. The actual day of the solstice occurs when the sun reaches its southernmost position along the horizon. This happens on the shortest day and longest night of the year. The following day the sun begins to move north along the horizon, and the days slowly begin to lengthen while the nights shorten. The days continue to grow longer until the summer solstice, after which they begin to shorten again as the sun once more turns southward.

The explanation for this yearly cycle lies in the mechanics of the earth's orbit around the sun. The earth's axis, the hypothetical line connecting the North and South Poles, does not meet the plane of the earth's orbit around the sun at a perpendicular angle. Instead, the earth is tilted 23 degrees to one side. This tilt causes the earth's exposure to the sun to vary throughout the year.

During one six-month period of the earth's yearly orbit, the tilt points the **North Pole** towards the sun. During this period the Northern Hemisphere gradually gains exposure to the sun, while the Southern Hemisphere loses exposure. In the north the days lengthen and the sun crosses the sky more directly overhead; hence the weather grows warmer. Three months after the winter solstice, the Northern Hemisphere arrives at the spring equinox, the twenty-four hour period in which night and day are of equal lengths. Night and day are also of equal lengths in the Southern Hemisphere on that same date. There, since the days are growing shorter, the event is called the autumn equinox. In the north the days continue to lengthen and the nights to shorten until the very last day of this six-month period, summer solstice, the longest day of the year.

This situation reverses itself during the next six months. As the earth continues its orbit around the sun, the tilt begins to turn the South Pole towards the sun and the North Pole away from it. This decreases the Northern Hemisphere's exposure to the sun's warming rays while increasing the Southern Hemisphere's exposure. As a result, the days lengthen in the Southern Hemisphere, bringing spring and summer to that zone, while the people of the Northern Hemisphere experience fall and winter. The solstices as well as the equinoxes are reversed. The same day on which northerners experience winter solstice, southerners experience summer solstice.

The effect of this yearly cycle increases as one moves away from the equator and is greatest near the Poles, which undergo months of unbroken light or darkness near the solstices. The prolonged darkness may strongly affect those who live in the far north (*see also* **Depression**). Only the people living along the earth's equator are not affected by this cycle, since the equatorial zones receive about the same exposure to

the sun throughout the year. The length of the days and nights does not change at the equator, so seasonal differences all but disappear.

## Winter Solstice in Ancient Rome

According to the Julian calendar used by the ancient Romans, winter solstice fell on December 25. Although for most of their long history the Romans did not celebrate the winter solstice per se, two important Roman festivals fell on either side of this date. **Saturnalia** was celebrated from December 17 to December 23. **Kalends**, the new year festival, began on January 1 and lasted until January 5.

In the late third century A.D., however, the Roman emperor Aurelian added a new celebration to the calendar, the **Birth of the Invincible Sun**. He chose December 25, the winter solstice, as the date for this festival honoring the sun god. In fact, by the late third century the solstice did not occur on December 25. A flaw in the design of the Julian calendar caused this error. The creators of the Julian calendar believed the year to be 365.25 days long. The actual length of the solar year is 365.242199 days. This tiny discrepancy caused the calendar to fall behind the actual sun cycle by one day every 128 years. In 46 B.C., when the Julian calendar was established, the winter solstice really did occur on December 25. By the late third century, winter solstice was arriving two and one-half days early. Nevertheless, the twenty-fifth had engraved itself in the minds of the populace as the date of the solstice, and so was retained as the date of the new solstice holiday (*see also* **Old Christmas Day**).

## Winter Solstice and the Date of Christmas

In the middle of the fourth century, when Christian officials in Rome chose a date for the celebration of the Nativity, they, too, selected December 25. Most scholars believe that they chose this date in order to draw people away from the pagan holidays celebrated at that time of year. In fact, a document written by a Christian scribe later in that century explains that the authorities chose December 25 for the feast of the Nativity because people were already accustomed to celebrating on that date. Moreover, some Christian leaders found celebrating the birth of **Jesus** at the time of the winter solstice especially appropriate as they considered him "the sun of righteousness" (Malachi 4:2) and the "light of the world"(John 8:12). With the new festival date in place, Christian leaders exhorted the populace to dedicate their midwinter devotions to the birth of Jesus rather than to the birth of the sun.

## Winter Solstice and Other Ancient Celebrations

The people of Egypt used a slightly different calendar than did the Romans, one in which winter solstice fell on January 6. Egyptians also honored the sun god on the day of the winter solstice. Other Egyptian festivals that took place on January 6 included the birthday of the god Osiris and the birth of the god Aeon from his virgin mother, Kore. As early as the second century, Egyptian Christians adopted January 6 as one of their feast days, too. They began to celebrate **Epiphany** on that day.

Some researchers speculate that the ancient peoples of northern Europe celebrated a festival called **Yule** around the time of the winter solstice. Other researchers disagree, however, arguing that the festival took place in November.

People who lived in close contact with the natural world and who did not possess modern astronomical knowledge may well have viewed the gradual shortening of the days and the cooling of the weather with apprehension. It is easy to understand why many of these ancient peoples honored the gods on the shortest day of the year and gave thanks for the return of the sun.

### Contemporary Celebrations

In recent years, renewed interest in pagan or "earth" religions in the developed countries has prompted some people to begin celebrating the solstices again. Although we now understand the astronomical mechanisms behind this cycle in the earth's seasons, our lives still depend on these celestial maneuvers and the seasonal rhythms they create. The new solstice celebrations honor these life-giving processes with ceremony and festivity.

# Wrapping Paper

How would you feel if, instead of finding a pretty arrangement of wrapped **gifts** under the tree on Christmas morning, you discovered a naked jumble of store-bought merchandise with the price tags still on? What is it that turns an ordinary purchase into a Christmas gift? Nineteenth-century Americans found the answer to that question in decorative wrapping paper. Once encased in the paper, the individual identity and

cost of each item disappeared. All that remained visible was the wrapping, a symbolic statement of the item's status as gift. Today we use the trick of wrapping paper to turn ordinary store-bought items into gifts for all sorts of occasions.

### History

Christmas gift giving was an uncommon practice throughout most of the nineteenth century (*see also* **America, Christmas in Nineteenth-Century**). Moreover, those who gave gifts seldom bothered to wrap them. Parents deposited trinkets in their children's **stockings** as is, and adults exchanged small homemade items without bothering to disguise them. In the late nineteenth century the idea of exchanging Christmas gifts grew more popular, and some people began to shop for them in stores.

Around 1880 people began to wrap their purchases in decorative paper or decorated boxes. At the same time, retailers were searching for a way to encourage people to give store-bought rather than homemade items as Christmas gifts. Many consumers objected that manufactured goods were too impersonal and commercial to serve as appropriate Christmas gifts. In the last decade of the nineteenth century, retailers began to wrap their customers' holiday purchases in paper decorated with Christmas symbols. They discovered that the special wrapping paper boosted sales enormously. Apparently, removing the price tag and encasing the item in wrapping paper transformed manufactured goods into acceptable gifts by disguising their true identity until the last moment and emphasizing instead their status as a gift.

At the turn of the century, manufacturers also adopted the new sales gimmick. They began to ship all kinds of wares in decorative holiday packaging. If consumers wondered whether these ordinary manufactured items could serve as appropriate gifts, the holiday packaging removed all doubt. By the 1920s manufacturers had added one more detail to this already successful strategy. Instead of shipping goods in special packaging, they slipped special decorative sleeves around standard packaging. Retailers could remove the holiday sleeve right after Christmas, thereby turning their special "Christmas stock" back into ordinary stock.

# Wreaths

Americans recognize evergreen wreaths as symbols of Christmas. Many people hang them on their front doors at Christmas time or display them in other parts of the house. No one seems to know the exact history of this custom. Some speculate that the front door wreath evolved out of the older, German Advent wreath. Others suppose it to be an old Irish custom.

The English word "wreath" comes from the old Anglo-Saxon verb *writhan*, meaning "to writhe" or "to twist." Indeed, Christmas wreaths are made by bending or twisting branches of **greenery** into a circular shape.

Wreaths have served as powerful symbols for millennia. In ancient Greece and Rome, wreaths of greenery worn as crowns sat on the brows of those believed to have won divine favor. Thus, wreaths adorned the heads of sacrificial animals, winners of athletic and artistic competitions, participants in religious festivals, and kings. The type of greenery used to make the wreath also sent a message. Winners of athletic and literary contests donned wreaths of **laurel**. Wreaths of **ivy** circled the brows of those honoring the wine god, Dionysus or Bacchus. Those whose achievements brought about military victories or peace wore wreaths of olive.

The Bible also makes frequent mention of wreaths, usually associating them with joy, triumph, and honor. As Christianity developed its own symbolic code, it turned the laurel wreath into a sign of the attainment of salvation. In more general terms, the wreath represents the same thing as the circle, often interpreted as a symbol of eternity.

# Yule

Many researchers believe that in the early Middle Ages people in northern Europe celebrated a midwinter festival called Yule, *Juul*, or *Jol*. Although the history of the word remains uncertain, some authorities believe it comes from an Anglo-Saxon word, *geol*, meaning "feast." Others argue that it derives from an old Germanic word, either *iol*, *iul*, or *guil*, meaning "wheel." Thus, the festival is thought by some to have celebrated the turning of the wheel of the year and the lengthening of days after the **winter solstice**. In medieval times, Yule became another term for Christmas or **Christmas season**.

### *Origins*

Some scholars believe that the ancient Celtic and Teutonic peoples of northern and central Europe observed a great autumn festival sometime in November. The customs connected with this festival highlighted the contrasting themes of death and abundance. With the coming of cold weather, many plants withered and died, including the grass that fed domesticated animals. Consequently, the people adopted this season for the slaughter of the herds and the preparation of preserved meat for the winter. The slaughter also furnished the festival tables with a feast of fresh meat. Special autumn beers may also have been brewed for this festival, and used to toast the gods (*see also* **Ales**). At this time of the year people lit ceremonial fires and honored their dead ancestors. Some authorities claim that this feast venerated the Germanic god Odin, others that it venerated the Norse god Thor. This festival probably marked the end of the old year and the beginning of the new year.

At least one scholar has suggested November 11 or 12 as the date of this festival. In medieval times, November 11 became St. Martin's Day, or **Martinmas**. Medieval Europeans celebrated Martinmas by feasting, commemorating the dead, slaughtering animals and preserving their meat, and enjoying the first taste of the year's wines.

Did these November celebrations evolve out of the practices of ancient Mediterranean peoples or were they native to the North? One group of experts argues for Roman origins. They note that the Germanic peoples and the Romans came into close contact as they battled each other for land and rule during the last centuries of the Roman Empire. As a result of this exposure, the Teutonic peoples adopted some Roman customs, such as the celebration of the new year around the time of the winter solstice. The festivities that characterized Roman midwinter festivals, such as decorations of **greenery**, fortune-telling, processions of singers and masqueraders, and the exchange of **gifts**, also infiltrated northern celebrations (*see also* **Kalends**; **Saturnalia**). The northerners combined these customs with those of their autumn celebration and shifted the date of the new festival to midwinter, creating a new holiday called Yule.

Other authors disagree with this line of reasoning, however. They believe that the northerners must have waited anxiously for the winter solstice and the lengthening of days, since the midwinter days are shorter and colder in northern Europe than they are in the Mediterranean. These writers contend that the pagan peoples of northern Europe always celebrated around the time of the winter solstice, rejoicing in the return of the sun and the lengthening of days. According to these authors, the customs associated with medieval Yule originated in the north.

### Yule in Medieval Scandinavia

Since the pagan Scandinavian peoples left no documents of their own, it is impossible to confirm any theory of the holiday's origin. Around the ninth century, Christian missionaries introduced the art of writing with pen and paper to the region. The years from around 900 to 1300 A.D. produced a few additional records describing the customs, stories, and beliefs of the pagan Scandinavians. From these records, researchers have reconstructed a speculative picture of medieval Scandinavian Yule celebrations.

Some say the festival began on the longest night of the year (the winter solstice), a day that ushered in the month known as "Yule Month." The Yule celebration lasted over a number of days and involved feasting, fires, and sacrifices. Bonfires blazed in honor of the sun's struggle against, and eventual triumph over, the darkness and cold of winter. People gathered around the fires listening to ancient legends, singing songs, eating, drinking, and offering sacrifices to the gods. They might save a piece of the great logs used for the fires, called **Yule logs**, in order to start the next year's bonfire. During the Yule festival those who had died during the year were remembered. Their **ghosts** were thought to rise from the grave and attend the festivities. The boar, a symbol of the god Frey, who represented sunlight, fertility, peace, and plenty, formed an important part of the Yule feast. The king offered the largest boar in the land in sacrifice. It was considered a holy object, and when it was brought into the king's hall, men swore binding oaths before it.

As Christianity gained momentum in Scandinavia, some Christian rulers attempted to mesh pagan and Christian observances. The tenth-century Norwegian king, Haakon the Good, ordered that Yule celebrations should be held around the time of Christmas. Nevertheless, he refused to participate in the full range of sacrifices that the pagan kings usually offered at this time. Eventually, customs compatible with the Christian seasonal observance, such as feasting and merrymaking, were absorbed into the celebration of Christmas. A trace of the old pagan festival lingers in the modern Danish, Norwegian, and Swedish word for Christmas: *Jul.*

## Yule in Medieval Britain

Although the word "yule" eventually passed into the English language, some say that the Britons did not observe the festival in early medieval times. The earliest written use of the word "yule" in Britain occurs in a manuscript written by the scholarly English monk St. Bede. He noted that the English people of his day (the Angles) used the word *Giuli*, an ancestor of the word "yule," as a name for both December and January. He continued, "The months *Giuli* get their names from the turning round of the sun towards the increasing of the day, because one of them precedes and the other follows it." Bede's evidence suggests that the word "yule" may indeed have derived from an old word that referred in some way to the concept of turning.

But did the English celebrate a special festival at this time? Bede claims that they did. He wrote that the Angles "began their year from the eighth day before the Calends of January [Dec. 25], on which we now celebrate the birthday of our Lord. And they called that night *Modranicht*, i.e., night of the mothers, as I suppose, because of the ceremonies which they performed in it, keeping watch all night." Bede speculates that this day was originally called "Giuli" and that the months of December and January derived their names from the festival, but he is not certain. No evidence exists to confirm this speculation. It is not until the eleventh century that we find other British manuscripts that refer to **December 25** as "Yule." Before that time, old English manuscripts referred to December 25 as "midwinter," "midwinter's mass," or "Nativity." From the eleventh century onwards, "Yule" gained gradual acceptance as another term for Christmas or the Christmas season.

Some argue that the Scandinavian Vikings brought the term and the festival with them when they conquered and settled in parts of England in the ninth through eleventh centuries. Others claim that the Anglo-Saxon people of early medieval Britain, along with the Scandinavians and northern Germans, did celebrate a midwinter festive season, regardless of what it may have been called. They point out that the strategy of early Christian missionaries was to convert pagan populations by allowing them to practice most of their old customs, but attaching new, Christian meanings to their observances. They believe that many British customs associated with Christmas in later centuries, such as the burning of Yule logs, **mumming**, the

**534**

wassailing of fruit trees, the hunting of small animals, and decorating with greenery, originated in this early winter festival.

# Yule Logs

## Bûche de Noël, Calignaou, Chalendal, Christmas Block, Christmas Log, Tréfoir, Yule Clog

In past eras many European people burned Yule logs in their homes at Christmas time. Often these enormous logs burned throughout the Twelve Days of Christmas. The many customs and beliefs associated with these logs suggest that at one time they were thought to have magical powers. According to a variety of folk beliefs, a burning Yule log or its charred remains could not only protect a household from evil powers, but also confer health, fertility, luck, and abundance.

### History

Many writers trace the Yule log back to the ancient pagan holiday of Yule. Although little can be determined regarding the early history of this celebration, most authors agree that it included the burning of great bonfires. The earliest historical record mentioning a Yule log for the fireplace, however, comes from medieval Germany. German documents from this time contain a number of references to such logs. At least one writer traces the French Yule log back to a medieval tax that required peasants to bring an enormous log to the local manor house each year on Christmas Eve (*see also* Medieval Era, Christmas in).

In England, however, the custom can only be traced back as far as the seventeenth century. The English had a number of names for the logs, including Yule log, Yule clog, Christmas log, and Christmas block. The English poet Robert Herrick wrote a poem in which he described the customs and beliefs surrounding the Yule log in Devonshire, England. Herrick's householders lit their "Christmas log" using a fragment of the previous year's log. Moreover, they serenaded the burning log with music in order to coax good luck and abundance from it. Lines from another of Herrick's poems advised that the singed remains of the Yule log could protect the household against evil during the coming year. By the nineteenth century the Yule log could also be found at Christmas celebrations in Germany, France, northern Italy, Serbia, and most of northern Europe.

## Selection and Preparation

The Yule log was bigger than the usual chunk of wood tossed on the evening fire. In some places tree trunks or parts of tree trunks were used. The Scots preferred the trunk of a birch tree, dried and stripped of leaves and bark; hence the Scottish saying, "He's a bare as a birk on Yule e'en," meaning "He's very poor." The French had many names for the Yule log. In Provence it was known as a *calignaou*, but in other areas it was called a *chalendal* or a *tréfoir*. In Provence people believed that the best Yule logs were taken from fruit trees. The Serbs chose their log from green oak, olive, or beech trees. In some parts of England people scoured the countryside for a Yule log on **Candlemas**. They set it aside to dry during the warm weather, thereby preparing an evenly burning log for the following Christmas.

## Ceremonies and Superstitions

The selection of the log and its entrance into the house were often accompanied by rituals and invocations. The Serbs poured wine on the log, sprinkled it with grain or other foodstuffs, made the sign of the cross over it, and officially welcomed it into the home with a blessing. In Provence, France, people sprinkled wine over the log and blessed it in the name of the Trinity. Moreover, as the Provençal family trooped out to get their log, they sang songs requesting that fertility and abundance grace their family and their farm. Before burning the log they drew a human figure on it in chalk. In other areas, a human figure was carved onto the log. In Brittany, France, the oldest and youngest family members lit the log together, while offering a prayer to **Jesus**. Another popular custom in many areas advocated decking the log with ribbons and **greenery**.

Many superstitions attached themselves to the Yule log. In England, many people believed that maidens should wash their hands before touching it. If they didn't, the log would not burn well. Other English folk beliefs warned that if a barefoot or squinting person came into the house while the log was lit, ill luck was sure to follow. According to some folk beliefs, the shadows cast by the light of the Yule log could be read as omens.

### Lighting the Log

In many places tradition demanded that the new Yule log be lit with a fragment of last year's log. In some areas people set flame to the Yule log on Christmas Eve, in other places on Christmas morning. Custom commonly dictated that the log be kept burning continuously on Christmas Day. If the fire went out, bad luck would dog the household during the coming year. In some parts of Italy and England the log was kept burning throughout the Twelve Days of Christmas. English families whose logs went out during the Twelve Days often found it difficult to relight them. In some areas folk beliefs warned that it was unlucky to lend fire to a neighbor during these days, a belief that can be traced back to the Roman celebration of **Kalends**. Some towns kept communal fires burning for the purpose of lending flame to the unlucky folk whose fires went out. Greek folklore also advised householders to keep a fire in the hearth every day between Christmas and **Epiphany**. According to Greek folk beliefs, the fires warded off the evil **elves** known as the **kallikantzari**.

### Gifts and Blessings

In some places Christmas **gifts** were distributed around the Yule log. In past times parents in some parts of Italy lit the Yule log, blindfolded their children, and instructed the tots to hit the burning Yule log with sticks, thereby releasing magical sparks. While the children were doing so, the parents brought out the children's gifts. When their blindfolds were removed the delighted children fell upon the gifts magically provided by the log. Eventually, the Italians adopted the Christmas pyramid as a way of displaying Christmas decorations, foods, and gifts. Nevertheless, they call the pyramid a *ceppo*, which means "log" in Italian. Only the name remains as a clue to the existence of an earlier custom. A similar custom was once practiced in Burgundy, France. Parents instructed their children to say their prayers in another room while they hid some treats underneath the log. When the children returned they hit the log with a stick to make it bring forth its hidden treasures.

Widespread beliefs attributed special powers to the remains of the Yule log. Many people spread the ashes on their fields to increase the fertility of the land. In addition, families often guarded a charred chunk of the log in their homes in the belief that it deflected evil forces from the household and contained curative powers. Folk beliefs found across Europe attributed many powers to the ashes, including the power to prevent chilblains, cure toothaches, rid farm animals of parasites and disease, make cows calve and poultry lay, keep mice out of the corn, and protect the house from lightning and fire.

### Decline

Yule logs fell out of favor in the nineteenth century. Their disappearance coincided with the decline in the importance of fires as sources of household light and warmth. This, in turn, led to the disappearance of large fireplaces. Indeed, today's tiny ornamental fireplaces cannot accommodate a proper Yule log. In France, a trace of the Yule log remains in a popular log-shaped **Christmas cake** called a *buche de Noël*, or "Christmas log."

# Zagmuk

## Akitu, Babylonian New Year, Zagmug

Some writers trace elements of traditional European Christmas celebrations back to ancient Mesopotamian new year festivities. Indeed, an examination of the Zagmuk, or Akitu, festivals of ancient Mesopotamia reveals some striking resemblances to European celebrations of **Twelfth Night** and the **Twelve Days of Christmas**.

### Myths

Two thousand years before the birth of Christ, the Mesopotamians, a people of the ancient Middle East, celebrated their new year festival around the time of the spring equinox. The land once occupied by the ancient Mesopotamians now lies within the modern nation of Iraq. The Sumerians, who inhabited southern Mesopotamia, called their version of the festival "Zagmuk," while the Babylonians called it "Akitu." Experts believe that the festival lasted eleven or twelve days. It honored the yearly renewal of the world by the sun god Marduk, who created the world out of chaos. The people viewed the last days of the year as a time of decay. The forces of life and order were weak, and the forces of death and chaos were strong. To prevent the god of chaos and destruction from gaining control, the sun god Marduk must again defeat him in battle.

## Ceremonies

The ceremonies enacted during Zagmuk reflected these beliefs. Priests recited the lengthy epic describing the original victory of Marduk over the forces of disorder. The king also played a special role in new year observances. In the temple of Marduk, the high priest ceremonially stripped the king of power and rank, reinstating him only after the king had knelt and sworn to the god that he had always acted in accordance with the god's will. Some scholars propose that Mesopotamian beliefs dictated that the king die at the end of the year in order to descend into the underworld and aid Marduk in his yearly battle. Historical evidence suggests that a mock king was selected from among the ranks of criminals. During the time of the festival, he was given all the luxuries and privileges that the real king enjoyed. At the end of the festival, however, some scholars believe that the mock king was executed and sent to the underworld in place of the real king. Other scholars doubt that this occurred. According to another custom, the king and a woman from the temple reenacted the marriage of the god Marduk and his consort.

## Popular Customs

Popular customs and festivities evoked not only the epic struggle between the forces of order and disorder, but also the joyful celebration of the birth of the new year. In anticipation of Marduk's victory, the people staged mock battles between the gods, watched the burning of ceremonial bonfires, gave **gifts**, paid visits, feasted, and paraded in masquerade (*see also* **Kalends; Saturnalia**).

## Similarities

Some of the customs and folk beliefs associated with Zagmuk resemble those of medieval European celebrations of the Twelve Days of Christmas and Twelfth Night (*see also* **Medieval Era, Christmas in**). Similar acts of revelry and topsy-turvy events characterized the observance of both festivals. During the Twelve Days of Christmas, mock kings and bishops assumed temporary authority, costumed figures masqueraded through the streets, and people feasted together and lit special fires (*see also* **Boy Bishop; Feast of Fools; Feast of the Ass; Lord of Misrule; Mumming; Yule; Yule Logs**). Moreover, both Zagmuk and the Twelve Days of Christmas were celebrated at the end of the calendar year. Folk beliefs associated with both festivals warned that the waning of the year unleashed potentially destructive supernatural forces (*see* *also* Berchta; Christmas Lads; Ghosts; Kallikantzari; Knecht Ruprecht; Wild Hunt; Yule). Finally, the length of these festivals—eleven or twelve days—presents another interesting similarity. Because both festivals were observed at the end of the year, some experts suggest that these festival days represented a kind of intercalary period, the additional 11.25 days needed to reconcile the lunar year of 354 days to the solar year of 365.25 days.

# Selected Bibliography

This bibliography lists a selection of the books, articles, and web sites consulted for this volume.

A&E Television Networks, "Christmas," no date. Available online at http://www.history .com/topics/christmas.

Abbey, Cherie D. *Holidays, Festivals, and Celebrations of the World Dictionary.* Fourth edition. Detroit: Omnigraphics, 2010.

Achtemeier, Paul J., ed. *The HarperCollins Bible Dictionary.* Revised edition. San Francisco: HarperSanFrancisco, 1996.

Ammon, Richard. *An Amish Christmas.* New York: Atheneum Books, 1996.

Armstrong, Edward A. *The Folklore of Birds.* Second edition, revised and enlarged. New York: Dover Publications, 1970.

Augustine, Peg, comp. *Come to Christmas.* Nashville: Abingdon Press, 1993.

Auld, William Muir. *Christmas Tidings.* 1933. Reprint. Detroit: Omnigraphics, 1990.

———. *Christmas Traditions.* 1931. Reprint. Detroit: Omnigraphics, 1992.

Ballam, Harry, and Phyllis Digby Morton, eds. *The Christmas Book.* 1947. Reprint. Detroit: Omnigraphics, 1990.

Basinger, Jeanine. *The It's a Wonderful Life Book.* New York: Alfred A. Knopf, 1986.

Bassett, Paul M. "Epiphany." In Everett Ferguson, ed. *Encyclopedia of Early Christianity.* Volume 1. New York: Garland, 1997.

Begley, Sharon. "The Christmas Star—Or Was it Planets?" *Newsweek* 118, 27 (December 30, 1991): 54.

Belk, Russell. "Materialism and the Making of the Modern American Christmas." In Daniel Miller, ed. *Unwrapping Christmas.* Oxford, England: Clarendon Press, 1993.

Bellenir, Karen, ed. *Religious Holidays and Calendars: An Encyclopedic Handbook.* Third edition. Detroit: Omnigraphics, 2004.

Bevilacqua, Michelle, and Brandon Toropov, eds. *The Everything Christmas Book: Songs, Stories, Food, Traditions, Revelry, and More.* Holbrook, MA: Adams Media Corporation, 1996.

Bigham, Shauna, and Robert E. May. "The Time O' All Times? Masters, Slaves, and Christmas in the Old South." *Journal of the Early Republic* 18, 2 (summer 1998): 263-88.

Bowler, Gerry. *The World Encyclopedia of Christmas.* Toronto, Ontario, Canada: McClelland and Stewart, 2000.

Branley, Franklyn M. *The Christmas Sky.* Revised and newly illustrated edition. New York: Crowell, 1990.

Brewster, H. Pomeroy. *Saints and Festivals of the Christian Church.* 1904. Reprint. Detroit: Omnigraphics, 1990.

Brockman, Norbert C. *Encyclopedia of Sacred Places.* New York: Oxford University Press, 1998.

Brunvand, Jan Harold. "Urban Legend." In his *American Folklore: An Encyclopedia.* New York: Garland, 1996.

Burns, Charlene P. E. *Divine Becoming.* Minneapolis: Fortress Press, 2002.

Chambers, Robert. *The Book of Days.* 2 volumes. 1862-64. Reprint. Detroit: Omnigraphics, 1990.

*Christmas in Colonial and Early America.* Chicago: World Book, 1996.

Comfort, David. *Just Say Noel!* New York: Fireside Books, 1995.

Crippen, Thomas G. *Christmas and Christmas Lore.* 1923. Reprint. Detroit: Omnigraphics, 1990.

Crump, William D. *The Christmas Encyclopedia.* Jefferson, NC: McFarland, 2001.

Dipeiro, Diane. "Together at Christmas (Christmas Traditions of African-American Slaves)." *Colonial Homes* 20 (December 1, 1994): 28(2).

Duncan, Edmondstoune. *The Story of the Carol.* 1911. Reprint. Detroit: Omnigraphics, 1992.

Ferguson, Everett, ed. *Encyclopedia of Early Christianity.* Volume 1. New York: Garland, 1997.

Foley, Daniel J. *Christmas in the Good Old Days.* 1961. Reprint. Detroit: Omnigraphics, 1994.

Freedman, David Noel, ed. *Eerdmans Dictionary of the Bible.* Grand Rapids, MI: William B. Eerdmans Publishing Company, 2000.

Green, Thomas A., ed. *Folklore: An Encyclopedia of Beliefs, Customs, Tales, Music, and Art.* 2 volumes. Santa Barbara, CA: ABC-CLIO, 1997.

Griffin, Robert H., and Ann H. Shurgin. *Junior Worldmark Encyclopedia of World Holidays.* Volume 4. Detroit, MI: UXL, 2000.

Griffin, Robert H., and Ann H. Shurgin, eds. *The Folklore of World Holidays.* Second edition. Detroit: Gale, 1999.

Gulevich, Tanya. *Encyclopedia of Easter, Carnival, and Lent.* Detroit: Omnigraphics, 2002.

Guttman, Peter. *Christmas in America: A Photographic Celebration of the Holiday Season.* New York: Skyhorse Publishing, 2007.

Gwynne, Walker. *The Christian Year: Its Purpose and History.* 1917. Reprint. Detroit: Omnigraphics, 1990.

Halpert, Herbert, and G. M. Story, eds. *Christmas Mumming in Newfoundland.* Toronto, Ontario, Canada: University of Toronto Press, 1969.

Harper, Howard. *Days and Customs of All Faiths.* 1957. Reprint. Detroit: Omnigraphics, 1990.

Highfield, Roger. *The Physics of Christmas.* Boston: Little, Brown and Company, 1998.

Hottes, Alfred Carl. *1001 Christmas Facts and Fancies.* 1946. Reprint. Detroit: Omnigraphics, 1990.

James, E. O. *Seasonal Feasts and Festivals.* 1961. Reprint. Detroit: Omnigraphics, 1993.

Jameson, Anna. *Legends of the Madonna.* 1890. Reprint. Detroit: Omnigraphics, 1990.

Kane, Harnett. *The Southern Christmas Book.* 1958. Reprint. Detroit: Omnigraphics, 1998.

King, Constance. *Christmas Antiques, Decorations and Traditions.* Woodbridge, Suffolk, England: Antiques Collectors Club, 1999.

Lantos, James, ed. *Christmas.* Carlisle, MA: Applewood Books, 2009.

Lawrence, Elizabeth Atwood. *Hunting the Wren.* Knoxville: University of Tennessee Press, 1997.

Lewis, James R., and Evelyn Dorothy Oliver. *Angels A to Z.* Detroit: Visible Ink Press, 1996.

Lizon, Karen Helene. *Colonial American Holidays and Entertainments.* New York: Franklin Watts, 1993.

Marling, Karal Ann. *Merry Christmas!* Cambridge, MA: Harvard University Press, 2000.

McBrien, Richard P. *Lives of the Saints.* New York: HarperCollins, 2001.

McKibben, Bill. *Hundred Dollar Holiday.* New York: Simon and Schuster, 1998.

McKissack, Patricia, and Frederick McKissack. *Christmas in the Big House, Christmas in the Quarters.* New York: Scholastic, 1994.

Miles, Clement A. *Christmas in Ritual and Tradition.* 1912. Reprint. Detroit: Omnigraphics, 1990.

Nissenbaum, Stephen. *The Battle for Christmas.* New York: Alfred A. Knopf, 1996.

Northpole.com, no date. Available online at http://www.northpole.com.

Philip, Neil, ed. *Christmas Fairy Tales.* New York: Viking, 1996.

Pimlott, J. A. R. *The Englishman's Christmas.* Atlantic Highlands, NJ: Humanities Press, 1978.

Porter, J. R. *The Illustrated Guide to the Bible.* New York: Oxford University Press, 1995.

Restad, Penne. *Christmas in America.* New York: Oxford University Press, 1995.

Roberts, Paul William. *In Search of the Birth of Jesus.* New York: Riverhead Books, 1995.

Sammon, Paul. *The Christmas Carol Trivia Book.* New York: Citadel Press, 1994.

Santino, Jack. *All Around the Year.* Urbana, IL: University of Illinois Press, 1994.

Scheel, Eugene. "Recalling Joys of Christmas, Big and Small." *The Washington Post* (December 3, 2000): V03.

Schmidt, Leigh Eric. *Consumer Rites: The Buying and Selling of American Holidays.* Princeton, NJ: Princeton University Press, 1995.

Sechrist, Elizabeth. *Christmas Everywhere.* 1936. Reprint. Detroit: Omnigraphics, 1998.

Siefker, Phyllis. *Santa Claus, Last of the Wild Men.* Jefferson, NC: McFarland and Company, 1997.

Spicer, Dorothy Gladys. *The Book of Festivals.* 1937. Reprint. Detroit: Omnigraphics, 1990.

Talley, Thomas J. *The Origins of the Liturgical Year.* Second, amended edition. Collegeville, MN: Liturgical Press, 1991.

Thompson, Sue Ellen, ed. *Holiday Symbols.* Detroit: Omnigraphics, 1998.

Trexler, Richard C. *The Journey of the Magi: Meanings in History of a Christian Story.* Princeton, NJ: Princeton University Press, 1997.

Tyson, Ann Scott. "Christmas Without Shopping." *Christian Science Monitor* (Thursday, December 11, 1997): 1.

Urlin, Ethel. *Festivals, Holy Days, and Saints' Days.* 1915. Reprint. Detroit: Omnigraphics, 1992.

Waggoner, Susan. *Christmas Memories: Gifts, Activities, Fads, and Fancies, 1920s-1960s.* New York: Stewart, Tabori & Chang, 2009.

_____. *It's a Wonderful Christmas: The Best of the Holidays 1940-1965.* New York: Stewart, Tabori & Chang, 2004.

Waits, William. *The Modern Christmas in America.* New York: New York University Press, 1993.

Wakefield, Charito Calvachi. *Navidad Latinoamericana, Latin American Christmas.* Lancaster, PA: Latin American Creations Publishing, 1997.

Weaver, William Woys. *The Christmas Cook.* New York: HarperPerennial, 1990.

Webber, F. R. *Church Symbolism.* Second edition, revised. 1938. Reprint. Detroit: Omnigraphics, 1992.

Weiser, Francis X. *The Christmas Book.* 1952. Reprint. Detroit: Omnigraphics, 1990.

Wernecke, Herbert H. *Celebrating Christmas Around the World.* 1962. Reprint. Detroit: Omnigraphics, 1999.

Young, Joanne B. *Christmas in Williamsburg.* New York: Holt, Rinehart and Winston, 1970.

# Index

Guaraldi, Vince, 74
guising. *See* mumming
Gwen, Edmund, 309–10

Hackett, Albert, 211–12, 213
Handel, George Frideric, 298–302
Hans Muff. *See* Knecht Ruprecht
Hans Trapp. *See* Knecht Ruprecht
"Hansel and Gretel," 172
**Hanukkah, 191–93**
Harrison, Benjamin, 510, 514
Harrison, Caroline, 510
Henry VIII, King, 259, 305–6
Hereford Cathedral, 60
**Herod, King, 193–95**
    death of, 228–29
    Flight into Egypt, 153
    Jesus' birth, 178–79, 227
    St. Stephen's Day, 455–56
Herrick, Robert, 535–36
Hertha, 41
Hoffmann, E. T. A., 354
Holda. *See* Holde
Holde, 41
*Holiday Inn,* 504–7
Holle. *See* Holde
holly, 184–85, 195–98, 216
Holy Family. *See* Flight into Egypt; Jesus;
    Joseph; Mary, Blessed Virgin
**Holy Innocents' Day, 59, 199–201**
Hoover, Herbert, 509, 510
Hoover, Lou, 509, 510, 513
Horner, Jack, 305–6
horses, 456, 457–58
*How the Grinch Stole Christmas,* 202–4
hymns, 22, 46, 50

Iceland, 101–2
illuminations, 261–62
Incarnation, 222–23
incense, 155–56
Innocents' Day. *See* Holy Innocents' Day
**interfaith family holiday celebrations,**
    207–9
Irving, Washington, 414
Italy, 34–35
*It's a Wonderful Life,* 209–14
Ivanov, Lev, 355
ivy, 184–85, 195–96, 198, **215–17**

Jackson, Andrew, 508, 512
Jamaica, 230–33
Jamestown, Virginia, 12–13
Jefferson, Thomas, 508
Jennens, Charles, 298, 300
**Jesse tree, 221**
**Jesus, 222–26**
    Adam and Eve Day, 3–4
    angel, 27, 29
    Bethlehem, 42, 44–45
    birth date of, 121–24
    birth of, Gospel according to Luke,
      176–77, 286, 288
    birth of, Gospel according to
      Matthew, 177–79
    birth of, Gospel accounts, 181, 183
    cherry trees, 75, 77
    circumcision, 288
    Feast of the Ass, 149
    Feast of the Circumcision, 150–52
    festival celebrating birth of, 225–26
    Joseph, 233–34

V

W